The Churchlands and their Critics

PHILOSOPHERS AND THEIR CRITICS

General Editor: Ernest Lepore

Philosophy is an interactive enterprise. Much of it is carried out in dialogue as theories and ideas are presented and subsequently refined in the crucible of close scrutiny. The purpose of this series is to reconstruct this vital interplay among thinkers. Each book consists of a contemporary assessment of an important living philosopher's work. A collection of essays written by an interdisciplinary group of critics addressing the substantial theses of the philosopher's corpus opens each volume. In the last section, the philosopher responds to his or her critics, clarifies crucial points of the discussion, or updates his or her doctrines.

1 Dretske and his Critics *Brian McLaughlin*

2 John Searle and his Critics *Ernest Lepore and Robert van Gulick*

3 Meaning in Mind: Fodor and his Critics *Barry Loewer and Georges Rey*

4 Dennett and his Critics *Bo Dahlbom*

5 Danto and his Critics *Mark Rollins*

6 Perspectives on Quine *Robert B. Barrett and Roger F. Gibson*

7 The Churchlands and their Critics *Robert N. McCauley*

The Churchlands and their Critics

Edited by
Robert N. McCauley

BLACKWELL
Publishers

Copyright © Blackwell Publishers Ltd, 1996

First published 1996

2 4 6 8 10 9 7 5 3 1

Blackwell Publishers Inc.
238 Main Street
Cambridge, Massachusetts 02142, USA

Blackwell Publishers Ltd
108 Cowley Road
Oxford OX4 1JF
UK

Library of Congress Cataloging-in-Publication Data has been applied for.

ISBN 0-631-18968-8; ISBN 0-631-18969-6 (pbk.)

British Library Cataloguing in Publication Data

A CIP catalogue record for this book is available from the British Library.

Typeset in 10 on 12pt Times
by Wearset, Boldon, Tyne and Wear
Printed in Great Britain by TJ Press, Padstow, Cornwall

This book is printed on acid-free paper.

This book is dedicated to my parents,
Leland M. McCauley
and Muriel McCauley.

Contents

List of Figures   x

Notes on Contributors   xii

Acknowledgments   xiv

Introduction   1
    ROBERT N. McCAULEY

Part I   Essays Addressed to the Churchlands   15

1   Explanatory Pluralism and the Co-evolution of   17
    Theories in Science
    ROBERT N. McCAULEY

2   From Neurophilosophy to Neurocomputation: 48
    Searching for the Cognitive Forest
    PATRICIA KITCHER

3   Dealing in Futures: Folk Psychology and the Role   86
    of Representations in Cognitive Science
    ANDY CLARK

4   Paul Churchland's PDP Approach to Explanation   104
    WILLIAM G. LYCAN

5   What Should a Connectionist Philosophy of Science   121
    Look Like?
    WILLIAM BECHTEL

6   Paul Churchland and State Space Semantics   145
    JERRY FODOR and ERNIE LEPORE
    Reply to Churchland   159
    JERRY FODOR and ERNIE LEPORE

7   Images and Subjectivity: Neurobiological Trials and   163
     Tribulations
     ANTONIO R. DAMASIO AND HANNA DAMASIO

8   The Furniture of Mind: A Yard of Hope, a Ton of   176
     Terror?
     JOHN MARSHALL and JENNIFER GURD

9   The Moral Network   192
     OWEN FLANAGAN

Part II   Replies from the Churchlands   **217**

A   The Future of Psychology, Folk and Scientific   219

10   McCauley's Demand for a Co-level Competitor   222
11   Connectionism as Psychology   232
12   Kitcher's Empirical Challenge: Has There Been   239
     Progress in Neurophilosophy?
13   Clark's Connectionist Defense of Folk Psychology   250

B   The Impact of Neural Network Models on the   256
     Philosophy of Science

14   On the Nature of Explanation: William Lycan   257
15   Bechtel on the Proper Form of a Connectionist   265
     Philosophy of Science

C   Semantics in a New Vein   271

16   Fodor and Lepore: State-Space Semantics and   272
     Meaning Holism
17   Second Reply to Fodor and Lepore   278

D   Consciousness and Methodology   284

18   Neuropsychology and Brain Organization: The   285
     Damasios
19   Conceptual Analysis and Neuropsychology: John   290
     Marshall and Jennifer Gurd
20   Do We Propose to Eliminate Consciousness?   297

E   Moral Psychology and the Rebirth of Moral   301
     Theory

21   Flanagan on Moral Knowledge   302

Index   311

Figures

1.1	Three notions of co-evolution situated on the Churchlands' continuum	28
1.2	Mapping degrees of intertheoretic continuity (the Churchlands' continuum) onto intralevel and interlevel contexts	35
5.1	Neuberg and Kerb's (1913) model of the chemical reactions involved in alcoholic fermentation	134
6.1	Color state space	149
7.1	Pat Churchland's brain	164
10.1	A feedforward network for discriminating facehood, gender, and personal identity as displayed in photographic images	226
10.2a	An activation state space	228
10.2b	A dendogram representing the same set of hierarchically organized categories	228
11.1a	A simple recurrent network	233
11.1b	The activation space of the recurrent network's middle layer	233
11.2a	The basic architecture of Elman's grammatically competent network	236
11.2b	One surface within the hyperspace of the 70-unit middle or hidden layer	236
14.1	A degraded visual stimulus that resists recognition of what it is	262

16.1   A typical feedforward network   273

17.1   Six of the 80 "holons" that constitute the coding   280
       axes of the hidden-layer activation space of the
       face-recognition network of figure 10.1

19.1   Some of the connections mediating emotional   293
       responses in humans

19.2   The ascending and descending connections that   295
       unite the intralaminar system (ILS) with the
       many different areas of the cerebral cortex

Notes on Contributors

WILLIAM BECHTEL is a Professor in the Department of Philosophy and the Philosophy-Neuroscience-Psychology Program at Washington University, in St Louis. His research focuses on the foundations of cognition and the development of scientific research disciplines. He is the author of numerous books, including *Connectionism and the Mind* (co-authored with Adele Abrahamsen) and *Discovering Complexity* (co-authored with Robert C. Richardson).

ANDY CLARK is a Professor of Philosophy and Director of the Philosophy-Neuroscience-Psychology Program at Washington University, in St Louis. He is the author of *Microcognition: Philosophy, Cognitive Science, and Parallel Distributed Processing* and *Associative Engines: Connectionism, Concepts, and Representational Change*.

ANTONIO R. DAMASIO is the Van Allen Professor and head of the Department of Neurology at the University of Iowa College of Medicine. He is also Adjunct Professor at the Salk Institute. He is the author of *Descartes' Error: Emotion, Reason and the Human Brain*.

HANNA DAMASIO is Professor of Neurology and Director of the Human Neuroanatomy and Neuroimaging Laboratory at the University of Iowa College of Medicine. She is also Adjunct Professor at the Salk Institute. She is the author of *Lesion Analysis in Neuropsychology* and *Human Brain Anatomy in Computerized Images*.

OWEN FLANAGAN is chair of the Department of Philosophy, Psychology, and Neurobiology and Adjunct Professor in the Graduate Program in Literature at Duke University. He is the author of *Varieties of Moral Personality* and *Consciousness Reconsidered*.

JERRY FODOR   is Professor of Philosophy at Rutgers University. He is the author of many books, including *The Language of Thought*, *Modularity of Mind*, *Representations*, and *The Elm and the Expert*.

JENNIFER GURD   is a Professor in the Neuropsychology Unit of the University Department of Clinical Neurology at the Radcliffe Infirmary at Oxford University. Her research focuses on disorders of language and memory in degenerative brain disease. She is the author of numerous articles in such journals as *Neuropsychologia*, *Advances in Neurology* and *Archives of Neurology*.

PATRICIA KITCHER   is Professor of Philosophy at the University of California at San Diego. She is also a member of the Cognitive Science Program and is the author of *Kant's Transcendental Psychology* and *Freud's Dream: A Complete Interdisciplinary Science of Mind*.

ERNIE LEPORE   is Professor of Philosophy at Rutgers University. He is the author of many articles on the philosophy of language and the philosophy of mind. He is the co-author (with Jerry Fodor) of *Holism: A Shopper's Guide*.

WILLIAM G. LYCAN   is the William Rand Kenan, Jr. Professor of Philosophy at the University of North Carolina. His principal areas of research are the philosophy of language, the philosophy of mind, and epistemology. He is the author of *Logical Form in Natural Language*, *Consciousness* and *Judgement and Justification*.

JOHN MARSHALL   is a Professor in the Neuropsychology Unit of the University Department of Clinical Neurology at the Radcliffe Infirmary at Oxford University. His research focuses on disorders of language and visuo-spatial perception after brain damage. He is the co-editor (with M. Coltheart and K. E. Patterson) of *Deep Dyslexia* and (with P. W. Halligan) of *Spatial Neglect: Position Papers on Theory and Practice*.

ROBERT N. McCAULEY   is the Massee-Martin/NEH Professor of Philosophy and Adjunct Professor of Psychology and Anthropology at Emory University. His research focuses on models of cross-scientific relations and the connections between cognition and culture. He is the co-author (with E. Thomas Lawson) of *Rethinking Religion: Connecting Cognition and Culture*.

Acknowledgments

A book of this sort requires the cooperation of many people. I wish to express my gratitude to Ernie Lepore, who played an important role in the project's initiation.

I also wish to express my gratitude to the editors and publishers of *Philosophy and Phenomenological Research* for their permission to reprint the second part of chapter 6 and the Churchlands' reply in chapter 16, which originally appeared as:

Fodor, J. and Lepore, E. (1993). "Reply to Critics," *Philosophy and Phenomenological Research* **53**: 679–82.
Churchland, P. M. (1993). "State Space Semantics and Meaning Holism," *Philosophy and Phenomenological Research* **53**: 667–72.

Steve Smith at Blackwells has been cheerful, helpful, and patient throughout the entire process of bringing this book to print. His consistent kindness and support alleviated many worries at various points. Thanks, too, go to Meg Worley for fourscore chores along the way, to David Green for his help with the typescript, and to Becky Cohen for her photograph of the Churchlands.

This book would not exist without its contributors. In addition to hearty thanks to each for their papers, I wish to extend special words of appreciation to Bill Lycan for his promptness, to Owen Flanagan for his understanding, and to Bill Bechtel for his wise counsel.

I also wish to express my sincere gratitude to Pat and Paul Churchland for their friendship and support. They were always faithful, cooperative, and prompt with their replies and their encouragement. That was all the more remarkable in light of the fact that they composed those replies during a period of considerable adversity and concern.

Finally, my gratitude to Drindee and Ellen is profound for their love and support and for their patience through all those hours when I was holed up in my study.

Introduction

Robert N. McCauley

The Churchlands

The influence of Patricia and Paul Churchland's work in contemporary philosophy is unmistakable. That influence is not a function of mere philosophical fashion but, rather, of their work's ground-breaking importance. The best evidence for this is the fact that so many philosophers concede its importance begrudgingly – begrudgingly because the Churchlands challenge so many prevailing doctrines concerning the character of knowledge, science, language, and mind.

For more naturalistic philosophers, the importance of the Churchlands' projects stems even more from their *constructive* successes. No one's work more clearly exemplifies the advantages and accomplishments of naturalism within philosophy. Their pursuits are interdisciplinary at every turn, reflecting command of the research not only within the various subdisciplines of philosophy but within relevant areas of psychology, connectionism, and, especially, the neurosciences. The Churchlands are famous for carefully probing technical scientific research, regularly revealing its philosophically intriguing implications, and deftly integrating those results into their neurophilosophical and neurocomputational programs. Their achievements on these fronts are distinguished and consistent (and extended in their replies in this volume). No contemporary philosophical program is more imaginative, more productive, more empirically responsible, or more comprehensive. Recent neurocomputational proposals about moral knowledge and the virtues in Paul Churchland's *The Engine of Reason, the Seat of the Soul* (1995) as well as discussions of these and related topics by Patricia Churchland in chapter 19 and by Paul Churchland in chapter 21 in this volume contribute to the case for the comprehensiveness of their vision.

Neurophilosophy and neurocomputationalism reconsider and

reformulate Quine's naturalized epistemology, Kuhn's account of scientific revolutions, Sellar's attack on the Myth of the Given, and Feyerabend's discussions of theory incommensurability and eliminative materialism in the light of the most up-to-date advances in the cognitive and neuro-sciences. The suggestiveness of the Churchlands' proposals regularly startles sympathetic philosophers. Those proposals' affronts to orthodoxy just as regularly provoke traditional philosophers.

Epistemology should be naturalized not only because we generally have greater confidence in scientific findings than in traditional epistemological conclusions but also because so many of that traditional approach's central assumptions concern cognitive systems (perceptual, mnemonic, inferential, etc.) that have become the objects of focused scientific scrutiny in the past two decades especially. Attention to neuroscientific findings and neurocomputational modeling suggests that most cognitive processes yield to the sort of sentential characterizations that dominate traditional analytic epistemology usually roughly, at best, and only at the most abstract levels of description if at all. Unburdened by preoccupations with sentence-like representations, the Churchlands invite philosophers to rethink their models of the epistemic virtues – seeking, as always, accounts that are more attentive to pertinent scientific findings, that are more comprehensive (and more liberal), and that enjoy greater verisimilitude with cognizers' situations.

With both courage and creativity the Churchlands have resisted the considerable cultural and intellectual inertia that the legacy of common sense and ordinary language use contribute to the dominant philosophical tradition. Of a piece with their concerns about sentential epistemologies is their skepticism about the common-sense conception of psychology that inspires them. Maintaining that folk psychology offers a woefully inadequate program for research on the explanation of human behavior and mental life, the Churchlands foresee its substantial alteration or possibly even its elimination (along with its attendant ontology), in the face of progress in the neurosciences. They advance numerous arguments in support of this prognosis, focusing on folk psychology's explanatory failures or outright silence about a host of central psychological phenomena, its relative stagnancy as a blueprint for scientific research, its frequent discontinuity with reigning theories in the cognate sciences, and the general bankruptcy of folk theories in other empirical domains.

Ultimately, however, what gives the Churchlands' criticisms bite is that they buttress them by outlining alternative, scientifically informed pictures of such phenomena as visual perception, sensorimotor integration, learning, memory, sensory qualia, and (explanatory) understanding. In response to their critics in this volume, the Churchlands not only refuse to moderate their attack on folk psychology, they press it forward with even greater vigor.

Paul Churchland has begun to develop a case for the continuity between these pictures of our mental life in terms of neural networks and his account of the semantics of natural language – the origins of which extend at least as far back as his discussion of the semantic and systemic importance of sentences and their bearing on the problem of translation in *Scientific Realism and the Plasticity of Mind* (1979). Churchland's network theory of meaning, contrary to the major orthodoxies in the philosophy of language for the last hundred years, holds that (1) referential connections between language and the world and (2) causal connections between the world and language are both secondary, perhaps incidental, considerations in developing a satisfactory theory of meaning. Overshadowing both, according to the Churchlands, are the roles a term plays in the collection of beliefs in which it figures and the unique pattern of inferences those roles endow. Even alleged observation terms have material consequence only by virtue of their connections with various background assumptions. Further empirical inquiry can always reveal how thoroughly corrigible and conjectural those background assumptions are. Thus, the Churchlands hold all judgments, even basic perceptual ones, to be theory laden. This results at times (the title of Paul Churchland's first book notwithstanding) in a decidedly pragmatic approach to the metaphysics of science.

Sometimes the neuroscientifically informed pictures that the Churchlands draw of our mental goings-on resemble those of common sense; however, often they do not. In "Consciousness: the Transmutation of a Concept" (1983), Patricia Churchland first made most philosophers aware of a wide array of clinical and experimental findings concerning conscious phenomena. Her point was not to eliminate conscious phenomena but rather to substantially increase the amount of it that any satisfactory philosophical account of consciousness must illuminate. Even when resemblances remain between common-sense conceptions and neurophilosophically transmuted ones, the precision, fecundity, explanatory power, and coherence with the scientific facts of the Churchlands' proposals have improved upon previous philosophical accounts and enriched philosophers' subsequent discussions.

This claim does not rest solely on the relative assets of the Churchlands' alternative pictures. Their account of intertheoretic relations in science offers a further rationale for the value of the neurosciences instructing psychology and epistemology. The Churchlands' treatments of intertheoretic relations have substantially improved upon discussions of traditional theory reduction inspired by the work of Ernest Nagel. The Churchlands have brought coherence to the superficially disparate accounts of intertheoretic reductions on the one hand and scientific revolutions on the other, construing them as end points on a single continuum of theory commensurability. Their model leaves space for a wide range of intermediate cases of approximate reduction. It also justifies reinterpreting the classical account of theory reduction as a question about the preservation of an equipotent image of the reduced theory's central principles within the framework of the reducing theory.

Patricia Churchland's discussion of the co-evolution of theories in *Neurophilosophy* (1986) (and in various papers) might be understood as inserting a dynamic element into this continuum model. Her co-evolutionary model is probably better understood though as simply superseding the earlier continuum model, since the co-evolutionary metaphor not only allows for the movement over time on this continuum of the relationship of a pair of theories, but also introduces the means for far more detailed examination of the myriad considerations contributing to that movement, such as experimental design, technique, apparatus, sources of evidence, and theoretical and conceptual resources.

Talk of "equipotent images" and metaphors of "co-evolution" reflect a very different orientation in the philosophy of science than does talk of the formal reduction of scientific theories (construed as rigorously structured systems of propositions). This orientation is completely in accord with the Churchlands' attention to scientific research in all matters epistemic and, therefore, with their circumspection concerning sentential accounts of knowledge. In their view, finally, the philosophy of science – as a subdiscipline of epistemology – stands in no less need of naturalization. Reconceiving its central notions in the light of our knowledge about mind/brain operations will only improve our appreciation of both human cognitive accomplishments in general and their role in the process and progress of science in particular.

Paul Churchland pursues this approach to the philosophy of science in the second half of *A Neurocomputational Perspective* (1989), where he exhibits its many benefits as a particularly productive way of regarding theories, explanatory understanding, and conceptual change in science. Churchland's accounts of these notions are consonant with some of the best models of concept representation and cognitive processing advanced today in cognitive psychology and computational neurobiology. The crucial feature of these neurocomputational analyses is that each new advance in these sciences has potential implications for the meta-scientific interests of philosophers.

Adequate appreciation of these advances requires that the philosopher achieve a level of literacy in the sciences of the mind/brain that has been, at least since the eighteenth century, *almost* without precedent. (See chapter 8 by John Marshall and Jennifer Gurd.) It demands, in short, the competencies of the neurophilosopher. Mere "literacy" does not suffice to describe the Churchlands' expertise. The facility they have achieved with these materials comes from immersion not only in the literature but in the activity of science. The first half of Patricia Churchland's *Neurophilosophy* (1986) directs philosophers through the basic neuroscience necessary to appreciate her innovative proposals.

On this front some philosophers complain that the Churchlands' projects blur the distinctions between philosophy and science. By contrast, the world of science, displaying generally better judgment, has welcomed their endeavors. The Churchlands have generated a rich commentary on the implications of connectionist and neuroscientific research for philosophy. They have also produced insights of direct use to scientists, concerning everything from broad theoretical programs to the designs and details of experiments. (Patricia Churchland's replies to the papers in this volume by Antonio and Hanna Damasio and by John Marshall and Jennifer Gurd supply further illustrations.) Concerning broad theoretical programs, in *The Computational Brain* (1992) Patricia Churchland and Terrence Sejnowski advance a theory of neural representation and computation grounded in connectionist network modeling. This theory integrates hypotheses and empirical findings concerning various visual, cognitive, and motor functions from a wide range of investigative venues. In order to maximize the empirical tractability of their proposals, Churchland and Sejnowski focus on network models that simultaneously track the relevant neurobiology (so far as the modeling techniques permit) and address functions familiar to psychological and neuropsychological researchers. The Churchlands have also proposed specific models of their own. For example, in *The Engine of Reason, the Seat of the Soul* (1995) Paul Churchland advances an original connectionist model of stereoptic vision. Concerning experimental designs and details, Patricia Churchland's various collaborations with scientists, for example her work with V. S. Ramachandran (Churchland and Ramachandran 1993; see too McCauley 1993), have provided welcome correctives to philosophical speculations about neural and psychological phenomena.

The Churchlands' efforts bridge rather than blur the regions between philosophy and the sciences of the mind/brain. The connections they construct offer avenues of exchange between philosophy and these sciences – exchange that promises to invigorate and improve both philosophical reflection and scientific inquiry. Among philosophers, naturalists are pleased to contribute in this effort, however much they may differ with the Churchlands about details, whereas traditionalists demur explicitly, sometimes at remarkable length. Still, for both intellectual friends and foes, the Churchlands' efforts have proved as profound a stimulus to investigation in epistemology, the philosophy of science, and the philosophy of mind as any in this generation.

The Critics

The immediately preceding summary of the Churchlands' impact on contemporary thought in philosophy and the sciences signals points where I am sympathetic with some of their projects (or, at least, approximations thereof); however, intellectual[1] resemblance to either of the Churchlands was not a prerequisite for inclusion in this volume. Within the broad context of contemporary English-language philosophy, at least, some of the critics included in this volume agree with very few of the Churchlands' views. All nine critical papers in the book discuss a wide range of the issues the Churchlands' works raise.

My own chapter questions the Churchlands' account of intertheoretic relations in science and its implications for the status of psychology, especially of the scientific sort.

I argue that the Churchlands' earlier continuum model involves a decisive oversimplification that unjustifiably encourages their expectations about the elimination of psychology in the face of neuroscientific advances. The history of the last century's science and of the relevant social, political, intellectual, and institutional forces would suggest that the sort of *interlevel* (as opposed to *intralevel*) eliminations in science the Churchlands envision have occurred rarely, if at all, and are not obviously desirable, if they have. Although the metaphor of co-evolution could constitute a promising corrective, in fact, the Churchlands' discussions of specific cases too often reflect implausible assumptions about the possibilities of interlevel eliminations. Those discussions frequently presume that the selection pressures are *overwhelmingly* exerted from the bottom up. Examination of one of the Churchlands' favorite illustrations, however, strongly suggests that preserving a multiplicity of explanatory proposals from different, *semi*-independent levels of analysis will more likely abet scientific progress. Interlevel elimination of all forms of psychology involving attributions of propositional attitudes (which would include much of cognitive, developmental, and social psychology) would impoverish scientific research. It would eradicate fruitful technical, experimental, conceptual, theoretical, and evidential resources.

Certainly Patricia Kitcher should also be counted among the friends of psychology. She argues that Patricia Churchland does not succeed in defending the neurophilosophical thesis that significant progress with a host of traditional philosophical problems will ultimately depend upon aid from the neurosciences. Kitcher maintains that none of a half dozen representative examples that Churchland cites of such potential aid is convincing. She highlights various problems, including the relevant theories' inadequacies of precision and failures to inspire subsequent research. Concerning Churchland's case on behalf of connectionist modeling, in particular, Kitcher thinks that it is not clear (even now) whether primary credit for most advances in connectionist research should go to neuroscience or "non-neural psychology." She argues that the case for computational neuroscience also fails to establish the critical neurophilosophical thesis, since (1) the pivotal role of vector coding and the accompanying representational capacities in Churchland and Sejnowski's examples does not turn on any neurophysiological discoveries; (2) the similarity metric network models naturally supply is insufficient to explain the psychological facts about similarity judgments; and (3) there is little evidence that accounts of "inner representations" in networks like NETtalk show anything about human cognitive processes. Kitcher does hold, though, that Churchland's case for computational neuroscience suffices to establish the conclusion that neuroscience *will* have an important and ongoing impact on the development of psychology – the science that, according to Kitcher, can rightfully lay claim to deserving influence in current philosophical discussions, as another half dozen examples she supplies aim to illustrate.

In contrast to Kitcher, Andy Clark approves of the Churchlands' arguments that connectionist models offer valuable, new resources for understanding human cognition, yet he rejects (even more forcefully than Kitcher) the claim that this outcome impugns folk psychology. Clark emphasizes the non-sentential character of the representational resources of connectionist nets. He holds that research on connectionist nets and evolvable cognition indicates that accounts of learning need not be confined to analyses of hypothesis generation and testing as quasi-linguistic structures composed of fixed symbols from an innate symbol system. Instead, connectionist learning algorithms demonstrate the general possibility of rational learning that involves the generation and modification of representations over time and, thus, offer new insights into the "non-representational origins of representation itself." Even though Clark enthusiastically endorses the Churchlands' challenges to standard conceptions of both representation and its explanatory role within cognitive science, he does not draw the Churchlands' austere conclusions concerning folk psychology. Clark adopts an abstemious interpretation not only about the consequences of folk psychology for cognitive processing but also about its proper explanatory obligations.

In Clark's view the characterizations of folk psychology concern a global complex of capacities usefully read as "an effective social adhesive."

William Lycan's paper considers Paul Churchland's prototype activation account of explanatory understanding. Lycan argues that if explanation concerns either quasilogical relations between sentences and/or the natural relations between the affairs those sentences express, then Churchland's objections to the traditional deductive-nomological model of explanation are ineffective. In short, for the logical empiricists explanation and explanatory understanding were very different matters. If, however, explanation *is* best explicated in terms of explanatory understanding, then, Lycan argues, Churchland's proposal avoids a long-standing problem that all previous pragmaticist proposals have faced, viz., clarifying which types of understanding are examples of *explanatory* understanding without answering that they are the ones that involve correct explanations! Churchland's prototype activation account faces a different problem, though, since it explicates explanatory understanding in terms of particular psychological, indeed neural, states, which might arise from utterly fortuitous causes. Considering Churchland's prototype activation model on its own terms, Lycan thinks it manifests some obvious virtues, including its ability to make some sense of an underlying unity of all the things we call explanations. A series of questions that Lycan offers, however, press Churchland's account for greater clarity on various fronts.

Agreeing with Lycan that traditional philosophy of science has been little concerned with the psychology of scientists, and with Clark that its broadly sentential approach renders it ineffective at characterizing that psychology, William Bechtel disputes Paul Churchland's claim that theories and explanations are best understood in terms of representations in scientists' heads. He holds that renderings of theories, explanations, and even models in external symbols are not mere translations of internal representations that occur incidentally and after the fact but rather, a *pivotal* part of the process of their acquisition and development. Successful accounts employing external symbols are not recordings of human memory, but representations designed precisely for subsequent human interaction. External symbol systems, according to Bechtel, *extend* our cognitive capacities. Bechtel maintains that the principal contribution of connectionist inspired philosophy of science will probably concern our *use* of representations. Bechtel concurs with Churchland's contention that ascertaining deductive consequences is not usually what we do with the information at our disposal. Instead, we typically seek to arrange it and the new information we acquire into coherent wholes, where some elements (inevitably) enjoy a heightened prior credibility that imposes soft constraints (i.e., constraints that can be overcome in the right circumstances) on subsequent constructions. In short, one of connectionism's greatest strengths is solving multiple soft-constraint satisfaction problems. This will prove useful in understanding the theoretical and conceptual progress of science in general as well as the contributions of instruments and research techniques in particular. Toward these ends Bechtel explores the history of accounts of fermentation and the development of techniques of cell fractionation.

In the first part of chapter 6, Jerry Fodor and Ernie Lepore find Paul Churchland's state space version of a network account of semantics wanting. Fodor and Lepore argue that Churchland has remained committed to two positions that are (almost certainly) incompatible.

1 He has consistently *endorsed* a network account of semantics in which a term gains its meanings by virtue of both (a) the character of its semantically relevant connections to other terms in the network and (b) the term's place in the network's overall configuration.
2 He has just as consistently *rejected* the empiricist assumption that some of these semantically relevant relations must (sooner or later) involve connections with an observational vocabulary.

Rejecting that assumption forces Churchland to jettison appeals to the analytic/synthetic distinction as well, leading Fodor and Lepore to insist that Churchland must provide, as a substitute for content identity, an account of content similarity. Churchland's state spaces can possess indefinitely many semantic dimensions. Proximity within these spaces constitutes semantic similarity. Fodor and Lepore argue, however, that Churchland must supply criteria for the identity of the semantic dimensions that define the state spaces and that this must either involve some sort of return to observables or a solution to the problem of the identity of content. Fodor and Lepore think Churchland aims to solve that problem by characterizing the semantic dimensions by means of psychophysical criteria. They contend, first, that this is just to "assume the 'empiricist principle' that all our concepts are functions ... of our psychophysical concepts" and, second, that this principle is false.

This exchange between Fodor and Lepore and Churchland has gone a number of rounds. Churchland wrote a response to their criticisms, which constitutes chapter 16 of this volume. Fodor and Lepore reply to that response in the second section of chapter 6. Now, in the newest round (chapter 17), Churchland argues that the pivotal problem in this exchange has been Fodor and Lepore's failure to appreciate just how radically new his proposal is.

Antonio and Hanna Damasio advance hypotheses about the neuro-biological foundations of human consciousness, specifically consciousness of mental images. Lesion studies, neurophysiological studies of non-human primates, and reflection on patterns of neural activity jointly suggest that the representations that sustain mental images arise in the early sensory cortices, aided by such structures as the thalamus and the colliculi; however, activities in these areas do not suffice to insure *experiences* of those images. Mental images involve temporally and spatially arranged patterns of activation, which are often topographically organized. Stored, non-topographically organized representations ("dispositional representations") can regenerate these topographical representations in the early sensory cortices.

The Damasios also address the problem of integrating and coordinating inputs from the various sensory modalities into a single mental image. Since the early sensory cortices are neither contiguous nor directly interconnected, it looks as if concurrent activity at various sites in the brain sustains our multimodal experiences. The Damasios hypothesize that interactions with both cortical and subcortical "convergence zones," which receive convergent signals from and dispense divergent signals to the early sensory cortices, provide the necessary temporal coordination of brain activities.

Once constructed, though, how are mental images experienced? Questions about such forms of subjective experience presuppose a subject or self who experiences. The Damasios reject Cartesian Theaters and homunculi, but they do attribute to many nonhuman animals simpler-than-human selves, each of which possesses some consistent point of view but remains unenhanced by participation in linguistic communities. According to the Damasios, the self is the "cognitive/neural instantiation of a concept" that involves incessant signals from and indelible representations of the most invariant aspects of bodily structure, interactions with the environment, activities, preferences, relationships, and more. They propose that consciousness *of images* consists of the simultaneity or near simultaneity of an organism reacting to some entity while its brain sustains (with the elementary representational tools of the sensory and motor systems) images of that entity, of the self, of the organism's responses to that entity, and of the organism in the act of perceiving and responding to that entity.

John Marshall and Jennifer Gurd applaud Patricia Churchland's rejection of analytic philosophy's attempt to turn the philosophy of psychology "into a commentary on the Oxford English Dictionary." They highlight antecedents of Churchland's neurophilosophy in Ernst Cassirer's third volume of *The Philosophy of Symbolic Forms* (1929/1957). Like Churchland, Cassirer spent many hours in neurological clinics discovering how the effects of brain injury and disease provide valuable insights into the fundamental categories of experience.

Marshall and Gurd worry, however, that unlike Cassirer, Churchland has drawn needlessly reductionistic conclusions, which they regard as neither plausible nor desirable. Marshall and Gurd stress, as I do in the first chapter, that the empirical and theoretical success of what Kitcher calls "non-neural" psychology suggests not only that it should sometimes constrain research at neuroscientific levels but that it may redirect or even correct it. Along such lines, they point out that, although Churchland focuses on various functional dissociations patients manifest, she too often ignores the creditable and, on occasion, even insightful theoretical proposals psychologists have offered to organize and explain these and related phenomena.

Marshall and Gurd largely concur with Churchland that brain structure can provide critical clues about brain function and that understanding functional architecture is the key to ascertaining the brain's computational and representational capacities. Nevertheless, they warn that "form can be misleading." They raise the same general concerns raised by functionalists in philosophy (though with a good deal more clinical and experimental insight!). In different subjects the same functional disorder can result from different types of neurological damage in different areas of the brain. In short, they suggest that the route from form to function is not as direct as Churchland sometimes seems to suppose. They suspect that Churchland's first response to such objections, viz. denying that functions must have unique physical realizations, in fact amounts to embracing the same sort of token physicalism functionalists endorse. They acknowledge, though, that her second response, that connectionist and neurocomputational research has shown how the plethora of possible physical states that might underlie some function can still be usefully systematized and explained, may put many functionalist objections to rest.

Owen Flanagan defends Paul Churchland's "moral network theory" by examining its promise for making sense of our moral learning, knowledge, practices, and standards. The theory's "descriptive-genealogical" component sorts through the biological, psychological, and social forces shaping our moral lives, while its normative component assesses right and wrong, good and bad. Flanagan asserts that the key to making sense of a normative naturalism is the recognition that reason is a *natural*, not a transcendental, faculty of the mind/brains of socially situated humans. Thus, practical wisdom is an instance of successfully employing prototype-driven "ampliative discriminations" in human affairs – where success pertains primarily to the relative quality of a person's continuing navigation through the social world. In this view moral argument is the attempt to highlight (and downplay) various features of a situation so that persons will access one prototype rather than another.

Flanagan explores the social, developmental, and conceptual complexities that surround our views of lying and truth-telling in particular. He emphasizes that (a) our cognitive representations of each in terms of prototypes, (b) the evolution of those conceptions in the course of development and (c) divergences between proposed definitions and ascriptions in particular cases all pose fundamental problems for classical assumptions about categories and about rule-based accounts of moral thinking and judgment.

For the normative naturalist, socialization is not *mere* socialization when it includes mechanisms (such as individual and collective reflection, conversation, and debate) that, in response to changing social experience, encourage ongoing refinement and adjustment of current conceptions. Churchland looks to the fundamentality, ubiquity, and sensitivity-to-experience of the underlying cognitive processes as grounds for optimism about moral progress. Flanagan is less sanguine. Since, among other things, moral matters are inevitably interwoven with a host of other practical considerations (tact, prudence, etiquette, etc.), the adjustments required by changing social circumstances may not always or even usually arise in persons' *moral* networks. Because the development and subsequent adjustment of moral networks turns so centrally on humans' experiences of their immediate social environments, Flanagan also thinks that Churchland underestimates just how *local* much moral knowledge is. Flanagan maintains that both of these problems with Churchland's view are finally rooted in his "excessive dependence on the analogy between scientific and moral knowledge."

Suffice it to say that in their replies to these nine papers, the Churchlands remain their delightfully provocative and insightful selves!

Notes

I wish to express my gratitude to Marshall Gregory and Robert Louden for their helpful comments on an earlier version on this introduction.
1 let alone physical!

References

Cassirer, E. (1929/1957). *The Philosophy of Symbolic Forms*, Volume 3. New Haven: Yale University Press.

Churchland, P. M. (1979). *Scientific Realism and the Plasticity of Mind*. Cambridge: Cambridge University Press.

Churchland, P. M. (1989). *A Neurocomputational Perspective: The Nature of Mind and the Structure of Science*. Cambridge: MIT Press.

Churchland, P. M. (1995). *The Engine of Reason, the Seat of the Soul: A Philosophical Journey into the Brain*. Cambridge: MIT Press.

Churchland, P. S. (1983). "Consciousness: The Transmutation of a Concept," *Pacific Philosophical Quarterly* **64**, 80–95.

Churchland, P. S. (1986). *Neurophilosophy: Toward a Unified Science of the Mind-Brain*. Cambridge: MIT Press.

Churchland, P. S. and Sejnowski, T. J. (1992). *The Computational Brain*. Cambridge: MIT Press.

Churchland, P. S. and Ramachandran, V. S. (1993). "Filling in: Why Dennett is Wrong," in B. Dahlbom (ed.), *Dennett and His Critics*. Oxford: Blackwell.

McCauley, R. N. (1993). "Why the Blind Can't Lead the Blind: Dennett on the Blind Spot, Blindsight, and Sensory Qualia," *Consciousness and Cognition* **2**, 155–64.

Part I

Essays Addressed to the Churchlands

1
Explanatory Pluralism and The Co-evolution of Theories in Science

Robert N. McCauley

1 Introduction

Over the past decade or so Patricia and Paul Churchland have made major contributions to philosophical treatments of intertheoretic reduction in science. The historic importance of this issue in the philosophy of science is patent and so, therefore, is the importance of the Churchlands' contributions. Their insistence on the centrality of this issue to discussions in the philosophy of mind may, however, be even more praiseworthy in an era when many in that field (even among those who claim the mantle of naturalism) make repeated declarations about the status of the pertinent sciences and the mind-body problem generally in what often appears to be blithe ignorance of both those sciences and the relevant literature in the philosophy of science since 1975.

In a recent joint paper the Churchlands (1990) discuss and largely defuse five well-worn objections (concerning qualia, intentionality, complexity, freedom, and multiple instantiation) to the reduction of psychology to neurobiology. My concerns with that putative reduction and with the Churchlands' account of the overall process are of a very different sort.

Two models have traditionally dominated discussions of intertheoretic relations. After briefly surveying the contrasts between them, section 2 examines how the Churchlands' account of these relations in terms of a continuum of intertheoretic commensurability captures those models' respective advantages in a single proposal. That section ends by examining how Patricia Churchland's subsequent discussions of the co-evolution of theories enhances this account by exploring some of its underlying dynamics. In short, the co-evolution of theories concerns cross-scientific interactions that change the position of a particular intertheoretic relationship on the Churchlands' continuum.

In section 3 I locate some revealing equivocations in the Churchlands' discussions of "the co-evolution of theories" by distinguishing three possible interpretations of that notion that wind their ways through the Churchlands' work and through *Neurophilosophy* in particular. With the aid of a distinction concerning levels of analysis that I have developed elsewhere, I argue, in effect, that the Churchlands' account of the co-evolution of theories and their model of intertheoretic reduction obscure critical distinctions between three quite different types of intertheoretic relations. Section 4 positions these three types within a more fine-grained account of intertheoretic relations, which will offer a basis for evaluating their relative merits as analyses of the interface of psychology and neuroscience.

One of these three, the picture of co-evolution modeled on the dynamics of scientific revolutions, has attracted the most attention. This interpretation has encouraged the recurring eliminativist inclinations concerning folk psychology for which the Churchlands are renowned, but, of the three, it is also the interpretation that is least plausible as an analysis of the relations between psychology and neuroscience. Psychology (folk or otherwise) may well undergo substantial revision, and future scientific progress may well lead to the elimination of some psychological theories, but the Churchlands have offered an unhelpfully oversimplified account of the intertheoretic dynamics in question.

In section 5 I shall support and elaborate upon another of the interpretations of co-evolution that emerges from *Neurophilosophy* by, among other things, examining a case (concerning the connectionist network NETtalk) that the Churchlands and their collaborators have highlighted. This third interpretation recognizes the value not merely of integrating scientific disciplines but of preserving a plurality of semi-autonomous explanatory perspectives. Although the Churchlands now often seem to favor this third interpretation too, some of their comments continue to conflate the three distinct types of intertheoretic relations.

2 Three Philosophical Models of Intertheoretic Relations in Science

Until the late 1970s (at least) two models of intertheoretic relations in science dominated philosophers' attentions. The first, a general purpose model was deeply rooted in logical empiricism; the second, in effect a model of theory change, emerged largely in reaction to the first (Bechtel 1986). I shall briefly discuss them in order.

Although Ernest Nagel's *The Structure of Science* (1961) contains the most time-honored treatment of theory reduction, Robert Causey's *Unity of Science* (1977) probably provides the most comprehensive discussion of the topic. Their general approach to theory reduction proceeds within the constellation of commitments that characterize logical empiricism, including the assumptions that a satisfactory account of scientific rationality requires heed to justificatory considerations only, that scientific theories are best understood as complex propositional structures and best represented via formal reconstructions, that scientific explanation results from the deduction of explananda from scientific laws, that scientific progress results from the subsumption of reigning theories by theories of even greater generality, and that science ultimately enjoys an underlying unity of theory and ontology.

This model conceives theory reduction as a special case of deductive-nomological explanation. It is a special case because the explanandum is not a statement describing some event but rather a law of the reduced theory. In order to carry out such reductions, the premises in the most complex cases of heterogeneous reductive explanations must include

1 at least one law from the reducing theory;
2 statements indicating the satisfaction of the requisite initial conditions specified in that law;
3 bridge laws that systematically relate – *within a particular domain* delineated by appropriate boundary conditions – the terms from the pertinent law(s) of the reducing theory to those from the law of the reduced theory;
4 statements indicating the satisfaction of those boundary conditions (under which the events described in the law of the reducing theory realize the events described in the law of the reduced theory that is to be explained).

Such premises permit a straightforward deduction of the law of the reduced theory.

Because the boundary conditions included in the bridge laws are cast in terms of predicates characteristic of the reducing theory, the reduction reflects an asymmetry between the two theories. The reducing theory explains the reduced theory, finally, because the reducing theory encompasses a wider array of events within its explanatory purview. Presumably this set of events includes all of the events the reduced theory explains and more, so that the principles of the reducing theory are both more general and more fundamental. The most popular showcase illustration is the reduction of the laws of classical thermodynamics to the principles of statistical mechanics.

When the reducing theory operates at a lower level of analysis than the reduced theory, the added generality of its principles is a direct function of this fact. These are cases of *microreductions*, where a lower-level theory and its ontology reduce a higher-level theory and its ontology (Oppenheim and Putnam 1958; Causey 1977). Microreductionists hold that if we can exhaustively describe and predict upper-level (or macro) entities, properties, and principles in terms of lower-level (or micro) entities, properties, and principles, then we can reduce the former to the latter and replace, at least in principle, the upper-level theory.

Virtually all discussions of intertheoretic relations presuppose this arrangement among (and within) the sciences in terms of levels of analysis. (See, for example, Churchland and Sejnowski 1992, pp. 10–11.) Numerous considerations contribute to the depiction of the architecture of science as a layered edifice of analytical levels (Wimsatt 1976). Ideally, moving toward lower levels involves moving toward the study of increasingly simple systems and entities that are ubiquitous, enduring, and small. Conversely, moving from lower- to higher-level sciences involves moving toward studies of larger, rarer systems of greater complexity and (often) less stability, whose history is less ancient. Because the altitude of a level of analysis is directly proportional to the complexity of the systems it treats, higher-level sciences deal with increasingly restricted ranges of events having to do with increasingly organized physical systems.[1]

Often, as a simple matter of fact, more than one configuration of lower-level entities can realize various higher-level kinds (especially when functionally characterized). The resulting multiple instantiations highlight both the importance and the complexity of the boundary conditions in the bridge laws of heterogeneous microreductions. Critics of the microreductionist program (e.g., Fodor 1975) see that complexity as sufficient grounds for questioning the program's feasibility in the case of the special sciences, while more sympathetic participants in these discussions, such as Richardson (1979) and the Churchlands (1990), suggest that when scientists trace such connections between higher- and lower-level entities in specific domains they vindicate the general strategy, while recognizing the *domain specificity* of its results.

Reductionists differ among themselves as to the precise connections between entities at different levels that are required for successful reductive explanation. They all agree, however, that the theories which are parties to the reduction should map on to one another well enough to support systematic connections, usually contingent identities, between some, if not all, of the entities that populate them. The test of the resulting contingent identities is met, ultimately, by the explanatory successes the reductions accomplish (McCauley 1981; Enc 1983).

Feyerabend (1962) and Kuhn (1970) are the most prominent proponents of the second main account of intertheoretic relations. They forged their early discussions largely in response to both the logical empiricist program and its reductionist blueprint for scientific progress. Feyerabend emphasized how scrutiny of many of the showcase illustrations of intertheoretic reductions revealed the *failure* of these cases to conform to the logical empiricists' model. Kuhn discussed numerous examples in the history of science where successive theories were not even remotely plausible candidates for the sort of smooth transitions the standard reductive model envisions. Instead, Kuhn proposed that progress in science consists of extended intervals of relative theoretical stability punctuated by periodic revolutionary upheavals. Both hold that the cases in question involve conflicts between *incommensurable* theories.

Although the subsequent literature is rife with assessments of this claim – Thagard (1992) offers the most suggestive of recent treatments – the critical point for now is that, whatever incommensurability amounts to, it stands in stark opposition to any model of intertheoretic relations that requires neat mappings between theories' principles and ontologies capable of supporting strict deductive-nomological explanations. The history of science provides ample evidence that where such incompatibility is sufficiently severe the theory and its ontology that are eventually deemed deficient undergo elimination. Stahl's system of chemistry is the preferred illustration, but Darwin's theory of inheritance could serve just as well.

The unmistakable sense that both of these models of intertheoretic relations describe some actual cases fairly accurately and that they each capture important insights about the issues at stake, their profound conflicts notwithstanding, could induce puzzlement. An account of intertheoretic relations in terms of a continuum of commensurability that Paul Churchland (1979) initially sketched, and which the Churchlands have subsequently developed (P. S. Churchland 1986, pp. 281f.; Churchland and Churchland 1990), substantially resolves that perplexity by reconciling those conflicts and allotting to each model a measure of descriptive force.

The Churchlands point out that, in fact, different cases of intertheoretic relations vary considerably with respect to the commensurability of the theories involved. So they propose that such cases fall along a continuum of relative intertheoretic commensurability, where, in effect, the two models sketched above constitute that continuum's end-points.

One end of the continuum represents cases where intertheoretic mapping is extremely low or even absent. These are cases of *radical* incommensurability where revolutionary science and the complete elimination of inferior theories ensue. Whatever vagueness may surround the notion of "incommensurability," the Churchlands are clearly

confident that the developments which brought about the elimination of
the bodily humours, the luminiferous ether, caloric fluid, and the like,
involve sufficiently drastic changes to justify the sort of extreme
departures from the traditional model of reduction that Kuhn and
Feyerabend advocated.

At the other end of this continuum, where the mapping of one theory
on another is nearly exhaustive and the former theory's ontology is
composed from the entities the latter theory countenances, the most
rigorous models of theory reduction most nearly apply (e.g., Causey
1972). The constraints proponents have imposed on theory reduction
are so demanding that it is a fair question whether *any* actual scientific
case qualifies. The Churchlands have urged considerable relaxation of
the conditions necessary for intertheoretic reduction. Instead of conformity to the rigorous logical and ontological constraints traditional
models impose, Paul Churchland (1979; see too Hooker 1981; Bickle
1992) suggests that the reducing theory need only preserve an "equipotent image" of the reduced theory's most central explanatory principles.
The reduction involves an *image*, since the reducing theory need not
duplicate every feature of the reduced theory's principles, but only
enough of their salient ones to suggest their general character and to
indicate their systematic import (see Schaffner 1967.). That image is
equipotent, however, since the reducing theory's principles will possess
all the explanatory and predictive power of the reduced theory's
principles – and more. From the standpoint of traditional models,
Churchland proposes a form of *approximate* reduction, which falls well
short of the logical empiricists' standards, but which also suggests how
true theories (e.g., the mechanics of relativity) can correct and even
approximately reduce theories that are false (e.g., classical mechanics).
Switching to the metaphor of imagery is appropriate, since, as Wimsatt
noted over a decade ago, if the standard models of reduction allege that
a false theory follows from a true one, the putative deduction had better
involve an equivocation somewhere! (1976, p. 218).

In recent years the Churchlands have each enlarged on this continuum model. For example, within his neurocomputational program
Paul Churchland has advanced a prototype-activation model of explanatory understanding that, presumably, includes the understanding that
arises from *reductive* explanations.

Churchland holds that the neurocomputational basis of explanatory
understanding resides in the activation of a prototype vector within a
neural network in response to impinging circumstances. A distributed
representation of the prototype in the neural network constitutes the
brain's current best stab at detecting an underlying pattern in the
blooming, buzzing confusion. For Churchland, explanatory understand-

ing is an array of inputs leading to the activation of one of these existing prototypes as opposed to another.

Churchland insists that the activation of a prototype vector increases, rather than diminishes, available information. It involves a "speculative *gain*" in information (1989, p. 212). Thus, contrary to anti-reductionist caricature, this account of explanatory understanding implies that reductive explanations *amplify* our knowledge. The originality of the insights that a reductive explanation offers depends upon the novel application of existing cognitive resources, i.e., of an individual's repertoire of prototype vectors. Consequently, reductive explanation involves neither the generation of new schemes nor the destruction of old ones. The approximate character of intertheoretic reductions is a function of this "conceptual redeployment" on which they turn (1989, p. 237). In conceptual redeployment a developed conceptual framework from one domain is enlisted for understanding another. In short, successful reductive explanation rests on an analogical inference by virtue of which we deem an image of a theory equipotent to the original. Having established the initial applicability of an existing, alternative prototype vector, it inevitably undergoes a reshaping as a consequence of exposure to the newly adopted training set. This reshaping of activation space is the neurocomputational process that drives the remaining co-evolution of the reductively related theories.

In her discussions of the co-evolution of theories, Patricia Churchland has introduced a dynamic element into the continuum model. She suggests that the position of two theories' relations on this continuum can change over time as they each undergo adjustments in the light of each other's progress.

The suggestion that scientific theories co-evolve arises from an analogy with the co-evolution of species and from the picture of the sciences briefly outlined above. On the co-evolutionary picture the sciences exert selection pressures on one another in virtue of a general concern to supply as much coherence as possible among our explanatory schemes. If the various sciences are arranged in tiers of analytical levels, then each will stand at varying distances from the others in this structure. Typically, proximity is a central consideration in assessing the force of selection pressures. Thus the pivotal relationships are those between a science and those sciences at immediately adjacent levels. For example, the presumption is that the neurosciences below and the sociocultural sciences above are more likely to influence psychology than are the physical sciences, since the latter are located below the neurosciences and, therefore, at an even greater distance.

It is this process of the co-evolution of theories and the Churchlands' account of it that will dominate the remainder of this chapter. I shall attend to its implications for the relation of cognitive psychology to the sort of neurocomputational modeling that the Churchlands endorse.

3 Three Ways Theories Might Co-evolve

Patricia Churchland's *Neurophilosophy* (1986) contains the most extensive discussion of reduction in terms of the co-evolution of theories that is available.[2] Churchland focuses on the relation between neuroscience and psychology, but her discussion clearly aspires to morals that are general. Her comments at various points seem to support three different co-evolutionary scenarios, though two of them are, quite clearly, closely related. The three are distinguished by the locations on the Churchlands' continuum to which they predict co-evolving theories will incline.

On some occasions Churchland suggests that psychology and the neurosciences will co-evolve in the direction of approximate reduction. She states, for example, that "the co-evolutionary development of neuroscience and psychology means that establishing points of reductive contact is more or less inevitable. . . . The heart of the matter is that if there is theoretical give and take, then the two sciences will knit themselves into one another." (1986, p. 374.) The metaphor of two sciences knit into one another implies an integration that is tight, orderly, and detailed. Although Churchland, presumably, does not think that that integration will satisfy the traditional microreductionists' stringent demands on intertheoretic mapping, talk of knitting two sciences into one another, the ongoing pursuit of a unified model of *reduction* (Churchland and Churchland 1990), and a new interest in establishing psycho-physical identities echo commitments of traditional microreductionism, where the sort of reductive contact in question led to talk of an "in principle replaceability" of the reduced theory in which the lower-level theory enjoys both explanatory and metaphysical priority. More recently, the Churchlands have been clear about the futility of attempts to replace upper-level theories, but they still generally subscribe to the explanatory and metaphysical priority of the lower-level theory – especially in the case of psychology and neuroscience. (See, for example, P. S. Churchland 1986, pp. 277, 294, 382.) Certainly a co-evolutionary account of intertheoretic relations has no problem translating the general microreductive *impulse*. Within this framework it amounts to the claim that the selection pressures exerted by the science at the level of analysis *below* that of the theory in question will have an overwhelmingly greater effect on that theory's eventual shape and fate than will the sciences above (see section 5).

On the Churchlands' account, such intertheoretic integration would enable the neurosciences to supply an equipotent image of psychological principles. Paul Churchland's speculations about the neural representation of the sensory qualia associated with color vision might constitute an appropriate illustration. The fit between our common sense notions about our experiences of colors and the system of neural representation he proposes is quite neat (1989, pp. 102–08). Hereafter I shall refer to this sense of the co-evolution of theories as "co-evolution$_M$," i.e., co-evolution in the direction of approximate microreduction. In the Churchlands' joint discussion (1990), where it plays both a predictive and normative role, this notion of reduction receives considerable attention. The Churchlands clearly hold that "it is reasonable to expect, and to work toward, a reduction of all psychological phenomena to neurobiological and neurocomputational phenomena" (1990, p. 249).

Co-evolution$_M$ is not the only account of co-evolution in *Neurophilosophy*, for, as the Churchlands have subsequently asserted, in the case of psychology and neuroscience, "there are conflicting indications" about the direction in which conjectures at these two levels of analysis will likely co-evolve (1990, p. 253). If integration is the fate of psychology and neuroscience, Patricia Churchland repeatedly hints that this will only occur *after* psychology's initial demolition and subsequent reconstruction in accord with the mandates of the neurosciences. She claims, for example, that " ... the possibility that psychological categories will not map one to one onto neurobiological categories ... does not look like an obstacle to reduction so much as it predicts a fragmentation and reconfiguration of the psychological categories" (1986, p. 365). With this second view, as with the first, no question arises about where the blame lies, if the theories of psychology and neuroscience fail to map onto one another neatly. (See Wimsatt 1976.) *At least for the short term*, Churchland seems to expect that this intertheoretic relation will migrate on the continuum of intertheoretic commensurability in the direction exactly *opposite* to the one co-evolution$_M$ predicts, i.e., toward a growing *in*commensurability that predicts a fragmentation of *psychological* categories.

If the "fragmentation and reconfiguration" of psychological categories involved only the elaboration or adjustment (or even the in-principle replaceability) of psychological theories by discoveries in the neurosciences, co-evolution$_M$ might suffice. In this second view, though, this process can lead to the eventual eradication of major parts of psychology. So, for example, Churchland remarks that "there is a tendency to assume that the capacities at the cognitive level are well defined ... in the case of memory and learning, however, the categorial definition is far from optimal, and *remembering stands to go the way of impetus*." (1986, p. 373, emphasis added[3].) Here Churchland anticipates that just as the new physics of Galileo and his successors ousted the late-medieval theory of impetus, so too shall advances in neuroscience dispose of psychologists' speculations about memory. This, then, is co-evolution$_S$ (co-evolution producing the eliminations of theories characteristic of scientific revolutions) in which the theoretical perspectives of two neighboring sciences are so disparate that eventually the theoretical commitments of one must go – in the face of the other's success.

Co-evolution$_S$ underlies the position for which the Churchlands' advocacy has been famous, viz., eliminative materialism.[4] They have contended that progress in the neurosciences will probably bring about the elimination of folk psychology as well as any other psychological theories that involve commitments to the propositional attitudes (presumably including much of mainstream cognitive and social psychology). Just as scientists banished phlogiston and caloric fluid, so too will the propositional attitudes be expelled as neuroscience progresses. The psychological conjectures in question (will) fail to match the descriptive, explanatory, and predictive successes of their neuroscientific competitors. Moreover, their substantial dissimilarities to those alleged competitors preclude any sort of reconciliation. Consequently, numerous theoretical notions in psychology stand to go the way of impetus. This is the predicted result when the Churchlands emphasize, among those "conflicting indications," the *uncongenial* relations between psychology and neuroscience.

Revising their extreme eliminativism, the Churchlands sometimes seem to intend these two interpretations to address different stages in the co-evolutionary process (as I suggested above): first, the demolition of much current psychology via co-evolution$_S$ followed by, second, the reconstruction of a neuroscientifically inspired psychology via co-evolution$_M$. The crucial point for now is that these two interpretations of co-evolution hold that the relationship between two theories will, over time, shift in one direction (as opposed to the other) on the Churchlands' continuum.

An obvious question arises, though. If either direction is possible, then what are the variables that determine the direction of any shift? (This question presses the revised version of eliminativism no less than the original.) The Churchlands have not addressed this question directly, because they have recognized that the complexities of the intertheoretic relations in question and of the relationship of psychology to neuroscience, in particular, require more. Enter the third interpretation.

One of Patricia Churchland's extended comments about her general model of reduction (1986, pp. 296–7) is especially revealing, since it reflects at various points the influence of all three interpretations.

... some misgivings may linger about the possibility of reduction should it be assumed that a reductive strategy means an exclusively bottom-up strategy ... These misgivings are really just bugbears, and they have no place in my framework for reduction.

... if the reduction is smooth, its reduction gives it [the reduced theory] – and its phenomena – a firmer place in the larger scheme ... If the reduction involves a major correction, the corrected, reduced theory continues to play a role in prediction and explanation ... Only if one theory is eliminated by another does it fall by the wayside.

...coevolution ... is certain to be more productive than an isolated bottom-up strategy.

The second paragraph traces points on the continuum. It alludes initially to co-evolution$_M$ – its final sentence to co-evolution$_S$. It is the first and third paragraphs, however, where shadows of a third interpretation appear.

Closely related to co-evolution$_M$ is co-evolution$_P$ (co-evolution as explanatory pluralism). Their many similarities notwithstanding, it is worth teasing them apart. As a first pass, where co-evolution$_M$ anticipates increasing intertheoretic integration largely guided by and with a default preference for the lower level, co-evolution$_P$ construes the process as preserving a diverse set of partially integrated yet semi-autonomous explanatory perspectives – where that non-negligible measure of analytical independence rests at each analytical level on the explanatory success and epistemic integrity of the theories and on the suggestiveness of the empirical findings. Co-evolution$_M$, in effect, holds that selection pressures are exerted exclusively from the bottom up, whereas co-evolution$_P$ attends to the constraints imposed by the needs and demands of theories operating at higher levels.

These apparently small differences are but the fringe skirmishes of some of the most basic epistemological and metaphysical battles in the philosophy of science. Space limitations preclude extensive development, but broadly, if they are not persuaded by co-evolution$_S$, physicalists prefer co-evolution$_M$, since it suggests a science unified in both theory and ontology that accords priority to the lower (i.e., physical) levels. More pragmatically minded philosophers opt for co-evolution$_P$, forgoing assurances of and worries about a unified science and metaphysical purity in favor of enhanced explanatory resources. For nearly a decade now the Churchlands have been negotiating their interests in unified science and metaphysical purity on the one hand with their interests in enhanced explanatory resources and internalism on the other. (See McCauley 1993 and note 10 below.) The relaxation of their eliminativism and their emerging preference for co-evolution$_P$ indicate the influence of pragmatic currents in their thought.

Co-evolution$_P$ is prominent in *Neurophilosophy* and even more so in subsequent work.[5] Patricia Churchland claims that "the history of science reveals that co-evolution of theories has typically been mutually enriching," that "[r]esearch influences go up and down and all over the map," that "co-evolution typically is . . . interactive . . . and involves one theory's being susceptible to correction and reconceptualization at the behest of the cohort theory," and that "psychology and neuroscience should each be vulnerable to disconfirmation and revision at any level by the discoveries of the other" (1986, pp. 363, 368, 373, 376).

Figure 1.1 seems the most plausible interpretation of the relationship between these three notions of co-evolution and the earlier continuum model; it roughly indicates the regions of that continuum where the cases covered by the three types of co-evolution end up. (See Churchland and Churchland 1990, p. 252.)

Section 4 will suggest that in figure 1.1 the picture of intertheoretic relations and co-evolution, in particular, is oversimplified to the point of distortion. The intertheoretic dynamics of scientific revolutions are quite different from those of approximate microreduction and explanatory pluralism. Crucially, co-evolution$_P$ is incompatible with co-evolution$_S$. The *mutual* intertheoretic enrichment co-evolution$_P$ envisions will not arise, if neuroscience is radically reconfiguring (let alone eliminating) psychology. Neither the history of science nor pragmatic accounts of scientific practice offer much reason to think that co-evolution$_S$ provides either an accurate description or a useful norm for the relationship between psychology and neuroscience or for any such relation between theories in sciences operating at *different* analytical levels.

The differences between co-evolution$_P$ and co-evolution$_M$ are also important. At stake is the question of the relative priority of neuroscientific (lower-level) and psychological (upper-level) contributions to the science of the mind/brain. This topic will dominate section 5. In criticizing co-evolution$_S$ and curtailing co-evolution$_M$, the next two sections aim, ultimately, to endorse and develop the notion of explanatory pluralism.

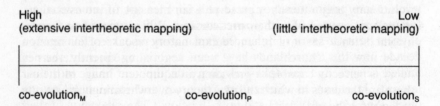

Figure 1.1 indicates, at the left:

High
(extensive intertheoretic mapping)

at the right:

Low
(little intertheoretic mapping)

along the bottom: co-evolution$_M$ co-evolution$_P$ co-evolution$_S$

Figure 1.1 Three notions of co-evolution situated on the Churchlands' continuum

4   Exploring Explanatory Pluralism: Debunking
Co-evolution$_S$

Enlisting a distinction Wimsatt (1976) introduced between *intralevel* and *interlevel* contexts, I have previously developed a model of inter-theoretic relations that discloses why we should not expect advances in neuroscience to eliminate much psychology directly (McCauley 1986). More generally, it suggests that co-evolution$_S$ does not very happily model the co-evolving relations of theories at different levels.

The sorts of unequivocal eliminations of theories and ontologies that co-evolution$_S$ countenances arise in *intralevel* contexts involving considerable incommensurability. These contexts concern changes *within* a particular science over time. They include the classic cases that philosophers group under the rubric of "scientific revolutions" – impetus, phlogiston, caloric fluid, and the like. Within a particular level of analysis some newly proposed theory proves superior to its immediate predecessor with which it is substantially discontinuous. When the scientific community opts for this new theory, most traces of its predecessor rapidly disappear. Since they offer incompatible accounts of many of the same phenomena, the new theory *explains* the old theory *away*.

By contrast, intralevel situations where the mappings between theories are reasonably good fall near the other end of the Churchlands' continuum. Here the new theory *explains* its predecessor, which it also typically corrects. Scientists regard the earlier theory's domain as a special case to which the new theory applies and for which the old theory continues to suffice as a useful calculating heuristic. Although corrected and incorporated as a special case into a more general theory, Newton's laws of motion work well for most practical purposes.

A new theory disrupts science less to the extent it preserves (rather than overthrows) the cherished insights and conceptual apparatus of its predecessors. It may require reinterpretation of established notions ("planets," "genes," "grammar acquisition," etc.), but changes are evolutionary only when they preserve a fair measure of intensional and extensional overlap with their predecessors. When succeeding theories in some science are largely continuous, no one speaks of elimination. The change is evolutionary, not revolutionary. Consequently, the new theory is perfectly capable of providing an equipotent image of the old. These are the cases in which the new theory overwhelmingly *inherits* the evidence for the old.

Revolutionary or evolutionary, progress within some science eventually eliminates features of earlier theories. In revolutionary settings the changes are abrupt and the elimination is (relatively) immediate. In evolutionary contexts incompatibilities accrue over time. Although the transition from one theory to its immediate successor may be more or less smooth, over a series of such transitions all traces of ancestral theories may completely disappear. Consider the fate of "natural motions" from Aristotelian through Newtonian mechanics (McCauley 1986, pp. 192–3). Similarly, over the past hundred years the "memory trace" has undergone considerable evolutionary transformation. Some theorists would argue that the reinterpretations have been so substantial that the original notion (and what it allegedly referred to) has virtually vanished.[6]

Interlevel relations concern theories at different (typically neighboring) levels of analysis at a particular point in time (in contrast to intralevel cases concerned with successive theories at the *same* level of analysis). The Churchlands' continuum maps onto interlevel cases too.

When sciences at adjoining levels enjoy substantial intertheoretic mapping (in situations approximating classic microreductions) they heavily constrain one another's form – otherwise, why would anyone have attempted to characterize their relations in terms of deductive logic and identity statements? This is the effect of the knitting of two sciences into each other that co-evolution$_M$ envisions. A well-integrated lower-level theory has resources sufficient to reproduce the explanatory and predictive accomplishments of the corresponding upper-level theory; however, this often comes at considerable computational expense. As the Churchlands have emphasized, this does not disgrace the higher-level theory or lead to the evaporation of the phenomena it seeks to explain.

When considering interlevel cases with relatively unproblematic intertheoretic relations, the Churchlands, like the traditional reductionists before them,[7] have focused exclusively on their *resemblances* to the intralevel settings described above. (See, for example, Churchland 1986, p. 294). After all, here too the elaborations of the upper-level theory's central concepts that the lower-level, *reducing* theory offers often correct the less fine-grained, upper-level theory's pronouncements. However, because the theories are tightly knit, the upper-level theory still provides a useful and efficient approximation of the lower-level theory's results. This sounds quite like the cases of scientific evolution described above.

Beneath these resemblances, however, lie small but revealing differences. First, unlike the evolutionary intralevel cases, the reduced theory in interlevel situations does not stand in need of technical correction in every case. For a few situations at least, its results will conform precisely with those of the lower-level theory, because for these cases it adequately summarizes the effects of all relevant lower-level variables.[8] This contrasts with the *inescapable*, if often negligible (from a practical standpoint), divergence of the calculations of some theory and its successor, such as classical mechanics and the mechanics of relativity. (See Churchland and Churchland 1990, p. 251.) In interlevel cases corrections can arise because the upper-level theory is insufficiently fine grained to handle certain problems. By contrast, in intralevel cases corrections always arise because the earlier theory is wrong – by a little in evolutionary cases, by a lot in revolutionary ones. It follows that the upper-level theory is not always a mere calculating heuristic (as the replaced predecessor is in cases of scientific evolution). Moreover, the upper-level theory's heuristic advantages in well-integrated interlevel contexts are typically enormous, compared with intralevel cases. The divergence of computational effort between the classical and statistical solutions for simple problems about gases (an interlevel case) dwarfs that between classical mechanics and the mechanics of relativity for simple problems about motion (an intralevel case). Of a piece with this observation, the Churchlands quite accurately describe the quantum calculations of various chemical properties (another interlevel case) as "daunting" (1990, p. 251). Finally, the upper-level theory lays out regularities about a subset of the phenomena that the lower-level theory encompasses but for which it has neither the resources nor the motivation to highlight. That is the price of the lower-level theory's generality and finer grain.

If these considerations are not compelling, scrutiny of interlevel circumstances that support relatively little intertheoretic mapping reveals far more important grounds for stressing the distinction between interlevel and intralevel settings. Here two sciences at adjacent levels address some common explananda under different descriptions, but their explanatory stories are largely (though not wholly) incompatible. In the Churchlands' view, this is just the relationship between neuroscience and most of folk psychology, and if remembering is to go the way of impetus, the relationship between neuroscience and some important parts of scientific psychology as well.

If all these intertheoretic relations should receive a *unified* treatment, as traditional reductionists, the Churchlands (e.g., Churchland and Sejnowski 1990, p. 229), and Figure 1 suggest, then it is perfectly reasonable to expect elimination in those interlevel situations involving significant incommensurability. The problem, though, is that neither the history of science, nor current scientific practice, nor the scientific research the Churchlands champion, nor a concern for explanatory pluralism offers much reason to expect theory elimination in such settings.

Incommensurability in interlevel contexts neither requires the elimination of theories on principled grounds nor results in such eliminations in fact. Admittedly, in the early stages of a science's history it is not always easy to distinguish levels of analysis nor, consequently, to distinguish what would count as an interlevel, as opposed to an intralevel, elimination. Crucially, though, the history of science and especially the history of late nineteenth- and twentieth-century science offer no examples of large-scale interlevel theory elimination (particularly of the wholesale variety that standard eliminativism and co-evolution$_S$ envision) once the upper-level science achieves sufficient historical momentum to enjoy the accoutrements of other recognized sciences (such as characteristic research techniques and instruments, journals, university departments, professional societies, and funding agencies). The reason is simple enough. Mature sciences are largely defined by their theories and, more generally, by their research traditions (Laudan 1977), hence elimination of an upper-level theory by a lower-level theory may risk the elimination of the upper-level scientific enterprise! (Presumably this is why Nagel always spoke of the reduction of a *science*, rather than of a theory, when addressing interlevel cases.)

A motive for undertaking interlevel investigation (especially when the intertheoretic connections are not plentiful) is to explore one science's successful problem-solving strategies as a means to inspire research, provoke discoveries, and solve recalcitrant problems at another level. (Bechtel and Richardson (1993) focus in particular on the problem of understanding the operation of mechanisms.) Monitoring developments in theories at neighboring levels is often a fruitful heuristic of discovery. The strategy's fruitfulness depends precisely on the two sciences maintaining a measure of independence from one another.

This is the mark of explanatory pluralism and co-evolution$_P$. A paucity of interlevel connections only enhances the (relative) integrity and autonomy of the upper-level science. As Wimsatt notes, "in interlevel reduction, the more difficult the translation becomes, the more *irreplaceable* the upper level theory is! It becomes the only practical way of handling the regularities it describes" (1976, p. 222). The theories at the two levels possess different conceptual and explanatory resources, which underscore different features of their common explanandum. They provide multiple explanatory perspectives that should be judged on the basis of their empirical success – not on hopes about their putative promise for the theoretical (or ontological) unification of science. For the pragmatically inclined, explanatory success is both sufficiently valuable and rare that it would be imprudent to encourage the elimination of any promising avenue of research. As Churchland and Sejnowski remark, "the co-evolutionary advice regarding methodological efficiency is 'let many flowers bloom'" (1992, p. 13).

The Churchlands have argued famously, however, that folk psychology is barren (P. S. Churchland 1986, pp. 288–312; P. M. Churchland 1989, pp. 2–11). Those arguments have provoked an entire literature in response (see Greenwood 1991; Christensen and Turner 1993). I am sympathetic with the Churchlands' arguments, at least when they wield them against positions in the philosophy of mind that deny the explanatory goals and the conjectural and fallible character of folk psychology. That folk psychology offers explanations and that it is conjectural and fallible are both correct. That is just not the whole story, though.

The pivotal question for a pragmatist is whether folk psychology can contribute to the progress of our knowledge or, better, whether folk psychology contains resources that may aid subsequent, more systematic psychological theorizing. Attribution theory, the theory of cognitive dissonance, and other proposals within social psychology employ as rich versions of the propositional attitudes as does folk psychology (Bechtel and Abrahamsen 1993). Moreover, as Dennett (1987) has emphasized, employing the intentional stance aids theorizing about operative subsystems in sub-personal cognitive psychology.[9] These are just two fronts where *psychological* science seems to be simultaneously employing and, ever so gradually, *transforming* familiar folk psychological notions. Arguably, then, the Churchlands may have underestimated the possible contribution of the resources of folk psychology, because they have been insufficiently attentive to their role in social psychological and cognitive theorizing (McCauley 1987, 1989). Indeed, they *sometimes* disregard the psychological altogether.[10] (See, however, note 14 below.)

I suspect that such neglect is born of insisting on a unified account of intertheoretic relations and of entertaining images of co-evolution$_s$, in particular. The Churchlands are correct to emphasize the salient role of theory elimination in scientific progress, but these eliminations are *intralevel* processes and most univocally so (1) when the levels in question concern scientific pursuits as well established as neuroscience and psychology and (2) when those levels are construed as thickly, i.e., as inclusively, as the distinction between those two sciences implies. The theories and characteristic ontologies informing Stahl's account of combustion and Young's account of the propagation of light were replaced by theories (with new ontologies) that operated at the same levels of analysis and that were identified, both now and then, as continuations of the research traditions associated with those levels. Elimination in science is principally an intralevel process.

That is not to assert, however that interlevel considerations play no role. Even with levels of analysis so thickly construed, I do *not* mean to deny that scientists' decisions at lower and higher levels influence theoretical developments at a given level. Nor do I wish to deny that at that targeted level such developments can involve eliminations. Rather, the critical point is that these influences are reliably *mediated* by developments in the conceptual apparatus and research practices that are associated with the research tradition of the targeted level. (See Bechtel and Richardson 1993, especially chapter 8, and Bechtel's chapter in this volume.)

If it is *construed as an explanatory construct*, I agree with the Churchlands that much of folk psychology may well undergo substantial revision and, perhaps, even elimination eventually.[11] What I am suggesting, however, is the following:

1 that those changes will occur primarily as a result of progress within social and cognitive psychology, i.e., that they will arise as the consequence of intralevel processes within the psychological level of analysis;
2 that, by virtue of the role of intentional attributions in the theories of social and cognitive psychology, this displacement will probably be quite gradual, i.e., that, so far, the changes are proving evolutionary, not revolutionary;
3 that theoretical developments within those sub-disciplines of psychology will mediate whatever co-evolutionary influence neuroscience has in this outcome.

Mapping the Churchlands' continuum on to the intralevel-interlevel distinction yields the arrangement in figure 1.2. It readily accommodates co-evolution$_M$ and co-evolution$_P$, but co-evolution$_S$ finds no obvious home. The point is that the interaction of psychology and neuroscience, like all co-evolutionary situations, is a case of *interlevel* relations. In short, co-evolution$_S$ embodies a category mistake. It conflates the dynamics of the co-evolution of theories at different levels of analysis with those of scientific revolutions, which are intralevel processes.[12]

What follows in this revised picture in figure 1.2 about interlevel cases that reflect substantial incommensurability? In fact, I think such cases are extremely rare, especially if the sciences in question are well established, since part of becoming a well-established science is precisely to possess theories that recognizably cohere with at least some features of theories at contiguous levels. Arguably, the distinctions between levels of analysis already presume the extreme improbability of such radical incompatibility between theories operating at adjoining *scientific* levels. (Of course, not all explanatory theories are scientific theories.) If analyses diverge in nearly all respects, then it may no longer be clear

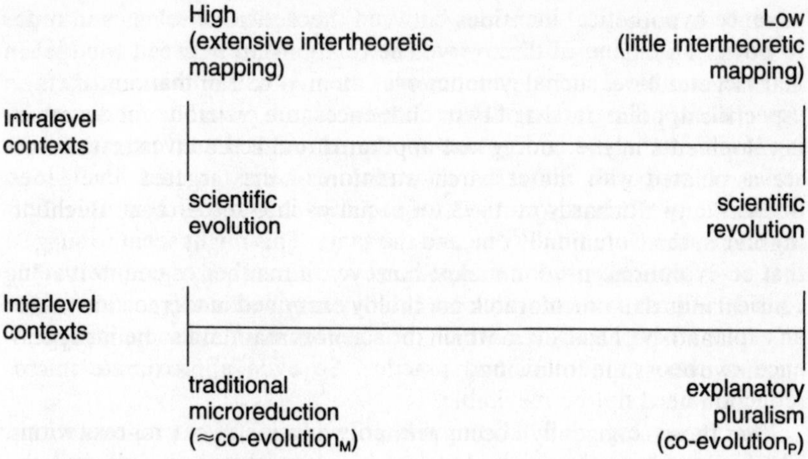

High (extensive intertheoretic mapping)		Low (little intertheoretic mapping)
Intralevel contexts		
	scientific evolution	scientific revolution
Interlevel contexts		
	traditional microreduction ($\approx$co-evolution$_M$)	explanatory pluralism (co-evolution$_P$)

Figure 1.2   Mapping degrees of intertheoretic continuity (the Churchlands' continuum) onto intralevel and interlevel contexts

that they share a common explanandum – tempting some researchers to adopt obscurantist strategies of metaphysical extravagance.[13]

The problems surrounding co-evolution$_S$ notwithstanding, in elaborating Wimsatt's metaphor of the co-evolution of theories the Churchlands have fundamentally reinvigorated the study of change in interlevel relations over time, arguably initiated by Schaffner (1967). As with this section, the next will say more about co-evolution$_P$ by opening with more about what it is not.

5   Exploring Explanatory Pluralism: Beyond Co-evolution$_M$

The demand in science for coherence of theories at adjacent levels of analysis is an additional motive, beyond the promise of new discoveries, for probing possible interlevel connections. The motive is to ascertain whether or not research at nearby levels coheres with and supports scientists' findings and, if it does not, to explore possible adjustments to increase the probability of such mutual support. This can, among other things, clarify respects in which the two sciences share a common explanandum.

In the long term scientists' concern for coherence among their results inevitably tends to encourage better intertheoretic mapping in interlevel settings. Forging such connections produces new discoveries in the respective sciences. One strategy, though certainly not the only one, is to advance hypothetical identities between theoretical ontologies in order to power an engine of discovery. The relationship between Mendelian genetics and biochemical genetics over the first half of this century is an especially apt illustration of two related research programs, at neighboring levels of analysis, aiding one another through the investigation of a series of proposals about which structures were, in fact, the genes. Scientists' two primary motives for inquiries into research at neighboring levels, then, are finally one and the same. This might seem to suggest that co-evolution$_M$ predominates; however, a number of countervailing considerations (some of which are briefly examined in this section) favor an explanatory pluralism in which the sciences maintain some independence of theory, method, and practice. So even approximate microreduction need not be inevitable.

Two issues especially distinguish co-evolution$_M$ and co-evolution$_P$. The first concerns the relative metaphysical, epistemic, and/or explanatory priority of upper- and lower-level theories in the co-evolutionary process. The second concerns the grounds offered for any disparate assignments of these priorities.

The default assumption adopted in an analysis of co-evolution$_M$ that accords with the traditional microreductionistic rationale for physicalism attributes comprehensive priority to lower levels. Classical microreduction would forecast a co-evolutionary process by which the overwhelming majority of the selection pressures are exerted from the bottom up. The upper-level theory may contribute in the process of discovery, providing an initial vocabulary and problems for research, but sooner or later it must conform to the lower-level theory's expectations. Here the grounds for this priority rest not merely on the theoretical maturity and superior precision lower-level theories typically enjoy (with which pragmatism has no complaint) but also on presumptions about those theories' metaphysical pre-eminence. (See note 10.)

Occasionally,[14] the Churchlands seem to subscribe to a version of co-evolution$_M$ that resembles this position. For example, Churchland and Sejnowski emphasize "the importance of the single neuron models [among the various sub-levels of analysis within neuroscience] as *the bedrock and fundament* into which network models *must* eventually fit" (1992, p. 13, emphasis added).[15] Although the Churchlands have avoided the traditional microreductionists' fervor about the replaceability of the reduced theory at the upper level (e.g., Churchland and Churchland 1990, p. 256), their repeated emphasis on lower-level theories' corrections of upper-level theories also suggests that selection pressures are largely unidirectional, especially when they treat these lower-level elaborations as of a piece with corrections in intralevel contexts where substantial ontological modification *is* sometimes part of the package.

Co-evolution$_M$ will prove relevant to but a small percentage of cases, at best. On the one hand, if co-evolution$_M$ is supposed to issue in the classical microreductionist program (presumably it is not), then all the familiar objections and caveats apply, plus at least one important additional one. The sort of tight integration with a dominant lower-level theory to which classical microreduction aspires must inevitably restrict research at the higher level. If there ever was a microreduction that conformed to all the logical and ontological constraints imposed by the classical model, for example Causey's (1977) version, it would endow the lower level with an explanatory and metaphysical priority that would discourage all motives for theoretical novelty at the higher level. It would encourage only those paths of research at the higher level that promised to preserve its tight fit with the theory at the lower level. Its effect, in short, would be to check imaginative scientific proposals.

On the other hand, if co-evolution$_M$ is supposed to result only in the weaker analogical relation to which the Churchlands' model of approximate reduction looks, then the points of reductive contact may prove less extensive than the knitting metaphor suggests, and the microreductionist case for the explanatory, epistemic, and metaphysical priority of lower levels ends up seeming somewhat less compelling, especially once we have teased apart the differences in the "corrections" that occur in interlevel and intralevel contexts.

The case for co-evolution$_P$, however, does not turn exclusively on the problems the two competing conceptions face. Scrutiny of actual cases, including those in cognitive neuroscience to which the Churchlands have devoted particular attention, strongly suggests that the outcome of the co-evolution of theories is usually as co-evolution$_P$ describes. Instead of driving inexorably toward comprehensive theoretical and practical integration, where the lower-level theory governs, scientific opportunism is usually closer to the truth in most interlevel forays. At least initially, scientists periodically monitor developments at nearby levels, searching for either interlevel support, tantalizing findings, or both.

Churchland and Sejnowski's survey of proposals concerning the neural basis of working memory is a fitting illustration (1992, pp. 297–305). Not only did the concept of "working memory" emerge out of theoretical developments in experimental psychology, but so did many of the findings that guide neural modeling. For example, Churchland and Sejnowski point explicitly to the discovery of a short-term memory deficit for verbal materials in some subjects. They also highlight the ability of various interference effects both to dissociate working memory from long-term memory in normal subjects and to dissociate subsystems of working memory (linked with auditory, visuospatial, and verbal materials) from one another. These discoveries in experimental psychology provided both inspiration and direction for neural modeling. They also constitute a set of findings that any relevant neuroscientific proposal should make sense of.

On even the most exacting philosophical standards, this last consideration is *epistemically* significant. Theoretical proposals and the research they spawn at the higher level do not merely contribute to the process of discovery at the lower level. The upper-level science provides a body of *evidence* against which the science at the lower level can evaluate competing models. This evidence is particularly useful, precisely because it frequently arises independently of the formulation of the specific lower-level models to whose assessment it contributes. It helps to ensure the independent testability of the models in question.

It has been widely conceded that upper-level theories can play a catalytic role in the process of *discovery* at the lower level. Indeed, sometimes the conceptual resources and research techniques of a lower-level science are basically insufficient to enable practitioners even to recognize some of that level's fundamental phenomena without aid and direction from an upper-level science. (Lykken et al. (1992) constitutes a particularly intriguing recent illustration.) In the previous section we also saw how microreductionistic proposals to subordinate upper-level explanations to lower-level explanations risk needlessly downplaying valuable resources for dealing with the often huge computational burdens lower-level theories entail. Upper-level theorizing (for example, in transmission genetics) contributes usefully to everyday scientific *problem solving*, even after lower-level research (for example, in molecular genetics) indicates the microlevel story is far more complicated. Scientific endeavors at different levels regularly display what Robert Burton (1993) has called a "strategic interdependence." Now we can see that upper-level theorizing also initiates research that can contribute to lower-level developments pertaining directly to *justification*. Microreductionistic proposals to subordinate upper-level sciences to lower-level sciences, either epistemically or metaphysically, risk needless evidentiary impoverishment.

The value of this evidence turns precisely on the fact that the research arose within a context of scientific theorizing and investigation sufficiently removed from and sufficiently autonomous of the lower-level research to ensure an honest check. These psychological findings do not occur in isolation. They arise in the course of ongoing theorizing and research at the psychological level. Their value to neuroscience rests in part on the fact that they emanate from a tradition of psychological theorizing and experimentation that neuroscience has not dominated. This is why it is worthwhile for each level of analysis to maintain a measure of independence.

As Churchland and Sejnowski note, experimental psychology has a century of findings (and theorizing) from which neuroscientists and neurocomputational modelers may draw (1992, p. 27; see too p. 240). Nothing more clearly illustrates the sort of scientific opportunism explanatory pluralism envisions than one of Sejnowski and Rosenberg's papers (1988) in defense of the claim that NETtalk plausibly models operative processes in human learning and cognition. (It is a fair question at what level of analysis connectionist modeling should be located. On the criteria I identified in section 2, it seems to occur at a level below that of social and cognitive psychology. Churchland and Sejnowski clearly regard it as a form of neurocomputational modeling. It is worth nothing that Michael Gazzaniga places Sejnowski and Rosenberg's chapter (1988) in the first half of his book, which concerns "*Neurobiologic* Considerations in Memory Function" rather than in the second half, which concerns "Psychological Dimensions of Memory Function in Humans.")

NETtalk is a connectionist system that converts English text into strings of phonemes (Sejnowski and Rosenberg 1987). It is a three-layer, feed-forward network that employs the standard back-propagation learning alogrithm. On any given trial NETtalk receives seven inputs corresponding to a window of seven letters (including punctuation and spaces between words, if they happen to arise). The desired output is the correct phoneme associated with the fourth item in the window. The three places on either side of the fourth item provide the network with information about how context affects pronunciation.

NETtalk's performance is nothing short of remarkable. It captures most of the regularities in English pronunciation and many of the irregularities as well. After 50,000 training trials with words, its accuracy with phonemes approaches 95 percent, and it is virtually perfect with stresses and syllable boundaries.

The critical question for now, however, is what evidence Sejnowski and Rosenberg might cite to support the claim that NETtalk models processes that resemble those involved in human learning and cognition. A model of co-evolution as explanatory pluralism suggests that attention to the findings of experimental psychology might prove just as helpful here as attention to research on neural structure, and, in fact, not only do Sejnowski and Rosenberg look to psychology, they also look to one of those century-old findings about *remembering*, the spacing effect.

The spacing effect is the finding that distributed practice with items enhances the probability of their long-term retention more than massed practice does. If occasions for rehearsal are spaced out over time, the probability is high that memory performance will exceed that from employing some small number of massed practice sessions of comparable duration at the outset. Massed repetition facilitates memory when retention intervals are extremely short. In practical terms, the spacing effect makes cramming for an exam not nearly so helpful as regular, daily preparation, whereas retention of two new telephone numbers supplied by Directory Assistance requires immediate, massed rehearsal if they cannot be written down.

In the course of investigating the various hypotheses that psychologists have offered for explaining the spacing effect, researchers have demonstrated its robustness across a huge variety of experimental settings, materials, and tasks. Thus, Sejnowski and Rosenberg suspect that it reflects "something of central importance in memory" (1988, p. 163). Consequently, if NETtalk can be induced to exhibit the spacing effect this is by no means trivial. It would be even more striking if its exhibition of the effect was similar in form to documented human performance.

Because of NETtalk's architecture the obvious comparison is with studies of cued recall. Sejnowski and Rosenberg chose a design after Glenberg (1976). The design called for training NETtalk up in the standard fashion and then presenting it with the cues from a list of 20 paired associates where those cues were strings of six random letters and their associated responses were randomly generated phoneme and stress strings six characters long. (This ensured that NETtalk's performance at the test could not be a function of any information it had acquired about English pronunciation.) During both the spacing interval between training opportunities and the retention interval before the test, NETtalk was presented with English distractor words that were part of its original training corpus. Both training on the paired associates and distractor episodes included feedback via back propagation. The order of the presentations to NETtalk in the experiment was as follows:

1   2, 10, or 20 presentations of each of the 20 paired associate cues;
2   a spacing interval of 0, 1, 4, 8, 20, or 40 distractors;
3   2, 10, or 20 re-presentations of each of the 20 paired associate cues;
4   a retention interval of 2, 8, 32, or 64 distractors;
5   a test of NETtalk's accuracy in cued recall of the 20 paired associates.

In short, NETtalk displayed the spacing effect: "A significant spacing effect was observed in NETtalk: Retention of nonwords after a 64-item retention interval was significantly better when presented at the longer spacings (distributed presentation) than at the shorter spacings. In addition, a significant advantage for massed presentations was found for short-term retention of the items." (Sejnowski and Rosenberg 1988, p. 167.) Moreover, although direct comparison was impossible, NET-talk's overall response profile resembled that of Glenberg's human subjects.

The interlevel interaction here benefits both cognitive psychology and neurocomputational modeling. Sejnowski and Rosenberg briefly review the two theoretical proposals for explaining the spacing effect in cognitive psychology, pointing out that neither the encoding variability hypothesis (e.g., Bower 1972) nor the processing effort hypothesis (e.g., Jacoby 1978) can account for all the available data. They then suggest a further hypothesis focusing on the form in which information is encoded in a connectionist network, i.e., on the form of the memory representation. They propose that the short-term advantage of massed practice and, particularly, the longer-term advantage of distributed practice are at least partially explicable in terms of the dynamics of connectionist nets.

Crucially, Sejnowski and Rosenberg do *not* construe their hypothesis as competing with (let alone correcting or eliminating) the two psychological proposals. (They have, after all, explored but one set of findings concerning cued recall.) Instead, they emphasize its compatibility with each. They claim correctly that it offers "a different type of explanation" at "a different level of explanation" (1988, p. 170). They explicitly discuss ways in which the notions of "encoding variability" and "processing effort" could map onto the dynamics of connectionist networks. These finer-grained accounts of these processes in terms of a network's operations suggest bases for *elaborating* the two hypotheses.

If the co-evolution of research in interlevel contexts yields the explanatory pluralism for which I have been plumping, then it is not only the lower level that offers the aid and comfort, nor is it only the higher level that receives it. As the neural modeling of working memory illustrates, here too psychological findings provide both evidentiary support and strategic guidance to lower-level modeling of brain functioning. Sejnowski and Rosenberg remark that "those aspects of the network's performance that are similar to human performance are good candidates for general properties of network models" (1988, p. 171). Their project reflects a general strategy for the testing and refinement of neurocomputational models that relies on the relative independence of work in experimental psychology. Features of particular networks that enable them to mimic aspects of the human performance that psychology documents themselves deserve mimicry in subsequent modeling of human cognition.

What is especially clear about the contribution of higher levels in this example is Sejnowski and Rosenberg's explicit acknowledgment of just how far "guidance" can go. "When NETtalk deviates from human performance, there is good reason to believe that a more detailed account of brain circuitry may be necessary." (1988, pp. 172.) Their comment accords nicely with the account of explanatory pluralism I have been developing. Unlike the picture of co-evolution inspired by the tradition of microreductionism, a pragmatically inspired explanatory pluralism permits no *a priori* presumptions about lower-level priority. Sejnowski and Rosenberg readily allow that our psychological knowledge enjoys sufficient integrity to forcefully urge further *elaboration* of analyses of brain systems formulated at lower levels.[16] This would be no less (and no more) a correction of the lower-level theory (and its ontology) than are the lower-level "corrections" of upper-level theories (and their ontologies) that the Churchlands have sometimes been wont to stress.

Such divergences, then, are not grounds for dismissal. They are, rather, opportunities for advance. The co-evolution of sciences (not just theories) at contiguous levels of analysis preserves the plurality of explanatory perspectives that the distinctions between levels imply, because leaving these research traditions to their own devices is an effective means of ensuring scientific progress.

Notes

I wish to express my gratitude to William Bechtel and Donald Rutherford for their many helpful comments on an earlier draft of this paper.

1 The story is even more complex, since each level of analysis has both a synchronic and a diachronic moment for which separate theories have been developed. See McCauley (forthcoming). At the biological level, for example, cell biology is one of the synchronic sub-disciplines focusing on the structures within the cell whereas evolutionary biology is devoted to the study of change in forms of life over time. The Churchlands have confined their discussions almost exclusively to synchronic examples.

2 One of the first, if not *the* first, is Wimsatt's (1976) classic discussion.

3 Although they concur with Churchland's judgment that the folk psychological notion of a unitary faculty of memory is probably wrong, Hirst and Gazzaniga (1988, pp. 276, 294, 304–5) seem to adopt a far more sanguine view about the contributions of psychology (both folk and experimental) to our understanding of memory. They recognize that the fragmentation of 'memory' need not lead to its elimination. (See section 5 below.)

4 – and the position from which they have generally (though not unequivocally) retreated over the past few years.

5 See Churchland and Sejnowski 1990, p. 229; 1992, pp. 10–13; Churchland, Koch, and Sejnowski 1990, pp. 51; 54.

6   Consider the discussion in Neisser (1967).

7   Interestingly, Ernest Nagel's *The Structure of Science* (1961), the *locus classicus* of traditional research on reduction, implicitly recognizes the importance of distinguishing between intralevel and interlevel contexts. Nagel consistently describes intralevel cases as involving the reduction of *theories* and interlevel cases as involving the reduction of *sciences*.

8   This is, in part, the result of the same considerations that motivate the Churchlands' and Richardson's (1979) arguments, which alleged that reductions that conform to traditional microreductionistic standards can only be domain specific.

9   – or in neuropsychology, as Churchland and Sejnowski's discussion of the role of the hippocampus in short-term memory illustrates (1992, p. 282). See also P. S. Churchland 1986, p. 361.

10 An interesting illustration arises in Churchland and Sejnowski's discussion of the major levels of organization in the nervous system (1992, pp. 10–11). Their diagram of the relevant levels tops out at the central nervous system with no mention of psychology. The obvious defense is to note that the diagram addresses *anatomical* structures of the nervous system only. Fair enough. What is telling, though, is a footnote (1992, p. 11, note 5) to this discussion. Churchland and Sejnowski concede that a more comprehensive account would include a *social* level above the central nervous system. At least for the purposes of this discussion, they seem not even to countenance the possibility that cognitive research may capture organizational structure of explanatory significance not immediately reducible to the neurophysiological. (See too Sejnowski and Churchland 1989, p. 343.)

A meta-level comment: the physicalist holds that metaphysical manifestness (which, remember, is *physical* manifestness for the physicalist) constrains what will count as *satisfactory* explanation, whereas the pragmatist proposes that explanatory success *should* constrain metaphysical commitment. If that diagnosis is correct, the ongoing negotiation in the Churchlands' work I described in section 3 is, at its root, one about competing norms.

11 I should emphasize that I am speaking of the elimination of folk psychology as an explanatory construct *within* scientific psychology. In physics the elimination of the principles of folk physics centuries ago has had little effect on its persistence among the folk.

12 The illustrations the Churchlands (1990) offer in support of their "overview of the general nature of intertheoretic reduction" (p. 249) proceed in the following order:

1   the reduction of Kepler's laws to Newton's (intralevel);

2   the reduction of the ideal gas law to the kinetic theory – emphasizing (p. 250, some emphasis added) that "this reduction involved *identifying* a familiar *phenomenal* property of common objects with a highly unfamiliar *micro*-physical property" (interlevel);

3 the reduction of classical (valence) chemistry by atomic and subatomic (quantum) physics (interlevel);

4 the reduction of Newtonian mechanics to the mechanics of Special Relativity (intralevel);

5 the elimination of phlogiston by Lavoisier's oxygen theory of combustion (intralevel).

13 But just as progress in tracing the relevant biological systems preserved the vitality of organisms without vitalism, so too is progress in tracing the relevant psychological systems slowly revealing how we can preserve the cleverness and wondrous experiences of intelligent creatures without dualism. The interlevel influences of neuroscience will no more co-opt or eliminate psychological theorizing than the interlevel influences of chemistry co-opted or eliminated physiological theorizing.

14 As noted near the end of section 3, the Churchlands more often seem to endorse an account of co-evolution resembling co-evolution$_p$. In Churchland and Sejnowski 1990 (p. 250) and 1992 (p. 240), they not only advocate a form of explanatory pluralism but also explicitly include the psychological sciences.

15 Conceding that it will not involve a single model nor direct explanations of higher levels in terms of events at the molecular level, Churchland and Sejnowski, none the less, aspire to a "unified account" of the nervous system, where "the integration [will] consist of a chain of theories and models that links adjacent levels" (Sejnowski and Churchland 1989, p. 343).

16 If neurocomputational modeling of networks constitutes a higher level of analysis than the study of particular neurons, and it certainly seems to on Churchland and Sejnowski's view (1992, p. 11), then their take on recordings of single cells' response profiles in the visual cortex (1992, pp. 183–8) is an illustration of just the sort of circumstances that the Sejnowski and Rosenberg citation allows for – one in which higher-level research impels a re-evaluation of lower-level doctrines.

Churchland and Sejnowski, following Lehky and Sejnowski (1988), argue that neurocomputational research on the visual system's ability to extract shapes exclusively from information about shading reveals that the conventional interpretation of the function of receptive fields of neurons in the visual cortex may well be wrong. That interpretation, which arose from single-cell studies, holds that these neurons function as edge and bar detectors. Churchland and Sejnowski maintain that this interpretation ignores the cells' projective fields. Hidden units in Lehky and Sejnowski's model developed receptive fields with similar response profiles, but these orientations were the result of training the network on the shape-from-shading task. "In a trained-up network, the hidden units represent an intermediate transformation for a computational task quite different from the one that has been customarily ascribed . . . they are used to determine the shape from the shading, not to detect boundaries." (Churchland and Sejnowski 1992, pp. 185–6.)

References

Bechtel, W. (ed.) (1986). "The Nature of Scientific Integration," *Integrating Scientific Disciplines*. The Hague: Martinus Nijhoff.

Bechtel, W. and Abrahamsen, A. A. (1993). "Connectionism and the Future of Folk Psychology," in R. G. Burton (ed.), *Natural and Artificial Minds*. Albany: SUNY Press.

Bechtel, W. and Richardson, R. C. (1993). *Discovering Complexity*. Princeton: Princeton University Press.

Bickle, J. (1992). "Mental Anomaly and the New Mind-Brain Reductionism," *Philosophy of Science* **59**, 217–30.

Bower, G. H. (1972). "Stimulus-Sampling Theory of Encoding Variability," in A. W. Melton and E. Martin (eds), *Coding Processes in Human Memory*. Washington: V. H. Winston & Sons.

Burton, R. G. (1993). "Reduction, Elimination, and Strategic Interdependence," in R. G. Burton (ed.), *Natural and Artificial Minds*. Albany: SUNY Press.

Causey, R. (1972). "Uniform Microreductions," *Synthese* **25**, 176–218.

Causey, R. (1977). *Unity of Science*. Dordrecht: Reidel.

Christensen, S. M. and Turner, D. R. (eds) (1993). *Folk Psychology and the Philosophy of Mind*. Hillsdale, NJ: Lawrence Erlbaum.

Churchland, P. M. (1979). *Scientific Realism and the Plasticity of Mind*. Cambridge: Cambridge University Press.

Churchland, P. M. (1989). *A Neurocomputational Perspective: The Nature of Mind and the Structure of Science*. Cambridge: MIT Press.

Churchland, P. M. and Churchland, P. S. (1990). "Intertheoretic Reduction: A Neuroscientist's Field Guide," *Seminars in the Neurosciences* **2**, 249–56.

Churchland, P. S. (1986). *Neurophilosophy: Toward a Unified Science of the Mind-Brain*. Cambridge: MIT Press.

Churchland, P. S., Koch, C., and Sejnowski, T. J. (1990). "What is Computational Neuroscience?" in E. L. Schwartz (ed.), *Computational Neuroscience*. Cambridge: MIT Press.

Churchland, P. S. and Sejnowski, T. J. (1990). "Neural Representation and Neural Computation," in W. Lycan (ed.), *Mind and Cognition: A Reader*. Oxford: Blackwell.

Churchland, P. S. and Sejnowski, T. J. (1992). *The Computational Brain*. Cambridge: MIT Press.

Dennett, D. C. (1987). "Three Kinds of Intentional Psychology," *The Intentional Stance*. Cambridge: MIT Press.

Enc, B. (1983). "In Defense of the Identity Theory," *Journal of Philosophy* **80**, 279–98.

Feyerabend, P. K. (1962). "Explanation, Reduction, and Empiricism," in

H. Feigl and G. Maxwell (eds), *Minnesota Studies in the Philosophy of Science*. Volume 3. Minneapolis: University of Minnesota Press.

Fodor, J. A. (1975). *The Language of Thought*. New York: Thomas Y. Crowell.

Glenberg, A. M. (1976). "Monotonic and Nonmonotonic Lag Effects in Paired-Associate and Recognition Memory Paradigms," *Journal of Verbal Learning and Verbal Behavior* 15, 1–16.

Greenwood, J. D. (ed.) (1991). *The Future of Folk Psychology*. New York: Cambridge University Press.

Hirst, W. and Gazzaniga, M. (1988). "Present and Future of Memory Research and Its Applications," in M. Gazzaniga (ed.), *Perspectives in Memory Research*. Cambridge: MIT Press.

Hooker, C. (1981). "Towards a General Theory of Reduction," *Dialogue* 20: 38–59, 201–36, 496–529.

Jacoby, L. L. (1978). "On Interpreting the Effects of Repetition: Solving a Problem Versus Remembering a Solution," *Journal of Verbal Learning and Verbal Behavior* 17, 649–67.

Kuhn, T. (1970). *The Structure of Scientific Revolutions* (2nd edition). Chicago: University of Chicago Press.

Laudan, L. (1977). *Progress and Its Problems*. Berkeley: University of California Press.

Lehky, S. R. and Sejnowski, T. J. (1988). "Network Model of Shape-from-Shading: Neural Function Arises from Both Receptive and Projective Fields," *Nature* 333, 452–54.

Lykken, D. T., McGue, M., Tellegen, A., and Bouchard, T. J. (1992). "Emergenesis: Genetic Traits that May Not Run in Families," *American Psychologist* 47, 1565–77.

McCauley, R. N. (1981). "Hypothetical Identities and Ontological Economizing: Comments on Causey's Program for the Unity of Science," *Philosophy of Science* 48, 218–27.

McCauley, R. N. (1986). "Intertheoretic Relations and the Future of Psychology," *Philosophy of Science* 53, 179–99.

McCauley, R. N. (1987). "The Role of Cognitive Explanations in Psychology," *Behaviorism* (subsequently *Behavior and Philosophy*) 15, 27–40.

McCauley, R. N. (1989). "Psychology in Mid-Stream," *Behaviorism* (subsequently *Behavior and Philosophy*) 17, 75–7.

McCauley, R. N. (1993). "Brainwork: A Review of Paul Churchland's *A Neurocomputational Perspective*," *Philosophical Psychology* 6, 81–96.

McCauley, R. N. (forthcoming). "Cross-Scientific Relations: Toward an Integrated Approach to the Study of the Emotions," in B. Shore and C. Worthman (eds.), *The Emotions: Culture, Psychology, Biology*.

Nagel, E. (1961). *The Structure of Science*. New York: Harcourt, Brace and World.

Neisser, U. (1967). *Cognitive Psychology*. New York: Appleton-Century-Crofts.

Oppenheim, P. and Putnam, H. (1958). "Unity of Science as a Working Hypothesis," in H. Feigl, M. Scriven, and G. Maxwell (eds.), *Minnesota*

Studies in the Philosophy of Science. Volume 2. Minneapolis: University of Minnesota Press.

Richardson, R. (1979). "Functionalism and Reductionism," *Philosophy of Science* **46**, 533–58.

Schaffner, K. (1967). "Approaches to Reduction," *Philosophy of Science* **34**, 137–47.

Sejnowski, T. J. and Churchland, P. S. (1989). "Brain and Cognition," in M. Posner (ed.), *Foundations of Cognitive Science.* Cambridge: MIT Press.

Sejnowski, T. J. and Rosenberg, C. R. (1987). "Parallel Networks that Learn to Pronounce English Text," *Complex Systems* **1**, 145–68.

Sejnowski, T. J. and Rosenberg, C. (1988). "Learning and Representation in Connectionist Models," in M. Gazzaniga (ed.), *Perspectives in Memory Research.* Cambridge: MIT Press.

Thagard, P. (1992). *Conceptual Revolutions.* Princeton: Princeton University Press.

Wimsatt, W. C. (1976). "Reductionism, Levels of Organization, and the Mind-Body Problem," in G. Globus, G. Maxwell, and I. Savodnik (eds), *Consciousness and the Brain.* New York: Plenum Press.

2

From Neurophilosophy to Neurocomputation: Searching for the Cognitive Forest

Patricia Kitcher

Introduction

Although the idea still seems very new and fresh and bold, if you count it has been more than a dozen years since Patricia Churchland launched the new sub-discipline of "neurophilosophy".[1] That is not a long time for a research program to be running, but perhaps it is long enough to get some sense of its accomplishments. I begin by presenting the central claims of Neurophilosophy and the general form of argument that Churchland has used to argue for those claims. Over the years, that form has been remarkably consistent. What has changed are the examples invoked to help make the case. I chart the progression of examples from "A Perspective on Mind-Brain Research" (1980) to *Neurophilosophy* (1986) to *The Computational Brain* (co-authored with Terrence Sejnowski, 1992). Hence my picture of the case for neurophilosophy will be neither broad nor timeless, but specific and historically dated.

Neurophilosophy: Theses and Argument

Neurophilosphy encompasses several distinguishable theses. The least controversial is the negation of the belief that Churchland attributes to philosophers right at the beginning of "A Perspective on Mind-Brain Research": "Direct study of the brain is not likely to be very fruitful in the endeavor to get a theory of how the mind-brain works" (1980, 185). Although the term "neurophilosophy" was not introduced until 1986, the clear implication of this article was a strong claim: Direct study of the brain is likely to be very fruitful in the endeavor to get a theory of those aspects of how the mind-brain works that are of special interest to philosophy. For ease of reference, I call the claim that neuroscience can contribute to philosophy the "contribution thesis."

This thesis is the heart of neurophilosophy. If it cannot be sustained, then the project will die. It is a very bold claim, for brief reflection on the sort of information philosophers would like to have about the mind indicates that cognition and perhaps emotion are the crucial explananda. Many students of epistemology and ethics are very interested in knowing how cognition happens, and the venerable debate between cognitivist and emotivist schools of ethics might be advanced by better information about these capacities. In distinguishing between cognition and emotion, I do not mean to imply that these are separate faculties or that faculties are the best way to conceptualize the mind's capacities. The point is only that the central philosophical areas of epistemology and ethics could well profit from a scientific understanding of those capacities we now place under the rubrics "cognition" and "emotion." Although novel in the context of twentieth-century Anglo-American and Continental philosophy as a whole, Churchland shares this part of her position with current efforts to "naturalize" epistemology and to introduce psychological realism into ethics (see Goldman, 1986; Kornblith, 1987; Flanagan and Rorty, 1990). It follows that her central thesis is a more specific claim than the general commitment to naturalism: direct study of the brain will be fruitful in advancing understanding of cognition and the emotions.

Churchland clearly appreciates that this is the point at issue (see Churchland and Sejnowski, 1992, 14). Examples such as habituation in sea slugs and bending reflexes in leeches are of interest only insofar as they hold out the promise of extension to higher-level capacities (e.g. habituation as a clue to more sophisticated kinds of learning, Churchland, 1986, 70ff.). The recognition that neuroscience must deliver in the cognitive domain permeates her writings (1980, 195ff.; 1986, 6ff.) and is nicely captured in the title of a piece she co-authored with Paul Churchland, "Stalking the Wild *Epistemic* Engine" (1983, my emphasis).

At times, Churchland advocates positions considerably stronger than the Contribution Thesis. She notes her "early conviction ... that neuroscience must contribute essentially to the theoretical enterprise [of a unified theory of the mind-brain that has implication for philosophy]" (1986, 6). Later writings contain no hint that this conviction has faded; if anything, it seems to grow stronger with the passing years (e.g. Churchland and Sejnowski, 1992, 17). Since I take the force of this conviction to be that philosophy cannot succeed in its traditional endeavors without the aid of neuroscience, I will call this the "*Sine qua non* Thesis."

Sometimes, Churchland seems to support another thesis, which is also stronger than the Contribution Thesis, but in a way slightly different from the *sine qua non* thesis. This is the view that neuroscience will be more important in understanding those areas of mentality of interest to philosophy than other candidate disciplines, e.g. linguistics or cognitive psychology or philosophy itself. So, for example, in *Neurophilosophy* she suggests that what will replace currently inadequate theories of mentality is "the conceptual framework of a matured neuroscience" (1986, 396; see also Churchland and Sejnowski, 1992 *passim*).

Still, Churchland's position on this issue is fairly complex, for she has also argued in many places that the best strategy for understanding the mind-brain involves the co-evolution of psychology and neuroscience into a new, unified science (1980, 169–70; 1986, 362 ff.; 1988, 393). From this, it would seem to follow that psychology and neuroscience would be roughly equal in importance for understanding cognition and emotion. On the other hand, Churchland also makes it quite clear that what she means by "scientific psychology" is a psychology that is itself reducible to neuroscience (1986, 382, chapter 7 *passim*; 1994, 2, 4, 5). Hence the co-evolution is importantly asymmetric. Although psychology can correct and guide research in neuroscience and vice versa, Churchland's expectation is that, in the end, neuroscience will provide the deepest understanding of mental phenomena, because it will explain why the psychological claims are true. Given the reducibility claim – which Churchland has repeated in virtually all her published writings – and its corollary, that neuroscience is the most fundamental science of the mind-brain, she appears to be committed to the view that it is the "most important contributor" to understanding mentality, including those aspects of most importance to philosophy.

From a logical point of view, the three theses are quite different, since a contributing condition is very different from both a necessary condition and a most important contributing condition. The real issues in debates about the relations among the disciplines are, however, practical ones. How should philosophy students be trained? How should individuals entering the profession orient their careers? And, practically speaking, the differences among these positions are matters of degree. If neuroscience can make some contributions to understanding cognition and emotions, but no essential contributions and less important contributions than say, psychology, then the Contribution Thesis might be true, but not very interesting. In particular, although those with a philosophical agenda might wish to devote some effort to understanding neuroscience (or hope some members of the community do so), most of their resources should go in the direction of whatever disciplines are more important contributors. Hence, informally but not formally, the fate of the core thesis of neurophilosophy – the Contribution Thesis –

depends on how well the *Sine qua non* Thesis and the Most-Important-Contributor Thesis fare. So, for example, the Contribution Thesis would be bolstered if neuroscience is among the more important contributors to explaining cognition and emotion, even if the Most-Important-Contributor Thesis itself is false.

Having distinguished these different claims, I am going to treat them all together for most of the paper. This is partly because, as a practical matter, they stand or fall *more or less* together, and partly because Churchland supports them by largely the same straightforward argumentative strategy. The case for Neurophilosophy always has two prongs: (1) criticisms of the adequacy of non-neural efforts to understand philosophically relevant aspects of mentality (henceforth "PR mentality") and (2) examples from neuroscience (or neurocomputation) intended to establish the ability to contribute to understanding some aspect of cognition.

The Case against Non-Neural Theories

The first prong itself typically has two sub-prongs. In many writings, Churchland criticizes the adequacy of non-neural accounts, by arguing against claims that these accounts enjoy some privileged position in explaining PR mentality. Her typical quarries are a priori arguments to the effect that, because dualism is true, or ordinary language is sacrosanct, or mentality must be approached via functions, or conscious life has a qualitative character, some non-neural account must be right. Although defeating these a priori arguments does not establish the inadequacy of non-neural accounts and makes Churchland vulnerable to the charge that she is fighting with straw men, this material is germane to her case. Real, live philosophers have offered these arguments and some have been quite influential (see Popper and Eccles, 1977; Vendler, 1984; Nagel, 1986). Further, if any of the a priori arguments were sound, then her project would be doomed.

The second half of the first prong is mostly a posteriori arguments from the history of science. I believe that the use of the ambiguous expression "folk psychology" in these arguments both undermines their validity and masks their radical character. "Folk psychology" is supposed to refer to the psychological beliefs or inchoate psychological theory held by ordinary people – the folk. In this meaning, "folk psychology$_1$," folk psychology is not a serious contender as an important contributor to an understanding of cognition and emotions. Some philosophers have offered a priori reasons for believing that any psychological theory must reflect folk wisdom, but consideration of these claims belongs with the part of the argument for Neurophilosophy already discussed. "Folk psychology$_2$" refers to the view that PR mental phenomena can best be understood by positing the existence of and transformations among propositional or sentence-like inner representations.[2] When "folk psychology" is used in the first sense, the arguments against it tend to be dismissive: The folk never get anything right. By contrast, Churchland offers direct arguments against folk psychology$_2$. One argument is described as an "infralinguistic catastrophe" for the sentential model (1980, 188; 1986, 388). There are some phenomena, such as the behavior of intelligent pre-linguistic children and animals, which do not appear to be easily accommodated by the model. The 1986 treatment also emphasizes two other problems, the closure problem and the frame problem. Both difficulties can be expressed as questions. If beliefs are sentential, are believers tacitly committed to all the consequences of their beliefs? If knowledge is organized by frames, how does the knower move between frames?

The arguments against the adequacy of folk psychology$_2$ are problematic. No one in the sententialist camp is going to abandon the position on the basis of Churchland's claims that there are problems with babies, animals, closure, and frames. Sententialists fully acknowledge the closure and frame problems and are actively working on solutions.[3] Further, they do not believe that babies and animals talk; they believe that the best way to model higher mental life is in terms of inner representational states that have features such as constituent structure in common with natural languages. In effect, Churchland's objection is that it is not obvious how the sentential model is going to handle these phenomena or that the model does not now have a satisfactory account of them. As she correctly points out, however, complaints that the current resources of neuroscience cannot handle a particular range of phenomena or that it is not clear how it could are "arguments from ignorance" and should not be taken very seriously (Churchland and Sejnowski, 1992, 2). By her own reasonable standards, her arguments against the sententialist model are too quick. They are given spurious plausibility only by the conflation with folk psychology$_1$. So the case against the sententialist model is pressed by noting the inadequacies of most folk theories (e.g., 1980, 189[4]; 1986, 395).

At times, Churchland appears to use "folk psychology" in yet another sense. On her account, eliminative materialism is committed to the following three claims:

1   that folk psychology is a theory;
2   that folk psychology is a theory whose inadequacies entail that it

must eventually be substantially revised or replaced outright (hence "eliminative");

3   that what will ultimately replace folk psychology will be the conceptual framework of a mature neuroscience (hence "materialism" (1986, 396).

Consider claim 3. It appears to divide psychological theories into just two camps: folk psychology and neurophysiologically based psychology. Seemingly, those parts of traditional psychology that cannot be grounded in neurophysiology are consigned to the folk psychology (call this folk psychology$_3$) to be replaced.

Churchland has vigorously resisted this interpretation of her view: It is a mistake to read her attack on folk psychology as an attack on scientific psychology, for "criticism of folk physics is not *eo ipso* an attack on physics, criticism of folk biology is not an attack on biology. Quite the reverse. Criticism lays the essential background for discovering a more adequate physics, biology, *and* psychology" (1988, 394). Again, however, Churchland's position is complex, and again the key is the reducibility claim. Perhaps the clearest statement of her view on reducibility occurs in *Neurophilosophy*. First she considers two possibilities, one in which psychological states are discovered to have a neurofunctional property in common, the other in which there is no common neurophysiological state that can be paired with psychological states, even at a high functional level of organization.

> In that [the latter] event readjustment of macrolevel theory and macrolevel description may be elicited, and in a science fiction [description] . . . it may eventually be said that there is no neurophysiology of individual beliefs; there is only a neurophysiology of information fermenphorylation (to take a made-up name). On either scenario, and this is the important point, there will be an explanation of macrolevel effects in terms of microlevel machinations, or macrolevel categories in terms of microlevel business. Insofar as there are such explanations, reductive integration will have been achieved (1986, 382).

I take Churchland's point to be that psychological categories will be either identified with high-level neurobiological categories or replaced with neurobiological categories.[5] And this entails that non-neurally-based psychological theories will be either revised or replaced (see 1994, 5, for a more recent statement of the same view). Hence, although Churchland may not intend to tar non-neural scientific psychology with the brush of folk psychology, she regards it as sharing the same fate.

Of course, it is one thing to say that folk psychology$_1$ will be replaced by a mature neuroscience and quite another to say that, in the end, any parts of psychology that cannot be reduced to neurophysiology must give way to neurophysiological theories. The radical nature of the latter position becomes clear if we consider a different vision of the co-evolution of psychology and neuroscience, that offered by William James. Like Churchland, James believed that psychology and neurophysiology had to inform each other. Mindful of recent discoveries in neurophysiology, he tried to ground the well-entrenched psychological principle of association in the "law of neural habit": "When two elementary brain-processes have been active together or in immediate succession, one of them, on reoccurring, tends to propagate its excitement into the other" (James, 1892/1961, 123). Still, James thought that something was left to be explained. Why should the nervous system behave in this way? Not surprisingly, given the time, he appealed to natural selection. This led to a somewhat paradoxical but nevertheless balanced view of the the roles of the macro and micro sciences in explaining human mentality: Neurophysiology explains why the laws of association are true in terms of the law of neural habit, and the theory of natural selection explains why the law of neural habit is true – in terms of the selective advantages of the laws of association (James, 1890, vol. 2, 626).

On a Jamesian view, psychology and neuroscience co-evolve, by touching base with each other as often as possible, but there is no presumption that the integration can be completed or that neuroscience is more explanatorily basic. To see the latter point, consider one of Churchland's examples, habituation in the sea slug. She finds this case interesting, because habituation is a kind of learning, and hence hopes that learning in more complex creatures might be explained by the same mechanism. For a Jamesian, however, the neural hardware underlying habituation would be interesting – something that should be part of scientific psychology – because it is a way of realizing the psychologically important capacity for learning. Thus the existence of, and the scientific importance of, the microlevel mechanism is explained by the macrolevel theory. Were such an explanation impossible for a particular neural mechanism – if it neither realized nor contributed to the realization of a recognizable psychological capacity – then presumably the microlevel account would cease to be part of a future scientific psychology, although it might still be part of "brain mechanics" (like descriptions of the circulation of blood in the brain).

On a Jamesian view, neither psychology nor neuroscience is explanatorily privileged relative to the other. They answer different questions. Neuroscience explains how a psychological capacity is realized (in some instances); psychology explains how (in certain circumstances) a neural structure contributes to cognition, emotion, or some other mental capacity. Further, in this scenario, non-neural psychological terms and theories are not replaced; indeed, they continue to function in explanations precisely because a psychological capacity is not identified with just one neurophysiological property. Otherwise, the second type of explanation would be circular: the A, B, C structure contributes to the capacity for learning (the A, B, C structure).

So far, Churchland's case against the adequacy of non-neural theories is not very compelling. The discussion of folk psychology$_1$ is irrelevant, and the objections to folk psychology$_2$, while serious, are not clearly fatal. What I have just been arguing is that her appeal to the unity of science to cast doubts on non-neural theories is also unavailing, for, as the Jamesian option makes clear, the unity of science itself does not entail the revision or replacement of non-neural explanatory constructs. That conclusion only follows from the further assumption that the only (or best) type of intertheoretic unity is produced by the reduction of macrotheories to microtheories. This view is, however, extremely controversial. Many general philosophers of science have tried to move beyond what they regard as the unfruitful notion of "reduction" (e.g., Putnam, 1967; Wimsatt, 1976 Garfinkel, 1981; Cartright, 1983; Sober 1984); many of the very philosophers Churchland opposes have shown the compatibility of anti-reductionism with at least a weak version of the unity of science, viz., materialism (e.g., Boyd, 1980; Putnam, 1967; Fodor, 1968). Churchland also argues against anti-reductionism, directly challenging what she correctly perceives to be its strongest point: multiple realizability.[6] She appeals to the classic case of temperature as a counterexample to the view that multiple realization blocks reduction (1986, 356). As Gary Hatfield has argued (1988, 734), however, the counterexample is not convincing, because what she presents as different instantiations of temperature were all viewed as mean kinetic energy; further, they do not posses the heterogeneity thought to raise problems in the case of psychological states. So the claim for reductionism is at best moot, and, without it, the ideal of the unity of science provides no grounds for rejecting non-neural theories.

In a recent paper, Churchland suggests that she might be willing to modify her reductionist position somewhat. Given that the details are almost never completely filled in, perhaps it would be better to describe the relation between psychology and neuroscience as one of "reductive contact" rather than "reduction" (1994, 8). She finds philosophers enthusiastic about this change, whereas scientists find it "quaintly pedantic." As the preceding discussion suggests, however, careful examination of the implications of intertheoretic integration is not mere pedantry, for different models have importantly different implications.

Suppose that we abandon not just the idea of complete reduction, but reduction itself, adopting instead a Jamesian approach that sees neuroscience and psychology as performing different but equally basic explanatory jobs. Interesting consequences follow, for now there is no reason to believe that neuroscience is likely to be the Most Important Contributor to an understanding of the mind-brain, including those aspects that are of interest to philosophy. Instead, one might think – as in fact I think – that neuroscience's contributions to philosophy are likely to be fairly indirect. Roughly, neuroscience enables psychology to develop more adequate accounts of the high-level capacities of interest to philosophy. Neuroscience may be important to psychology and psychology important to philosophy, but without the assumption of reduction, transitivity cannot be invoked to argue that neuroscience is *eo ipso* important to philosophy. Under these circumstances, the practical questions raised at the beginning about the allocation of effort between psychology and neuroscience are given answers quite different from those implied by Neurophilosophy.

This is not the occasion to explore fully the relative merits of a symmetric versus a reductive model of intertheoretic integration. I will just note, however, that Churchland's reductive or eliminativist (and hence asymmetric) approach to co-evolution leads her to overstate the successes of neuroscience in ways that she probably wants to avoid. So, for example, in a recent paper, she writes: "Very crudely speaking, current neurobiological data suggest that when one sees an apple, the brain is in some state that can be described as representing an apple" (Churchland and Ramachandran, 1993, 30). As it stands, this statement is quite inaccurate. The suggestion that the brain represents an apple does not come from contemporary neuroscience: It is a direct implication of materialism, plus the representational theory of the mind, which dates from the beginnings of modern philosophy. Presumably, current neurobiology has found some activities in the brain that are plausible candidates for instantiating apple representations. But why philosophers might care about these discoveries is explained by reference to the representational theory of mind and materialism. In eschewing a symmetric approach that has psychology and philosophy explaining the relevance of certain brain mechanisms (and neuroscience explaining the mechanisms of psychological capacities), Churchland runs the constant risk of re-describing – and mis-describing – psychological or philosophical contributions as purely neuroscientific ones. This is a way to establish the importance of neuroscience to philosophy, but not a way she wants any part of. On the other hand, as already noted, dropping reductionism in favor of an expected co-existence of neuroscientific and psychological constructs undermines a part of the motivation for *Neuro*philosophy.

Although the arguments from folk psychology and reductionism are problematic, Churchland does offer a compelling a posteriori consideration for preferring neurophysiologically grounded theories. The history of science shows that micro-level theories can often presage breakthroughs in understanding important ranges of phenomena. Further, dramatic recent developments in molecular genetics, and molecular biology more generally, demonstrate the power of micro approaches outside their traditional domains of physics and chemistry. Hence, she can correctly claim that, given the history of science, it is more reasonable to expect revolutionary advances in those areas of psychology that can be directly linked to the neural level than in other areas.

Churchland does not usually make this claim in precisely these terms,[7] because she tends to cast the issue in terms of folk theories being replaced by scientific theories. Although this may be a more diplomatic way of expressing her view than to predict the ultimate demise of non-neurally based areas of psychology, as noted, the arguments from folk psychology are invalid, whereas this point has considerable merit – however unwilling parties to the debate may be to say or hear it. Further, if Churchland wanted to be even less diplomatic, but still truthful, she could call attention to the disappointing history of psychology itself. After 100 years, psychology is somewhat long in the tooth still to be indulged as an infant science, and progress has been much slower than anyone would like.

In Defense of Non-Neural Psychology

I hope that I have reconstructed Churchland's best case against the adequacy of non-neural theories. In particular, I have tried to give sufficient weight to the historical case for micro-level theories. Before turning to her positive arguments that neuroscience can enlighten philosophy, it will be useful to offer some defense. Mine is very simple. In spite of the generally superior performance of micro-level theories and the fact that whenever psychology has appeared to be on the brink of a revolutionary theoretical breakthrough (psychoanalysis, Gestalt psychology, behaviorism, drive-reduction theory) the hope has faded, traditional scientific (but non-neural) psychology has discovered a number of facts of great relevance to philosophy. Getting some of these out on the table will also provide a benchmark for evaluating Churchland's case for the importance of neuroscience in understanding PR mentality. Since I will consider six of Churchland's examples, I choose the same number of examples from recent work in cognitive psychology.

In picking the examples, I have followed two guidelines: The psychological results are widely accepted and their relevance to traditional issues in philosophy is clear. Although sometimes tempting, arguments of the form "*if* this or that theory is true, then it is very important for philosophy" are interesting only when there is good reason to believe that the antecedent can be discharged. Similarly, arguments that a particular discovery *may* have some bearing on traditional philosophy are unhelpful unless that bearing can be indicated.

I start with some examples that are already familiar in the philosophical literature. For a variety of reasons, philosophers as diverse as Locke and Frege believed that a concept was represented in human beings in the form of a set of necessary and sufficient conditions for its application. This enabled Locke to explain how complex theoretical concepts might be constructed from sensory primitives; it allowed philosophers in the post-Fregean tradition to give substance to the notion of a "sense." The well-known experiments of Eleanor Rosch and her colleagues imply, however, that (at least for the majority of concepts) this picture is incorrect. Rosch first asked her subjects to rate the typicality of various instances of concepts as examples of those concepts. This turned out to be an easy task. She then engaged in a prototypical, traditional psychological experiment. She measured the reaction time that it took subjects to classify various instances under concepts. The result was that the typicality measure predicted the speed at which an instance would be classified. So a robin, which rated highly as a typical bird, was quickly classed as a bird; a goose, which was not thought to be a very typical member, was classified more slowly (Rosch, 1973).

The problem for the definitional view is that if people apply concepts to objects by going through a checklist of necessary and sufficient conditions, then since there are the same number of items the times should be the same. Further, and perhaps more telling, the definitional view of the representation of concepts has no explanation for the typicality effects that appear to be a prominent feature of concept application.[8] Beyond the obvious questions of how concepts are represented and acquired, these results also bear on philosophical questions of translation and theory change.[9] For if concepts are not fixed by definitions, then it is not clear exactly what is to be captured in translation and exactly what changes when new theories are accepted. Even more importantly, perhaps, these discoveries raise serious questions about the preoccupation of much of twentieth-century philosophy with finding definitions (see Bishop, 1992). I take their relevance to philosophy to be clear.

Perhaps the second-best-known psychological results among epistemologists were those obtained in Tversky and Kahneman's studies of reasoning. They found that laypeople – in particular Stanford and University of British Columbia undergraduates – deviated in important ways from accepted norms of statistical reasoning. So, for example, when asked whether it was more probable that a shy man with a passion for detail was a librarian or a farmer, they answered "librarian." What a good Bayesian should do, however, is consider the relative numbers of farmers and librarians and conclude that the individual is far more likely to be a farmer, just because there are so many more farmers than librarians (Kahneman, et al., 1982, 4). Even worse, consider the subjects' responses when asked which of the following two statements was more likely to be true:

1 "Linda is a bank teller."
2 "Linda is a bank teller and is active in the feminist movement."

Since the latter statement is a conjunction containing the former as a conjunct its truth can be no more probable than the less probable of its two conjuncts. Yet, 80 percent of the students took the conjunction to be more probable than the conjunct! (Kahneman, et al., 1982, 92ff.)

Although these results are not controversial, their implications for philosophy have been the subject of some debate (e.g., Cohen, 1981). I will not try to settle those issues, but will just observe one of the interesting effects that this work has had on philosophical discussions of rationality. Tversky and Kahneman and their colleagues did not just debunk the idea that Bayesian analyses were commonly used (even among those who had studied statistics). They also described the heuristic principles that were guiding these and other apparently sub-rational decisions. So, for example, subjects appeared to rely on a "representativeness" heuristic, that is, on the fact that the description they were given was of a stereotypical librarian (Kahneman, et al., 1982, 4–5). Beyond stereotypes, this heuristic can also involve the representativeness of a particular outcome, given its causal antecedent. So, for example, when asked which sequence of male and female births is more likely, BBBBBB, GGGBBB, or GBBGGB, students rated the final sequence as much more probable. (Presumably the same sort of process underlies the bank teller data, with subjects assuming either that working is likely to produce feminist leanings or that the same traits that lead Linda to work at all also make her a feminist.) In laying out their results, these psychologists noted that since human beings are very bad at detecting actual covariation, it is not surprising that other, albeit inaccurate, methods come into play (Nisbett and Ross, 1980, 90ff.). One result of this work is that philosophers have been led to open up their concept of rationality. In particular, they have been led to consider whether the use of some inferential shortcuts might be rational, given available cognitive resources (e.g., Solomon, 1992). Without trying to resolve these matters, the debates about the nature of rationality engendered by this work are themselves clear evidence of its relevance for philosophy.

As philosophers from Kant to Kuhn have recognized, whether perception is a constructive process is a central question in understanding and assessing the objectivity of our knowledge claims. In a series of experiments, Anne Treisman and her colleagues have found evidence that even fairly simple perceptions are constructed. (Although less well known among philosophers than the two previous examples, this work is widely recognized in psychology.) Treisman's stimuli were very simple: rapidly displayed colored letters. When presented with a green R, a red S, an orange V, and a purple E, in a row, some subjects will report seeing an orange E. This result is both robust and subjectively compelling. Subjects will often resist the experimenter's claim that they are mistaken (Treisman and Gelade, 1980; Treisman and Schmidt, 1982).

Treisman dubs these errors "illusory conjunctions." Illusory conjunctions – the mis-combinations of color and shape in a percept – imply that, even in normal cases, subjects must combine color and shape information. Given that color and shape are straightforwardly perceptible properties, this work also strongly suggests that, in general, perceptions are produced by the construction of complex representations from more simple parts. What processes guide this construction? In particular, how similar are the processes that lead to complex perceptions to those that produce complex beliefs? Philosophers have a great stake in the answers to these questions, since they will constrain any debate on the objectivity of perception.

Alan Leslie's work on autistic children is beginning to be recognized in philosophical discussions (e.g., Gordon, 1987, 133, 147; Goldman, 1993.) Interestingly, Leslie used a variation of an experimental paradigm introduced by Wimmer and Perner, which they credit to independent suggestions from Jonathan Bennett, Daniel Dennett, and Gilbert Harman. Bennett, Dennett, and Harman were trying to devise a test to determine whether monkeys attributed mental states to conspecifics. Wimmer and Perner used their suggestions to test small children. Children aged three to five were set the following task: Figure out where another child will look for some chocolate when he puts the chocolate in a box, and, after his departure his mother then moves the chocolate to a cupboard. Little children (three and under) opt for where the chocolate is, the cupboard. Older children seem to realize that what matters is where the child *thinks* the chocolate is.

Leslie used this experimental paradigm to test autistic children with an average age of 12. Although these children had fairly normal IQs (mean 82), almost all of them gave the three-year-old's answer. He then tested Down's syndrome children, who had much lower IQs (mean 64, average age 11). Oddly, these children performed the task very well. These results indicate that the ability to attribute mental states to others is not a matter of general intelligence, but something like a specialized capacity (Leslie, 1987, 423–4).[10] Leslie's results have a number of implications for philosophy, of which I will note just two. They strongly suggest that one implication drawn from Sellar's famous "myth of Jones" (1963, 178ff.), that our ability to attribute mental states to others is best understood as a cultural achievement, is wrong.[11] Second, Alvin Goldman has observed that work in this area also bears on the thesis of eliminative materialism (1993, 96). For, as Churchland notes, the eliminativist regards the attribution of mental states to others as theory-driven and, thus, as completely plastic to changes in theory. If this ability does not rest on any theories – and hence not on any theories that might be refuted – it seems less likely that such attributions will be eliminated with the advancement of science.

I turn to some psychological results whose implications for philosophy have been less widely appreciated. Despite Nelson Goodman's indictment of the notion of "similarity," (1972, 437ff.), few empiricist epistemologists have been able to resist appealing to similarity to explain concept acquisition and application. Most famously, Goodman's colleague, W. V. Quine, argued that children originally acquire natural-kind concepts through the mediation of innate qualitative similarity spaces, which are then replaced by theories born of trial and error with the original concepts (1969, 28). Similarity is also frequently invoked in explanations of scientific and other forms of creativity. A standard view is that acts of creativity are mediated by making analogies between old and new domains, that is, by recognizing that old and new domains are similar in some respects.

Beginning with Tversky's classic paper (1977), recent work in psychology implies that several assumptions underlying these philosophical appeals to similarity are mistaken. Perhaps the most dramatic is Tversky's own demonstration that the geometric representation of similarity fails to accord with experimentally obtained data about similarity judgments. The geometric representation models similarity relations as distances, with smaller and larger distances indicating

greater and lesser degrees of similarity. Since similarity is often measured on more than one dimension, this leads to the idea of similarity
spaces, a notion introduced into philosophy by Quine and adopted by a
number of others, including the Churchlands.

As Tversky observed (1977, 328), the geometric representation presupposes three axioms of metric distance (δ):

Minimality:
$$[\delta (a,b) \geqslant \delta (a,a) = 0.]$$
Symmetry:
$$[\delta (a,b) = \delta (b,a).]$$
The triangle inequality:
$$[\delta (a,b) + \delta (b,c) \geqslant \delta (a,c).]$$

However, none of these correctly predicts subjects' similarity judgments.
Thus, the minimality assumption requires that the similarity of all
objects to themselves be the same, but subjects do not always judge
identical objects to be the same. Even more striking, similarity judgments clearly violate the symmetry requirement. So, to adapt one of
Tversky's examples, I can say that my sons are similar to their father, but
it would be quite a different matter to observe that my husband is
similar to my sons. Tversky concedes that the triangle inequality is
difficult to test empirically. Still, he offers quite a persuasive argument,
by adapting an example of William James's. If the triangle inequality is
true, then if a and b are very similar and b and c are very similar, then a
and c should be fairly similar. But, he notes that while Jamaica is similar
to Cuba (geographically) and Cuba is similar to Russia (politically (as of
1977)), Jamaica and Russia are very dissimilar (1977, 329).

More recent work suggests that similarity judgments – even those of
very young children – typically depend on specific knowledge bases
(Medin, et al., 1993, 256–7). Work on analogy indicates that what
matters in constructing or recognizing analogies is not qualitative
considerations, but deeper systematic relations among features (Clement and Gentner, 1991, 90). Hence, although it may still be possible to
explain the development of new knowledge by appealing to mechanisms
like similarity and analogy, those processes themselves appear to be
mediated by pre-existing knowledge. I take the clear morals of this work
for philosophy to be at least

1 that we should be wary of geometric models of similarity;
2 that although "similarity" may continue to appear in the explanans
   of philosophy, it is itself a rather complex explanandum;

3   that Quine's simple picture of the development of natural-kind terms
     is probably much too simple.[12]

Late in the next section, I will also consider the implications of this work
for one of Churchland's arguments for Neurophilosophy.

Although Leslie's work probably also has implications for ethics, I
chose my last example because its relevance to moral theory is obvious.
Recall Hume's elegant turn of the tables (1739–40, 411) on the
libertarian argument that free will is a necessary condition of moral
responsibility:

> Actions are by their very nature temporary and perishing; and where they
> proceed not from some cause in the characters and disposition of the
> person, who perform'd them, they infix not themselves upon him, and can
> neither redound to his honour, if good, nor infamy, if evil. The action itself
> may be blamable ... But the person is not responsible for it; and as it
> proceeded from nothing in him that is durable or constant, ... 'tis
> impossible he can, upon its account, become the object of punishment or
> vengeance.

Hume is not alone in assuming that characters or dispositions are
relatively fixed features of individuals. So, for example, it is a precondi-
tion of Rawls's mechanism of reflective equilibrium that people are able
to sustain their moral attitudes along enough to adjust them rationally in
the face of new evidence.[13] However, a number of studies indicate that
the evidence for believing in dispositional stability is systematically
flawed. This does not show that people are fickle, but it should lead
ethicists to question whether they have any good reasons for assuming
stable character traits.

According to Nisbett and Ross's summary of the literature, we all
engage in what they stigmatize as the "fundamental attribution error."
That is, when confronted with some type of action, we assume –
regardless of other salient factors – that the action flowed from a fairly
enduring disposition of the actor. Two examples will give a sense of the
studies. In one experiment, some subjects were paid a reasonably large
sum to write essays that went contrary to their stated beliefs; other
subjects were asked to do the same thing, but were given very little or no
money for their efforts. When asked why they complied, the first group
pointed to the money. However, the second group inferred that their
writing of the essays reflected their own views. They gave no weight to
the subtle pressures created by the experimental situation in which they
were asked to perform (Nisbett and Ross, 1980, 123). Even more telling
was a study of lay people's expectations of subjects' behaviors in the
well-known Milgram experiments. Subjects were given an exact

re-enactment of one of the original subject's actions, including delivering the maximum shock to the alleged learner. Yet they consistently underestimated how much other subjects would give in to the same situational pressures to obey, because they assumed that the sample subject's reactions were a reflection of his particular character (Nisbett and Ross, 1980, 123).

Given these results, Hume was right to expect his readers to agree with him that most actions flow from something "constant" in the actor. However, the results cast serious doubts on whether he or they were justified in this belief. Beyond providing grounds for attributing moral praise and blame, the belief in fairly stable character traits stands behind many theories of punishment and moral education. Moral philosophers have a considerable stake in its correctness and ought to urge their colleagues in psychology to try to obtain further evidence to help determine if it is not just unjustified, but actually false.

The Case for Neurally Based Theories

Before taking up Churchland's examples, it will be helpful to characterize the challenge that she is trying to meet in a little more detail. How can she demonstrate that neuroscience can contribute to the understanding of PR mentality? As she well understands, there is a large gap between neurons and epistemology. To begin to close this gap, we need neuroscientific theories that go beyond the individual neuron to functional and global properties of the whole neural system (1980, 205; 1986, 6, especially 8–9; Churchland and Sejnowski, 1992, 7). In considering the case against the adequacy of non-neural approaches, I conceded that the history of traditional psychology is not particularly encouraging. It is very important to realize that the search for general theories of the nervous system has gone no better than the search for large-scale psychological theories. Nearly 100 years ago Sherrington gave an eloquent plea for trying to understand not just individual neurons but the "integrative action" of the nervous system (Sherrington, 1906). But, as Churchland concedes, there is no "governing paradigm" in neuroscience (1986, 6), and the field is frequently described by its own practitioners as "data rich, but theory poor" (Churchland and Sejnowski, 1992, 16).

An important part of Churchland's brief for neurophilosophy is that things are changing and that it is now possible and profitable to start searching for the cognitive forest in the billions of dendrites. More prosaically, there are now or soon will be higher-level theories in neuroscience that have important implications for understanding emotion and, especially, cognition (1986, 5).[14] That is the thesis that the examples are intended to make plausible. In assessing this argument by example, I make a simplifying assumption. I assume that no one is in a better position to know the work in neuroscience that might bear on her project than Churchland herself. Hence, I take her examples to be the most compelling available.

In her original 1980 argument for neurophilosophy, Churchland appealed to three examples, habituation in sea slugs, Mountcastle's theory of directed attention, and Pellionisz and Llinas's model of the cerebellar cortex. Because the sea slug has a tiny nervous system composed of only about 10,000 neurons, it has been possible to figure out its neuronal organization in some detail. The particular experiments Churchland highlights concern habituation to a splash of sea water. The tractability of this nervous system made it possible to hypothesize and test a small number of possible mechanisms for habituation. It turned out that habituation was caused by changes in the amount of neuro-transmitter passed from sensory neurons to motor neurons (1980, 199–200).

As Churchland sees, for her purposes, the important question is whether there is reason to believe that this result can be generalized to other behaviors and organisms. In the 1980 paper, she cites work on crayfish and some preliminary studies on dogs and cats, but notes that the work on sea slugs is so recent that it is hard to say very much about implications (201). This work is also discussed in 1986 (70), but there is no mention of further developments. It does not recur in her 1992 discussion (with Sejnowski) of habituation in the leech (350–1). Because all neuronal action is similar in some respects, more complex organisms may have similar mechanisms of habituation. What is not clear is whether such mechanisms would play an important role in explaining any aspect of PR mentality. Of course, this work may eventually be very illuminating for learning, or for behavioral plasticity more generally. But Churchland's discussions provide no reason to think that these outcomes are particularly likely.

Churchland's next example is deliberately more cognitive. She describes Vernon Mountcastle's hypothesis about the mechanisms subserving directed attention. In brief, Mountcastle's suggestion is that since micro-electrode recordings indicate that various neurons in the parietal lobe are involved in such activities as visual fixation and visual tracking, then it is this area of the brain that coordinates foveal vision with the operations of the oculomotor system (the system that controls eye position relative to the motion of the body) (1980, 202–3). As Churchland realizes, knowing the location of a particular function in the brain is not immediately illuminating, and she considers no implications of this hypothesis. Churchland discusses the vestibulo-ocular reflex (which enables the eyes to adjust to motion so as not to lose the object of the vision) again in 1986 and 1992 (with Sejnowski), but with no reference to Mountcastle's hypothesis. In 1986, she returns to the topic of attention, but the theory she discusses is not Mountcastle's, but a new theory of Francis Crick's. I infer that Mountcastle's hypothesis did not lead to a widely accepted higher-level theory of attention.

Churchland devotes more attention to her third example, Pellionisz and Llinas' efforts to describe the network properties of the cerebellar cortex and the nervous system more generally. She concludes her discussion with the conjecture that "this work may constitute a major breakthrough in the attempt to describe neuro-functional concepts" (1980, 206). Pellionisz and Llinas' theory is discussed at greater length in 1986, and I take my presentation partly from that source. Their candidate for a global account of the functioning of the nervous system is tensor network theory. A tensor is a generalized mathematical function that permits vector to vector transformations across different co-ordinate systems. It is very plausible to regard the nervous system as a device for relating different co-ordinate systems, e.g., the eye with the head, the hand, the foot, or even the elbow. Further, it has seemed to many that perception requires the construction of representations that are at least partially independent of angle of view.

On Churchland's account, it was not such top – down functional considerations that gave rise to the tensor network hypothesis, but detailed study of the neural structure of the cerebellum. In particular, Pellionisz and Llinas were impressed with the fact that different cerebellar neurons had significantly different numbers of synaptic connections with incoming neurons and also with the number of neurons to which they project (1986, 416). Although the cerebellum has remarkably orderly neural structures, it still has about 10^{10} neurons. So to study this structure, Pellionisz and Llinas created a more manageably sized computer model. Starting with the idea that connectivity was the key and reflecting on the patterns generated by their model, they came to the hypothesis that the network of cells in the cerebellum could usefully be understood as a tensor (1986, 416–17). Churchland's 1986 discussion offers a cartoon illustration of this idea (Roger the crab), but she also suggests possible real applications, including the problem of the vestibulo-ocular reflex (henceforth VOR).

Neurocomputational models of the VOR occupy a prominent position in the 1992 book with Sejnowski, but there is no further discussion of the tensor network hypothesis. Again, I assume that this is because Pellionisz and Llinas' attempt at a grand theoretical breakthrough (1986, 411) came up short. I say this not to carp but as a partial assessment of the thesis at issue: we now have reason to believe that, after a long drought of theory (almost exactly as long as that in psychology), neuroscience shows promise of providing functional or network level theories that bear on PR mentality.

Besides tensor network theory, Churchland's 1986 argument appeals to two other examples, parallel distributed processing (PDP) models of visual recognition and Crick's proposed solution to Treisman's "binding" problem. Because PDP is also discussed extensively in the 1992 co-authored book, I consider Crick's theory first.

Recall that Treisman's work implied that different qualities of a stimulus, such as shape and color, must be combined in order to produce a perception of, say, a colored letter. Crick's hypothesis concerns the neural mechanisms that might subserve this "binding" of two properties in a single percept. First assume that the basic problem is how the nervous system can create temporary associations between different groups of cells, say those representing "green" and those representing "S". Crick's theory takes off from an unusual feature of some thalamic neurons: If they are first hyperpolarized (i.e., the inner surface of the neural membrane is made more negative than its outer surroundings) and then depolarized (i.e., the membrane is made more positive with respect to outer surroundings), they will engage in a short burst of activity followed by a resting state. Were these neurons to be hyperpolarized by some neurons (perhaps some in the reticular system that seems to be concerned with attention) and then depolarized by a visual stimulus, they might begin a rapid firing that could be the type of neural activity that would realize association. Churchland provides some further details of Crick's hypothesis, which I omit, because, as she notes, the theory is both imprecise and radically incomplete (1986, 477–8). Further, as in the previous cases, the initial promise of this hypothesis has not been borne out, at least so far.

Churchland discusses PDP models of various processes in both 1986 and 1992 (with Sejnowski). Although it may seem somewhat odd, I will present her reflections on PDP as two somewhat distinct examples in support of the thesis of neurophilosophy. I adopt this procedure because PDP made very rapid advances and changes in these years, changes that affect the role that it can play in the argument for Neurophilosophy.

As everyone knows, parallel distributed processing (also know as "connectionism") offers an alternative to traditional sequential methods of computing. Traditional methods employ explicit algorithms that orchestrate a sequence of separate operations on distinct representations. By contrast, via the strength of the connections across a collection of nodes, PDP computing involves the simultaneous (parallel) activation of a collection (distributed) of nodes, with each node potentially participating in the computation of many different responses. To come immediately to the two questions at issue: Is PDP modeling a neurophysiologically-based theory (or theory-schema)? Can it illuminate any aspects of PR mentality? Notice that if both these questions can be given affirmative answers, then the case for Neurophilosophy has been made.

Despite the appealing quickness and tidiness of this argument for Neurophilosophy, Churchland did not embrace it in 1986. Of the 66 pages she spent "In Search of Theory," 46 dealt with tensor network theory, five with Crick's fledgling account of attention, and 16 with PDP modeling. I believe that this material was less prominent in 1986 partly because Churchland had doubts about the answer to the first question: Is PDP grounded firmly enough in neurophysiology to be a good case for her thesis? Toward the end of her discussion, she explicitly raised the question, "Do real neuronal systems work this way?" Her answer was mixed. The units of a PDP model are "neuron-like" with their connectivity "grossly patterned to simulate neuronal connections," but she would be much happier if these models incorporated more anatomical and physiological facts (e.g., about the visual system) (1986, 470–1). Further, she noted that in many respects the units are quite unlike neurons: These units are simple on-off units, whereas real neurons are not; real neurons have spontaneous rates of firing that can be affected by processes like hyperpolarization; the type of firing can also be affected by the recent history of the neuron, its extracellular environment, and so on.

Thus, by itself, Churchland seems to regard the analogy between PDP units and neurons as too weak to sustain a claim of neurological grounding. In this estimation, she was probably correct in 1986, although history could offer a different verdict. She was correct for two reasons. When PDP models were first introduced, their authors were clear that, even though these were more neural-like than serial computers, their real appeal lay in their ability to solve certain kinds of computational problem involving, for example, multiple constraint satisfaction (Rumelhart and McClelland, 1986, 11; Smolensky, 1986, 394ff.) Second, the information used in the parade cases of PDP models – speech, reading, memory, past tense, and so forth – did not come from neurophysiology but from traditional psychology. Hence, from 1986, PDP models did not supply a particularly good case of what Churchland wanted – a model or theory of some aspect of PR mentality that was importantly informed by neuroscience.

Still, history could prove Churchland wrong on this point if PDP models become more and more infused with neurobiological realism, for, given this continuation, it would be reasonable to give more weight to the fact that PDP models were neurally inspired. I am not suggesting that the facts change – the models were always loosely based on connections among neurons – but that a changed context changes the best way to interpret those facts. Perhaps an analogy will clarify my point. As a number of sportswriters observed at the time, whether or not the sixth game of the 1991 World Series will become a baseball classic depends somewhat on Kirby Puckett's future career. If he continues to grow in stature, then that game will become more important as a clear demonstration of his talent; if he fades, then the game will not be as salient in baseball history. Similarly, if neurobiological realism becomes a characteristic feature of PDP models, then the biological inspiration of early models will be seen as more significant.

I have belabored the question of whether or not PDP models reflect neurological theories *per se* – regardless of any other neurological information they may incorporate – because it is critical to the thesis at issue. Although many philosophers have raised questions about the ability of PDP models to capture higher cognitive processes, I think there is no question that this movement has importantly altered the way mentality is approached. Even if such models never extend beyond sensory processes, as already noted, perception itself has long been of interest to philosophers. Even if PDP models turn out to be yet another dead end in the search for global theories of mental functioning, for now at least they offer a new range of theoretical concepts to apply to this very difficult set of phenomena. Hence I think it is reasonable to view PDP models as making important contributions to our understanding of mentality (even if PDP is not the most important contributor) and perhaps as providing vital (if not absolutely essential) information in the form of solutions to constraint satisfaction problems. Hence, were PDP models correctly viewed as based in neurophysiology, they would establish the Contribution Thesis. As already observed, however, this is a delicate call, and a positive answer depends on the successful development of future neurocomputational theories. Hence, the final judgment on Churchland's third example in the 1986 book depends on the fate of the project she undertook in 1992 (with Sejnowski).

Churchland's 1992 co-authored book does not focus directly or exclusively on the thesis of Neurophilosophy. Rather, it is an extended argument for the virtues of a new way of approaching the study of the brain, computational neuroscience. A chief virtue of this approach is, however, that it might lead to network-, if not global-, level theories of neural functioning (Churchland and Sejnowski, 1992, 4, 6, 239, 415). Hence computational neuroscience is another example of the search for higher-level theories in neuroscience that might have some bearing on PR mentality. Churchland and Sejnowski make this point clear (1992,

14), when they list philosophy among the disciplines that stand to benefit from their approach. Given Churchland's efforts to produce this large monograph, I assume that she now takes computational theories in neuroscience to be among the most promising avenues for the development of the higher-level theories needed to make the connection to epistemology.

Since I consider Churchland and Sejnowski's argument only as it bears on PR mentality, what follows is in no way a complete assessment of the project of computational neuroscience. Whether this is an especially fruitful way to model, for example, fairly low-level systems of neurons is an issue that I am not qualified to discuss. The only observation I make is one made by others within and without computer science. It is somewhat unfortunate that certain types of computer models of neural systems and/or psychological processes are referred to as "neural nets." These neural nets are intended to be models of actual neural systems (in which case the label presupposes the point at issue), models of mental processes (in which case the label itself implies that they are neural models, regardless of the degree of neurobiological faithfulness), or both (in which case their faithfulness to both neurophysiology and psychology has to be argued). Churchland is well aware of the celebrated error of confusing the conceptual nervous system (CNS) with the central nervous system (Hebb, 1982, 32–41) and so probably rues the use of the potentially confusing "neural net."

Before turning to Churchland and Sejnowski's empirical argument from computational neuroscience to Neurophilosophy, I think it is important to understand the very powerful a priori or quasi-a priori considerations that stand behind computational neuroscience. For over a hundred years, psychologists from Freud and Köhler to Hebb and Lashley have been anxious to tie their psychological theories as closely as possible to a physiological substratum. Opinion has often differed as to how close was possible, but not on the desirability of clear ties. Where no hypotheses of links were in the offing, possible evolutionary scenarios were sometimes substituted to help establish the physical plausibility of a particular psychological hypothesis. The ascendence of computational modeling as a touchstone for psychological theories is much more recent, but just as pervasive. Whether a theory is neurological, experimental, or completely top–down in its origin, current practice is to test its viability by constructing a computer model. Given these two methodological imperatives, the appeal of computational neuroscience is almost overwhelming. The basic idea is to construct computer models of low- and high-level processes with enough neural realism to make plausible links to potential physiological substrates. If this program can be advanced, then the two currently critical tests for psychological theories would be passed in a single step.

Churchland and Sejnowski's argument for Neurophilosophy centers on the issue of representation.[15] Churchland has long regarded the use of neurological information in developing "a new paradigm for characterizing representations and computations" as an important desideratum for Neurophilosophy (1986, 9; cf. 1980, 194; Churchland and Sejnowski, 1992, 168–72). If their case for a new model of representation with implications for PR mentality is sound, then that would go some way toward meeting this desideratum. I say "some way", because the question of whether PDP models *per se* should be regarded as neurophysiological persists. For the moment, however, I ignore that issue in order to consider their argument that models in computational neuroscience provide a way of looking at representation that is likely to be quite helpful in understanding PR mentality.

Perhaps it is easiest to understand the notion of representation at issue by looking at the road not taken. As Sejnowski observes, one way representation in the nervous system has been modeled is in terms of "local coding." That is, different features of the environment are represented by particular neurons, and it is possible to tell which neurons represent what features by the famous micro-electrode studies initiated by, among others, Hubel and Wiesel.[16] By contrast, models in computational neuroscience do not use local coding but "vector coding," or coding by a set of numbers. This would appear to be an intrinsic feature of the models, because they compute by passing activation from a set of input units through a set of hidden units to a set of output units. So all three steps – input, hidden processing, output – can be understood as involving a set of values (levels of activation) of each of the nodes involved. If the nodes are thought of as different dimensions, then "an occurrent representation is a position in the activation state space as specified by the vector whose elements are the activity values of all the participating units" (Churchland and Sejnowski, 1992, 167).

Churchland and Sejnowski suggest that in addition to these occurrent representations, it is possible to regard a trained network as instantiating an implicit representation, in the form of the weights of the connections across its nodes (1992, 168).[17] They also note that since a three-layer network can instantiate any well-behaved mathematical function, "any representable world can be represented in a network, via a configuration of weights" (Churchland and Sejnowski, 1992, 168).

Here then is an important equivalence between traditional methods of computation and PDP networks. Any computable function is both Turing-computable and computable by a PDP network. It is the next part of Churchland and Sejnowski's argument that is critical to the thesis of Neurophilosophy: PDP computation is not just powerful but likely to be especially illuminating for a number of issues of PR mentality. I quote their remarks at some length and letter the excerpts for ease in reference:

[A] An activation space will also be a similarity space, inasmuch as similar vectors will define adjacent regions in space. This means that similarity between objects represented can be reflected by similarity in their representations, that is, proximity of positions in activation space. Similarity in representations is thus not an accidental feature, but an intrinsic and systematic feature (Churchland and Sejnowski, 1992, 167).

[B] The idea expands to encompass more complex representations. . . . To put it in economic terms, coding by vectors gives us the similarity metric for free . . . (Churchland and Sejnowski, 1992, 169–79).

[C] In the domain of simple models, this hand-in-glove conception of representation and computation is powerful. In one encompassing theory, we can see, albeit roughly, how learning and representing fit together, how perceptual prototypes can be developed, how similarities in perception, cognition, and motor control reflect similarities at the network level . . . (Churchland and Sejnowski, 1992, 171).

[D] A major perceptual problem is to explain similarity relationships in perceptual recognition, and it is important to see that a general account falls quite naturally out of the vector-coding approach. Recognizing similarities and analogies in many domains, including perception, cognition, and motor control can be seen as a matter of position (or trajectory) in similarity space, as defined by n-dimensional vectors . . . (Churchland and Sejnowski, 1992, 172).

The plausibility and fruitfulness of regarding the nodes in a PDP network as dimensions of a representational space or a space of representations is reinforced and illustrated by reference to Sejnowski and Rosenberg's oft-cited program NETtalk:

[E] Analysis of units' activity in computer models of networks make it comparatively easy to observe the nuts and bolts of vector-coding and vector-matrix transformations, and how artificial neural nets can produce highly specific representations; for example, the representation of vowels in NETtalk (Churchland and Sejnowski, 1992, 173).

Putting these observations together yields the following, *prima facie* persuasive argument for Neurophilosophy.

1   Many problems of PR mentality depend on exploiting relations of similarity and analogy. [C, D]

2   Hence, a theory that illuminates how similarity relations are exploited would be valuable in explaining PR mentality.

3   The nodes in a PDP network can easily be regarded as dimensions in a similarity space. By using vector-coding, one automatically creates a similarity space. [A, B]

4   Hence, in computing similarity relations via a PDP network, the similarity relations among the objects represented will be a reflection of the [end]-positions in activation space of the process that did the computation. [A]

5   Hence, given this model, we have some understanding of how similarity judgments (or processes that rely on similarity, such as analogy) come out as they do. [A, C]

6   Moreover, if this is how actual systems of neurons process information, then we would have some understanding of how actual similarity judgments come out as they do.

7   Further, although not all vector-coding can be regarded as coding micro-features, some can (Churchland and Sejnowski, 1992, 165). In particular, NETtalk provides an illustration of how specific representations can be produced, because we can understand what features the system is exploiting and how it does it. (E, see also Churchland and Sejnowski, 1992, 115.)

Conclusion   Therefore, contemporary neuroscience can make significant contributions to philosophy, because the development of the notion of representation as vector-coding in a PDP network by computational neuroscience appears to be a promising means of approaching central problems in PR mentality.

Through the ubiquitous notion of similarity, a plausible link has been bruited between issues in epistemology and what happens in networks of neurons. Given the methodological desirability of connecting epistemological issues to real psychological processes and psychological processes to a real physical substratum, it almost seems churlish to demur from this demonstration, but demur I must. My reservations are neither logical nor philosophical, but empirical.

The first reservation comes from the psychological work on similarity already discussed. What Churchland and Sejnowski emphasize is that vector-coding brings with it a geometric representation of similarity. The similarities between represented objects are reflected by the distances between the positions their "representations" occupy in activation space, and, of course, those positions are a straightforward geometric function of the values of each of the nodes[18] (which may be interpretable as representing the micro-features through which the similarity is calculated). However, Tversky's widely recognized work on similarity judgments indicates that, whatever its intuitive plausibility, the geometric representation of similarity is inaccurate as a predictor of actual practice. Thus, either the neural system does not work as Churchland and Sejnowski suggest or the workings of the neural system *per se* do not explain how we make similarity judgments (or both). Further, later psychological research suggests (1) that simple featural similarity may be much less important in similarity judgments than systematic relations among features (Clement and Gentner, 1991, 90) and (2) that future progress in understanding similarity depends on specifying the respects in which things are similar and the constructive processes involved in making similarity judgments (Medin et al., 1993, 255, 274).

It may be tempting to reply that although similarity is a more complex matter than Churchland and Sejnowski's work suggests, PDP networks still might contribute to its solution. Their discussion of NETtalk indicates that by analyzing the activation patterns of hidden units, it is possible to "discover how the different letter-to-sound correspondences were coded" (Churchland and Sejnowski, 1992, 115). Generalizing from this case, it seems that it might be possible to analyze the hidden units in a network that was trained to group items together as similar (or to make analogies) in order to determine the respects (and hence possibly the processes) that were exploited in the responses.

This brings me to my second reservation. If, as appears likely at present, the key to understanding the notion of similarity (which is indeed crucial to so many aspects of PR mentality) is to determine the relevant respects and the particular processes involved in making similarity judgments, then the kind of models Churchland and Sejnowski discuss are not likely to be helpful. To understand why, we need to consider the illustrative case of NETtalk in more detail.

NETtalk maps graphemes to phonemes (which are then fed into the speech synthesizer unit of DECtalk, so the phonemes may be "played" (Sejnowski and Rosenberg, 1987, 152)). As anyone who has heard this dramatic demonstration can attest, the resulting string of sounds sounds very like speech. However, it is important to realize the somewhat limited role of NETtalk itself in the demonstration. Of course, it does not create the sounds. But neither does it determine either the graphemic input or the phonemic output categories. These are, as Sejnowski and Rosenberg put it, "innate" (1987, 158). That is, the graphemes are simply the letters plus three units for spaces and punctuation, and the phonemic categories are represented in terms of 21 articulatory features (voiced, palatal, fricative, etc.) that the experimenters borrow from standard linguistics and give to the network. Besides these 21 output units, there are five units to represent syllable and word boundaries. The network is trained to take a letter as input, in the context of three letters (or punctuation marks) to its right and three to its left, and produce as output the "right" set of articulatory features. Training is via the back-propagation of error.

Beyond the input and output units, NETtalk uses varying numbers of hidden units, and the number affects performance. The crucial point at issue is how these hidden units are analyzed to reveal information about the strategies used by the network to produce the letter-to-sound correspondences (Sejnowski and Rosenberg, 1987, 156–8; Churchland and Sejnowski, 1992, 115). Seemingly the only resources available to answer this question are the activations produced among the hidden units and the input and the output categories. That is, it is possible to find correlations between the activation levels of the hidden units and particular interpreted input and/or output units.

Sejnowski and Rosenberg analyzed the hidden units by computing the average activation level of each of the 80 hidden units for each of the 79 letter-to-sound correspondences in the training set. They then applied clustering techniques to group the letter-to-sound vectors into hier-archies. The result was what they describe as a "striking" pattern: Hidden units were completely segregated into those that dealt with vowels and those that dealt with consonants (Sejnowski and Rosenberg, 1987, 157). Churchland and Sejnowski characterize the same result as "interesting" (1992, 115).

These terms suggest that the analysis of hidden units is a discovery procedure for determining how the network is producing its responses – and in a sense it is, but only in quite a limited sense. NETtalk is given a set of letter-to-sound correspondences that it must learn to replicate. How can it succeed in the task? Presumably only by extracting whatever regularities there are in the correspondences between the inputs and the outputs. However, these regularities depend completely on the pre-existing categories in which the inputs and outputs are represented. In a very real sense the "theory" of the process, or account of how it is done, provided by analyzing the activity of hidden units can be no more informative than the theory of the process already present in the input and output categories.[19] The hidden units have no access to either graphemes or phonemes. All they can operate with are the input and output categories.[20]

Paul Vershure (1992) has argued this general point in detail for the case of NETtalk. He focuses on the "discovery" that the system treats vowels and consonants differently. If one does not look at articulatory features accompanying phonemes but starts with articulatory features and considers the letters in whose pronunciation they play a role, a very different picture emerges.[21] In particular, the features that are used to code 95 percent of the vowels only code about 5 percent of the consonants. In all only eight of the 24 articulatory features[22] are present in both vowels and consonants and the overlap is slight: It is never more than one letter in the other category. So, for example, "velar" is used to describe eight consonants and one vowel (Vershure, 1992, 655). Further, since each phoneme involves more than one articulatory feature, the set of features effectively separates the vowels from the consonants.

Vershure concludes: "The vowels are always translated to a set of articulatory features of which we know beforehand that they distinguish vowels from consonants. Therefore, it is not surprising that NETtalk learns to discriminate them from the category of patterns coding consonants." (1992, 655.)[23] Churchland and Sejnowski acknowledge that in the rock-mine example, the features revealed by analysis of hidden units could also have been discovered by data analysis (1992, 113; but see Gorman and Sejnowski, 1988, 81–4). Perhaps they recognize that analyzing hidden units does not provide much insight into higher cognitive processing.[24]

Let me pause to take stock. The foregoing considerations suggest that computational neuroscience does not work very well as an example of a network-level theory of neural functioning that possesses significant implications for PR mentality, and particularly for our understanding of either similarity or representation. This is so for three independent and largely empirical reasons. First, although parts of computational neuro-science discussed by Churchland and Sejnowski appear to be "neurally close" (1992, 13), the considerations invoked in the argument about PR mentality concerning the nature of vector coding and the representa-tional capacities of NETtalk are not tied to any neurophysiological discoveries.[25] Insofar as this model is neurological, it is only because all PDP models are loosely modeled on systems of neurons. Second, the empirical evidence suggests that the kind of similarity metric provided for free in network models is not the kind that underlies actual similarity judgments. Further, the notion of similarity is important for many aspects of PR mentality, and network models do not seem to be helpful in uncovering the qualitative respects that current research suggests are crucial to understanding similarity. (I should add, however, that once some of these parameters are found, network models may be very helpful in modeling the multiple-constraint satisfaction that seems to be involved in similarity judgments.) Finally, examination of the exemplary network model NETtalk casts serious doubts on the claim that a new paradigm of "representation" has been presented. The difficulty does not concern the term "representation." My reservation derives from the theoretical purpose of talking about inner representations, namely to understand how the cognizer acts and thinks. If it provides no clues about the inner processes through which knowers acquire or exercise their cognitive capacities, then what is the point of describing the activation patterns of hidden units as a kind of representation?

As already noted, Churchland and Sejnowski's discussion ranges far beyond the issues I have considered.[26] Further, to a lay person at least, computational neuroscience appears to be a promising way to approach larger systems of neurons. Hence the conviction may arise that other discussions, those that involve the modeling of lower-level capacities, actually present a stronger case for Neurophilosophy than the explicit argument just considered. Notice, however, that this move begs the very question at issue, for it assumes that any good approach to understanding the behavior of the nervous system will have relatively direct implications for PR mentality. As also noted, the methodological imperatives embodied in computational neuroscience are extremely compelling. Under these circumstances, it is easy to succumb to wishful thinking and assume that since some such approach must be the right way to bridge the gap from neural functioning to cognitive processes, the empirical support is stronger than it actually is.[27] As presented by those best able to present it, however, the empirical case is not strong: Neurophysiological facts are largely irrelevant to the demonstration, the psychological facts imply that the proposed model is inappropriate, and the computational facts do not support the idea that the model provides insight into cognitive processes.

Conclusion

For the reasons given, Churchland's efforts to establish the Contribution Thesis by offering examples of higher-level neuroscientific theories with implications for PR mentality are unsuccessful, at least for the moment. This result should have been expected, for, as noted – and as she observes – the search for higher-level theories in neuroscience has turned out to be extraordinarily difficult. What about the more controversial *Sine qua non* and Most-Important-Contributor Theses? Presumably the most straightforward way to assess the Most-Important-Contributor Thesis is to do so comparatively – hence my examples from psychology. Using Churchland's own "proof of the pudding" standard (Churchland and Sejnowski, 1992, 135), traditional psychology has demonstrated its ability to illuminate philosophical problems, and, to date, neuroscience has not.

Beyond the cases, Churchland offers an independent argument (or series of reflections) for each of these positions. To give credence to the *Sine qua non* Thesis, she raises the specter of the failure of "folk theories" and hints at the lack of solid progress in traditional psychology. Neither of these considerations stands up to scrutiny, however. As already argued, the reflections about folk theories involve vitiating ambiguities, and the history of neuroscience has been just as disappointing as the history of psychology in discovering global theories of mental functioning.

As we have seen, Churchland also tries to bolster the importance of potential contributions from neuroscience by invoking reductionist arguments. Given a proper – i.e., reductionist – relation between psychology and neighboring sciences, the basic explanatory concepts of a unified theory of the mind-brain will be those of a "matured neuroscience." The reductionist move is, however, highly controversial. Besides the problems already noted, the history of attempts to reduce higher processes to relatively simple neurological or biological properties has been fairly embarrassing, and Churchland should not be eager to align her project with this tradition. (Think of nineteenth-century theories of reflexes or instincts, Freud's libido theory, Köhler's appeal to the "electrotonus" of the brain, and so on.[28])

Although Churchland does not make a persuasive case for any of the theses of Neurophilosophy, several points have emerged along the way that clearly indicate the importance of neuroscience to understanding mentality. Oddly, one of the strongest considerations is methodological or quasi-a priori: It is always best to tie accounts of mentality to the physical structure of the brain when possible. Another consideration is a very general lesson from the history of science: Micro-level sciences are more likely than macro-level theories to produce quantum leaps in understanding. Finally, there is an empirical consideration from neuroscience itself: Partly through developments in molecular biology and partly through new techniques, a wealth of data is now accumulating about various neuronal activities.

Together, these three points make a powerful argument for a thesis about neuroscience, although not for any of the theses of neuro*philosophy*. What they show is that neuroscience is extremely likely to be critical to the development and testing of future psychological theories. Given naturalism, future psychologies will be very important to epistemology, ethics, and perhaps other areas of philosophy. But, as the earlier discussion of the unity of science reveals, even taken together, these two claims do not establish that neuroscience itself is likely to exert a significant influence on the advancement of philosophy. That conclusion follows only by invoking the additional premise of reductionism, and, as we have seen, the goal of the unity of science may also be served by viewing the relations of explanatory dependence between psychology and neuroscience as symmetric. Given that option and the examples currently available, the more likely outcome is that neuroscience will affect philosophy only indirectly, via its contributions to psychology. Although this difference may seem slight, it has considerable practical significance. Contrary to the implications of Neurophilosophy, it suggests that for the time being the preponderance of the limited resources of the naturalistic wing of philosophy should be devoted to the science that is directly relevant to its concerns, viz. psychology.

Notes

1   The name dates from P. S. Churchland 1986, but the idea was clearly present in P. S. Churchland 1980.
2   "Folk psychology$_2$," would be equivalent to "folk psychology$_1$," if it could be shown that the average person believes that mental states are inner representational propositional states. *Prima facie* this seems quite dubious, since ordinary people take their minds to be populated by images, ideas, feelings, and half-formed thoughts, as well as fully expressed propositional beliefs. To confirm this, compare any dictionary's entries for "sentence" and "proposition" with its entries for "thought," "idea," "concept," and "image."
3   See Lycan, 1988, 63–4 for discussion of some recent strategies.
4   In this case, the slide is from the linguistic model to "common sense psychology."
5   Churchland's discussion of reduction is somewhat confusing because she endorses both a modified version of classical intertheoretic reduction and Philip Kitcher's notion (1984, 1989) of "explanation extension," which was intended as a refined replacement of the traditional approach to reduction. One important feature of the latter view is that it is possible to capture important connections without supposing that there is one privileged level. By contrast, I think that Churchland's position is that psychological phenomena must be able to be explained in neurophysiological terms. See below for further elaboration of this contrast.
6   Multiple realizability is also crucial to the Jamesian option presented above. For, as noted, it is only because learning, for example, is not identified with a particular state of the nervous system that it is possible to explain the significance of a bit of hardware by noting that it is a mechanism that can instantiate learning.
7   Although she comes very close in the 1992 co-authored book, 1–4.
8   For a thorough discussion of ways to get the definitional view out of trouble see Smith and Medin, 1981.
9   This is clear in some of the literature on the causal theory of reference and

scientific change. See, for example, Putnam, 1975; Devitt and Sterelny, 1987.

10 I should note that Leslie offers some hypotheses about how mental states are represented in children. My appeal is not to his own hypotheses, but only to the well-replicated result that the ability to do this task varies independently of IQ.

11 It does not, however, touch his basic logical point that "appearance" talk is dependent on "is" talk.

12 This conclusion is also strongly supported by other work in psychology, e.g., Keil, 1989, 269ff.

13 I owe this point to Eleanor Wittrup.

14 One of Churchland's section titles is "In Search of Theory" (1986, 407).

15 Chapter 5 is loosely about learning, the plasticity of cells, and, in some cases, systems. I do not discuss these projects for several reasons. A main consideration is length. Another is that large parts of the chapter concern long-term potentiation and so are at the level of the single cell. And as Churchland and Sejnowski recognize recognize (e.g., 1992, 241), connecting individual neurons with PR mentality is a significant problem. Another is that, as they periodically acknowledge, this discussion largely eschews question of higher-order functions (e.g., 1992, 287). Further, when the discussion leaves the level of cellular mechanisms in an effort to make the connection to some dramatic results with lesion studies, the theories become quite speculative. For example, Damasio's hypothesis that deficits caused by hippocampal lesions can be understood in terms of neural networks (as opposed to modules) is quite recent, 1990, and one way among others of making sense of the data (Churchland and Sejnowski, 1992, 320ff.; see also the discussions of Rolls (284ff.) and Zipser (301ff.). Finally, the argument that computational neuroscience can enlighten us about PR mentality is much more developed in the discussion of representation.

16 Churchland and Sejnowski offer a formidable challenge to the single-cell recording paradigm that produces this straightforward account of representation (1992, 183–8, especially, 186, see note 25).

17 They say implicit "representations," but since there is just one set of synaptic values that defines the final position on the network in weight space, this would seem to be just one representation (the vector defined by the synaptic values), although it could be said to represent the "total knowledge" of the network.

18 Since the values in a vector make independent contributions to it, this model implies that features are independent of each other in producing similarity judgments, and this also appears to run counter to current evidence (Goldstone, et al., 1989, 131).

19 This point is implied by Churchland and Sejnowski's own critique of the inferences drawn from micro-electrode recording from single cells (see also note 15):

Their inputs were exclusively smoothly varying gray levels. Therefore, bar and edge receptive-field properties do not necessarily mean that the cell's function is to detect bars and edges in objects ... The general implication is that there is no way of determining the function of each hidden unit in the network simply by "recording" the receptive-field properties of the unit. (1992, 186, my italics.)

20 It was exactly this kind of reflection that led Kant to adopt transcendental idealism (see e.g., 1781/87, A105). He realized that to explain our cognitions, it was unavailing to appeal to the properties of *objects* outside us. All that mattered in our cognitive lives were those aspects of objects conveyed to us via the senses. Applied to computer simulations, Kant's point is perfectly general: all that can be discovered by the hidden units – and hence by analyzing the hidden units – are the correlations contained in the input–output correspondences. It makes no difference what actual objects are like.

21 Contrast Sejnowski and Rosenberg's chart (1987, 161–2) with Vershure's (1992, 655).

22 Sejnowski and Rosenberg list 24 different articulatory features, although they equate some. I do not believe that this difference affects the argument.

23 I should note that Vershure's general point was to argue that too much emphasis has been placed on the "subsymbolic" computation allegedly exemplified by PDP network as a bridge between the cognitive and neural domains.

24 But see Churchland and Sejnowski's discussion of hidden units in networks modeling absolute depth judgments and the activities of the vestibular nucleus (1992, 231, 359). I should note that even though the hidden unit analysis cannot discover anything beyond the regularities present in the input–output correspondences, network simulations do establish something very important: that the output can be produced from the input by non-miraculous means.

25 As Churchland and Sejnowski partially acknowledge, "we are still in the realm of simple computer network models" (1992, 171). On the other hand, they sometimes seem to suggest something stronger: "only enough neurobiological realism, namely geniculate-like input, vector coding, vector-matrix transformations" (1992, 188). This is perhaps just an optimistic slip of the pen, for the hypothesis of vector coding comes from PDP modeling, not from neurobiological discoveries.

Churchland and Sejnowski also forthrightly acknowledge that there may be a very serious problem with applying PDP models to the nervous system. The models involve a principled distinction between current activation and (longer duration) weight changes, and the nervous system does not make such a sharp distinction. There may be enough temporal variation in neural changes to make this a useful idealization, but the question remains open (1992, 174 ff.).

26 Besides those discussed in their note 20, Churchland and Sejnowski offer three examples of attempts to construct (large portions of) synthetic brains on the basis of computer modeling. This work is presented in their very brief concluding chapter. All three projects are at very early stages and are consequently quite hard to evaluate.

27 This type of mistake seems pervasive in the history of psychology. On my 1992 reading of Freud, it was exactly this type of methodological conviction that led him to vastly over estimate the strength of the "evidence from the couch."

28 For example, Freud, 1915; 1920; Köhler, 1969, see especially 104. Brazier, 1988, provides an account of nineteenth-century reflex theories, Murphy, 1949, of the use of instinct concepts in psychology – a use that led to the virtual banishment of the concept from psychology.

References

Bishop, Michael, 1992. "The Possibility of Conceptual Clarity in Philosophy," *American Philosophical Quarterly* **29**: 267–77.

Boyd, Richard, 1980. "Materialism without Reductionism: What Physicalism Does not Entail," in N. J. Block (ed.), *Readings in the Philosophy of Psychology*, vol. I. Cambridge, Mass.: Harvard University Press.

Brazier, Mary A. B., 1988. *A History of Neurophysiology in the 19th Century*. New York: Raven Press.

Cartright, Nancy, 1983. *How the Laws of Physics Lie*. New York: Oxford University Press.

Churchland, Patricia S., 1980. "A Perspective on Mind-Brain Research," *Journal of Philosophy* **77** 185–207.

Churchland, Patricia S., 1986. *Neurophilosophy: Toward a Unified Science of the Mind-Brain*. Cambridge, Mass: MIT Press.

Churchland, Patricia S., 1988. "Replies," *Biology and Philosophy* **3**: 393–402.

Churchland, Patricia S., 1995. "Can Neurobiology Teach Us Anything About Consciousness?," forthcoming, in H. Morowitz and J. Singer (eds.), *The Mind, The Brain, and Complex Adaptive Systems*.

Churchland, Patricia S. and Churchland, Paul M., 1983. "Stalking the Wild Epistemic Engine," *Noûs* **17**: 5–18.

Churchland, Patricia S. and Ramachandran, V. S., 1993. "Filling in: Why Dennett is Wrong," in B. Dahlbom (ed.), *Dennett and His Critics*. Oxford: Blackwell.

Churchland, Patricia S. and Sejnowski, Terrence J., 1992. *The Computational Brain*. Cambridge, Mass.: MIT Press.

Clement, Catherine A. and Gentner, Dedre, 1991. "Systematicity as a Selection Constraint in Analogical Mapping," *Cognitive Science* **15**: 89–132.

Cohen, L. Jonathan, 1981. "Can Human Irrationality Be Experimentally Demonstrated?" *Behavioral and Brain Sciences* **4**: 317–31.

Devitt, Michael and Sterelny, Kim, 1987. *Language and Reality*. Cambridge, Mass.: MIT Press.

Flanagan, Owen and Rorty, Amelie (eds.), 1990. *Identity, Character, and Morality*. Cambridge, Mass.: MIT Press.

Fodor, Jerry A., 1968. *Psychological Explanation*. New York: Random House.

Freud, Sigmund, 1915. "Instincts and their Vicissitudes," *The Standard Edition of the Complete Psychological Works of Sigmund Freud*, vol. XIV., ed. James Strachey. London: Hogarth Press.

Freud, Sigmund, 1920. "Beyond the Pleasure Principle," *The Standard Edition of the Complete Psychological Works of Sigmund Freud*, vol. XVIII., ed. James Strachey. London: Hogarth Press.

Garfinkel, Alan, 1981. "Reductionism," chapter 2 of *Forms of Explanation*. New Haven: Yale University Press; reprinted in Richard Boyd, Philip Gasper, and J. D. Trout (eds.), *The Philosophy of Science*, Cambridge, Mass.: MIT Press.

Goldman, Alvin I., 1986. *Epistemology and Cognition*. Cambridge, Mass.: Harvard University Press.

Goldman, Alvin I., 1993. *Philosophical Applications of Cognitive Science*. San Francisco: Westview Press.

Goldstone, Robert L., Gentner, Dedre, and Medin, Douglas L., 1989. "Relations Relating Relations," in *Proceedings of the Eleventh Annual Conference of the Cognitive Science Society*. Hillsdale, NJ: Lawrence Erlbaum: 131–38.

Goodman, Nelson, 1972. "Seven Strictures on Similarity," in *Problems and Projects*. Indianapolis: Bobbs-Merrill: 437–47.

Gordon, Robert M., 1987. *The Structure of Emotions*. New York: Cambridge University Press.

Gorman, R. Paul and Sejnowski, Terrence, 1988. "Analysis of Hidden Units in a Layered Network Trained to Classify Sonar Targets," *Neural Networks* 1: 75–89.

Hatfield, Gary, 1988. "Neuro-philosophy Meets Psychology: Reduction, Autonomy and Physiological Constraints," *Cognitive Neuropsychology* 5: 723–46.

Hebb, D. O., 1982. "Drives and the C. N. S. (Conceptual Nervous System)," reprinted in Henry A. Buchtel (ed.), *The Conceptual Nervous System*. New York: Pergamon.

Hume, David, 1739–40. *A Treatise on Human Nature*, ed. L. A. Selby-Bigge. Oxford: Oxford University Press, 1962.

James, William, 1890. *The Principles of Psychology*. New York: Dover, 1962.

James, William, 1892. *Psychology, The Briefer Course*. New York: Harper, 1961.

Kahneman, Daniel, Slovic, Paul, and Tversky, Amos, 1982. *Judgment under Uncertainty: Heuristics and Biases*. New York: Cambridge University Press.

Kant, Immanuel, 1781/87. *Immanuel Kant's Critique of Pure Reason*, tr. Norman Kemp Smith. New York: MacMillan, 1968.

Keil, Frank, 1989. *Concepts, Kinds, and Cognitive Development*. Cambridge, Mass.: MIT Press.

Kitcher, Patricia, 1992. *Freud's Dream: A Complete Interdisciplinary Science of Mind*. Cambridge, Mass.: MIT Press

Kitcher, Philip, 1984. "1953 and All That: A Tale of Two Sciences," *Philosophical Review* 93: 335–73.

Kitcher, Philip, 1989. "Explanatory Unification and the Causal Structure of the World," in Philip Kitcher and Wesley Salmon (eds.), *Scientific Explanation: Minnesota Studies in the Philosophy of Science*, vol. 13. Minneapolis: University of Minnesota Press.

Köhler, Wolfgang, 1969. *The Task of Gestalt Psychology*. Princeton: Princeton University Press.

Kornblith, Hilary (ed.), 1987. *Naturalizing Epistemology*. Cambridge, Mass.: MIT Press.

Leslie, Alan, 1987. "Pretense and Representation: The Origins of 'Theory of Mind'," *Psychological Review* **94**: 412–26.

Lycan, William C., 1988. *Judgment and Justification*. New York: Cambridge University Press.

Medin, Douglas L., Goldstone, Robert L., and Gentner, Dedre, 1993. "Respects for Similarity," *Psychological Review* **100**: 254–78.

Murphy, Gardner, 1949. *Historical Introduction to Psychology*. New York: Harcourt Brace and World.

Nagel, Thomas, 1986. *The View from Nowhere*. New York: Oxford University Press.

Nisbett, Richard and Ross, Lee, 1980. *Human Inference: Strategies and Shortcomings of Social Judgment*. Englewood Cliffs, NJ: Prentice-Hall,.

Popper, Karl R. and Eccles, John C., 1977. *The Self and Its Brain*. Berlin: Springer-Verlag.

Putnam, Hilary, 1967. "The Nature of Mental States," in W. H. Capitan and D. D. Merrill (eds.), *Art, Mind, and Religion*. Pittsburgh: University of Pittsburgh Press.

Putnam, Hilary, 1975. "The Meaning of 'Meaning'," in Keith Gunderson (ed.), *Language, Mind, and Knowledge: Minnesota Studies in the Philosophy of Science*, vol. 7. Minneapolis: University of Minnesota Press.

Quine, W. V., 1969. "Natural Kinds," in *Ontological Relativity and Other Essays*. New York: Columbia University Press, 114–38.

Rosch, Eleanor, 1973. "On the Internal Structure of Perceptual and Semantic Categories," in T. E. Moore (ed.), *Cognitive Development and the Acquisition of Language*. New York: Academic Press.

Rumelhart, David E. and McClelland, James L., 1986. *Parallel Distributed Processing*, vols. I and II. Cambridge, Mass.: MIT Press.

Sejnowski, Terrence and Rosenberg, Charles, 1987. "Parallel Networks that Learn to Pronounce," *Complex Systems* **1**: 145–68.

Sellars, Wilfrid, 1963. "Empiricism and the Philosophy of Mind," in *Science, Perception, and Reality*. New York: Routledge and Kegan Paul, 127–96.

Sherrington, Charles S., 1906. *The Integrative Action of the Nervous System*. New Haven: Yale University Press.

Smith, Edward E. and Medin, Douglas L., 1981. *Categories and Concepts*. Cambridge, Mass.: Harvard University Press.

Smolensky, Paul, 1986. "Neural and Conceptual Interpretations of PDP Models," in Rumelhart and McClelland, op. cit., 1986.

Sober, Elliot, 1984. *The Nature of Selection: Evolutionary Theory in Philosoph-*

ical Focus. Cambridge, Mass.: MIT Press.

Solomon, Miriam, 1992. "Scientific Rationality and Human Reasoning," *Philosophy of Science* **59**: 439–55.

Treisman, A. M. and Gelade, G. A., 1980. "A Feature Integration Theory of Attention," *Cognitive Psychology* **12**: 97–130.

Treisman, A. M. and Schmidt, H., 1982. "Illusory Conjunctions in the Perception of Objects," *Cognitive Psychology* **14**: 197–41.

Tversky, Amos, 1977. "Features of Similarity," *Psychological Review* **84**: 327–52.

Vendler, Zeno, 1984. *The Matter of Minds*. Oxford: Clarendon Press.

Vershure, Paul, 1992. "Taking Connectionism Seriously: The Vague Promise of Subsymbolism and an Alternative," *Proceedings of the Fourteenth Annual Conference of the Cognitive Science Society*. Hillsdale, NJ: Lawrence Erlbaum, 653–8.

Wimsatt, William, 1976. "Reduction, Levels of Organization, and the Mind-Body Problem," in G. Globus, G. Maxwell, and I. Savodnik (eds.), *Consciousness and the Brain*. New York: Plenum.

3
Dealing in Futures: Folk Psychology and the Role of Representations in Cognitive Science

Andy Clark

1 Folk Psychology Loses, Neuroscience Gains?

For well over a decade now, P. S. and P. M. Churchland have been prominent speculators on the scientific futures market. Two of their most important targets can be identified as (1) the attempt to establish the low long-term value of the framework of daily mentalistic explanations now known (a little unfortunately) as folk psychology, and (2) the attempt to demonstrate that the scientific study of cognition will increasingly deal in the somewhat different representational and explanatory resources emerging from work in neuroscience and broadly connectionist kinds of computational modelling. Though both the Churchlands are sympathetic to each of the two projects, it is probably fair to say that it is P. M. Churchland who has made much of the running on (1) (see especially P. M. Churchland, 1979, 1981, 1989) and P. S. Churchland who has pursued the most detailed investigations of (2) (see P. S. Churchland, 1986; 1992, the latter being co-authored with the neuroscientist T. Sejnowski). The separation is none the less clearly artificial – a full half of P. M. Churchland's 1989 is devoted to matters which concern the explanatory resources of connectionism and neuroscience, while works such as P. S. Churchland's 1978, 1980, and 1986 leave us in no doubt that she too shares a deep-rooted pessimism about the ultimate integrity of folk psychology.

Intense philosophical interest in the claims about folk psychology has, I believe, served to obscure some of the Churchlands' important observations concerning the changing nature of the explanatory resources of the scientific study of mind. This is unfortunate because, in my view at least, the two issues are more or less orthogonal, and the insights concerning the methodology and explanatory profile of future cognitive science should be valued even by those (myself included) who reject their strong claims concerning the poverty of the folk framework.

My strategy will therefore be to pursue each of these issues in its own right. I begin (section 2) by summarizing briefly some of the results and conjectures that play pivotal roles in both debates. These concern the nature of representation and learning in recent, neurally inspired, models of mental processing. The potential impact of such results on both cognitive scientific practice and our assessment of folk psychology are briefly discussed. Section 3 homes in on issues concerning the future role of representation-talk in cognitive science. In this section I attempt to add even more fuel to the Churchlands' fire by highlighting the availability of a new and stronger model of learning and conceptual change, and introducing some recent studies concerning the effects of the interplay of evolution and individual learning. The emerging lesson – which I see as a central implication of the Churchlands' overall view – is that we may well need to re-think the role of representations in the future explanatory projects of cognitive science. Representations will often be alien (unrelated to folk items), sometimes inward looking (concerning states of other neural systems), module-specific (no global or "central" cognitive code) and as much the objects of our explanatory endeavours as their foundation.

I end (section 4) by returning to the issue concerning the probable lack of fit between the ontology and explanatory resources of a future cognitive science and those of folk psychology. This lack of fit is, I argue, paradoxically our best clue to the peculiar virtues of the folk framework. In particular, I suggest (building on some brief comments made in section 2) that the folk are best seen as engaged in a kind of global knowledge detection and that scepticism about the value of the folk enterprise cannot therefore be justified by appeal to results that rather concern the form of representation in cognitive *sub-systems*. More positively, I suggest that once we are clear that the mere lack of inner quasi-linguistic items is not itself sufficient to undermine the folk discourse the way is open to build a balanced image of the folk project. Once such an image is in place it becomes clear that the most likely impact of scientific advance takes the form not of an eliminative but of an augmentative materialism.

2 The Impact of Non-sententialism

The Churchlands' philosophical projects are powerfully rooted in ongoing work in neuroscience and in (broadly) connectionist artificial intelligence. Two aspects of this recent work bear centrally on the topics of this paper. The first directly concerns the nature of the story about internal representational states which is emerging from such studies: it is a story that challenges any deeply sentential or quasi-linguistic (symbol system and grammar) vision of the inner cognitive economy. The second (related) aspect concerns the nature and scope of processes of individual learning. The new representational forms which challenge the sentential vision can, it seems, emerge as the products of powerful learning processes. These learning processes constitute existence proofs of the broad possibility of types of learning that outstrip the kinds of learning associated with the classical Fodorian vision in which learning is depicted as a process of hypothesis generation and testing using the restricted (and restricting) resources of a fixed innate symbol system (see Fodor, 1975). I would like to offer a word on each.

Regarding the basic form of internal representation, both P. S. and P. M. Churchland stress that the inner representational resources posited by connectionist artificial intelligence do not look much like quasi-linguistic declarative structures. Seen through the lens of connectionist AI "the basic kinematics of cognitive creatures is a kinematics not of sentences but of high-dimensional activation vectors being transformed into other such vectors by passing through large arrays of synaptic connections" (P. M. Churchland, 1989, xvi). In similar vein, P. S. Churchland, writing with the neuroscientist T. J. Sejnowski, comments that: "Instead of starting from the old sentence-logic model, we model information processing in terms of the trajectory of a complex non-linear dynamical system in a very high-dimensional space" (P. S. Churchland and T. Sejnowski, 1990, 234).

This is not the place to review the detailed and ever growing body of evidence for such claims. Suffice to say that it is widely accepted, even among its detractors, that connectionist AI really does offer a new and in some genuine sense non-sentential vision of inner processing (for fuller descriptions see P. M. Churchland, 1989; Clark, 1989). But suppose then that some such non-sentential model really does characterize information processing in the brain. What would follow, either for cognitive science or for the folk vision of the mind?

The implications for cognitive science are clearly direct and profound. Called into question would be the attempt to model reasoning as a kind of proof theory defined over internal data structures (see Oaksford and Chater, 1991) and with it the very notion of a clean boundary separating perceptual and cognitive processes (see P. M. Churchland, 1989, chapter 10). At the same time the usefulness of familiar distinctions (processing/ data, algorithm/implementation) would be challenged (see P. S. Churchland and T. J. Sejnowski, 1990; Clark, 1990a). Even the once unimpeachable methodology of seeking a symbolic competence theory as both the starting point and explanatory core of our cognitive scientific endeavours is revealed as embodying illegitimate assumptions (see Clark, 1990a). These are serious implications indeed.

By contrast, the implications for the folk framework (or, more properly, for our considered assessment of the integrity of that framework) are far less obvious. The folk do indeed use sentential formulations as a means of specifying one another's mental states. Thus I may say of Pepa that she believes that the sun will shine; in so doing I rely on a proposition embedded in a that-clause and expressed by a sentence of English. But what can this reasonably be supposed to commit me to (philosophically) as regards the form of internal representation in Pepa's head? In general, it is certainly *not* the case that the use of a sentential description language commits one to the existence of even quasi-sentential structure *in* the domain described (think of sentences about protein folding, or about geology, or about cooking. . . .). On the face of it, at least, the very most that the sentential folk discourse might seem to saddle us with is the commitment to there being some kind of internal state or states which are causally potent and which somehow support the specific mental contents alluded to in a given (supposedly true) folk psychological account. (And see Van Gelder, 1993; Clark, 1993, for some broadly Rylean doubts (Ryle, 1949) even about this!)

But this latter kind of claim is not obviously contradicted by work in the connectionist or neuroscientific paradigms.[1] Thus we might reflect that many existing connectionist networks happily succumb to useful knowledge ascriptions couched in the folk vocabulary. Thus P. M. Churchland (1989, chapter 9) describes a single net which is fairly happily described, at times, as believing that an object is a mine and not a rock. By this I mean that, although the system is surely too impoverished to count as really believing that it is confronting a mine (ibid., p. 177), our doubts about the belief-invoking description are not rooted in its non-sentential character: we would have equal reservations about a classical, rule and symbol device that could (only) partition inputs into mine and rock indicating signals. Similarly, P. M. Churchland is seen to claim that a good connectionist encoding might capture the prototypical structure of fine-grained types of situation whose contents he is willing to describe as, for example, depicting a mouse eating sesame seeds or hickory nuts (P. M. Churchland, 1989, 207). It is thus hard to see what, in such cases, can be amiss with the folk psychological framework – the creature whose behaviours are as complex as our own (and this *must* be on the cards if connectionism is put forward as a potential new model of human thought) and whose inner connectionist network includes a distinctive sub-volume devoted to representing the fact that the mouse that is eating sesame seeds is surely a being ripe for folk psychological description.

Does P. M. Churchland depict the mere non-sentential form of connectionist internal representation as inimical, in and of itself, to the integrity of the folk framework? I am not sure. In a revealing passage originally published as part of a commentary on D. Dennett's book *The Intentional Stance* he writes that: "We both (i.e. D. Dennett and P. M. Churchland) accept the premise that neuroscience is unlikely to find 'sentences in the head' or anything else that answers to the structure of individual beliefs and desires. On the strength of this shared assumption I am willing to infer that folk psychology is false and that its ontology is chimerical." (P. M. Churchland, 1989, 125.)

It seems, from this passage at least, that the mere failure of a putative internal representational system to evince some kind of sentential form is not itself sufficient to compromise folk psychology. Instead we would need to discover that nothing in the scientific description "answers to the structure of individual beliefs and desires". But if we are faced with a connectionist system in which a distinctive sub-volume of activation space is dedicated to representing, for example, that the mouse is eating sesame seeds, it is unclear in what sense we lack an inner item that "answers to" the description of the being as, for example, believing that the mouse is eating sesame seeds.

Perhaps, however, we should be taking these descriptions (of sub-volumes of activation space as representing such familiar states of affairs) with a pinch of salt. My own view (developed at length in Clark, 1993) is that it is unrealistic to expect sub-volumes in the activation space of single networks to turn out to encode such familiar contents. Instead, the contents that figure in the folk discourse may refer, at best, to rather global properties of systems (like us) comprising multiple networks whose individual tasks are to represent specific aspects of the input: aspects not postulated as components of the folk-individuated mental states. Some partial and preliminary evidence for such a view is already available in the range of unexpected deficits and dissociations revealed by studies of brain-damaged patients. Thus the Churchlands observe elsewhere "that the accidental destruction of isolated brain areas (lesions) leaves people with isolated and often very curious cognitive deficits" (P. M. and P. S. Churchland, 1990, 309). Indeed so – see, for example, Ellis and Young (1988); Warrington and McCarthy (1987); Shallice (1988); Humphreys and Riddoch (1987); P. S. Churchland and Sejnowski (1992), chapter 5. In the inner realm, folk psychological items (knowledge of persons, recognition of faces, identification of everyday objects) fragment. But even this, I claim, fails to undermine the folk ontology of mental states. Thus imagine now a sophisticated connectionist device whose range of behaviours (verbal, sensor-motor, recognitional etc.) is so great as to incline us to say that it really does know about rocks and mines, i.e. it is not an impoverished single net but a complex organism comprising multiple input channels and processing modules. Such a device has, I would like to say, a variety of global skills: as a result it is able (courtesy of the operation within it of some multitude of networks which act as mini-experts dealing with unintuitive fragments of the gross tasks that confront the overall system) to satisfy us as to its right to be described as knowing, for example that such and such an input signifies the presence of a mine. In such a case, any inner fractionability is surely neither here nor there: what the folk talk is a comment upon is rather some global complex of capacities and skills not even plausibly subserved by any single inner resource. Potential frag-mentation is thus the empirical price of the complex of behaviours we rightly *demand* before engaging in the full-blooded use of the folk vocabulary. The inner economy can be both non-sentential and fragmentary/distributed relative to the folk's descriptive practice with-out that practice being in any obvious way compromised.

I conclude that we do not really have any clear sense of what it would be like to discover, scientifically, that nothing inside us "answers to the structure of individual beliefs and desires". We *do* know what it would be like to discover that the inner story is non-sentential. And we *do* know what it would be like to discover that our inner resources divide up the task of representing the world in ways that the folk practice would never lead us to predict. But once we see the folk practice as commenting on the overall body of skills and knowledge our daily behaviour exhibits even the latter discovery seems compatible with the truth of the folk descriptions. To say of people that they believe such and such is, on this account, to locate them in a web of possible actions and responses whose inner roots may be both non-sentential and highly various. The inner facts which "answer to the structure of individual beliefs and desires" are thus not *localized* inner facts. They are not facts about some specific inner *sub-system*. One (misguided) source of apparent pressure on the folk framework is surely the drive to identify beliefs and desires (and all the rest) with scientifically respectable *sub-states* of the cognitive system. This expectation is fuelled, I believe, by the ubiquitious talk within cognitive science of the inner *vehicles* of folk psychological content. The folk explanatory framework, however, leaves it quite open that the only vehicles of *those* kinds of content are whole situated organisms. This kind of view is clearly expressed in Ryle (1949) and echoed, with some unnecessary instrumentalist baggage, in Dennett (1978; 1987). It is also pursued, in somewhat different ways, in Van Gelder (1993) and in Clark (1993).

Time now to shift the focus to our second issue, the nature and scope of learning. Although the issues concerning folk psychology can be raised again here, I do not propose to do so. P. M. Churchland does, famously, claim that the failure of folk psychology to itself illuminate processes of learning and conceptual change constitutes another reason to question its integrity (see P. M. Churchland, 1981, reprinted in 1989, 6–9). But it has been argued elsewhere (Clark, 1989, chapter 3; Horgan and Woodward, 1990) that these alleged explanatory failures are of uncertain import as it is entirely plausible to insist that the folk discourse was never committed to the explanation of such phenomena in the first place. I do not propose to cover this terrain again here. Instead, I propose to highlight an issue concerning the potential impact of alternative scientific models of learning on our conception of the explanatory project of cognitive science.

The place to start is with the broadly Fodorian view that there really is not (and cannot be) any process of truly radical but rational conceptual change and learning. Instead, all such "change" is really conservative, in that it merely involves the recombination of original innate representational resources. The problem of explaining the origins of these representations is then shunted onto biological species level evolution (see Fodor, 1975).

The Churchlands are rightly critical of this evasive tactic. It certainly looks as if human beings engage in processes of real representational change and development, and passing the representation-generating buck entirely to evolution seems to postpone the problem rather than to solve it (see P. S. Churchland, 1978). The good news (and for lots more on this see Clark, 1993) is that connectionist learning algorithms offer a clear existence proof (one which remains despite the biological implausibility of the standard learning algorithms) of the general possibility of representation-generating yet rational learning and hence of the possibility of representational change unbounded by the expressive limitations of a pre-existing symbol system base. This is because such systems are provably capable of inducing new representations to facilitate success at a problem-solving task. In addition, even if some innate representational resources *are* provided, the form of learning does not limit the future representational growth of the system to the quasilogical manipulation and recombination of those resources (see Rumelhart et al., 1986, 141; Clark, 1993, chapter 2).

Connectionist approaches to learning thus extend a fascinating invitation to try to understand the non-representational origins of representation itself. This project will, I predict, increasingly come to dominate cognitive science. By contrast, most of the work of traditional cognitive science consisted in trying to discover or guess what the mature representational resources of the brain looked like. Once the representations were on the table, most of the work of classical, Fodorian cognitive science would have been finished (see, e.g., Fodor, 1987, 147). The new explanatory endeavour clearly embodies a new conception of the *aspirations* of cognitive science in so far as it is at heart a representation-generating and not a representation-assuming approach. Such a framework provides an exciting opportunity to begin to probe forms of representational content very far removed both from those specified in familiar folk psychological talk and from those that have figured in previous competence-theoretic speculation. In the next section I try to capture some of the flavour of these new possibilities.

3   The Role of Representation in the Future of Cognitive Science

The scientific study of cognition is replete with talk of representation. What I find most suggestive in the Churchlands' work is the persistent attempt to challenge our conception both of representation itself and of its role in the explanatory projects of cognitive science. To illustrate this, I shall briefly rehearse one aspect of their treatment and then offer an illustration which may help reveal the potential radicalness of the proposed reconception.

In a co-authored paper (P. M. and P. S. Churchland, 1981)) the Churchlands draw a useful contrast between what they term calibrational and translational kinds of content. The ascription of translational content involves first the mapping of a whole system of representations onto the system embodied in a public human language, and second the systematic translation, in the light of that mapping, of propositional contents between the two representational schemes. Calibrational content, by contrast, is assigned on a much simpler and less globally systematic basis: a calibrational content of X can be assigned to any physical state which repeatedly and reliably indicates the presence of the feature X in the system's accessible environment. Thus we assign the calibrational content of "temperature 0°C" to a certain height in a column of red alcohol (see P. M. and P. S. Churchland, 1981, reprinted in P. M. Churchland, 1989, 42–3). Given the putative absence of any quasi-sentential inner code, it becomes plausible to suppose that the basic method of assigning contents to the states of inner sub-systems will need to be calibrational rather than translational.

One immediate benefit of giving up on the search for translational contents "in the head" is that it opens the door to a far-reaching multiplicity of internal representational systems. We no longer need search for a single representational system able to underpin all processes of rational learning and higher cognition. Instead, it seems likely that we deploy an integrated hierarchy of quite different computational/ representational systems (P. M. and P. S. Churchland, 1990, 309). Once we give up the dream of translational content, we can treat each such system in its own right as a target for the assignment of calibrational content.

In addition, the contents of calibrational content can be arbitrarily removed from those of daily talk, whereas translational content is required to connect directly and systematically to the kinds of contents suitable for report in our public language. It is this last virtue of calibrational content that comports most elegantly with the idea of a changing role of representation in cognitive science. To illustrate this, consider some recent work in the evolution of learning.

In a fascinating series of simulations Nolfi and Parisi have investigated what happens when evolution is allowed to work on complex systems in which one component acts as a kind of trainer/teacher for another. Nolfi and Parisi modelled 'organisms' consisting of two linked connectionist sub-networks. The two sub-nets both begin with random weights and share an input signal indicating the angle and distance of the nearest food source in a small grid-world. One sub-net (the "teacher") would then determine the target output patterns to be presented to the other sub-net (the "student"). The student net's task is then to learn (using the familiar – though admittedly biologically unrealistic – back-propagation learning algorithm) the mapping specified by the combination of the input (common to both student and teacher) and the internally (teach-net) generated target output. These target outputs were to take the form of motor commands, i.e. the task was to learn to respond to the sensory input data by issuing a command whose effect is (ideally) to move the simulated organism into the food-containing square on the grid, at which point the food is counted as consumed. Food items were placed randomly and re-distributed at the start of each simulation.

As it stands, of course, the set-up is hopeless. It is a case of the blind leading the blind. For since the weights in the teacher sub-net (which do not change during the organism's lifetime) are random, the target outputs it sends to the student will be chaotic relative to the task. The student net will learn this mapping, whatever it is, but it is unlikely to constitute any advance in the organisms eating skills, which will remain at the level of chance. But what will happen if we allow an analogue of genetic evolution to operate on a population of such organisms?

To find out, Nolfi and Parisi created an initial population of 100 organisms (teach-net/student-net pairings) each with different random weights in the two sub-nets. Each organism was allowed to "live" for a fixed time (5,000 movements in the grid-world). At the end of that time, the number of successful ingestions was counted and the twenty organisms that had done best were each used to create five "offspring", i.e. five close copies of the initial (note, initial – this is not a Lamarkian simulation) weights of the organism, with minor mutations (a few of the original initial weights changed at random). A new generation of 100 organisms was thus produced and the procedure repeated. After some 200 generations very successful eating was being achieved. This success, however, depended heavily on individual learning. At birth the student nets of the successful organisms were hopeless. More interestingly, the teacher nets themselves, if allowed *directly* to control motor output at birth, did significantly worse than their associated student nets after lifetime learning. So evolution had not simply hard-wired the optimal solution into the teacher sub-net, leaving it merely to transfer it to the student via back-propagation training. To emphasize this, Nolfi and Parisi showed that if the weights in the student sub-net are once more randomized at the outset, then the whole system (the student-net/teach-net pairing) fails to learn any useful food-approaching behaviour over its individual lifetime. Thus the weights in the student net, although of no direct use in solving the problem at birth, are still crucial in some way to the organism's general ability to *learn* to solve the problem.

The way to understand what has happened here is to see that the weights in the student net "are not selected for directly incorporating good eating behaviours ... but they are accurately selected for their ability to let such a behaviour emerge by life-learning" (Nolfi and Parisi, 1991, 10). Unpacking this, we may note that, first, the weights in the student net will have been selected so as to afford a good (local minima avoiding) starting place for learning. And, second, that since the teach-net and the student-net have co-evolved, the teach-net may be in a somewhat extended sense calibrated to the particular initial location of the student in weight space, i.e. it can generate training signals that reflect the specific needs of that student-net, the one whose initial weights are thus and so.

In a final twist, Nolfi and Parisi repeated the experiment, but this time allowed each sub-net to pass a training signal to the other; thus, in this simulation (unlike the previous one) the weights in the teach-net were *themselves* changeable by back propagation learning during the organism's individual lifetime. Once again good eating behaviour evolved. But this time neither sub-net was clearly acting as teacher and both were completely hopeless at birth. What we see in this final simulation is thus the power of evolution to select cleverly co-evolved complexes of networks whose joint activity, given processes of individual learning dependent upon realistic environmental inputs, is able to determine successful mature behaviour.

Suppose we then tried to understand the computational roots of such success by seeking a mapping, in terms of translational content, between the inner representational resources of some highly complex version of such a system and the daily fodder of human language. In all likelihood, we would fail dismally. We would fail to illuminate the process of learning as the systems would not have proceeded by performing quasi-linguistic operations on a rich initial representational base. Instead, if we ask what exactly is the content of the innate knowledge embodied in the initial weights of the evolved nets, we find ourselves talking rather of one net's knowledge of the other's location in weight space, of initial positions which avoid local minima, etc.: i.e. we are confronting a form of innate knowledge that is fully independent of the usual resources of daily language. This is not even calibrational content in any simple sense, as the states do not directly track features of the external environment. Instead, it is a kind of inward-looking calibrational content; it concerns the delicate evolved harmonization of the resources of a complex of sub-networks evolved so as to yield successful learning given realistic input data.

The force of this observation is not, I believe, restricted to the understanding of learning. For once we see how alien and inward-looking the initial representational base may be, we must begin to wonder whether the mature system likewise depends for its success on the exploitation of multiple delicately and probably non-intuitively harmonized inner resources. We may even begin to wonder whether the attempt to understand even the mature information processing of the human brain will finally revolve around a body or bodies of representations whose contents are in any way well depicted by sole and direct reference to the kinds of external states of affairs by means of which we fix the meanings of public language terms. Perhaps it will not. Perhaps the cognitive scientific wisdom we seek will require us to treat the inner processing economy as itself a kind of ecology *within* which we must attempt (at times) to determine crucial calibrational contents. The useful notion of calibrational content may thus serve us best once it is expanded to refer not just to states of the gross external environment, but to states of the internal one as well.

This notion of important but inward-looking cognitive resources can also be found in some recent work in cognitive neuroscience. Thus Van Essen et al. (forthcoming) argue that the brain is best seen as a system evolved to treat information as "an essential commodity" and that this in turn leads to the development of very specialized systems whose task is not to represent the external world but rather to control the path and flow of information within the system. Van Essen et al. go so far as to postulate the existence of "control neurons" whose task is to modulate the connectivity between other groups of neurons and hence to ensure that the right information arrives in the right place at the right time, thus gaining maximal benefit from information stored anywhere in the system. These inward-looking control resources might enable the flexible linkage of a multiplicity of distinct modules and so result in a more plastic and efficient system. But they would clearly *not* be well understood in terms of any external representational role.

I conclude that the present role of representation in cognitive science is indeed due for a full re-evaluation. Considered as the content-bearing states of cognitive sub-systems, such internal representations as we are eventually driven to posit may turn out to bear rather alien (non-folksy) and at times purely inward-looking contents. In addition there need be no single central code, and content fixation may thus depend on calibrational rather than translational techniques. Finally, representations thus reconceived will not be taken for granted as a necessary innate bedrock upon which cognitive scientific explanation has only to build. Representational states will be considered as much the object of cognitive scientific explanations as their foundation. Churchland's radical belief that the explanatory apparatus of future cognitive science will owe little or nothing to the "sentential categories of current common sense" (P. M. Churchland, 1989, 177) is thus one I fully and unambiguously endorse. It is a belief whose full implications we are only beginning to glimpse.

4 Blunt Instruments and Augmentative Materialism

Cognitive scientific theorizing about mind, I have conceded, will indeed very probably depart radically from the vocabulary and assumptions of daily mentalistic talk. To the extent that it does so, must we view such talk as at best amounting to the opportunistic use of a rather blunt instrument? Must the folk vision be, if not exactly eliminated, at least relegated to the status of a one-dimensional projection of much higher-dimensional internal cognitive states, or a "partial and unpenetrating gloss on a deeper and more complex reality" (P. M. Churchland, 1989, 7)?

The view I have been developing (section 2 above; Clark, 1989) depicts it instead (and here I obviously follow, for example, Dennett 1978; 1987) as offering a different kind of information. Thus, suppose someone were to complain of the simple thermometer that it is flawed because it is just too blunt an instrument to reveal the precise nature of an illness. Several different illnesses, after all, can result in one and the same temperature reading! It would be fair to reply to this that the objection misconstrues the nature of the information the thermometer is meant to supply. Its job is more global, and more mundane. It is supposed, amongst other things, to reveal a specific state (someone's temperature) that is an indicator not of specific facts concerning what particular illness is present, but rather acts as a general indicator of (a range of types of) ill health. Likewise, as I suggested in section 2, we may see folk psychology as a device whose purpose is to inform us ONLY of the overall states of knowledge and motivation of other agents. For most social and daily purposes, we care not at all about the specific details of inner representational form or neural configuration. Instead, we care only, for example, whether so and so believes the film will begin at 10 p.m. Should he instead believe it begins at 11.00, that fact (whose internal roots may be distributed and fragmentary, involving several possibly competing or inconsistent kinds of information stored in disparate inner resources) will explain and predict his lateness. It is this more coarse-grained level of detail that folk psychology is adapted to provide. What P. M. Churchland sees as an unpenetrating gloss is thus fruitfully reconceived as an effective social adhesive.

One common response to such claims is to castigate them as placing too few constraints on the acceptability of the folk "theory". Thus both in his 1981 paper and in subsequent pieces (e.g. the commentary on Dennett reproduced in his (1989) pp. 125–7) P. M. Churchland accuses this type of defence of folk psychology of being too powerful. If we restrict the commitments of some discourse to the correct plotting of a few global properties that are revealed in gross behaviour, then we could defend alchemy, for example, or the astronomical theory of nested crystal spheres, as acceptable. This worry deserves more attention than I have space to give it here. But I should at least note that depicting the role of the folk discourse in the way I have does not commit us to the claim that the discourse makes *no* assumptions that concern inner facts. My claim is just that one kind of inner fact that it does *not* concern is the question whether we do or do not rely on some kind of sentential inner code. To give a single example, it is commonly assumed that some of my actions and verbal outputs draw on stored information concerning my previous experiences. But if it were discovered that I was a pre-programmed Giant Look-up Table with a distinct stored output for every possible input (in every possible sequence of inputs!) then that assumption would be undermined. It would then be unintelligible to suppose that my present action or utterance was caused by the stored trace of a previous experience, and it might reasonably be judged that I was not, after all, a proper object of folk psychological descriptions. The particular example is unimportant. The point is just that the stress on global behaviour does not make the folk discourse immune to inner evidence: it just makes it immune to the wrong kinds of inner evidence.

The more positive vision of the nature of folk psychology rehearsed above accords surprisingly well with P. M. Churchland's own favoured model of explanatory understanding. The model in question is one in which explanatory understanding is depicted as involving prototype activation. Thus the basic form of representation in mature con-nectionist systems, and probably in brains, is, Churchland argues, prototype-involving. This means that a neural network learns to use the resources of its high-dimensional weight space so as to generate partitions in activation space corresponding to the features it needs to distinguish in order to perform a set task. Each partition separates off a sub-volume of activation space such that activity defining the centre point of the space indicates the presence of a prototypical instance of the feature (see P. M. Churchland, 1989, chapters 6, 9, 10). These prototype-style representations are best seen, I suggest, as bearing contents that are calibrationally determined (see section 3). One appealing fact about them is that the objects of such calibration can be arbitrarily complex. To repeat an example already used, activity in the centre of one such space might be assigned the calibrational content that the mouse is eating sesame seeds. Explanatory understanding thus consists, P. M. Churchland suggests, of the activation of correct, perhaps highly abstract and complex, prototypes (see P. M. Churchland, 1989, chapter 10).

Endorsement of such a model recently led P. M. Churchland to depict our individual folk psychological understanding *not* as "consisting of an internally stored set of general sentences" (P. M. Churchland, 1989, 112), but as consisting of a body of stored prototype-style representa-tions. That is, our own internal encoding of the folk wisdom need not *itself* be stored in sentential form. Instead we are to expect complex partionings reflecting "typical configurations of desires, beliefs, prefer-ences and so forth" (P. M. Churchland, 1989, 124). The folk framework could still mislead, he goes on to insist, as such configurations may offer only a shallow and inadequate vision of the inner roots of action. But the internal representation of the (putatively flawed) folk theory need not itself be conceived as sentential.

The worries about shallowness we have already tried to rebuff; folk psychology is not shallow so much as coarse-grained. Remove the taint of shallowness and we are left with a nice model of why the folk discourse, sententially couched, actually works. It works because the belief/desire (etc.) sentences successfully evoke complex non-sentential inner representations of (on our account) coarse-grained behaviour patterns and trends. What P. M. Churchland says in partial defence of deductive-nomological explanation now applies wholesale to folk psychological explanation. I quote. "What a well-turned deductive-nomological argument certainly can do is successfully evoke explanatory understanding in the hearer by provoking activation of the relevant prototype ... D-N arguments are therefore entirely appropriate things to exchange in a great many explanatory contexts..." (P. M. Churchland, 1989, 224). Ditto, I suggest, for the sentential repertoire of folk psychology. Propositional attitude talk, exchanged between competent speakers of a natural language, will reliably evoke a host of inner (prototype encoding) resources, whose cumulative effect is to induce in the hearer useful knowledge and expectations concerning the likely overall behaviour patterns and responses of some other individual.

In addition, and to close on a truly positive note, this conception lays our folk psychological understanding nicely open to the advances of what I shall dub an augmentative materialism. Augmentative materialism allows that scientific advance may indeed contribute to the enrichment of the knowledge the folk psychological sentences reliably evoke. It may do this by, for example, adding some broad conception of the varied panoply of types of internal event which may be causing a behaviour or by expanding the repertoire of types of behaviour pattern which can be reliably identified. The process I have in mind is thus one in which the likely impact of scientific advance is to endorse and enrich the explanatory understandings reliably evoked by the folk discourse. In contrast, the kinds of scientific discovery that would genuinely undermine such discourse are, once we have disposed of the red herring of inner sentences, just the unworkable and bizarre imaginings of philosophers: pure look-up table organizations, radio-controlled puppets, chance behaviours of chaotic matter etc. But these are marginal phantasms, whose shadowy presence is unsubstantiated by the actual conjectures of working connectionists and neuroscientists.

5 Conclusions: Provoking Prophets

The exposure of folk psychology to scientific refutation has, I have argued, been somewhat exaggerated. The single most potent source of such exaggeration is the image of the folk discourse as targeted, for some peculiar reason, on *sub-states* of organisms. If it is instead seen as commenting on overall skills and bodies of knowledge, the argumentative dialectic is significantly altered.

But whatever the fate of the speculations regarding folk psychology, the profound conceptual impact of the scientific advances upon which the Churchlands draw is real enough. We have indeed reached some kind of crossroads in our conception of the nature and form of explanation in cognitive science. Where once the starting point of such explanation was a conception of representation quite closely modelled on our experiences with language, proof theory and artificial grammars, we now reach a point where the nature and role of representation in the brain is almost entirely up for grabs. Several factors contribute to this healthy but challenging state of affairs. We have existence proofs of the possibility of powerful yet non-sentential modes of storing and exploiting information. We are glimpsing the possibility of models of learning and representational change that are neither constituted by nor bounded by the expressive power of any pre-existing symbol system. And in exploring the relations between evolution and individual learning we are beginning to see in concrete detail the role of unexpectedly inward-looking kinds of knowledge in promoting successful learning and the more efficient exploitation of information. Both the explanatory targets and the explanatory tools of cognitive science are in a state of flux. As both participants in this new ongoing work and philosophers pursuing a unified vision of mind and its place in nature, the Churchlands' critical contribution to this emerging re-evaluation is unique and crucial. Long may they provoke!

Notes

This paper was prepared while the author was in receipt of a Senior Research Leave Fellowship granted by the joint Council (SERC/MRC/ESRC) Cognitive Science and Human Computer Interaction Initiative.
1 But see Ramsey, Stich and Garon (1991) for a valiant attempt to generate a non-obvious contradiction. I reply to their argument in Clark (1990b).

References

Ackley, D. and Littman, M. (1992). Interactions between learning and evolution. In C. Langton, C. Taylor, O. Farmer and S. Rasmussen (eds), *Artificial Life II, Santa Fe Institute Studies in the Sciences of Complexity*, vol. 10, Reading, Mass.: Addison-Wesley.

Churchland, P. M. (1979). *Scientific Realism and the Plasticity of Mind*, Cambridge: Cambridge University Press.

Churchland, P. M. (1981). Eliminative materialism and the propositional attitudes. *Journal of philosophy*, **78**, 2, pp. 67–90. Reprinted in P. M. Churchland (1989).

Churchland P. M. (1989). *The Neurocomputational Perspective: The Nature of*

Mind and the Structure of Science, Cambridge, Mass.: MIT Press.

Churchland, P. M. and Churchland, P. S. (1981). Functionalism, qualia and intentionality. *Philosophical Topics*, **12**, 1, pp. 121–45. Reprinted in P. M. Churchland (1989).

Churchland, P. M. and Churchland, P. S. (1990). Stalking the wild epistemic engine. In W. Lycan (ed.), *Mind and Cognition: a Reader*, Oxford: Blackwell, pp. 300–11.

Churchland, P. S. (1978). Fodor on language learning. *Synthese*, **38**, 1, pp. 149–59.

Churchland, P. S. (1980). A perspective on mind-brain research. *Journal of Philosophy*, **77**, 4, pp. 185–207.

Churchland, P. S. (1986). *Neurophilosophy: Toward a Unified Science of the Mind-brain*, Cambridge, Mass.: MIT Press.

Churchland, P. S. and Sejnowski, T. J. (1990). Neural representation and neural computation. In W. Lycan (ed.) *Mind and Cognition: a Reader*, Oxford: Blackwell, pp. 224–51.

Churchland, P. S. and Sejnowski, T. (1992). *The Computational Brain*, Cambridge, Mass.: MIT Press.

Clark, A. (1989). *Microcognition: Philosophy, Cognitive Science and Parallel Distributed Processing*, Cambridge, Mass.: MIT Press.

Clark, A. (1990a). Connectionism, competence and explanation. *British Journal for the Philosophy of Science*, **41**, 195–222.

Clark, A. (1990b). Connectionist minds. *Proceedings of the Aristotelian Society*, **XC**, pp. 83–102.

Clark, A. (1991a). Radical ascent. *Proceedings of the Aristotelian Society*, supp. **65**, pp. 211–27.

Clark, A. (1991b). In defence of explicit rules. In W. Ramsey, S. Stich and D. Rumelhart (eds), *Philosophy and Connectionist Theory*, Hillsdale, N. J.: Erlbaum.

Clark, A. (1993). *Associative Engines: Connectionism, Concepts and Representational Change*, Cambridge, Mass.: MIT Press.

Dennett, D. (1978). *Brainstorms: Philosophical Essays on Mind and Psychology*, Cambridge, Mass.: MIT Press.

Dennett, D. (1987). *The Intentional Stance*, Cambridge, Mass.: MIT Press.

Ellis, A. and Young, A. (1988). *Human Cognitive Neuropsychology*, London: Erlbaum.

Fodor, J. (1975). *The Language of Thought*, New York: Crowell.

Fodor, J. (1987). *Psychosemantics: the Problem of Meaning in the Philosophy of Mind*, Cambridge, Mass.: MIT Press.

Horgan, T. and Woodward, J. (1990). Folk psychology is here to stay. In W. Lycan (ed.), *Mind and Cognition: a Reader*, Oxford: Blackwell, pp. 399–420.

Humphreys, G. and Riddoch, M. (1987). *To See but Not to See: a Case Study of Visual Agnosia*, London: Erlbaum.

Nolfi, S. and Parisi, D. (1991). Auto-teaching: networks that develop their own teaching input. Technical Report PCIA9103, Institute of Psychology, CNR, Rome.

Oaksford, M. and Chater, N. (1991). Against logicist cognitive science. *Mind and Language*, **6**, 1, 1–38.

Ramsey, W., Stich, S. and Garon, J. (1991). Connectionism, eliminativism and the future of folk psychology. In W. Ramsey, S. Stich and D. Rumelhart (eds), *Philosophy and Connectionist Theory*, Hillsdale, N. J.: Erlbaum.

Rumelhart, D., McClelland, J. and the PDP Research Group (1986). *Parallel Distributed Processing: Explorations in the Microstructure of Cognition*, Cambridge, Mass.: MIT Press, Bradford Books.

Ryle, G. (1949). *The Concept of Mind*, London: Hutchinson.

Shallice, T., (1988). *From Neuropsychology to Mental Structure*, Cambridge: Cambridge University Press.

Van Essen, D., Anderson, C., and Olshausen, B. (in press) Dynamic routing strategies in sensory, motor and cognitive processing. In C. Koch and J. Davis (eds), *Large Scale Neuronal Theories of the Brain*, Cambridge, Mass.: MIT Press.

Van Gelder, T. (1993). The distinction between mind and cognition. Paper presented to "Mind and Cognition: an International Symposium" at the Institute of European and American Studies Academia Sinica, Taipei, Taiwan, May.

Warrington, C. and McCarthy, R. (1987). Categories of knowledge: further fractionations and an attempted integration. *Brain*, 110, 1273–96.

4
Paul Churchland's PDP Approach to Explanation

William G. Lycan

Or rather, Paul Churchland's PDP approach to explanatory under-standing. As we shall see, there is a big difference.

Many years ago, in a now badly underappreciated article (1970), Churchland allied himself to the deductive-nomological (D-N) theory of explanation, indeed so strongly as to defend it for the case of folk-psychological explanation of human actions.[1] But that allegiance he would now regard as a young man's folly. Notoriously, he has since (1979; 1989; Churchland and Churchland, 1983) rejected all of what he calls "sentential epistemologies," which take the units of cognition and of cognitive norms to be sentences or propositions or propositional structures of the sort found in the epistemological literature without exception.

Most recently, he has rejected in particular the idea that *scientific theories* are propositional structures such as sets of sentences, and that scientific explanation is the deduction of sentences from other sen-tences.[2] His main objection to sentential epistemologies is that they are radically unsuited to human organisms as those organisms (we) are found in nature; sentential theories are both psychologically and bio-logically unrealistic. He draws a less traditionally philosophical but allegedly far more plausible picture of theory and explanation from neural-network models of sensory processing and of associative mem-ory: as we shall see, its units are configurations of *synaptic weights* and *activation patterns*, defined over large populations of neurons in a cognizer's brain – not sentences or even "sentences," but points in umpteen-dimensional phase spaces.

Churchland vs. Hempel and Oppenheim

Accordingly, Churchland now vehemently rejects the D-N model of explanation.[3] In fact, he takes Hempel and Oppenheim's garishly sententialist D-N model explicitly as his foil. Granting that criticism of the D-N model has clamored and resounded for decades, he offers objections claimed to be new or at least atypical. ("Relatively little [attention] has been paid to ... [the D-N model's] shortcomings when evaluated from a *psychological* point of view" (p. 199, italics original).) The objections are:

1 Although "if someone has just come to understand why a is F, the D-N model requires that we ascribe to that person knowledge of some universally quantified general statement having Fx as its consequent, plus knowledge of a series of initial conditions ..., plus the successful deduction ...," real people who have explanatory understanding nonetheless can seldom "voice either the general law ... or the set of initial conditions," much less perform complex deductions (p. 199).
2 All that assembling of facts and laws (let alone the deducing) would take significant amounts of real time, but explanatory understanding is often "almost instantaneous" (pp. 199–200).
3 Nonhuman animals "display behavior that indicates the achievement of explanatory understanding ... But the assembly of discursive premises and the execution of formal inferences is presumably beyond their capacities" (p. 200).

Thus (very probably), D-N explanation is neither psychologically nor biologically real; and, since for Churchland psychology and biology exhaust what is real about human beings, that leaves no sense in which human beings engage in D-N explanation.

But there is evident mismatch between Churchland's subject-matter and that of Hempel and Oppenheim. Arguments 1–3 concern explanatory *understanding* considered as a psychological state or condition. Yet the title of Hempel and Oppenheim (1948) was "Studies in the Logic of Explanation," not "Studies in the Psychology of Explanation." Its authors evinced no interest whatever in explanatory understanding, at least not in explanatory understanding considered as an actual psychological state of a person. Their concern was rather to explicate the relation "being a correct explanation of," considered either as a quasi-logical relation between sentences (as befitted a logical empiricist) or as a natural relation between the states of affairs in the world expressed by those sentences,[4] without reference to actual human psychology either particular or generic. Arguments 1–3 have little to do with "being a correct explanation of," in either its sentential or its natural-physical version; so, as launched against Hempel and Oppenheim, they are rubber arrows, not new and formidable objections.

There is a more charitable reading of Churchland's critical stance: If one were to *extrapolate* the D-N model to explanatory understanding psychologically understood, then presumably it would incur Churchland's criticisms; for the natural route of extrapolation would be to explicate a person's possession of explanatory understanding as that person's psychological *grasping of* a real D-N explanation – laws, initial conditions, computation and all – which grasping is, in the real world, rare to nonexistent.

Hempel and Oppenheim certainly never intended any such extrapolation. (The point is not just that they had not gotten around to the topic of explanatory understanding; they cared nothing for explanatory understanding or any other psychological condition in the first place.[5]) To make 1–3 stick even on the present charitable reading, therefore, Churchland would need a premise to the effect that any theory of explanation *ought* to extrapolate to explanatory understanding. Some theorists, those who think that the term "explanation" first and foremost nominalizes the activity of explaining as it occurs between human beings, would find that premise plausible. But Hempel and Oppenheim would never grant it, nor would anyone who thinks of explanation as a relation between states of affairs in the world. So I believe Churchland's objection fails even on the more charitable interpretation.

(It is still reasonable to ask any proponent of any account of explanation to say *something* about the relation between that account and explanatory understanding. Failing total grasp of a real D-N explanation, what must a person grasp in order to qualify as understanding it? Hempel and Oppenheim did address or at least touch on that question when they conceded (p. 139) that a person is sometimes counted as "having an explanation of" a phenomenon even though that person is far from grasping a "complete" (i.e., real D-N) explanation, by virtue of knowing "some positive correlation between the antecedent conditions adduced and the type of phenomenon to be explained" and knowing "a direction in which further research might be carried on in order to complete the explanatory account." Subsequent theorists, notably Railton (1980) and Salmon (1984; 1989),[6] have said more about understanding as felicitously partial grasp of an ideal total explanation. Thus, I think Hempel and Oppenheim are in no immediate danger on this score.)

Churchland and the Pragmaticist Move

There is of course a vigorously anti-D-N movement that does focus on explanatory understanding: what is sometimes called the "pragmaticist" school, represented by Scriven (1962), Bromberger (1965; 1966), van Fraassen (1980), Achinstein (1983), and Sintonen (1989). The pragmaticist idea is precisely to explicate explanation in terms of understanding, considered as the actual or hypothetical perlocutionary effect of a speech act on an audience. Thus, Scriven (p. 224): "What is a scientific explanation? It is a topically unified communication, the content of which imparts understanding of some scientific phenomenon. And the better it is, the more efficiently and reliably it does this, i.e., with less redundancy and a higher *over-all* probability." Likewise, Achinstein takes "explanation" to derive from the illocutionary verb "explain" and requires of the speech act "explaining q" that the speaker intend his or her utterance to "render q understandable" (p. 16). Other pragmaticists focus on related psychological states of putative hearers that figure in the linguistic pragmatics of "why-" and other questions; for example, van Fraassen explicates "explanation" ultimately in terms of a body K of background knowledge.

The pragmaticist move has a besetting flaw, foreshadowed by Zaffron (1971) and well documented by Salmon (1989): If we are to explicate explanation in terms of understanding, we cannot understand understanding in the most obvious way, as the possessing of a correct explanation; we need an independent account of understanding which in no way presupposes the relation "being a correct explanation of." But, in fact, pragmaticists have uniformly failed to jettison that presupposition. Scriven's own remarks on "understanding" itself (pp. 224–5) follow immediately upon the preceding quoted passage: "What is understanding? Understanding is, roughly, organized knowledge, i.e., knowledge of the relations between various facts and/or laws. These relations are of many kinds – deductive, inductive, analogical, etc. (Understanding is deeper, more thorough, the greater the span of this relational knowledge.)" But this is no help, for Scriven does not say *what sorts of* relations between facts and/or laws are the operative ones, leaving us only to guess that it must be the *explanatory* relations that matter.

Likewise, according to van Fraassen, an explanation of a state of affairs S is a "direct answer" to the "why"-question directed upon S; a "direct answer" has roughly the form "S in contrast to the rest of X [a contrast-class] because A," where A is true, no member of X other than S obtains, and A bears a "relevance" relation R to S modulo X.[7] But, as was argued by Kitcher and Salmon (1987), the relation R is essentially unexplicated, and we are left to guess that the "relevance" van Fraassen has in mind is *explanatory* relevance. Let us call Scriven's unspecified relations and van Fraassen's R "Zaffron points" in those authors' accounts. A Zaffron point in general can be considered a spot at which a key notion is left unexplicated and where the only obvious explicans-candidate involves "being a correct explanation of." A key Zaffron point in Achinstein's discussion is his unexplicated appeal, in his analysis of "understanding," to the *correctness* of a "complete content-giving proposition" with respect to an explanation-seeking question, i.e., roughly, the correctness of a statement having the form "The reason *a* F'ed is that *p*."[8]

Now, a striking feature of Churchland's account of explanatory understanding is that it contains no obvious Zaffron point; an activation pattern exhibited by a population of neurons does not seem to pre-suppose any notion of correct explanation. So perhaps Churchland's view might be invoked to save the pragmaticist cause. Can we, then, analyze explanation in terms of explanatory understanding thus conceived?

Not on the first pass. For explanatory understanding in Churchland's sense is a neurological condition, if slightly fancifully described; it is a rather extreme example of a specific psychological state of a person at a time (extreme as compared with, say, a reference to someone's "background knowledge"). The trouble with treating understanding as a concrete psychological state, from the pragmaticists' point of view, is that such a state might be induced by any means, however noncognitive and/or fortuitous: a blow to the head, a psychoactive pill, a freakish burst of Q-radiation from the sky. Thus, an explanation cannot simply be something that actually or potentially produces explanatory under-standing in some suitable hearer, for the means aforementioned are not explanations, even though they do happen to produce explanatory understanding.

One would have to add a further condition as to *how* explanatory understanding was produced, and, as before, the further condition had better not be, or presuppose, "produced by giving the hearer a correct explanation." Though Churchland's discussion manifests no specific Zaffron point, it still moves us no nearer to an adequate explication of explanation.[9]

The present objection is hardly specific to Churchland's view; it points toward a general moral that is slightly surprising: The more concretely one understands "explanatory understanding," as a psychological state of a person, the less closely are explanation and understanding related. That is because the more concrete a psychological state one takes understanding to be, the wider is the range of possible noncognitive and/or fortuitous sources that understanding might have; and the more abstract a notion one has of understanding – say, as "grasping a D-N deduction" – the less psychologically realistic that notion is. It is a virtue of Churchland's work to have underscored this general point in a particularly vivid way.

Finally Getting Around to Churchland's Own Concerns

Until now I have been reading Churchland from the viewpoint of the orthodox scientific-explanation literature and going by a sadistically literal interpretation of his chapter title "On the Nature of Explanation." My excuse is that he started it, by purporting to draw blood from Hempel and Oppenheim. But explanation itself is far from Churchland's main concern, especially since, as anything-like-traditionally conceived, explanation is an artifact and/or tool of the despised "sentential epistemologies." He wants to focus on explanatory understanding and say illuminating things about that, not to solve the traditional problem of explicating explanation, for (I dare say) he thinks the latter will go the way of the Raven paradox, the Gettier problem, and other sententialist bogies. So, for the rest of this paper, I shall read him more sympathetically and assess what he says of explanatory understanding on its own terms. When we do that, we shall find that his theory has much to recommend it.

I shall have to assume that readers of this volume know the basics of connectionist AI, at least the elements of a connectionist network.[10] Churchland's view of explanatory understanding is expounded in connectionist terms: any network is essentially a sorter or classifier (it classifies acoustical signatures as rock echoes or mine echoes, or written English words as particular sequences of phonemes, or the like); once it has been trained up, a network assumes an arrangement of "synaptic" connection weights that yields the correct output for each input in the training set and (its trainer hopes) only infrequent error for novel inputs.

It is particularly interesting that in the course of training, the network's hidden layer comes to exhibit a *similarity gradient*, as follows. Think of each hidden unit as one axis of a vector. Then each activation pattern across the hidden units is a point in a vector space, an n-space where n is the number of hidden units. Now in learning to classify, during the training process, the network partitions that space into discernible sub-regions corresponding to its categories of classification ("mine" vs. "rock," the various phonemes, or whatever). Each sub-region takes the form of a rough "hot spot" with vague boundaries. Churchland suggests we think of these sub-regions as prototypes. Any central point in such a sub-region represents a prototypical so-and-so, e.g., a prototypical mine echo; more peripheral points represent less typical but similar inputs, according to the network's instinctively developed measure of similarity. Moreover, Churchland maintains, the network does not *only* classify, thereby losing information: Any prototypical point "represents the extended family of relevant (but individually perhaps non-necessary) features that collectively unite the relevant class of stimuli into [what is for the network] a single kind" (p. 206). And (p. 212) "... the prototype vector embodies an enormous amount of information. Its many elements – perhaps as many as 10^8 elements was our earlier guess – each constitute one dimension of a highly intricate portrait of the prototypical situation. That vector has structure, a great deal of structure, whose function is to represent an overall syndrome of objective features, relations, sequences, and uniformities." A prototype is *activated*[11] when the network's hidden layer is caused by an input to assume a configuration of (in the quasi-neural sense) activation levels whose vector falls within the rough sub-region that is the prototype.

A key connectionist insight is that prototype activation is strikingly reminiscent of *perceptual recognition* in humans and other animals. It responds to a confusing variety of input patterns, according to no easily statable rule (cf. "... our ability to recognize a horse in almost any posture and from almost any perspective" (p. 206) and, Churchland might have added, partially occluded in almost any way); it makes fine and heavily context-bound discriminations; it is virtually instantaneous, even when the given input is complex and subtle; it (as they say) degrades gracefully; and, most importantly for Churchland's present project, the activation of a prototype classifies its input

> ... as an instance of a general type, *a type for which the creature has a detailed and well-informed representation*. Such a representation allows the creature to anticipate aspects of the case so far unperceived, and to deploy practical techniques appropriate to the case at hand. (p. 210, italics original)

> [Because a] vector represent[s] an overall syndrome of objective features [etc.] ..., its activation by a given perceptual or other cognitive circumstance ... represents a major and speculative gain in information, since the portrait it embodies typically goes far beyond the local and perspectivally limited information that may activate it on any given occasion. That is why the process is useful: it is quite dramatically ampliative. (p. 212, italics omitted)

For these reasons, Churchland hypothesizes that perceptual recognizing is simply prototype activation or something very like it.

The previous paragraphs of this section have been only a preamble, lengthy but necessary exposition. Now, finally, we may state Churchland's main conjecture as regards explanatory understanding: that explanatory understanding, like perceptual recognition, is prototype activation also. (Recall our original formulation of the view: An explanation of a particular state of affairs is "the activation pattern defined over a population of neurons in a cognizer's brain.") Thus, explanatory understanding is like perceptual recognition in being an often nearly instantaneous, finely articulated and importantly ampliative classification of an explanandum considered as an input.[12] But its inputs are not exclusively sensory; they may be the outputs of prior networks or of other agencies. "A brain is not a single network, but a committee of many cooperating networks.... And ... the input to a given bank of hidden units comes not *just* from the sensory periphery, but from elsewhere in the brain itself" (p. 208). In that way the higher-order networks will give rise to more abstract explanatory classifications, more abstract understanding; eventually, we reach quantum-mechanical and other prototype activations (mathematical? metaphysical? religious?) whose inputs are hardly perceptual at all.[13]

Churchland's Theory Praised

Here are some of the theory's significant virtues.

First, explanatory understanding as a psychological state does seem closely analogous to perceptual recognition. Besides the similarities just mentioned, it can result from, or perhaps be constituted by, a Gestalt shift of perceptual set or "seeing as";[14] it need not be immediately articulate (though, I would note as a *dis*analogy with perceptual recognition, we would be suspicious of one who claimed explanatory understanding but was *persistently* unable to offer an explanation out loud); it can co-classify very disparate input states of affairs; it "allows the creature to anticipate aspects of the case so far unperceived, and to deploy practical techniques appropriate to the case at hand" (p. 210).

Second, Churchland's view is consilient with rejection of the "argument" or "inferential" conception of scientific explanation (pp. 224–5). Though explanation often does take the form of deductive inference or other argument retrodicting the explanandum, it need not (as has been argued by Adams (1947), Jeffrey (1969), Salmon (1971), Railton (1978; 1981), and Humphreys (1981; 1989)). A standard example illustrating this is that of radioactive decay (Railton, 1978). For example, an alpha-particle is emitted during a time interval Δt from a U^{238} nucleus; the probability of such emission is very low. But since (a) that probability is a *de re* property of the nucleus, (b) such probabilities fall under a well-

established though irreducibly probabilistic law, and (c) we understand
the underlying mechanism at work, from the quantum-mechanical
theory of tunnelling, the emission is genuinely explained by the law, at
least in that we know everything there is to know about the emission's
etiology and we can exhibit it as part of a familiar law-like pattern. This
is grist to Churchland's mill, since he posits specifically etiological
prototypes (pp. 213–14) and since seeing events as parts of patterns is
just what prototype activation can constitute.

Third, Churchland argues (p. 212),

> One prominent fact, ill addressed by any existing account of explanation, is
> the variety of different *types* of explanation. We have causal explanations,
> functional explanations, moral explanations, derivational explanations, and
> so forth. Despite some procrustean analytical attempts, no one of these
> seems to be the basic type to which all of the others can be assimilated. On
> the prototype-activation model, however, we can unify them all in the
> following way. Explanatory understanding is the same thing in all of these
> cases: what differs is the character of the prototype that is activated.

Churchland proceeds (pp. 212–18) to catalogue "property-cluster"
prototypes, etiological prototypes, and several other dramatically different types of prototype.

Two related points have been run together here. One is that there are
different though heavily overlapping paradigms for scientific explanation, no one of which strikes a neutral philosophical observer as pre-
eminent: There are subsumptions; there are etiologies or causal
narratives; there are unifications; there are arguments to show that a
phenomenon was to be expected; there are fillings of gaps in understanding; there are exhibitings of the phenomenon as part of an
important pattern; there are functional flow-chart diagrams; there are
Just-So Stories; and more. No going theory of explanation itself can
comprehend all these.[15] The other point is that different subject matters
seem to call for different styles of explanation. Mathematical and even
some physical explanation is not causal; computer science and auto
mechanics seem to call for function-analytical rather than D-N or
etiological explanation; legal explanation essentially involves particular
codes; moral and aesthetic explanations are up for grabs.

Each point is dead right, and each is "ill addressed by any existing
account of explanation."[16] If prototype activation is common to all these
different styles and subject matters, that raises more hope for the
pragmaticist program, though it does nothing to alleviate the problem of
fortuitous causes posed above.[17]

The Theory Questioned

I shall close by raising a few queries, in diminishing order of friendliness.

1   What makes one explanation better than another? Churchland addresses this, on pp. 218–23, mentioning four marks of goodness. He summarizes (p. 223):

> A virtuous mode of explanatory understanding (that is, an activated prototype vector) should be a *rich* portrait of the general type at issue; it should be strongly *warranted* (that is, have low ambiguity in the input that occasions it); it should be *correct* (relative to the library of currently available alternative prototypes); and it should be part of the most *unified* cognitive configuration possible.

As Churchland recognizes, each of these four desiderata needs a good deal more spelling out than he has had space to give it. "Correctness" of a prototype activation is particularly problematic, in that it depends on cooperation from the external world in each of two ways, statistical "reliability" of the prototype activation's cause and adaptive "appropriateness" of the behavior it then instigates (cf. note 9). Since explanatory goodness – as opposed to truth – is usually thought of as a matter of the explanation's role in the cognizer's internal organization, Churchland would do well here to distinguish purely internal desiderata and components of desiderata from external or "wide" ones, since their rationales will be quite different.[18]

2   If sentientialist epistemology is to be cast out, what are explananda? Churchland says (p. 198) we have explanatory understanding of "a problematic *thing, event, or state of affairs*. The linguistic expression, exchange, or production of such understanding, should there be any, is an entirely secondary matter" (italics mine). Presumably the things, events, and states of affairs in question are those whose microfeatures are represented by a coherent succession of input vectors (distributions of activation levels across the network's input layer). But that holds only for the system at its most sensory and peripheral. Most of the system's explanatory understanding will be of explananda at one or more removes from the periphery, and the relevant networks' inputs will be the classificatory outputs of prior networks (again, "mine" as opposed to "rock," a phoneme sequence, or whatever). But these are representations in the brain, not external things, events or states of affairs. I

presume it will not be the represent*ings* themselves that are explananda for the next-higher-order prototype activation, but those representings' represent*eds*, either the states of affairs reported by the original peripheral classifiers or those depicted by the outputs of intermediate networks. If the higher-order prototypes have representeds as their explananda, does this not put Churchland back in the, or a, sententialist business? – for some of the explananda will be representations like "That's a mine" and "That (or 'choir') is pronounced /kwayr/."

3   How, exactly, is explanatory understanding related to perceptual recognition other than by being another species of the same interesting genus? Churchland remarks (p. 198) that understanding differs from perceptual recognition "primarily by being a response to a wider variety of cognitive situations: it is not limited to sensory inputs," and goes on to suggest   (p. 228) that perceptual recognition itself is "just a case of *explanatory understanding at the sensory periphery*" (italics original). It seems to follow that perceptual recognition entails explanatory understanding, hence that it is simply a sub-species of explanatory understanding. It is a further question whether there are prototype activations that are not cases of explanatory understanding at all.

Reid (1992) notes the apparent implication and tries to refute it. In what sense do we have explanatory understanding at the sensory periphery? If I simply see a duck and accordingly my "duck" prototype fires, what is explained or (explanatorily) understood? Not obviously anything; I have merely made a perceptual identification, sophisticated and wonderful though that achievement is from the neurobiological point of view.

The obvious reply to this is to say, along with some well-grounded perceptual psychology (Teuber, 1960; Gregory, 1966; 1970; Rock, 1983), that my perceptual identification is indeed an explanatory hypothesis. Its explananda are the microfeatures represented by sectors of the relevant well-trained hidden layer, those to which the peripheral network as a whole responds, the ones exhibited by ducks despite differences of perspective, occlusion, and so on. But two further objections loom.

First, though there may well be an explanatory relation between my perceptual judgment and the set of micro-features that prompted it, that would do little to show that the subject has explanatory *understanding*. Certainly I do not understand why the duck has such-and-such microfeatures, for I am entirely unaware that it has them. And never mind awareness, with its connotation of consciousness and such elite capacities: I see no useful sense in which *I* understand anything about the microfeatures, even subconsciously. Here we find ourselves on the other side of the widening split between explanation and understanding: It seems I have an explanation, but not understanding. (On the other hand, perhaps what is true is that I contain a homunculus, a sub-personal agency, that has understanding even though I do not have it.)

Second, there are intuitive recognitions, plausibly supposed to be prototype activations, that are abstract and in no interesting sense perceptual, that do not seem to involve understanding in any way. Reid offers the example of reading a philosophy article, perusing a particular argument, and getting the strong feeling that the argument is unsound; one may do this without having an inkling of what it is that is wrong with the argument. Thus it seems my bad-argument prototype may fire without constituting explanatory understanding of the argument beyond the bare knowledge of what it says. Here it is less plausible to suppose that any sub-personal Philosophical Argument Analyst of mine has explanatory understanding even though I do not.

Of course, this example may be a case of prototype activation that is neither a perceptual recognition nor explanatory understanding of any other sort; again, Churchland has in no way ruled out such a *tertium quid*. But then we would need to hear what distinguishes the explanatory prototype activations from the nonexplanatory ones, and we are back in the saddle again.

4   *What of* good old scientific explanation in the robustly sentential, discursive, deductive, left-brained, etc. sense? Physicists and chemists do, after all, produce explanations that are elaborate propositional structures, by laborious deduction from fully axiomatized theories in the traditional sense of sets of statements. Hempel and Oppenheim's paradigm is sometimes realized.[19, 20] And those scientists would not count themselves as having genuine explanatory understanding until the derivations had been carried out. (Yet, as always, not every deduction of laws from laws, or of particular statements from laws plus initial condition, is genuinely explanatory; so the traditional problem remains.) This is unmistakably scientific explanation, yet Churchland's theory is ill suited to encompass it.

Perhaps we should recall a previous quote: "The linguistic expression, exchange, or production of [explanatory] understanding, should there be any, is an entirely secondary matter" (p. 198). Churchland might reply, to the present objection, that I am confusing what is only a useful means toward explanatory understanding with explanation itself. My physicists and chemists do indeed axiomatize, perform deductions and the rest, but those exercises merely massage the relevant neural networks into readiness. Their sententialist products are not themselves disembodied, Platonic "explanations" but only detritus left after the axiomatizings and derivings have caused explanation, i.e., prototype activation, to occur within the scientists' brains.

In rejoinder, I plead only the acceptability of ordinary usage. It is entirely proper to point to a page of a physics text and call a derivation appearing thereon an explanation, say of one law by another, or to speak of a scientist as explaining this or that phenomenon by deducing its occurrence from an articulate theory and some initial conditions, regardless of what is happening in the brain of any particular person. If Churchland wants to pooh-pooh this steam-age sense of "explanation," he should at least reconstruct it in his own preferred terms, as an honorable paronym.

Despite its remoteness from the traditional problems of scientific explanation (I suspect Churchland would say *because of* that remoteness) his model is even more powerful than I have been able to indicate here. It should be, and doubtless will be, extensively explored and developed.[21]

Notes

1   The opening footnote of that article offers "major acknowledgement" to one Miss Patricia Smith, for conversations on the topic during the summer of 1968. No astute reader will fail to identify Miss Smith with Professor P. S. Churchland, co-honoree of the present volume. (And see note 3 below.)

2   Chapters 9 and 10 of Churchland (1989), respectively entitled "On the Nature of Theories: A Neurocomputational Perspective" and "On the Nature of Explanation: A PDP Approach." Subsequent page references will be to Churchland (1989) unless otherwise indicated.

3   So far as I know, Patricia Churchland has not (in print) rejected the D-N model. In Churchland (1986) she "declared ... [her] preference for" the model "as a first approximation" (p. 294), though in the next paragraph she adds,

> ...I think the theory of explanation is bound to be provisional, since I expect that as theories of brain function mature, we will acquire a far deeper sense of what the brain is doing when it seeks explanations, what it counts as explanatory fit, what understanding comes to, and so on. And my conviction is that this deeper sense will take us beyond the paradigm in which explanations in general are characterized on the model of *logical* relation [*sic*] between *sentences*.... Indeed, some of the shortcomings visible in the DN model cut so deep as to suggest the need for a very different paradigm. (Italics original.)

4   The D-N model confounds taxonomy by exemplifying each of what Coffa

(1977) called the "epistemic" and the "ontic" conceptions of explanation (cf. Salmon, 1989, pp. 118ff.). But even its "epistemic" aspect is drastically nonpsychological.

5 Indeed, they were criticized on just this point by Scriven (1962) – but in their own terms, by means of counterexamples, not because Scriven thought the D-N model was intended as psychology in any form.

6 See particularly Salmon, 1989, pp. 159ff.

7 That formulation is directed upon "explanation" in the linguistic sense, but it is easily adjusted to cover the ontological sense instead.

8 Achinstein recognizes this problem and tries (on pp. 71–2) to circumvent it; in my view he is unsuccessful. To say exactly why would require a tortuous forced march through Achinstein's labyrinth of technical notions. The short version is this: Achinstein claims that neither his definition of explaining nor his definition of understanding invokes explanatory terms such as "reason," because he has invoked only "the general notion of a complete content-giving proposition with respect to [a given explanation-seeking question]." But the unexplicated explanatory concepts surface in the "with respect to" relation; a complete content-giving proposition cannot be such a proposition *with respect to* an explanation-seeking question unless its "content-noun" is "reason" or something too closely related.
Sintonen's paper contains two sparkling Zaffron points, on pp. 258 and 265.

9 Churchland does put forward a notion of "correct" explanation (pp. 220–1). An explanation (= prototype activation) can be incorrect either by resulting from an input situation that "is not a member of the class of situations that will reliably activate [that particular prototype] from almost any perspective," or by leading to behavior that is "highly, even lethally inappropriate to the problematic situation in question." But the correctness of a prototype activation in that sense has little to do with the correct explanation of Hooke's Law by Newtonian physics, or that of an economic recession by the government's taxation policies, neither of which has anything obviously to do with the neurological condition of a particular creature. Churchland continues to flout the "ontic" conception of explanation (cf. note 4 above).

10 I myself know no better exposition of connectionist basics for philosophers than Churchland's own: pp. 159–94, 200–6.

11 Churchland uses this verb equivocally, as applying to prototypes in a sense different from that in which a unit has an "activation" level.

12 Interestingly (if I read Churchland correctly), it is not *theories* that explain particular phenomena directly, for in his view (chapter 9) theories are configurations of synaptic weights, not of unit activation levels. Rather, the theories lead to explanations, i.e., prototype activations, given inputs. But that is not so different from Hempel and Oppenheim's sententialist picture, since theories in their sense need to be applied to particular initial conditions in order to D-N-explain particular explananda.

13 Churchland does not explicitly mention *philosophical* explanation; but

surely there are philosophical prototypes that are vehemently activated by experience.

14 Cf. Churchland's graphic example (1979, pp. 30–4) of learning to see the heavens and the earth in Copernican style, by taking the plane of the ecliptic rather than the local plane of the earth's surface as the "horizontal floor" of one's visual space. I hope that at some point Churchland will explicitly address the topic of perceiving-as, since his view can be expected to illuminate traditional a priori puzzles about that notion (on which see Lycan, 1971).

15 Lycan (in preparation) argues in detail that scientific explanation is a classic Wittgensteinian family-resemblance concept, and that, accordingly, the orthodox explanation literature has been committing the classic Socratic fallacy of seeking a set of necessary-and-sufficient conditions where none can be expected.

16 Kitcher (1989), however, makes an attempt to deal with the second point, in the name of his Unification Church.

17 A fourth point worth mentioning, though not specific to issues of explanation, is that Churchland's prototype-activation model will undoubtedly be fruitful in suggesting experiments – not actual biological experiments on living lab animals, but computer simulations of networks of different sorts encountering who-knows-what "environmental" inputs and perhaps interacting with each other in variously structured and unstructured ways. I expect a connectionist Axelrod daily and with keen anticipation.

18 Reid (1992) suspects a Zaffron point in Churchland's notion of correctness, though (even if we impose a pragmaticist interpretation on his project) I am not convinced. Reid also raises some useful questions about his notion of unification, first having noted that he slides without acknowledgement from the well-described and well-motivated "unifiedness" of a *prototype* to the unexplicated "unifiedness" of a "cognitive configuration" in which the prototype is embedded.

19 Or nearly so, save for the literal and exceptionless truth of the laws.

20 In general, both P. M. and P. S. Churchland are concerned to emphasize the *extent* of the nonlinguistic, nondiscursive, etc. cognition that we share with the rest of the animal kingdom, as opposed to the comparatively tiny excrescent bit of cerebral, articulate linguistic cognition that we do not – 99.9 percent, if you like. And rightly so. But that does nothing to show that the remaining 0.1 percent is not perfectly real, and neither Churchland nor Churchland nor anyone else should be surprised that this distinctive faculty and its products are what interest philosophers 99.9 percent of the time and most other people 100 percent of the time.

And perhaps this is the place to register my dissent from Churchland's claim (p. 200) that nonhuman animals often achieve explanatory understanding. One would be foolish to rule out the possibility that animals do that, but if Churchland finds it *obvious* that they do he is too firmly in the grip of his own picture.

21 For very helpful discussion of Churchland's theory, I thank the students in

my 1992 graduate seminar on scientific explanation, particularly Jane Reid and David Weber.

References

Achinstein, P. (1983), *The Nature of Explanation*, Oxford University Press.

Adams, E. M. (1947), "An Analysis of Scientific Explanation," doctoral dissertation, Harvard University.

Bromberger, S. (1965), "An approach to explanation," in *Analytical Philosophy, Second Series*, ed. R. J. Butler, Blackwell.

Bromberger, S. (1966), "Why-Questions," in *Mind and Cosmos*, ed. R. G. Colodny, University of Pittsburgh Press.

Churchland, P. M. (1970), "The logical character of action explanations," *Philosophical Review*, **79**, 214–36.

Churchland, P. M. (1979), *Scientific Realism and the Plasticity of Mind*, Cambridge University Press.

Churchland, P. M. (1989), *A Neurocomputational Perspective: The Nature of Mind and the Structure of Science*, MIT Press.

Churchland, P. M. and Churchland, P. S. (1983), "Stalking the wild epistemic engine," *Noûs*, **17**, 5–18; reprinted in *Mind and Cognition: A Reader*, ed. W. G. Lycan, Blackwell, 1990.

Churchland, P. S. (1986), *Neurophilosophy: Toward a Unified Science of the Mind-Brain*, MIT Press.

Coffa, J. A. (1977), "Probabilities: reasonable or true?", *Philosophy of Science*, **44**, 186–98.

Fraassen, B. van (1980), *The Scientific Image*, Oxford University Press.

Gregory, R. L. (1966), *Eye and Brain*, McGraw-Hill.

Gregory, R. L. (1970), *The Intelligent Eye*, McGraw-Hill.

Hempel, C. G., and Oppenheim, P. (1948), "Studies in the logic of explanation," *Philosophy of Science*, **15**, 135–75.

Humphreys, P. (1981), "Aleatory explanation," *Synthese*, **48**, 225–32.

Humphreys, P. (1989), *The Chances of Explanation*, Princeton University Press.

Jeffrey, R. C. (1969), "Statistical explanation vs. statistical inference," in *Essays in Honor of Carl G. Hempel*, ed. N. Rescher, D. Reidel.

Kitcher, P. (1989), "Explanatory unification and the causal structure of the world," in Kitcher and Salmon (1989).

Kitcher, P. and Salmon, W. (1987), "Van Fraassen on explanation," *Journal of Philosophy*, **84**, 315–30.

Kitcher, P. and Salmon, W., eds (1989), *Minnesota Studies in the Philosophy of Science*, vol. XIII: *Scientific Explanation*, University of Minnesota Press.

Lycan, W. (1971), "Gombrich, Wittgenstein and the duck-rabbit," *Journal of Aesthetics and Art Criticism*, **30**, 229–37; reprinted in *The Philosophy of Wittgenstein: Aesthetics, Ethics and Religion*, ed. J. V. Canfield, Garland Publishing, 1985.

Lycan, W. (in preparation), "Scientific explanation," MS.

Railton, P. (1978), "A deductive-nomological model of probabilistic explanation," *Philosophy of Science*, **45**, 206–26.

Railton, P. (1980), "Explaining explanation," doctoral dissertation, Princeton University.

Railton, P. (1981), "Probability, explanation, and information," *Synthese*, **48**, 233–56.

Reid, J. (1992), "Problems with prototypes," unpublished MS.

Rock, I. (1983), *The Logic of Perception*, Bradford Books/MIT Press.

Salmon, W. (1971), "Statistical explanation and statistical relevance," in *Statistical Explanation and Statistical Relevance*, ed. W. Salmon, University of Pittsburgh Press.

Salmon, W. (1984), *Scientific Explanation and the Causal Structure of the World*, Princeton University Press.

Salmon, W. (1989), "Four decades of scientific explanation," in Kitcher and Salmon (1989).

Scriven, M. (1962), "Explanations, predictions, and laws," in *Minnesota Studies in the Philosophy of Science*, vol. III: *Scientific Explanation, Space, and Time*, ed. H. Feigl and G. Maxwell, University of Minnesota Press.

Sintonen, M. (1989), "Explanation: in search of the rationale," in Kitcher and Salmon (1989).

Teuber, H. L. (1960), "Perception," in *Handbook of Physiology*, vol. 3, ed. J. Field, H. W. Magoun, and V. E. Hall, American Physiological Society.

Zaffron, R. (1971), "Identity, subsumption, and scientific explanation," *Journal of Philosophy*, **68**, 849–60.

5
What Should a Connectionist Philosophy of Science Look Like?

William Bechtel

The re-emergence of connectionism[1] has profoundly altered the philosophy of mind. Paul Churchland has argued that it should equally transform the philosophy of science. He proposes that connectionism offers radical and useful new ways to understand theories and explanations.

An individual's general theory of the world, Churchland proposes, is not a set of propositions, but "a specific point in that individual's synaptic weight space. It is a configuration of connection weights, a configuration that partitions the system's activation-vector space(s) into useful divisions and subdivisions relative to the inputs typically fed the system. 'Useful' here means 'tends to minimize the error messages'" (1989, p. 177). In a connectionist network, the weights on the various connections determine the response of the network to a particular input that is supplied by providing activations to a set of units. The response of a network is a pattern of activation over a designated set of units.[2] As a result of acquiring a certain set of weights (reaching a specific point in weight space), a network will learn to categorize input patterns into different groups, each member of which generates either the same or a similar response. Thus, what Churchland is terming a *theory* in a connectionist network determines the response categories of the network.

Within the range of responses a trained network gives to members of a category, there is one pattern that constitutes the central or prototypical response for that category. No actual input the network has yet received may trigger this response, but it represents the central tendency amongst the response. Responses to actual inputs will tend to cluster around this prototypical response. It is the activation of a response close to the prototypical response that Churchland proposes constitutes the system's explanatory understanding of its input circumstances. New examples are *explained* as they activate the same (or nearly the same) pattern: "I wish to suggest that those prototype vectors, when activated, constitute the creature's recognition and concurrent *understanding* of its objective situation, an understanding that is reflected in the creature's subsequent behavior"(1989, 208).

I shall briefly review Churchland's case for these radical construals of theories and explanatory understanding in part 1. What makes Churchland's view of theories and explanatory understanding novel is that it bypasses the sentential paradigm. One of my concerns in the rest of this chapter will be whether it is wise to bypass the sentential paradigm so completely. While I am no fan of it as an approach to explaining human cognitive activity and concur with Churchland that connectionism has much to offer philosophy of science, I contend that Churchland is mistaken in localizing the focus of philosophy of science exclusively in activities occurring in the heads of scientists.[3] Representations are central to scientific activity, but the representations that matter are not exclusively mental representations. They are also external representations such as are found in sentences of natural language as well as in tables, figures, and diagrams. In part 2 I will argue that it is in terms of these representations that we need to understand the notions of *theory* and *explanation* and will explore how recognizing the role of these external symbolic representations in science changes Churchland's conception of the role of connectionism in modeling the cognitive activities of scientists. In parts 3 and 4 I will then attempt to illustrate this revised conception of a connectionist philosophy of science, showing how it might apply to actual cases of scientific research.

1   Churchland's Case for a Connectionist Philosophy of Science

Churchland advances his case for a connectionist philosophy of science partly by pointing to what he takes to be failures in sentential approaches that connectionism can overcome and partly by showing how a connectionist perspective provides positive accounts of such central notions in recent philosophy of science as simplicity, theory-ladenness of observation, and paradigm.

Among shortcomings of the sentential approach, Churchland identifies a number of well-known problems, such as the paradoxes of confirmation that afflict the hypothetico-deductive framework, the problem of determining which among many propositions used to make a prediction are falsified in a Popperian framework, and the inability of probabilistic accounts of theory choice to account for the rationality of large-scale conceptual change. Except for some comments relevant to the last point, Churchland does not make it clear how a connectionist perspective overcomes these problems. Large-scale conceptual change arises, in Churchland's connectionist framework, when a network gets trapped in a local minimum and must be bumped out of it by an infusion of noise that significantly alters the current weights in a network. With luck, the network will then be able to find a deeper minimum. But there is no guarantee that a network will find one. While this account may characterize what occurs within a scientist as he or she undergoes large-scale conceptual change, it neither explains what causes the change (the sort of noise that will bump a network out of a local minimum) nor its rationality (especially since most such bumps fail to lead to deeper minimums).[4]

In "On the nature of explanation: a PDP approach" (in 1989) Churchland raises two objections directed specifically at the deductive-nomological (D-N) model of explanation. According to this model, explanation involves deduction from laws. But, Churchland argues, people often cannot articulate the laws on which their explanatory understanding is supposed to rest. So explanation does not seem to require sententially-stated laws. Further, people arrive at an understanding of phenomena for which they seek an explanation in much less time than it would likely take them to perform a deduction. Thus, Churchland questions both the need for laws and the appeal to logic as the way of relating laws to the phenomena to be explained.

The other objections Churchland raises against the sentential framework have to do with features of science that it cannot address. For example, the sentential view offers no account of learning to make perceptual discriminations or of learning to use the propositional system itself. Likewise, it cannot account for the learning of skills, which, as Kuhn has argued, is just as important as learning the facts of a discipline. From a connectionist perspective, these are accounted for in the same manner as all other learning: through the adjustment of weights within the network. Further, the sentential perspective cannot explain how we retrieve relevant information in the process of reasoning about theories. This, it might seem, would require a massive search through all the propositions stored within the system. From a connectionist perspective, all stored knowledge is stored in the weights through which processing will occur. These weights *coarse-code* the stored knowledge so that a particular weight will figure in the network's response to many inputs and does not provide a representation of a discrete bit of knowledge. But when a set of inputs similar to one on which a given response was learned is presented, these weights will cause the network to generate a similar response. Hence, the knowledge stored in connection weights automatically is brought into play whenever relevant. Finally, Churchland contends that sentential perspectives cannot explain the progress of science. In some sense it seems that current theories are closer to the truth than previous ones, and so many sentential theorists have tried to explain progress in terms of how new theories are better approximations of the truth. But Churchland contends that no adequate account has been developed of what it is to be closer to the truth. Indeed, the notion of truth has itself become problematic.

Among the positive features Churchland cites for a connectionist approach is that it provides an account of why simplicity is a cognitive virtue. He construes simplicity in terms of the number of hidden units in a network and points out that the ability of networks to generalize depends upon their utilizing the minimum number of hidden units needed for a particular problem. Networks with greater numbers of hidden units usually fail to develop weights on connections that generalize well. Rather, they will use different weights to generate the same response to different inputs that are supposed to be members of the same category, and thus will neither acquire the common category nor be able to extend it to new cases. Thus, he argues that the preference for simplicity can be understood from a connectionist perspective not simply as an aesthetic nicety, but as an important epistemic virtue: The point in weight space (i.e., the theory) found in simpler networks generalizes better to new cases.

Churchland also links the virtue of simplicity with the virtue of explanatory unity. He proposes that explanatory unity arises not from arranging theories in a deductive hierarchy, but from finding one set of weights that enables a single network to solve a multitude of problems. The virtue of this arrangement over using distinct subsets of weights to deal with each sub-type of problem is that this set of weights will allow the network to generalize to many new problems. These are problems whose inputs lie within the region (not necessarily contiguous) in the input space that generates that response. Generally this region will be larger than the sum of the regions defined by the separate sets of weights that might otherwise determine the common response; hence a side benefit of using just one set of weights is that new cases (for which the network otherwise might have no solution) now fall within the region that will generate the same response as well.

Another feature that Churchland contends points to the strength of the connectionist framework is that it can explain features of science to which Kuhn (1970) had drawn attention: the theory-ladenness of observation and the role of paradigms in science. Since all processing in a network is determined by the weights, and these are constituents of the network's global theory, it follows directly that any processing of inputs by a network will be governed by its theory. Theory-laden observations are the expected case, not something requiring further justification. The notion of a paradigm was central to Kuhn's account. Normal research, for Kuhn, is directed by the paradigm with the goal of filling in the general perspective on phenomena encoded in the paradigm. But, as Churchland notes, Kuhn was severely criticized for the vagueness of this notion. Churchland contends, however, that connectionism provides a way both to make the notion more specific and to explain why paradigms often seem vague (1989, p. 191):

> For a brain to command a paradigm is for it to have settled into a weight configuration that produces some well-structured similarity space whose central hypervolume locates the prototypical application(s). And it is only to be expected that even the most reflective person will be incompletely articulate on what dimensions constitute this highly complex and abstract space, and even less articulate on what metric distributes examples along each dimension. A complete answer to these questions would require a microscopic examination of the person's brain.

Churchland thus sees connectionism providing for a radical advance in philosophy of science. By understanding theories in terms of weights in a network and explanations in terms of prototypical responses of a network, he claims that we can overcome some of the problems that have afflicted the classical approaches that took theories to be sets of propositions and explanations to involve derivations from theories or laws.

2   The Use of Symbolic Representations in Science

An interesting feature of Churchland's construal of the deductive-nomological form of explanation as a major element in the sentential paradigm is his portrayal of its use in the mental lives of scientists. Thus, in commenting on the failures of the classical approach described above, he says (p. 154): "Those failures suggest to me that what is defective in the classical approach is its fundamental assumption that languagelike structures of some kind constitute the basic or most important form of representation in cognitive creatures, and the correlative assumption that cognition consists in the manipulation of those representations by means of structure-sensitive rules." However, most of the positivists who formulated the classical conception of theories and explanation had very little interest in the representations used in cognitive creatures or in the nature of cognition generally. When they construed laws and theories as involving specific kinds of universal generalizations and explanation as a matter of deduction from these laws or theories, they seemed to be focused on the representation of laws in natural language inscriptions and deductions that could be carried out in terms of such inscriptions. Many of them took the extreme position of denying any interest in how scientists justified laws and theories or generated explanations, focusing rather on how these activities might be logically reconstructed to show the warrant of laws and theories or the adequacy of proffered explanations. (See Lycan's chapter in this book).

Churchland has moved the positivists' account of explanation inside the head of scientists and argues that it fails to give an adequate account of cognition. I concur that it fails to give an adequate account of the cognitive activities of scientists, but want to resist the idea that laws and theories are primarily representations in the head and that explanatory understanding is localized in internal cognitive activity. The common view is that scientists "write up" their ideas in papers for publication, and that they often find it most useful to present their ideas in figures and diagrams. I want to suggest, however, that these natural language representations and figures and diagrams are *not* translations of representations in the head (except insofar as scientists and other people often rehearse privately the sentences they will speak publicly or image the diagrams they will draw, an activity that depends upon their mastery of the external representational systems). Rather, constructing natural-language accounts of the phenomena they are studying and creating diagrams is part of developing theories and acquiring explanatory understanding of the phenomena. Constructing an explanation is an interactive activity involving both the cognitive agent and various external representational systems.

The view I am advancing is suggested by Rumelhart, Smolensky, McClelland, and Hinton (1986) in their account of multiplying two three-digit numbers. For most people, this is too complex a task to carry out in one's head. So, we "work on paper." That is, we represent the problem in a canonical form such as

$$
\begin{array}{r}
343 \\
\underline{822}
\end{array}
$$

We then proceed in a step-wise manner, having learned to break the task into component tasks that are much simpler. We begin with the problem 2×3, whose answer we have already memorized (have trained up our networks to solve). As a result, we write 6 directly beneath the 2 and the 3:

$$343$$
$$822$$
$$\underline{822}$$
$$6$$

We then proceed to the next step, multiplying 2×4, and so on. What is important here is that we solve the problem by working interactively with external representations. In fact, as long as we have learned the procedures for approaching such a problem, we do not need any internal representations to solve it.

Elsewhere I have argued that our ability to make logical inferences (Bechtel and Abrahamsen, 1991; Bechtel, 1994) and our ability to use natural languages (Bechtel, in press) have a similar character. Focusing for now on language, what I propose is that we learn to use the symbols of a language as they are initially embodied in an external medium (sound, print, etc.) as representational devices. These symbols afford concatenation in various ways, so we also learn the ways of concatenating these symbols employed in our native language as we participate in interpersonal communication. According to this view, our knowledge of grammar, for example, may consist in knowledge of *procedures* for comprehending and producing sentences in spoken or written speech. The grammar is not, as is often thought, a set of rules for operating on internally represented strings of symbols. Just as a Turing machine consists of a finite-state device, which employs a finite set of rules to determine responses to different possible situations, supplemented by a potentially infinite tape on which symbols are written and from which they are read, so the cognitive system may possess sets of procedures that enable the system to produce and comprehend spoken or written symbols.

Can syntactically correct speech be processed by a system that does not process internal symbols according to explicit rules? In addressing this question we should bear in mind that we are addressing linguistic performance only, not competence. Moreover, performance is generally far better in written language, in which it is possible for the user to backtrack and correct errors, than it is in spoken language. Finally, sophisticated language users are able to rehearse their performances privately, storing a trace in echoic memory, before actually producing it.[5] This process does allow some error correction. So, in evaluating whether a system that does not manipulate internal symbols in rule-governed ways can account for linguistic capacities, we need to be careful not to overestimate what is required. Nonetheless, accounting for linguistic abilities constitutes a major challenge for connectionism. St. John and McClelland's (1990) network for sentence comprehension, however, suggests how a network might learn to respect grammatical constraints in a natural language. It learned to develop case role representations from an impressive variety of sentences in which the correct interpretation often depended on grammatical as well as semantic structure.

I want to emphasize that, if this account is correct, we can view natural language as providing a powerful extension to our cognitive capacities. It provides an external representational system which allows us to encode information that can be useful in guiding our actions. For example, we can write down the steps in a procedure we do not execute very often (e.g., a recipe for chicken marbella) and extract from the written representation the information we need when it comes time to execute the procedure again. We can also record descriptions of events that have transpired so that we can consult these records again. These written documents are not transcriptions of our mental representations, but specifically constructed representations with which we have learned to interact. In fact, these linguistic representations possess features that may not be found in our internal cognitive representations. For example, written records can endure unchanged for extended periods of time, whereas our internal "memory" appears to rely on reconstruction, not retrieval of stored records. Moreover, through the various syntactical devices provided by language, relations between pieces of information can be kept straight (e.g., that a tree fell and a person jumped) that might otherwise become confused (e.g., when linked only in an associative structure such as a simple connectionist network). Thus, by acquiring language, a system acquires capacities to represent information and use that information in its own activities which it would otherwise lack. (In this discussion I have abstracted from the use of language in coordinating behavior amongst agents. This is a not insignificant further role that language plays, which is crucial to the operation of science.)

Given the potential usefulness of language as a representational system, it is natural that scientists should avail themselves of it. And of course they do in their conversations and publications. But I would contend that language plays a much greater use than merely a medium for transmitting ideas to other scientists. It is also the medium in which laws, theories, and models are often developed. The first two of these ideas are familiar from positivist philosophy of science. Laws are universal, counterfactual, supporting generalizations, while theories also consist of universal statements that are supposed to provide a more fundamental account (i.e., in terms of more basic entities and processes) from which laws can be derived. Recently a number of philosophers have charged that laws do not play quite the role they have generally been taken to play in positivist philosophy of science. Cartwright (1983), for example, argues that, strictly interpreted, most laws of physics, let alone the special sciences, are false. They present an idealized structure that is never quite realized in the natural world. Other philosophers, such as Giere (1988), have argued that most science involves less-abstract entities, which he calls *models*. In part, models are more concrete as a result of filling in specifications of parameters left unspecified in more general laws.

Starting not from physics but from the life sciences, one is impressed by how infrequently scientists appeal to structures having the character of laws. The challenge is not to subsume individual cases under generalizations. Rather, scientists frequently find themselves confronted with systems in nature that generate a certain kind of output. What they want to know is how a system uses the inputs it receives to generate this output. For example, biochemists seek to detail the substrates and the enzymes that operate upon them in the course of performing a physiological function. Thus, scientists construe the systems they are confronting as machines, and their goal is to determine how these machines work. This involves identifying the parts of the machine and the contributions each makes to the performance that is of interest. The result is not a set of laws, but rather a blueprint or model of a possible machine that is thought to be capable of carrying out the activities of the system in nature. There are some notable respects in which models are different from laws. First, they are often quite particular, describing how specific components behave in specific circumstances (e.g., the enzymes and cofactors involved in fermentation under specific conditions in a particular species of yeast cells), not general. Second, they are often incomplete, and sometimes known to be incomplete. For example, Mitchell proposed the basic chemiosmotic mechanism of oxidative phosphorylation in the 1960s, and it was widely accepted by the 1970s, despite the recognition that parts of the account were incomplete and required further investigation. Third, characterization of entities and processes in models are sometimes known to be false but nonetheless to provide a useful basis for initially understanding and reasoning further about a phenomenon, as in Kauffman's (1993) models of gene control networks (see also Wimsatt, 1987).

I will return to this notion of a model in the next section, in which I consider how connectionism can help us understand the process through which scientists construct such models. What I want to stress is that scientists frequently formulate their models linguistically: They name the various actors in processes and describe the transactions they envision occurring. Language provides one way of representing these actors and processes; diagrams provide another. (We should note that diagrams are often labeled linguistically and are often uninterpretable except with linguistic commentary.) Therefore, we should not attempt to develop our whole account of what scientists do by focusing on what is going on in their heads; we should also consider how they manipulate these external representations that are crucial to science.

Churchland is not unaware of the relevance of public discourse in science. Indeed, in his closing remarks in "On the Nature of Theories" he comments (1989, p. 195):

> It remains for this approach to comprehend the highly discursive and linguistic dimensions of human cognition, those that motivated the classical view of cognition. We need not pretend that this will be easy, but we can see how to start. We can start by exploring the capacity of networks to manipulate the structure of existing language, its syntax, its semantics, its pragmatics, and so forth.

The approach Churchland outlines for dealing with this public discourse seems to be close in spirit to what I have sketched above. I contend, however, that this is not a task we can put off until we have worked out notions of theories and explanatory understanding. Scientific theorizing and explanation depend upon this external representational capacity. The weights on connections and activation patterns in the head are only part of the story. They may explain how scientists are able to employ these representations and specifically how they relate them to particular phenomena to be explained. If the connectionist account of cognition is correct, it has a major role to play in our understanding of scientists. But so have linguistic structures, diagrams, and other external representational systems.

Before leaving this issue there is one objection that Churchland makes to a related position that needs to be addressed. He argues that focusing on the public level fails to account for important differences between individuals. Churchland himself raises this when he considers whether, in his connectionist account, one should identify a theory with a particular point in weight space or with a set of points that would produce the same classifications of inputs. He objects that the latter fails to account for the differences in dynamics between agents/systems. The details of how a particular network solved a problem are important for determining how that network will generalize and learn in the future (1989, p. 177). This information is lost when we move to the external level, either by focusing on how the network partitions inputs or by looking to the external representations that the network might use. I grant part of Churchland's contention: The process of conceptual change is partly determined by the details of internal processing. Change those details, and a different trajectory will be followed. But this is not all that will determine future trajectories; external representations also affect them. The same model of a system can be presented in different ways even within language. These different ways will highlight different aspects of the model. What is highlighted is particularly important when the model must be revised, for those are the features one is likely to change. Further, different sorts of external representational systems afford different manipulations and restrict others. Stereoscopic representations of a system may make salient possible alterations that are not apparent in non-stereoscopic representations. For example, since one is aware of three-dimensional relations, one may see multiple ramifications of altering a part that would not otherwise be noticed. The process of theory revision is thus controlled at many points, both at points within the mental processes of scientists and at points in a theory's external representations.

3   Model Building as Multiple Soft-Constraint Satisfaction

Having allowed a central place for symbolic representations (albeit external, not internal, ones), one might wonder what role connectionism could still play in altering our philosophy of science. To see this, we need to look not at the representations themselves, but at the way in which these representations are used. In the positivists' account, logical relations, especially deduction, were the model of relations between propositions. While it is certainly possible for humans and connectionist networks to use logical relations in connecting propositions (e.g., to construct a natural deduction out of propositions – Seé Bechtel, 1994), this is not the only or even the primary way of relating propositions. In fact, most inferences people make are not logically valid. People often seem to be quite good at determining what would likely be the case when certain propositions are true even when what is inferred does not follow logically. Thus, it seems that the way in which people interact with even propositionally encoded information is not primarily through logical deduction.

An alternative view is that people seek to fit information together into coherent wholes. Some of the information available is viewed as having especially high prior credibility. This information serves as a constraint on the whole pattern of information constructed. (For example, knowledge of a person's previous behavior and expressed moral views may make it extremely unlikely that the person would act in a certain way.) Constraints, however, cannot always be respected. Sometimes the only ways that can be envisioned for fitting pieces together require rejecting some of the constraints.

The idea of constraint satisfaction is one that resonates with a connectionist perspective. When a connectionist network tries to solve a problem, it too seeks to find a solution that respects the various constraints presented to it (either in the form of inputs to the network or weights on connections). But the best solution it can generate sometimes violates these constraints. The constraints are thus often referred to as *soft constraints*. In what follows, I will suggest that this is quite characteristic of scientific reasoning and that it is by encouraging us to adopt this perspective on scientific reasoning that connectionism may make its major contribution to philosophy of science.

In the previous section I suggested that, at least in the life sciences, models of mechanisms rather than deductively organized sets of laws were the primary explanatory tool. Richardson and I (Bechtel and Richardson, 1993) have developed an account of the processes by which scientists construct such models. I want to emphasize here that when scientists engage in such model construction, they are typically confronted with a number of constraints. Some of these constraints stem from data they have about the behavior of the system to be explained, others from knowledge of possible mechanisms. Their task is one of constructing a description or diagram of a mechanism that is compatible with these constraints. Often the problem is that the researcher cannot find any way to do this. Any approach violates one or more of the constraints. The reasoning task turns into one of doing least damage to these constraints.

An example will make this clear. After Buchner's discovery (1897) that fermentation could be carried out in cell extracts, it became clear to investigators that fermentation did not depend upon special properties of living cells but was a chemical process. Their goal was to explain the reaction. The general chemical change was well known. In the case of alcoholic fermentation, sugar was transformed to alcohol:

$$C_6H_{12}O_6 \rightarrow C_2H_5OH$$

Since this is not a simple or basic chemical reaction, the task was to determine the intermediate reactions and their products. The researchers were constrained by beliefs about what reactions were possible and what chemical formulae corresponded to actually occurring substances. Since it was fairly clear that fermentation involved splitting a molecule of sugar (a compound with six carbon atoms) into two molecules of a compound with three carbon atoms, researchers focused their attention on a number of three-carbon compounds known from organic chemistry: lactic acid, methylglyoxal, glyceraldehyde, dihydroxyacetone, and pyruvic acid. The initial question was, Which of these might be intermediates in fermentation?

In evaluating whether these compounds could be inserted into their proposed pathways, researchers imposed two constraints. They required evidence (a) that the substances were found in fermenting cells and (b) that they metabolized[6] as rapidly as sugar. Both of these are reasonable, if ultimately problematic.

First, if it was not possible to find any evidence that a substance ever occurred in living cells, then it was not plausible to assume that it was indeed an intermediate in a chemical reaction in the cell. This criterion can nonetheless be problematic: In tightly linked systems, such as those found in cells, the product of one reaction is rapidly employed in other reactions, so there will be little buildup of the substance. Thus one must often develop ingenious ways to interrupt the normal processes in the cell in order to find evidence of the intermediary. If the substance appears when normal processes are interrupted, however, it is always possible that it does so as a consequence of these perturbed conditions and is not generated under normal conditions in the cell.

Second, if something is an intermediary, it is reasonable that the reaction from that point on takes no longer than the reaction from the initial starting point. However, this is plausible only if the reactions are independent and comprise a linear chain of reactions. If later reactions are coupled to earlier ones, then an intermediate might not react as rapidly as the initial substance, since the early coupled reactions will not occur. Thus, in imposing the second condition, researchers are implicitly adopting the idea that a mechanism is decomposable into a linear chain of reactions. This, however, is such a natural and powerful constraint on human thinking that it is natural to impose it as an additional constraint on possible models.

Pyruvic acid ($C_3H_4O_3$) satisfied both constraints on possible intermediates: It was found in living cells and reacted rapidly to yield alcohol. It was, therefore, provisionally assumed to be part of the pathway. The challenge was to fill in the rest of the pathway. One proposal stemmed from Carl Neuberg (Neuberg and Kerb, 1913). He proposed (see Figure 5.1) that a molecule of sugar was first scissioned into two molecules of methylglyoxal (step 1). The course of the subsequent reactions depended upon whether a supply of aldehyde was available. Before it was available, two molecules of methylglyoxal would react with two molecules of water to generate a molecule of glycerol and of pyruvic acid (step 2a). A molecule of carbon dioxide would then be removed from the pyruvic acid, yielding aldehyde (step 3). The molecule of aldehyde would then react with another molecule of methylglyoxal to yield pyruvic acid and alcohol (step 2b). After a supply of aldehyde was created, step 2a would drop out and the aldehyde generated at step 3 in a previous cycle of the reaction would react with methylglyoxal

(1) $C_6H_{12}O_6$ $\Rightarrow$ $2C_3H_4O_2 + 2H_2O$
       (hexose)   (methyglyoxal + water)

(2a) $2C_3H_4O_2 + 2H_2O$ $\Rightarrow$ $C_3H_8O_3 + C_3H_4O_3$
       (methylglyoxal + water)   (glycerol + pyruvic acid)

(2b) $C_3H_4O_2 + C_2H_4O + 2H_2O$ $\Rightarrow$ $C_3H_4O_3 + C_2H_5OH$
       (methylglyoxal + aldehyde + water)   (pyruvic acid + alcohol)

(3) $C_3H_4O_3$ $\Rightarrow$ $C_2H_4O + CO_2$
       (pyruvic acid)   (aldehyde + carbon dioxide)

Figure 5.1 Neuberg and Kerb's (1913) model of the chemical reactions
involved in alcoholic fermentation

generated in step 2b to create alcohol and pyruvic acid.

Neuberg's account is often cited as the first coherent model of
fermentation (Fruton, 1972; Florkin, 1975). It does provide an account
in terms of known intermediates and known reactions. One thing to note
about this proposal is that the constraint of linearity has already been
violated. After the initial stage, a reaction earlier in the pathway (2b)
depends upon a reaction later in the pathway (3). The constraint of
linearity was sacrificed not for principled reasons, but because a nonlinear organization provided the only way to account for the overall
reaction using known intermediates and known reactions.

Two other features of Neuberg's pathway were problematic. First, the
investigations of Harden and Young in the first years of the century had
indicated that in order to sustain fermentation in extracts from which all
whole cells had been removed, inorganic phosphate had to be added to
the extract (Harden and Young, 1906). Although the added phosphate
would induce a spurt of rapid fermentation, it was soon taken up into a
hexosediphosphate ester, a stable compound of sugar and phosphate,
and the reaction rate slowed dramatically. The fact that adding phosphates caused a spurt of rapid fermentation suggested that they played
some role in the reaction, but Neuberg had provided no role for them.
His exclusion of phosphates, however, is quite understandable. Hexosediphosphate reacted very slowly in yeast extract. Thus, it failed to
satisfy the criterion that any intermediate must ferment as rapidly as
sugar itself. Neuberg explained away the need for adding phosphate to
cell-free extracts as an artifact of the experimental procedure.

The second problematic feature, however, was that methylglyoxal,
when added to yeast extract, would itself not ferment. This would seem
to be a telling evidence against Neuberg's proposal, especially since he
had used failure to ferment as grounds for rejecting hexosediphosphate's role in the pathway. But Neuberg did not so regard it. He
assumed that the failure of methylglyoxal to ferment was due to the

experimental arrangement, and he and others continued to seek evidence that, if supplied in the correct way, it would metabolize in normal yeast cells. He also considered the possibility that the form of methylglyoxal occurring in normal fermentation was different from laboratory methylglyoxal. (Another factor Neuberg cited as supporting the role of methylglyoxal in the pathway was that it could account for the methyl that was found in the yeast extract.)

About 20 years later Neuberg's model of fermentation was supplanted by one in which phosphorylated compounds figured throughout the pathway, and methylglyoxal was removed from the pathway (for details of this history, see Bechtel and Richardson, 1993). The reason hexosediphosphate seemed to build up and not ferment in cell-free extracts also came to be understood: The overall reaction requires a supply of ADP to which to transfer the high-energy phosphate bonds that are developed through the fermentation reaction (forming ATP). In normal cells, this ADP is made available by the breakdown of ATP in the course of cell work, but this process was not available in the extracts. The cell is not the nearly-decomposable system that early researchers assumed, but a highly integrated system. Nonetheless, for about 20 years Neuberg's model was regarded as the most plausible model of fermentation.

It is of interest here that Neuberg's model was pieced together in an attempt to satisfy a number of constraints. It succeeded in satisfying many of them, using known intermediates and known reactions to construct a coherent pathway. This success largely explains its acceptance. But the constraints it *failed* to satisfy are also noteworthy: It could not explain the need for phosphates, and methylglyoxal failed to satisfy the criterion of metabolizing as rapidly as sugar. Thus it satisfied some constraints but not others. This suggests that in science, as in ordinary life, many constraints are soft constraints, and can be violated if the overall result is the best that can be obtained. Insofar as this is a mode of reasoning that connectionism leads us to expect, connectionism may have an important role in helping us understand the reasoning processes scientists employ when developing such models. (Moreover, it suggests that connectionism may eventually provide a useful framework for modeling such reasoning.)

4 Evaluating Research Techniques and Data as Soft-Constraint Satisfaction

One of the virtues Churchland cites for his connectionist account of theories is that it can account for Kuhn's contention (1970) that observation is theory-laden. The theory-ladenness claim opposed the view that scientific knowledge was built on foundations such as observation reports that were immune to challenge. But the traditional account of theory-ladenness only focuses on the role of theories in fixing our characterization of what we observe. In many scientific disciplines, what is observed is not just the product of our unaided senses and our theories, but rather depends upon a variety of instruments and research techniques. Outside of Hacking (1983), the development of these instruments and techniques for using them has not received much discussion in philosophy. (Sociologists of science such as Latour (1987), on the other hand, have made much of the role of the development of instruments and research techniques, seeing in them further support for the view that science is a social construction not guided by epistemic considerations.) But explaining the reasoning involved in development and evaluation of instruments and research techniques should be a prime objective for philosophy of science, since these techniques play a pivotal role in determining what is taken to be the evidence for scientific models or theories.

Although philosophers of science have said little about how scientists reason about instruments and research techniques, these topics are an important part of the ongoing discussion of many sciences. Some of the greatest controversies in the scientific literature are not about theories, but rather about the instruments and techniques that give rise to data. What is taken to be data by one scientist is not informative about the natural system under study but is a product only of the instruments or techniques used to study those systems. Reasoning about instruments and research techniques is therefore a central activity of scientists.

If we cannot give an account of how scientists reason about and decide upon instruments and research techniques, then we can give no account of why they should put such faith in their evidence. Insofar as we maintain our focus on logical relations between linguistic propositions, we may not be able to account for reasoning about instruments, since much of the development of instruments and research techniques is not grounded on theories or propositions, but on physical explorations conducted with the instruments. Instruments and techniques are not justified because they are built on already justified principles. Churchland briefly suggests that a connectionist framework can help us understand the development of skills as an important part of learning to be a scientist, since, like all knowledge, knowledge of skills for connectionists consists in weights in a network. But, as in the last section, I want to urge that if we are to understand the development of the knowledge scientists have of instruments and research techniques, we cannot, as Churchland suggests, focus just on what occurs inside the head. Rather, there is a crucial interaction between scientists and physical parts of the world, including both the physical instrument and the physical actions of scientists and technicians. Further, as with models themselves, as scientists develop instruments and techniques, they are frequently attempting to satisfy multiple soft constraints.

The modern discipline of cell biology emerged with the development of new instruments and research techniques that made it possible to identify structures within the cell and determine their contributions to cell life. Very important among these was cell fractionation, which provided a tool for isolating cell organelles to determine their bio-chemical function. The potential for artifact presented by this technique is obvious: It involves subjecting cellular materials to forces several thousand times that of gravity in order to effect the separation. But one hopes that the cellular components themselves will not be adversely affected by the process. In the early development of cell-fractionation techniques, various approaches to fractionation were developed, many of which succeeded at some part of the task but then failed in others, requiring constant compromise. This is clearly brought out by Allfrey (1959, p. 198):

> The ideal isolation procedure is easy to define: it is the method which yields the desired intracellular components as they exist in the cell, unchanged, uncontaminated, and in quantitative yield. Unfortunately, all cell fractiona-tion techniques known at present fall short of this ideal, and some compromise becomes necessary. Methods which give quantitative yields often involve serious alterations of form, structure, or composition, and procedures which preserve the morphology often destroy activity and function. Purity and homogeneity of the product are rarely, if ever, achieved.

I will focus on three aspects of the overall fractionation process, in each case showing how researchers were trying to satisfy competing con-straints.

A first challenge in cell fractionation is to break the cell membrane. This requires subjecting the cell to disruptive forces. At the same time, however, one seeks to do the least damage to the internal components. For example, one wants to prevent them from releasing enzymes into the medium in which the fractionation is occurring. A host of instru-ments were employed by researchers in breaking the cell: the Waring Blendor, mortar and pestle, various piston-type homogenizers, colloid mills, and sonic vibrators. In fact, during the 1940s and 1950s scientists were actively exploring various techniques. Allfrey (1959) presents a diagram of nine different designs for homogenizers alone, each of which produced the shearing force required to break the cell membrane in somewhat different ways and hence led to to different results. In each case, researchers faced competing goals: to insure that all cell membranes were broken, but not to disrupt internal membranes. If one failed to break all the cells, then their materials would be deposited in the first fraction (together with nuclei), distorting the analysis of that fraction and the attempt to secure quantitative information about what substances appeared at each location in the cell. On the other hand, too violent a technique would break up the internal organelles as well.

Typically techniques for breaking cells were evaluated in terms of their products: Did the technique break all the cells without harming the organelles (for example altering their biochemistry)? Whether all the cells were broken could be evaluated by microscope, but evaluating whether organelles were harmed was far more problematic. The process of fractionation was the primary tool for determining the nature of these organelles, so there was no independent standard by which to judge harm. Here researchers relied on two strategies. The first was to compare the results of one technique for breaking the cell with others that were already held in some repute. But if the technique was to be judged an improvement, it should not just produce results that could already be obtained otherwise. The second criterion therefore was crucial: Did the fractionation process as a whole yield results compatible with an emerging theory? To a foundationalist it may seem circular to evaluate the technique by this appeal to theories, which are supposed to be grounded on the evidence provided *by* the technique, but it is in fact the sort of reasoning that often figures in scientists' evaluations of their techniques, as we shall see by turning to the other components of the cell-fractionation process.

As the cell membrane is broken, its contents must be released into a fluid medium. The challenge was to find a medium that would cause the least disruption of the cell organelles. Among the variables considered were the substances for inclusion (salt, sucrose, citric acid, etc.), the concentration of each of these (hypotonic, isotonic, or hypertonic), and the pH for the medium. Each of these would affect the organelles differently. Claude's early fractionation work used a solution consisting of a few drops of NaOH at a pH of about 9.0 (Claude, 1943); he later used a saline solution buffered at a pH of 9.0 to 9.5. This led to serious distortion of the shape of organelles such as mitochondria, but did provide a basis for identifying the mitochondrion as the locus of some of the crucial enzymes in cellular respiration (Hogeboom, Claude, and Hotchkiss, 1946). Subsequently, Hogeboom, Schneider, and Palade (1948) employed hypertonic sucrose solution, which allowed the mitochondria to retain their normal rod-like shape and staining, though they failed to synthesize ATP. Schneider (1948) then introduced isotonic sucrose, which preserves the ATP synthesis but compromises shape. Again, whether the results cohered with those using other investigatory strategies (microscopy for determining the shape of particles, staining for identifying particles) and with developing theories (for example that the mitochondrion was the "power plant" of the cell) was critical to judging whether a new medium represented an improvement. Moreover, a perfect solution was not possible.

After the cell membranes have been broken and the contents released into an aqueous medium, the preparation is ready for centrifugation. Here the underlying principle is clear: Depending upon their density and shape, particles will travel at different speeds in a centrifuge. Drawing on Stokes' Law, it was possible to specify the rate at which different particles should move, but a variety of factors generated results different from the ideal. For example, particles would hit the side of the vesicle, and often slide down it at a very different rate. Also, particles might agglutinate, resulting in particles of different size and shape traveling together. Finally, some of the lighter materials would start closer to the bottom than some of the heavier materials and would sediment out in the same time it took for the heavier materials (de Duve and Berthet, 1954). The result was that prolonging centrifugation to secure all the heavier particles increased the amount of contamination in that layer. If one shortened the time, then the heavier particles would contaminate other fractions.

In his early fractionation work, Claude (1940) discovered a technique (three or four alternate long and short runs of a high-speed centrifuge under 18,000 g) for producing a fraction of small particles, which he compared with particles he had isolated from viruses. Finding them in all cells, normal and pathological, he developed the idea that they might be mitochondria, or pieces of mitochondria. He contrasted them with somewhat larger particles previously separated and identified as mitochondria by Bensley and Hoerr (1934) and argued that Bensley's particles were really secretory. Claude subsequently reversed his judgment, deciding that the larger particles, which were sedimented faster, were the mitochondria, and he identified the new particles as small particles or microsomes. As the techniques were refined (the establishment of different speeds and different times for different fractions and the use of washing and resedimenting to increase purity), it became clear that the two fractions have very different chemical make-ups. Two other fractions were also distinguished: a nuclear fraction that was sedimented even more quickly or at lesser speed and a supernate consisting of the fluid materials left after the last sedimentation. The separation of these four fractions became the standard approach for many years.

What justifies these four fractions? One factor is that the particles were of significantly different sizes. Further, they were clearly different in chemical make-up. Claude comments (1948, pp. 127–8): "It should be pointed out that division of the cell in this manner is not arbitrary and is not based on size differences alone since . . . these various fractions are also distinct in chemical constitution, in biochemical functions, and even in color." While many enzymes and other compounds were common to all fractions, some were predominantly recovered in a single fraction: DNA and DPN-synthesizing enzyme in the nuclear fraction, succinic dehydrogenase, cytochrome oxidase and cytochrome c in the mitochondrial fraction, and glucose-6-phosphatase in the microsomal fraction. Some researchers developed the strategy of trying to demonstrate that the enzymes each originated in a different fraction of the cell, and they used the ability to produce fractions of this sort as a criterion of the correctness of their approach (Claude, 1948; de Duve and Berthet, 1954). Accepting the principle as a constraint provided the basis for differentiating yet more fractions and arguing that they originated in different loci in the normal cell, an approach that turned out to be very fruitful. Other researchers (e.g., Dounce, 1954) strongly resisted this move, arguing that it was highly plausible that the same enzyme or chemical compound might function in different parts of the cell.

The first thing to note is that cell fractionation is a complex process. Small variations in the technique could yield very different results. De Duve and Berthet make this point clearly (1954, p. 226): "Differential centrifugation is a delicate method, and small modifications in the procedures applied may in many cases alter quite significantly the manner in which a preparation is finally fractionated." No approach achieved the ideal described in the passage by Allfrey above. Yet some of the techniques were taken to provide authoritative information about the natural state of cells. How did the scientists determine which results were authoritative? As in the building of models described in the previous section, alternatives were developed and evaluated against multiple constraints such as, How did the results of this technique correspond to those achieved with other approaches? How well did the results fit with an emerging understanding of cell function? Since no technique satisfied all criteria, some had to be sacrificed. Thus, once again scientists seem to be engaged in soft-constraint satisfaction, the sort of processing characteristic of connectionist networks.

In developing their instruments and techniques, we should note that scientists are typically not engaged in manipulating propositions. They use propositions and diagrams to communicate their techniques to others and to present reasons why a technique should or should not be respected, but generally not in the process of developing their techniques. Rather, they interact directly with the physical objects. The physical instruments and the scientist's body themselves provide additional constraints. Only some modifications of the material of the instrument or ways of maneuvering a person's body are possible. In this case it does not make sense to think of the reasoning as carried out in language. Linguistically-encoded information provides one source of constraint, but directly-apprehended physical factors provide others. The chief cognitive activity throughout is one of satisfying as many of the constraints as possible.

5 Conclusion

Churchland argues that connectionism can play an important role in helping us reconceptualize philosophy of science. I agree with this contention but claim that the role for connectionism is somewhat different from the one Churchland presents. For Churchland, the contribution is to move us away from a sentential construal of theories and explanation. In their stead, he proposes that theories consist of weights within a network and that explanatory understanding involves the activation of prototype vectors in the network. I have argued that sentential representations do have a role to play but that their primary locus is not in the heads of scientists. Scientists use representations in natural language as well as figures and diagrams to encode their models. These representations are not translations of what is in the heads of the scientists; rather, they are devices used by scientists. Scientific theories may take a sentential form even if, in using these theories, scientists rely on weights on connections within their heads. Consequently, we should not seek to localize the story of scientific development in representations and processes occurring in the head. Instead we need to take seriously the fact that scientists are situated cognizers whose cognitive processes involve interactions with external representations as well as physical devices.

While I do not foresee connectionism supplanting the sentential framework, I have suggested that when that framework is restricted to external representations, it can fundamentally alter our conception of what scientists do in their interactions with theories or with their research instruments. Connectionist networks treat connections and inputs as constraints; when solving a problem, they seek a state that maximally satisfies these constraints. Some of the constraints must be overridden in the process. Accordingly, the constraints in a network are *soft*. I have argued that this is the kind of reasoning scientists often

engage in when developing explanatory models. They seek a representation that maximally satisfies the various empirical and conceptual
constraints on the model. I have also argued that in their reasoning
about new instruments and research techniques, scientists likewise seek
to satisfy multiple soft constraints. Thus, connectionism can make an
important contribution to philosophy of science as it moves us away
from deductive and inductive logic as the model of scientific reasoning
to a model of soft-constraint satisfaction performed in the context of
interacting with external representations and physical devices.

Notes

Support for this research was provided by the American Society for Cell
Biology, the National Endowment for the Humanities (RH-21013-91) and
Georgia State University, all of which are gratefully acknowledged. I also thank
Robert McCauley for his comments on an earlier draft of this chapter.
1   This is not the place to present an introduction to connectionism, an
    approach to modeling cognitive phenomena that was first developed in the
    1950s and that once again gained prominence in the 1980s, in part with the
    publication of Rumelhart, McClelland, and the PDP Research Group (1986).
    Both Paul and Patricia Churchland have presented introductions to connec-
    tionism in their writings. See also Bechtel and Abrahamsen (1991) for an
    introduction. The understanding of connectionism varies significantly among
    authors. For both the Churchlands the importance of connectionism seems
    to be that the parallels between connectionist networks and real neural
    networks allows our emerging understanding of brain function to inform
    cognitive modeling. For many others the importance lies not so much in the
    similarity of connectionist networks to neural architecture as in the fact that
    connectionist models seem to exhibit features of cognition lacking in other
    approaches to cognitive modeling.
2   Often the units in a connectionist network will be layered so that a set of
    input units sends activations to one or more layers of other units, known as
    hidden units, which in turn send activations to a final layer of units known as
    output units. Such a network is known as a *feedforward* network. However,
    increasingly connectionists are pursuing architectures in which there are
    connections between units of a layer and feeding from a higher layer back to
    a lower layer. Moreover, there need not be any layering of units; units may
    be connected to all other units in the network or to a subset of them.
3   On the other hand, making the reasoning activities of scientists part of the
    concern of philosophy of science is certainly an advance. In *Discovering
    Complexity* (Bechtel and Richardson, 1993) Richardson and I bemoan the
    fact that the standard models in philosophy of science have excluded the
    scientists and their ways of understanding and working to solve problems.
    Below I will show how one of the case studies we presented in that book

lends itself to analysis within a connectionist framework. But the remedy to ignoring the minds of scientists is not to focus there exclusively.

4 Further, as historians of science have pointed out, many major conceptual changes have come from scientists who had not accepted or acquired the previous conceptual framework. Often the revolutionary scientist comes from a different conceptual field and brings ideas from that field to the new field, ideas that are often in radical conflict with those of the existing conceptual framework. As a result, in Churchland's terms the revolutionary scientist never encountered the local minimum.

5 This private use of language is, as Vygotsky (1962) argued, dependent upon having mastered the public use of language, and involves going through most of the steps of actually producing a public utterance, and then responding to the product that is generated (the sounds of inner speech) as input.

6 The researchers generally spoke of the intermediates themselves as *fermenting*. This reflects the conception, discussed below, that fermentation was simply a chain of independent reactions, not the result of a highly-integrated system.

References

Allfrey, V. (1959). The isolation of subcellular components. In J. Brachet and A. E. Mirsky (eds), *The Cell: Biochemistry, Physiology, and Morphology*, pp. 193–290. New York: Academic Press.

Bechtel, W. (1994). Natural deduction in connectionist systems. *Synthese*, **101**: 433–63.

Bechtel, W. (in press). What knowledge must be in the head that we might acquire language? In B. Velichkovsky and D. M. Rumbaugh (eds), *Naturally Human: Origins and Destiny of Language*. Hillsdale, NJ: Erlbaum.

Bechtel, W. and Abrahamsen, A. (1991). *Connectionism and the Mind: An Introduction to Parallel Processing in Networks*. Oxford: Blackwell.

Bechtel, W. and Richardson, R. C. (1993). *Discovering Complexity: Decomposition and Localization as Scientific Research Strategies*. Princeton: Princeton University Press.

Bensley, R. R. and Hoerr, N. (1934). Studies on cell structure by the freeze-drying method. VI. The preparation and properties of mitochondria. *Anatomical Record*, **60**, 449–55.

Buchner, E. (1897). Alkoholische Gährung ohne Hefezellen Vorläufige Mitteilung. *Berichte der deutschen chemischen Gesellschaft*, **37**, 417–28.

Cartwright, N. (1983). *How the Laws of Physics Lie*. Oxford: Clarendon Press.

Churchland, P. M. (1989). *A Neurocomputational Perspective: The Nature of Mind and the Structure of Science*. Cambridge, MA: MIT Press.

Claude, A. (1940). Particulate components of normal and tumor cells. *Science*, **91**, 77–8.

Claude, A. (1943). Distribution of nucleic acids in the cell and the morphological constitution of cytoplasm. In J. Cattell (ed.), *Biological Symposium*. Vol. X.

Frontiers of Cytochemistry, pp. 111–29. Lancaster, PA: Jacques Cattell Press.

Claude, A. (1948). Studies on cells: morphology, chemical constitution, and distribution of biochemical fractions. *Harvey Lectures*, **43**, 121–64.

de Duve, C. and Berthet, J. (1954). The use of differential centrifugation in the study of tissue enzymes. *International Review of Cytology*, **3**, 225–75.

Dounce, A. L. (1954). The significance of enzyme studies on isolated cell nuclei. *International Review of Cytology*, **3**, 199–223.

Florkin, M. (1975). *Comprehensive Biochemistry*. Vol. 31. *A History of Biochemistry*. Part III. *History of the Sources of Free Energy in Organisms*. Amsterdam: Elsevier.

Fruton, J. (1972). *Molecules and Life: Historical Essays on the Interplay of Chemistry and Biology*. New York: Wiley Interscience.

Giere, R. (1988). *Explaining Science*. Chicago: University of Chicago Press.

Hacking, I. (1983). *Representing and Intervening: Introductory Topics in the Philosophy of Natural Science*. Cambridge: Cambridge University Press.

Harden, A. and Young, W. J. (1906). The alcoholic fermentation of yeast-juice. *Proceedings of the Royal Society, London*, **B77**, 405–20.

Hogeboom, G. H., Claude, A. and Hotchkiss, R. (1946). The distribution of cytochrome oxidase and succinoxidase in the cytoplasm of the mammalian liver cell. *Journal of Biological Chemistry*, **165**, 615–29.

Hogeboom, G. H., Schneider, W. C. and Palade, G. E. (1948). Cytochemical studies of mammalian tissues. I. Isolation of intact mitochondria from rat liver: some biochemical properties of mitochondria and submicroscopic particulate material. *Journal of Biological Chemistry*, **172**, 619–35.

Kauffman, S. A. (1993). *The Origins of Order: Self-organization and Selection in Evolution*. Oxford: Oxford University Press.

Kuhn, T. S. (1970). *The Structure of Scientific Revolutions*. Chicago: University of Chicago Press.

Latour, B. (1987). *Scientists in Action: How to Follow Scientists and Engineers Through Society*. Cambridge, MA: Harvard University Press.

Neuberg, C. and Kerb, J. (1913). Über zuckerfreie Hefegärungen. XII. Über Vorgänge bei der Hefegärung. *Biochemische Zeitschrift*, **53**, 406–19.

Rumelhart, D. E., Smolensky, P., McClelland, J. L. and Hinton, G. E. (1986). Schemas and sequential thought processes in PDP models. In J. L. McClelland, D. E. Rumelhart and the PDP Research Group (eds), *Parallel Distributed Processing: Explorations in the Microstructure of Cognition*, Vol. 2. *Psychological and Biological Models*, pp. 7–57. Cambridge, MA: MIT Press.

Schneider, W. C. (1948). The intracellular distribution of enzymes. III. The oxidation of octanoic acid by rat liver fractions. *Journal of Biological Chemistry*, **176**, 259–66.

St. John, M. F. and McClelland, J. L. (1990). Learning and applying contextual constraints in sentence comprehension. *Artificial Intelligence*, **46**, 217–57.

Vygotsky, L. S. (1962). *Language and thought*. Cambridge, MA: MIT Press.

Wimsatt, W. C. (1987). False models as means to truer theories. In M. Nitecki and A. Hoffman (eds), *Neutral models in biology*, pp. 23–55. London: Oxford University Press.

6

Paul Churchland and State Space Semantics

Jerry Fodor and Ernie Lepore

Introduction

A number of philosophers believe that the notion of identity of meaning should be replaced by some graded notion of similarity of meaning. With a graded notion of similarity of meaning, intentional generalizations would be viewed as subsuming individuals in virtue of the similarity of their mental states; translation and paraphrase would be viewed as preserving not identity but similarity of meaning. The prospects, however, for constructing a "robust" notion of similarity of meaning – one adequate to the purposes of semantics and cognitive science – are, we believe, remote. This prognosis isn't widely shared. That may be because friends of semantic similarity have generally been careful not to say what they take semantic similarity to consist in. Paul Churchland, however, has proposed a sketch of the sort of similarity theory that is required, a notion of mental (or, anyhow, neural) representation that "... embodies ... metrical relations ... and thus embodies the representation of similarity relations between distinct items thus represented" (1989b: 102; barring notice to the contrary, emphases are Churchland's throughout).

Since Churchland's attitude towards the intentional/semantic generally tends to be eliminativist, it's unclear just what properties of contentful states his "state space" representations are supposed to preserve. Suffice it that, when he's in a "highly speculative" mode, he contemplates, for example, the possibility of "...a way of representing 'anglophone linguistic hyperspace' so that all grammatical sentences turn out to reside on a proprietary hypersurface within that hyperspace, with the logical relations between them reflected as spatial relations of some kind ... [This would hold out] the possibility of an alternative to, or potential reduction of, the familiar Chomskyan picture" (1989b: 109). This entails that state spaces can represent grammars and such. Like much else that he says, it certainly sounds as though Churchland has in mind a kind of representation that specifies the contents of neural states in which case he is into intensionality up to his neck. In any event, we propose to read him that way and ask how much of the intuitive notion of content similarity state space representation allows us to reconstruct.

In what follows, we hope to convince you that, for all that's on offer so far, the problem of semantic similarity appears to be intractable.

State Space Representation

"The basic idea . . . is that the brain represents various aspects of reality by a position in a suitable state space; and the brain performs computations on such representations by means of general coordinate transformations from one state space to another" (1989b: 78–9).

For our present purpose, which is semantics rather than the theory of mental processes, only Churchland's account of neural representation need concern us. We commence by trying to make clear how Churchland's state space proposal connects with the more familiar "network" picture of semantics. Churchland's state space proposal is, we suggest, profitably viewed as an attempt to generalize the more familiar "network" picture of semantics and to free it from its specifically empiricist assumptions.

Suppose we start with a roughly Quinean picture of the structure of theories (/languages/belief systems). According to this picture, there are two sorts of ways in which the (nonlogical) symbols belonging to a theory get semantically interpreted. The semantics of the "observation vocabulary" is fixed by conditioning (or other causal) relations between its expressions and observable properties of the distal or proximal environment. The semantics of the rest of the vocabulary is fixed by a network of inferential or (in case the semantics is intended to be naturalistic) causal/associative relations to one another and to the observation terms. The semantic theory of a language thus represents its vocabulary as nodes in a network, the paths of which correspond to semantically-relevant relations among the vocabulary items. Observation terms are at the "periphery" of the network; nonobservational vocabulary is further in. We take it that this geography is familiar.

Recall how the problem of content identity arises on this "network" picture. If the paths to a node are collectively constitutive of the identity of the node (as presumably they will be if, as Quine holds, no analytic/ synthetic (a/s) distinction is assumed), then only identical networks can token nodes of the same type. Identity of networks is thus a sufficient condition for identity of content, but this sufficient condition isn't robust; it will never be satisfied in practice. The long and the short of it is: a network semantics offers no robust account of content identity if it is denied access to an a/s distinction. But maybe a network semantics can nevertheless be made to offer a robust notion of content similarity? The present proposal is to make content similarity do the work that content identity did in semantic theories that endorsed the a/s distinction.

How, then, might a robust metric of content similarity be constructed; one which is defined for nodes belonging to networks that are (perhaps arbitrarily) different from each other? An immediate problem is this: according to the usual understanding, the only fixed points in a network are the nodes that correspond to observation vocabulary. It's only these peripheral nodes that can be identified without specifying the rest of the network that contains them. (We're supposing that we know what it is for two arbitrarily different theories to both have a node that expresses an observable property like red; it's for both to have vocabulary items that are appropriately connected – for example, conditioned – to redness.) It thus appears that, if we are to define a similarity relation over terms in the nonobservation vocabulary, it will have to be by reference to their (direct or indirect) relations to observation terms.

But this picture might well strike one as intolerably empiricistic. It just doesn't seem to be true that the dimensions of content along which words (concepts) can be similar are reducible to the various ways in which they can be connected to observables. There is plausibly something semantically relevant that everything subsumed by the concept uncle has in common with everything subsumed by the concept aunt; but a couple of hundred years of unsuccessful empiricism suggest that what they have in common is not expressible by reference to the observable properties of aunts and uncles. Similarly, mutatis mutandis, for the similarity between the things subsumed by the concept ice and the things subsumed by the concept steam; or between the thing subsumed by the concept the President of the US and the things subsumed by the concept Cleopatra. And so on, endlessly.

Churchland's state space story is best understood in this context. At least since *Scientific Realism and the Plasticity of Mind* (1979), he has been attracted to network semantics and inclined to think that a good semantics must make similarity, rather than identity of content its basic theoretical notion. But he is also suspicious of the sort of empiricism which reduces all semantically relevant relations eventually to relations to observation vocabulary.

The semantic identity of a term derives from its specific place in the embedding network of the semantically important sentences of the language as a whole. Accordingly, if we wish to speak of sameness of meaning across languages, then we must learn to speak of terms occupying analogous places in the relevantly similar networks provided by the respective sets of semantically important sentences of the two languages at issue (1979: 61).

However, he goes on to say a few pages later:

> ... the aims of translation should include no fundamental interest whatever in preserving observationality ... languages, and the networks of beliefs that they embody, have an identity that transcends and can remain constant over variations in the particular sensory conduits to which they happen to be tied, and in the particular locations within the language where the sensory connections happen to be made. Accordingly, any conception of translation that ties its adequacy to the preservation of "net empirical content" as conceived by Quine will lead to nothing but confusion (1979: 65–6).

For Churchland, the question is thus how to free the network picture of semantics from its empiricist assumptions, and somehow to generate a robust notion of content similarity in the course of doing so. We read his paper "Some reductive strategies..." (1989b) as a failed attempt at this, and we'll argue that a recidivist empiricism is in fact its bottom line.

Churchland's current proposal may now be summarized: A "Quinean" network semantics of the sort we have been discussing can be thought of as describing a space whose dimensions correspond to observable properties, and where each expression of the object language is assigned a position in the space. To say that the concept dog is semantically connected to the properties of barking and tail wagging is thus equivalent to saying that it occupies a position in semantic space that is (partially) identified by its value along the barkingness and tail-waggingness dimensions. Since the empiricism of the standard network proposal resides in the requirement that all the dimensions of the semantic space in which the concepts are located must correspond to observable properties, all you have to do to get rid of the empiricism is abolish this requirement. What's left are semantic state spaces of arbitrary dimensions, each dimension corresponding to a parameter in terms of which the semantic theory taxonomizes object-language expressions, and where similarity of content among the object language expressions is represented by adjacency relations among regions of the space.

Let's now see how Churchland proposes to develop a theory of the semantics of mental representation that accords with this conception. Rather surprisingly, Churchland's analysis starts, not with the paradigms of intensionality (propositional attitudes and concepts) but with sensations. The more or less explicit suggestion is that if we had a treatment that provided an illuminating semantical account for sensations it might generalize to mental representation at large. Let us, therefore, consider how the state space story is supposed to apply to sensations, bearing in mind that it is Churchland's account of mental representation, rather than his theory of qualitative content, that is our primary concern.

> The qualitative character of our sensations is commonly held to pose an especially intractable problem for any neurobiological reduction of mental states ... and it is indeed hard to see much room for deductive purchase in the subjectively discriminable but "objectively uncharacterizable" qualia present to consciousness. ... Even so, a determined attempt to find order rather than mystery in this area uncovers a significant amount of expressible information. ... Consider ... the abstract three-dimensional "color cube" proposed by Edwin Land, within which every one of the many hundreds of humanly discriminable colors occupies a unique position or small volume ... Each axis represents the eye/brain's reconstruction of the objective reflectance of the seen object at one of the three wavelengths to which our cones are selectively responsive. Two colors are closely similar just in case their state-space positions within this cube are close to one another. And two colors are dissimilar just in case their state-space positions are distant.

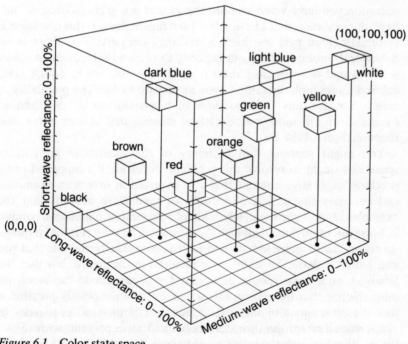

Figure 6.1 Color state space

We can even speak of the degree of the similarity, and of the dimensions along which it is reckoned (1989b: 102–3).

We emphasize that Churchland views this as an account of the qualitative content of color sensations, not just of the nervous system's capacity to discriminate among colors. As Churchland goes on to say,

> In particular, it suggests an effective means of expressing the inexpressible. The "ineffable" pink of one's current visual sensation may be richly and precisely expressible as a "95 Hz/ 80 Hz/ 80 Hz chord" in the relevant triune cortical system. ... This more penetrating conceptual framework might even displace the common-sense framework as the vehicle of inter-subjective description and spontaneous introspection (1991a: 106).

How plausible is this story for the representation of the qualitative content of sensations? And, how close does it get us to a robust notion of content similarity in general? We'll say just a word or two about the first question, saving most of our attention for the second.

There is, notoriously, a problem of qualitative content that philosophers of mind worry about. It's closely connected with problems about qualia inversion. For example, it seems conceptually possible that the sensation you have when you see things that are grass colored is "just like" the sensation that I have when I see fire engines. If this inversion is systematic, then perhaps there is nothing – in particular, there is no behavioral consequence of our capacity to respond selectively to colors – that would tell this case apart from the normal one in which grass colored things look the same to you as they do to me. The possibility of inverted qualia thus looks to show that behaviorism is false, and an extension of the same considerations suggest that it may show that functionalism is false too.

You might suppose that a theory of the qualitative content of sensations ought to resolve this problem. After all, it's supposed to be precisely qualitative content that gets inverted in inversion examples, and precisely the notion of identity of qualitative content that the examples render equivocal. Churchland's account of qualitative content is, however, of no help at all with these issues. The reason is that if qualia inversion makes any sense at all, it seems conceptually possible that you and I should share the state space pictured in the figure, but that the labels on your cube should be inverted with respect to the labels on mine. Notice that the reason this seems to be conceptually possible is that the dimensions of this state space specify physical properties of visual stimuli rather than parameters of qualitative content *per se*. Since the relation between the property of being a 95 Hz/ 80 Hz/ 80 Hz chord and being a sensation of ineffable pink would appear to be thoroughly contingent (or, at an any event, thoroughly nonsemantic), it would seem to be conceptually possible that something should have the first property but not the second. This just is the qualia inversion problem; there appears to be no property of a sensation except its qualitative content, upon which its qualitative content is guaranteed to supervene. (In particular, there appears to be no behavioral, or functional, or neurological property upon which it is guaranteed to supervene.) So if you were worried about the qualia problem before you read Churchland, what you should do is keep worrying.

To put this same point in an old-fashioned way, the dimensions of Churchland's state space appear to specify qualia by reference to properties they have nonessentially, and any such specification begs the inversion problem. (Or, if you think that it is "metaphysically necessary" that color sensations have the psychophysical properties that they do, then our point is that this necessity is not engendered by any semantical connection between sensation concepts and psychophysical concepts.) You could, in consequence, know perfectly well that a certain sensation corresponds to a certain "chord in the relevant triune cortical system" and have no idea at all of "what it's like" to have a sensation of that kind, or, indeed, that there is anything that it is like.

The problem so far is that the dimensions in terms of which Churchland proposes to taxonomize qualia don't specify their content. Rather, they appear to taxonomize qualia by psychophysically sufficient conditions for having them. But it might be thought that this is a defect of the example, not a defect of state space semantics as such. Why not stick to the state space notion of mental representation, but add the proviso that the dimensions of the semantic space must really be semantic; they have to taxonomize content bearing states by their contents. Perhaps concepts (like aunt, uncle, steam, ice, the President of the US, and Cleopatra) can be identified with positions in a state space of semantically relevant dimensions, so that similarities among these concepts could be identified with adjacencies in the state space. (The President of the US is close to Cleopatra on the politician dimension, but maybe less close on the nubile dimension.) This, as opposed to the vicissitudes of Churchland's treatment of qualia, is the issue we are really interested in.

In fact, however, we now propose to argue that this suggestion is without substance. The same problems that traditionally arose for theories of content identity also arise for this theory of content similarity, so the appearance of progress is simply an illusion. To begin with the crucial point: the state space story about content similarity actually presupposes (and therefore begs) a solution to the question of content identity.

Problems of State Space Semantics

The Individuation of Dimensions

What Churchland has on offer is the idea that two concepts are similar insofar as they occupy relatively similar positions in the same state space. The question thus presents itself: when are S1 and S2 the same state space? When, for example, is your semantic space a token of the same semantic space state type as mine? Well, clearly a necessary condition for the identity of state spaces is the identity of their dimensions; specifically, identity of their semantic dimensions, since the current proposal is that concepts be located by reference to a space of semantically relevant properties. We are thus faced with the question when x and y are the same semantic dimensions (for example, when positions along x and y both express degrees of being a politician, or of nubility). But this is surely just the old semantic identity problem back again. If we don't know what it is for two words both to mean nubile, then we also don't know – and for the same reasons – what it is for two spaces both to have a nubility dimension. Perhaps it will be replied that semantic similarity doesn't, after all, require concepts to be adjacent in the very same state space; perhaps occupying corresponding positions in similar state spaces will do. That a regress has now appeared is, we trust, entirely obvious.

It's worth getting clear on what has gone wrong. The old (empiricist) version of network semantics had a story about the identification of the dimensions by reference to which it did its taxonomizing; they were to express observable properties, and an externalist (for example, a causal) theory of some kind was to explicate the relation between observable properties and terms in the observation vocabulary. In particular, that relation was assumed to be specifiable independent of the interpretation of the rest of the vocabulary. However, as we've seen, Churchland's proposal comes down to the idea that the dimensions of semantic state space don't generally correspond to observable properties; they can correspond to whatever properties the brain may represent. This avoids empiricism, all right, but it begs the question how identity of state spaces is itself to be determined. On the one hand, we are assuming that dimensions of semantic state spaces can express whatever properties you like. And, on the other hand, we don't have and can't assume any identity criterion for dimensions that express other than observable properties. And, on the last hand, to take such a criterion for granted would just be to beg the semantic identity problem.

To repeat: We have a robust notion of semantic similarity only if we have a criterion for the identity of state spaces. We have a criterion for the identity of state spaces only if we have a criterion for identity of dimensions of state spaces. And we have a (nonempiricist) criterion for the identity of dimensions of state spaces only if we have a criterion of "property expressed by a dimension of a state space" that works for arbitrary properties, not just for observable properties. But a criterion for "property expressed" that works for arbitrary properties is just a criterion for identity of meaning. So Churchland's proposal for a robust theory of content similarity fails to avoid the problem of robust content identity. (And, of course, fails to solve it.)

In our book *Holism: A Shopper's Guide*, we offer it as a plausible methodological principle that you can't have a robust notion of content similarity (one that applies across languages, across minds, or across theories) unless you have a correspondingly robust notion of content identity. Churchland's space state semantics provides a graphic illustration of how this principle applies. His explication of an interpersonal notion of content similarity as proximity in semantic state space presupposes an interpersonal notion of identity for the semantic spaces themselves, a notion that Churchland leaves entirely without explication. In consequence, if you're worried about how concepts can be robust, Churchland's state space semantics provides no illumination at all.

We're claiming, in effect, that Churchland has confused himself by taking the labels on the semantic dimensions for granted. The label on a dimension says how positions along the dimension are to be interpreted; for example, it says that they're to be interpreted as expressing degrees of F-ness. To label a dimension as the F-ness dimension is thus invite the question "In virtue of what do the values of this dimension express degrees of F-ness rather than, say, degrees of G-ness?" (Equivalently, for these purposes "What makes it the case that a dimension in your state space expresses the same property F as some dimension in mine does?"). Patently, a semantic theory mustn't beg this sort of question on pain of assuming the very concepts it is supposed to explicate.

Cognitive scientists are forever getting themselves into trouble in this way; it's a fallacy that is particularly endemic among connectionists. Connectionists draw diagrams in which the label on a node tells you what the intentional interpretation of the excitation of the node is supposed to be. But no theory is offered to explain why a node gets the label that it does; it's just semantics by stipulation.

Churchland makes exactly this mistake, only it's the dimension labels rather than the node labels that he stipulates. This, however, is actually a distinction without a difference since stipulating a semantic interpretation for the dimensions just is stipulating semantic interpretations for points (regions, and the like) in the space they define. This fact is obscured in the figure because the labels that are provided for points in that semantic space (namely, the color labels "brown," "dark blue," and so on) are not actually the ones implied by the labels on the axes. The labelling of the axes implies that points in the space are ordered triples corresponding to values of short, medium and long wave reflectances. By contrast, the color labels represent not the semantics of the state space but Land's empirical proposal about how the qualitative character of sensations varies as a function of psychophysical properties of light.

This slight tension in Churchland's notation turns out, upon reflection, to be the tip of a substantial iceberg. It's worth a digression to make the issues clear. Consider the following question: How does Churchland decide what gets represented by dimensions of state spaces and what gets represented by regions in the state spaces that the dimensions define? What decides, for example, that "brown" and "dark blue" correspond to regions rather than dimensions? There is, after all, nothing obviously wrong with taxonomizing bananas according to their degree of brownness or oceans according to their degree of dark blueness, and there are presumably lots of cases where one's concept of an X includes information about the color of Xs – blondes for example.

One principled way of making this decision might be to stipulate that the dimensions of state spaces express, always and only, psychophysical (or possibly neurological) parameters; indeed, this may well be what Churchland has in mind. If so, however, what he is offering isn't a semantics at all. For, a semantics taxonomizes mental states by their contents, not by their causes. Churchland may be assuming that if a stimulus has such and such psychophysical properties, then if the brain responds to the stimulus, the brain thereby represents the stimulus as having those psychophysical properties. But the brain represents red things as red, not as reflecting light of such and such wave length; and it represents aunts as aunts, not as possessing whatever psychophysical properties we employ for purposes of aunt-detection (assuming, indeed, that there are such properties). Psychophysics would be a lot easier were this not so; we could do it by introspection.

Churchland's state spaces thus vacillate between being psychophysical spaces and being semantic spaces. Correspondingly – and this point really is essential – proximity in state space means quite different things in the two interpretations of Churchland's theory. According to the semantic reading, proximity expresses the similarity of the content of mental states; according to the psychophysical reading, it expresses the similarity, under physical description, of the (proximal) stimuli that elicit the sensations. Apparently Churchland hasn't decided which sort of similarity he has in mind, so that there's a crucial respect in which he hasn't decided what his space state theory is a theory of.

That Churchland really has confused the semantical with the psycho-physical enterprise is suggested by revealing hesitations like his sugges-tion that state spaces offer ". . . *an alternative to, or potential reduction of*, the familiar Chomskian picture (1989a, 109)" (our emphasis). One or the other, perhaps, but surely not both. An alternative to the Chomskian picture would be a new story about what a native speaker knows about his language; that is, a new story about the intentional content of the native speaker's knowledge of his language. *Qua* "alternative" it would, by definition, be in competition with Chomsky's picture. A reduction, by contrast, would presumably be a story about the neural format in which what the native speaker knows about his language is coded in his brain. By definition, a reduction is not in competition with the theory that it reduces. The semantic theory and the deductive theory are in quite different lines of work, and nothing can do both jobs.

The Analytic/Synthetic Distinction

As you might expect, all the other standard worries about content identity now come trooping back in. Consider the a/s question itself. It's analytic (let's say) that dogs are animals; it's not analytic (let's say) that they typically have wet noses. Consequently, to change to Churchland's notation, the space in which the concept dog is resident must have a dimension corresponding to the property of being an animal, but it needn't have a dimension corresponding to the property of typically having a wet nose. (In fact, it had better not have such a dimension if the location of an item in the space is to predict its behavior in modal inferences.) This is to say that it is constitutive of the concept dog that it subsumes only animals, but not constitutive of the concept dog that it subsumes only things whose noses are typically wet. Problem: If you are convinced that there is no principled way of drawing an a/s distinction, what principle will you appeal to to distinguish the dimensions that are relevant to defining semantic spaces from the dimensions that aren't? You can have the problem of individuating meanings as the a/s problem or as the problem of saying what makes something a bona fide dimension of semantic state space (as per Churchland). The point is that it's the same problem whichever way you choose to have it; in particular, it doesn't go away when you start to think of semantic relations among concepts as "metric."

A way out that Churchland would surely find congenial would be to take concepts as stereotypes; on that account the distinction between empirical and constitutive inference is statistical rather than semantic since the distinction between stereotypical properties and others is itself statistical. (The stereotypical properties for F-ness are, roughly, the ones that people are most prepared to infer F's have.) The stereotype account of concepts has, notoriously, problems of its own; but we don't propose to press them here. Suffice it to say that assuming that concepts are stereotypes, whatever other virtues it may have, does not help avoid the problem of how the dimensions of state spaces are individuated. This is because a robust notion of similarity of stereotypes presupposes a robust notion of identity for the stereotypical features. To say that the prototypical dog has a wet nose is to take the identity of the property of having a wet nose for granted.

If this problem doesn't worry stereotype theorists nearly as much as it should, that is because most of them, deep down, suppose that the stereotypical features are sensory/psychophysical. They thereby tacitly endorse the empiricism we have seen Churchland struggle unsuccessfully to avoid.

Collateral Information

If it is to turn out that your concept dog occupies much the same region of your semantic space that my concept dog occupies in mine, then it had better be that your semantic space has whatever dimensions mine has; as we've seen, this raises the question of how the dimensions of semantic state space are to be identified/individuated, which would seem to be the content identity problem all over again. Well, suppose the problem of individuating dimensions is somehow solved; it's still not guaranteed that your dog concept and my dog concept will turn out similar. The problem is that I know a lot of things about dogs that you don't. (And, of course, vice versa.) For example, I know that I once had a dog named Spot, and that my grandmother is allergic to dalmatians, and that there aren't any dogs in the room in which I'm writing this. But you wouldn't have known any of those things about dogs if I hadn't just told them to you. Nor is there any particular reason why the various beliefs about dogs that we fail to share must in general be token reflexive. If you're a dog buff, and I'm not, you have very many standing beliefs about dogs that I don't have and don't have any desire to acquire.

The point is that if a semantics recognizes dimensions of state space corresponding to all the properties of dogs about which our beliefs differ, then even assuming that your state space has exactly the same dimensions as mine, the location of the dog concepts in our respective spaces is likely to turn out to be quite significantly different. This should all be sounding like old news; it's just the worry, familiar from attempts to construct a notion of content identity, that a lot of what anybody knows about dogs counts as idiosyncratic; it's "collateral information," the sort of thing that Frege says belongs to psychology rather than semantics. If we are to have a notion of meanings as shared and public property, a robust notion of meaning, we must somehow abstract from this idiosyncratic variation. This holds just as much for similarity of meaning as it does for identity of meaning. Or, if it doesn't, an argument is needed to show why it doesn't. We're not aware that there's any such argument around.

If, in short, all dimensions (all the properties in respect of which the contents of concepts can be classified) count in determining positions in state space, then even if everybody's state space has exactly the same dimensions as everybody else's, the collateral information problem makes it quite unlikely that anybody's concepts will turn out similar to anyone else's. One way out would be to assume that the dimensions of state space are weighted; that agreement along some dimensions counts more for conceptual similarity than agreement along other dimensions does. In traditional theories of content identity, this weighting of dimensions was accomplished precisely by appealing to the a/s distinction: it matters that your concepts have the same values as mine on dimensions that correspond to properties that figure in the analysis of the concepts; with respect to the other dimensions, the concepts are allowed to vary idiosyncratically. Once again, nothing changes when the topic changes to content similarity. Our concepts are similar if they have similar locations along certain dimensions, whether or not they have similar locations along other dimensions. The collateral information problem is to find a principled way of deciding which dimensions count a lot, which ones count a little, and which ones don't count at all. And nobody has the slightest idea of how to do this without invoking an a/s distinction.

We hope the moral will now be clear. What Churchland's got is a dilemma: it may be that he doesn't require that the dimensions of his state space correspond to properties of the contents of the mental states (objects, events) that they taxonomize. In that case, he isn't doing semantics at all. He's doing, as it might be, psychophysics, and we have no quarrel with anything he says except that he is not really entitled to describe what he has on offer as a theory about how "the brain *represents* various aspects of reality by a position in a suitable state space" (our emphasis). If, on the other hand, Churchland is taking the talk about neural representation seriously, his move to state spaces

158   JERRY FODOR AND ERNIE LEPORE

leaves all the old problems about content identity still to be solved. We think that probably, given these options, Churchland would prefer the first. He is, as we remarked above, very much inclined to be an eliminativist about intentional/semantic properties when metaphysical push comes to shove. An eliminativist doesn't, however, need a notion of semantic similarity any more than he needs a notion of semantic identity. An eliminativist doesn't want to reconstruct semantical discourse; he wants to change the topic.

But couldn't Churchland somehow contrive to have it both ways; couldn't he somehow work it out that state spaces do semantics and psychophysics at the same time? Sure he could. What he has to do is just assume the "empiricist principle" that all our concepts are functions (possibly Boolean functions, but more likely statistical functions) of our psychophysical concepts. As far as we can tell, this is what connectionists, Churchland included, actually do assume (though, understandably, they aren't eager to put it that way).

Here, for example, is Churchland doing his level best to make a virtue of this necessity. Anyone who wants to understand what epistemological assumptions underlie the connectionist version of state space semantics should pay especially close attention to the passage that starts "it may be that ..."

> ... the activation-vector spaces that a matured brain has generated, and the prototypes they embody, can encompass far more than the simple sensory types such as phonemes, colors, smells, tastes, faces, and so forth. Given high-dimensional spaces, which the brain has in abundance, those spaces and the prototypes they embody can encompass categories of great complexity, generality, and abstraction ... such as harmonic oscillator, projectile, traveling wave, Samba, twelve-bar blues, democratic election, six-course dinner [etc.] ... It may be that the input dimensions that feed into such abstract spaces will themselves often [sic] have to be the expression of some earlier level of processing, but that is no problem. The networks under discussion are hierarchically arranged to do precisely this as a matter of course. In principle, then, it is no harder for such a system to represent types of processes, procedures, and techniques than to represent the "simple" sensory qualities. From the point of view of the brain, these are just more high-dimensional vectors (1989a, 191).

Take home exercise: What is there in this understanding of the relation between "abstract" and sensory concepts that Hume would not have endorsed?

The reason that assuming the empiricist principle is helpful in this context is that it provides a robust identity criterion for semantic spaces: If all concepts are ultimately sensory concepts, then every concept is a

location in a semantic space whose dimensions express sensory properties. So two organisms share a semantic space if they have their sensory
transducers in common. The reason why assuming the empiricist
principle is nevertheless to be avoided, however, is that it isn't true.
Most concepts are not Boolean or statistical functions of psychophysical
or sensory concepts, and most concept learning is not either Boolean or
statistical inference. *A fortiori*, one's concepts and theories are not to be
identified with points in a space whose dimensions express sensory or
psychophysical properties or constructs thereof. You might have
thought this was the one thing philosophers would have learned from
200 years or so of epistemological bad weather. But, no: the smoke
clears and the landscape is revealed as having hardly changed at all.

That Churchland's account of content similarity is question begging
doesn't, of course, constitute a proof that a robust notion of content
similarity can't compensate holistic semantics for its lack of a robust
notion of content identity. Somebody might come up with a robust
notion of content similarity that's not question begging by early
tomorrow afternoon (though one would, perhaps, be well advised not to
hold one's breath). But what's not a proof may nevertheless serve as an
object lesson. The current situation is that nobody has any idea what
content similarity is, just as nobody has any idea what content identity is
– and, as we remarked at the outset, for much the same reasons.

References

Churchland, P. M. (1979), *Scientific Realism and the Plasticity of Mind*, Cam-
bridge University Press: Cambridge.
Churchland, P. M. (1989a), *A Neurocomputational Perspective: The Nature of
Mind and the Structure of Science*, MIT Press: Cambridge, Mass.
Churchland, P. M. (1989b), "Some reductive strategies in cognitive neurobiol-
ogy," in *A Neurocomputational Perspective*, pp. 77–110.
Churchland, P. M. (1989c), "Perceptual plasticity and theoretical neutrality: a
reply to Jerry Fodor," in *A Neurocomputational Perspective*, pp. 255–80.
Fodor, J. and Lepore, E. (1992), *Holism: A Shopper's Guide*, Blackwell: Oxford.

The following was written in response to chapter 16.

Reply to Churchland

Churchland has much hope for semantic holism; connectionism, he says,
is its natural home. We do not share his optimism. The connectionist

theory of concepts, at least as Churchland presents it, adds nothing interesting to familiar empiricist accounts. Indeed, Churchland's connectionism appears to be bent on recapitulating the history of empiricism, only at the frenetic pace of a Mack Sennett two-reeler. Consider:

Naive empiricism was the idea that concepts are typically complexes built out of sensory primitives; in effect, concepts are stored sensory images. Similarly, Stage One Churchland – the Churchland whose papers we discussed in *Holism* (1992) – identified concepts with locations in a state space whose dimensions correspond to sensory parameters. Nothing distinguishes these views except their terminology: where naive empiricists speak of *sensory* properties of objects (that is, the properties of objects to which sense organs are responsive), the Stage One Churchland connectionist speaks of *transducible* properties of objects (that is, properties to which transducers are responsive).

There is a notorious (Berkeleyan) objection to naive empiricism, and, unsurprisingly, it holds against Stage One Churchland connectionism too: Most concepts aren't constructions out of sensory concepts. Justice and happiness, for example, can't be imaged, because, to put it crudely, what the just share *qua* just and the happy share *qua* happy can't be specified by reference to their sensory (= transducer detectable) properties. You can image a triangle, of course; but you can't have an image of triangularity as such; what triangles have in common *qua* triangles also isn't something that can be expressed in sensory terms. So far, there is nothing in Stage One Churchland except what Locke proposed and Berkeley refuted. Or so we claim.

Churchland, however, thinks the analogy between naive empiricism and Stage One Churchland connectionism is overplayed: Whereas empiricists thought of complex concepts as *constructed* out of sensory primitives, connectionists think of complex concepts as "filtered" out of the background of correlated properties. This is, however, a distinction without a difference. Suppose *glub* is the concept of something round and red. Then you can think of learning the concept as constructing *glub* from instances of the concepts of redness and roundness; or you can think of learning *glub* as filtering red-roundness out of a background of irrelevant concomitant stimulation. Suppose you sort a pile of rocks into the red ones and the brown ones. You can think of the process as selecting the red ones, or you can think of the process as filtering out the brown ones. To prefer one way of speaking over another is to prefer your cup half empty to your cup half full.

There is, to be sure (and as we remarked in *Holism*), one difference between the sort of concept learning that networks do and the sort of concept learning that naive empiricists contemplated: Whereas naive empiricists supposed concepts to be something like *Boolean* functions of sensory primitives, connectionists think of concepts as something like *statistical* functions of sensory primitives. Churchland finds this "marvellous," "almost magic." In fact, as far as anybody knows, what networks do (analogically) is much the same sort of thing that familiar statistical feature extraction procedures do (digitally). Networks are about as magical as factor analysis, and a lot slower.

As we pointed out in *Holism*, Stage One Churchland has a dilemma. If the dimensions of semantic state space are stipulated to be sensory, the connectionist theory of concepts reduces to naive empiricism and is thus born pre-refuted. The alternative is to liberalize the allowable dimensions. The concept *justice* can't be a location in a space of *sensory* dimensions; but, trivially, it could be a location in a space one of whose dimensions is *justice*. Or, to say the same thing without the intimidating talk of spaces and vectors: you can't define "justice" in terms of "red," "triangular," and such; but, of course, you can define it in terms of "justice." The options Churchland has on offer are therefore to do without *justice* or to resign yourself to empiricism. It was, of course, precisely this line of thought that led Hume, in some of his moods, to deny that we have concepts like justice, triangle, cause, etc.

Stage Two Churchland – the Churchland of the present paper – thinks he has a way out: let the dimensions of semantic space continue to be sensory, but suppose that positions in this space define not concepts but *prototypes*. What makes (as it might be) a kitten prototype a concept of kittens isn't its sensory constitution but its "downstream" role in certain inferences. The "prototype vector has rich causal and computational sequelae of its own . . . because of its own transformational significance . . . *downstream*" (p. 276). Thus Hume's solution to Berkeley's problem about abstract ideas: The concept of a triangle can't be an image, but it might be an image that is *appropriately employed in reasoning about triangles*. Having the abstract concept is having an image of some triangle or other, together with rules that tell you what to ignore when you use the image to think about triangles. Sophisticated empiricism thus distinguishes the concept of a triangle from the concept of a prototypical triangle, and identifies the former with the latter together with an inferential regime.

Stage Two Churchland's connectionism is thus Hume's sophisticated empiricism, the very kind of empiricism that Quine's "Two Dogmas" set its face against.

If having the concept triangle is identified with accepting an inferential regime, the crucial question is *which inferences define the regime*? What "transformations," "interactions," etc., does the triangle prototype have to undergo in order for having the prototype to count as having the concept? If you are prepared to answer this question, you thereby accept an analytic/synthetic distinction, and Quine will be displeased with you. If, on the other hand, you decline to answer this question, then, (according to the argument that we set out in *Holism*), you can have no coherent account of the compositionality of thought (/language), and, since compositionality isn't negotiable, *everyone* will be displeased with you.

So, then: Stage Two Churchland, like Stage One Churchland, thinks that concepts are (sensory) prototypes. It is natural that a connectionist should think this, since prototypes are bundles of statistical relations, and "neural" networks are analogue devices for computing statistical inferences; so networks and prototypes are made for one another. However, concepts *can't* be prototypes – sensory or otherwise – because prototypes aren't compositional and concepts are. What the concept *cat* contributes to the thought that the cat is on the mat is the content *cat*, not the content *prototypical cat*. Compare Berkeley: what the concept *triangle* contributes to thoughts about triangles is the content *triangle*, not the content *prototypical triangle*; and triangularity, unlike proto-typical triangularity, can't be imaged.

Faced with this sort of objection, Stage Two Churchland suggests that concepts are prototypes *together with inferential regimes*. But this leaves wide open Quine's question how the inferential regimes are themselves to be individuated. Connectionism makes *no* contribution to answering this question. *A fortiori*, it says nothing about how Paul and Patricia, whose kitten prototypes are associated with *different* inferential regimes, could nevertheless both have the concept *kitten*. We thought that Churchland thought that connectionism was going to answer this question by providing a viable notion of content similarity, thereby relieving holism of its chief embarrassment. Apparently, however, this project has now been quietly dropped.

Connectionism is just empiricism served cold the day after. But the empiricism in connectionism is so thickly disguised by the jargon of neuroscience, vector algebra, and computer high technology that it has become unrecognizable even to the connectionists. (Perhaps one should say that it has become unrecognizable *especially* to the connectionists.) It's like the old joke about the worm: Once upon a time, there was a worm that fell in love and offered his, so to speak, hand in marriage. "Don't be silly," came back the brusque reply, "I'm your other end."

7

Images and Subjectivity: Neurobiological Trials and Tribulations

Antonio R. Damasio and Hanna Damasio

This chapter is not for or against anything the Churchlands have ever said or written but rather about something that we, the Churchlands and their critics, are passionately interested in: consciousness. More specifically, it is about the possibility of investigating a neurobiology of consciousness.

We shall begin by considering the results of some experiments, in both humans and animals. The first is quite close to the Churchlands. Figure 7.1 shows a section taken through a 3-dimensional reconstruction of Pat Churchland's own and very-much-living brain. The image is based on a fine-resolution magnetic resonance scan, manipulated by Brainvox, a collection of computational techniques that allow the fine neuroanatomical analysis of the brain (H. Damasio and Frank, 1992). The stippled area marks the part of that section which contains Pat's "early" visual cortices. (The early visual cortices are a set of heavily interlocked cortical regions whose cellular architecture and connectivity are distinctive; one cortex within the set, the primary visual cortex, also known as V_1 or area 17, is the main recipient of visual input from the lateral geniculate nucleus.) The white circle marked within the early visual cortices signifies a peak of neural activation detected during a positron emission tomography (PET) experiment.

The activation peak shown on Pat's visual cortex was obtained as follows: In the course of an experiment aimed at understanding how the brain processes stimuli with emotional value, Pat and four other normal persons (not all philosophers, we might add, but all smart, normal people) were asked to visualize, in as much detail as they could muster, a series of familiar places and faces while their eyes were not only closed but covered. That is, they were asked to form mental images when neither their visually-related subcortical structures, such as the lateral geniculate nucleus or the superior colliculus, nor their primary visual cortices could receive any stimuli from the exterior. We will omit the details of the other experimental specifications and of the long and laborious process of data analysis that finally yielded the image you have in the figure (see H. Damasio et al., 1993a; H. Damasio et al., 1993b). We will simply say that the activation peak in the picture is an average for the activation peaks of the five experimental subjects, Pat included, plotted onto Pat's brain.

This striking image is an appropriate excuse for us to ask the following question: What is the neurophysiological meaning of this focal activation, within a specific set of brain structures, during the experience of a

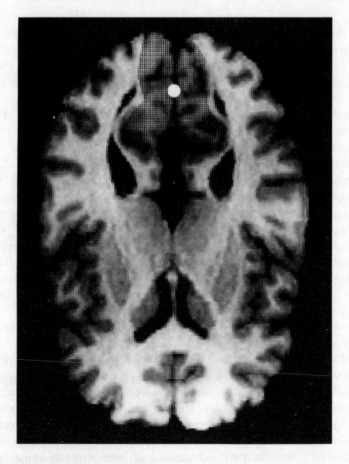

Figure 7.1   Pat Churchland's brain

particular set of images? Does the figure, along with the voluminous numerical data on the basis of which it was generated, mean that the images in the subjects' minds were being generated at this particular brain site? And if the answer is affirmative, were the subjects' "experiences of seeing" also generated at the same site? Or might neither be the case? Might it be that mental images as such cannot be correlated with any specific set of structures and that the experience of an image is even less correlatable with neural structures?

To make a long answer short we will say this. First, we *suspect* that a considerable part of the process of generating visual images was in fact taking place in the early visual cortices, in and about the area where the activity peaks were found. More about this later. Second, we *know* that the experience of those images did not depend on those early visual cortices *only*. With this short answer we encapsulate many of our assumptions, prejudices, hunches, and hypotheses concerning the neurobiology of consciousness. Rightly or wrongly, we believe consciousness can be approached neurobiologically. The effort has already begun, theoretically and practically, in the work of several colleagues. Rightly or wrongly, we believe that neurobiology must deal with two critical issues if it is to make progress in the understanding of consciousness. The first issue is the process whereby our brains create images in our minds. The second issue is the process that makes those images our own, in other words the process that lets images acquire the property of subjectivity. We do not suggest for a moment that the neurobiological solutions to both problems, were they to come, would explain comprehensively the neural basis of consciousness, but they would help elucidate the basis for two of its indispensable aspects. We do not think it is reasonable to discuss consciousness without invoking images *and* subjectivity (although we can conceive of images being formed in a brain that is pathologically deprived of subjectivity and thus deprived of consciousness).

Making Images

As we talk about images, some qualifications are important. First, when we use the term "images" we do not refer to visual images only but rather to images based on any sensory modality, e.g., sound images and images of movement in space.

Second, images convey both nonverbal and verbal entities. Word-forms or sign denotations, in auditory or visual modes, are images.

Third, there are images to describe both the world external to an organism as well as the world within the organism – that is, images of visceral states, images of musculoskeletal structure, body movement, and so forth.

Fourth, images may or may not be attended. When they are not attended we may still discover indirectly that they were formed and displayed (as happens in a priming experiment or when we turn attention to an unattended image and it suddenly is "on," from one moment to the next).

Fifth, images may or may not be held in working memory. When they are, they can be displayed for long periods – many seconds or minutes; this really means that the pattern of neural activity that constitutes them is being reiterated.

Sixth, images are usually not a luxury. In general, they help us optimize our responses. They probably evolved and endured because they allowed organisms to perfect movements and plan even more perfect movements. Humans use images for numerous purposes, from motor behavior to the long-term planning of actions and ideas.

Finally, as was probably made clear by our choice of illustration above, when we talk about images we refer both to images generated in perception and to images generated from memory, during recall.

Let us return to the experiment and discuss the comments we made on its interpretation. Why is it that we believe that a substantial part of image making depends on early cortices, such as those of vision, in the case of the experiment? The reasons are manifold. We cannot discuss all of them, but the main ones are as follows. We know that the partial destruction of early visual cortices precludes both the perception and the recall of certain aspects of vision. After damage in cortical areas V_2 and V_4, for instance, color is neither perceivable nor recallable. The patients so affected have no experience of color, looking *out* or thinking *in*. No consciousness of color is possible even if other aspects of vision can be appreciated and even if you are aware of the absence of the color experience. The fact that perception and recall are compromised by damage at the same site and that no other site of damage encountered so far produces such a defect is one among several findings to suggest that early sensory cortices are the critical base for processes of image making in the brain. Other relevant findings we must mention include the fact that damage to higher-order association cortices, which are located outside the early sensory region, does not preclude the making of images (see Damasio and Damasio, 1993; 1994).

Based on lesion studies in humans, neurophysiological studies in nonhuman primates, and reflection on the patterns of neuroanatomical connectivity currently known, we have hypothesized that the early sensory cortices of each modality construct, with the help of structures such as the thalamus and the colliculi, neural representations that are the basis for images. As far as the cortex is concerned, the process seems to require the concerted activity of several early cortical regions that are massively interconnected among themselves. The precise mechanisms behind this process are not known, but several current proposals suggest the problem is treatable (see Churchland, Sejnowski, and Ramachandran, 1994; Crick, 1994; Tononi, Sporns, and Edelman, 1992; Zeki, 1993). Whatever the mechanisms are, the temporally-coordinated activity of those varied early cortices and of the subcortical stations they are interconnected with yields a particular type of representation we call an "image." An important characteristic of such image representations is that they have spatially and temporally organized patterns. In the case of visual, somatosensory, and auditory images, those patterns are topographically organized (according, we believe, to a space grounded on body structure and body movement). The correspondence between the structure of the neural activity pattern in early sensory cortices and the structure of the stimulus that evoked the pattern can be quite striking, as shown by Roger Tootell and his colleagues (1988).

Topographic representations can be committed to memory in the form of dispositional representations and can be stored in dormant form, in cortical regions or subcortical nuclei. Their subsequent reactivation followed by signaling from their storage sites back to early sensory cortices can regenerate topographically-organized representations (the process uses the rich connectional patterns of feedforward and feedback that characterize the architecture of cortical regions and subcortical nuclei). In short, nontopographically organized representations (which we generally refer to as dispositional representations) can trigger topographically-organized ones; they can also trigger movements or other dispositional representations. Topographic representations arise as a result of signals external to the brain, in the perceptual process; or they arise, in the process of recall, in signals inside the brain, coming from memory records held in dispositional representation form.

Given the fact that most of our experiences are based on images of several sensory modalities occurring within the same window of time, and that the early sensory cortices for each sensory modality are not contiguous or directly interconnected, it follows that our polymodal experiences must result from concurrent activity in several separate brain regions rather than in a single one. The making of images is a spatially parcellated process. But since our experiences are "integrated" rather than parcellated – at least that is how they appear to our mind – we should consider how the integration occurs. Our idea is that timing – that is, a fair amount of synchronization of separate activities – is probably an essential condition for integration. However, synchronization does not happen by magic. We suspect that the neural mechanism behind it is based on signaling from both cortical and subcortical neuron ensembles, capable of simultaneous firing towards *many* separate neuron populations. Such ensembles are a neuroanatomical reality, and we have chosen to call them convergence zones (Damasio, 1989 a,b). They are the receivers of convergent signals and the originators of divergent signals toward the sites in which convergent signals originate. Convergence zones are located throughout the association cortices and subcortical nuclei, including the thalamus, a structure we believe to be critical both for making images and for generating the process of subjectivity, and they contain a storehouse of knowledge in the form of dispositional representations, ready to be activated. Knowledge and timing properties help convergence zones play a critical role in the coherent integration of perceptual images. Naturally, they play an indispensable role in generating images in recall and in making perceived and recalled images cohere.

Subjectivity

We turn now to the issue of subjectivity, one of the basic properties of consciousness. Inevitably we must also take on the issue of self. Without subjectivity we do not know what consciousness means, nor, for that matter, do we know what awareness is. But if our brain/mind is capable of generating states of subjectivity, it is not unreasonable to presume that a crucial agent in the process is something we may call "self," whatever the neurobiological nature of self may turn out to be. We know that the word "self" is ambiguous, even treacherous, but perhaps the word will be less of a problem if we can define what it means for *us*.

Jerome Kagan has keenly described the self as "the universal emergence in the second year of an awareness that one can have an effect upon people and objects, together with a consciousness of one's feelings and competences" (Kagan, 1989). What we have in mind when we talk about self and what we would like to understand in neurobiological terms is *the antecedent and foundation* for the process Kagan describes. It is the neural structure and neurobiological states that help engender the consistent perspective automatically conferred upon images as the brain processes them; it is what allows us to know unequivocally, without the help of inferences based on language, that the images we perceive are our own rather than somebody else's. This is our general idea of self – the core structures and operations necessary but not sufficient for subjectivity to emerge – and it does not include concepts such as "self-esteem" and "social self," although we see it as likely that the processes to which those terms refer develop from the same core.

Postulating that there is a cognitive sense of self and neurobiological structures and operations that support such a sense does not mean, we believe, that all images and image manipulations that take place in a brain are controlled by a single and central "knower" and "master," and even less that such a knower/master would be in a single brain place sitting in judgment as the audience in a Cartesian theater. Our view is thus compatible with the criticisms leveled at single-brain-region views of self or consciousness (Damasio, 1989 a,b; Dennett, 1991; Churchland and Sejnowski, 1992; P. M. Churchland, 1984; P. S. Churchland, 1986). We simply mean that many of the images that constitute our mind are perceived from a *consistent perspective*, which we identify as that of our individual persons, and that experiences have a *consistent point of view*, which is only diminished or suspended in pathological brain states (which include extreme forms of anosognosia, some types of seizure, multiple personality disorder, and schizophrenia).

Our idea of self does not require the pronouns "I" or "me" as anchors. Many nonlinguistic creatures must have a self, in the sense described above, or something like it. Most of the animals commonly used in neurobiological experimentation do, in our view. No single experiment of which we are aware can contradict this statement, although several experiments suggest, predictably, that the complexity of the self is maximal in higher primates and leaps to the highest level in humans. Needless to say, language does enrich the human self even if it does not serve as its base. In fact, it is hard to imagine how language-making devices would have been selected and would have evolved if animals had not possessed prelinguistic "selves."

The appropriately-maligned solution to the problem of the self, that is, the solution to the problem of ownership and inspection of images, is the *homunculus*. It consists of postulating a spatially-defined creature to whom images are referred within the brain and assuming that the creature is equipped with the knowledge necessary to interpret the images. The solution would have been fine were it not for the problem that the thinking homunculus would need to have its own brain and its own knowledge so that, in turn, its images could be interpreted. This "spatial homunculus" solution is no solution at all, since it simply removes us from the problem by one step, whereupon the problem starts again *ad infinitum*. In recent years, recognition of the homunculus pitfall has given way to homunculus phobia, presumably an adaptive mental condition. But because the self has traditionally been conceptualized in homuncular terms, the attempt to avoid homuncular thinking has entailed a denial of anything that sounds like the self and, by extension, subjectivity. This is simply not reasonable. Rejecting the idea of a homunculus in our brains does not alter the fact that most images in our minds are processed from a consistent perspective. To evade the problem by saying that our brains just form images and that we are aware of those images is not a satisfactory solution. The nature of the neural entity that is aware of those images remains unclear.

The task at hand then is to propose a plausible and preferably testable hypothesis for a neural structure of the self-related processes, such that the problems of the spatial homunculus may be avoided. The solution we propose includes the following features and components.

We conceptualize the self as a collection of images about the most invariant aspects of our organism and its interactions – certain aspects of body structure; certain aspects of body operation, including the repertoire of motions possible with the whole body and its varied parts; and identity-defining traits (kinships to certain persons, activities, places; typical motor and sensory patterns of response). These images have a high probability of being evoked repeatedly and continuously by direct signaling (as happens in body states) or by signals arising from stored dispositional representations (as happens with records concerning identity and typical response patterns).

In our framework, the cognitive/neural self is the cognitive/neural instantiation of a *concept*, no different in its essence from the concept of a particular object whose representation relies on the segregated mapping of its properties (such as shape, size, color, texture, characteristic motion, etc.) in varied neural systems from which they can be conjointly retrieved, momentarily, as the concept is activated. But if the essence of the concept of self and of, say, orange, need not be different in basic cognitive and neural specifications, they are different in one important respect. Objects come and go from the vicinity of the organism, and thus they come and go from the sensory sheaths that can signal their presence. Yet the body, its parts, and some of its operations, as well as the stable aspects of our autobiography, remain with us, the former signaling incessantly to the brain, the latter indelibly represented and ready to be reinstantiated.

We propose that the core components of the concept of self concern the body structure (the viscera and musculoskeletal frame) and fundamentals of one's identity (one's usual activities, preferences, physical and human relationships, etc.). These core components change substantially during childhood and adolescence and then change far less, and far more gradually, throughout the remaining life span. The anchor lies with visceral states, which change almost not at all, and with the neural mechanisms that represent and regulate basic biological processes, whose modifiability is minimal. The former are continuously signaled to the complex of somatosensory cortices in the insula, parietal operculum, and post-rolandic parietal cortices (the signaling is bilateral but there is a right hemisphere dominance effect in humans). The biological regulating machinery is represented in the brain core (hypothalamus and brain stem).

Skeptics may counter that we are usually unaware of our body states and that body signaling is thus an odd choice to anchor subjectivity. As argued elsewhere, however, the objection is weak (A. Damasio, 1994). Firstly, although our attention is more often than not centered in nonbodily signals, its focus may shift rapidly, especially in conditions such as pain or emotional upheaval. Secondly, the argument we are making is especially concerned with the historical development of the sense of self, in evolutionary and individual development terms, rather than with the situation of an adult. Thirdly, since we all agree that the mechanisms behind the emergence of subjectivity are hidden, there is no reason why the body states we propose as their scaffolding should be easily revealed in consciousness. The important issue to decide is whether the mechanisms we propose are a plausible base, not whether we are or should be aware of them.

As images corresponding to a newly perceived entity (e.g., a face) are formed in early sensory cortices, *the brain reacts to those images*. In our framework this happens

1 because signals arising in those images (rather than the images themselves) are relayed to several subcortical nuclei (for instance the amygdala and the thalamus) and multiple cortical regions (in temporal, parietal, and frontal sectors);
2 because those nuclei and cortical regions contain dispositions for response to certain classes of signal.

The end result is that dispositional representations in nuclei and cortical regions are activated and, as a consequence, induce some collection of changes in the state of the organism. In turn, those changes alter the body image momentarily, and thus perturb the *current* instantiation of the concept of self. In other words, the multifarious process of recognizing an object generates sets of responses – autonomic, hormonal, motor, imagetic – and those responses change the state of the organism for a certain time interval. We suspect that the essence of the neural mechanisms of consciousness may well reside with the perturbation of self images by newly occurring images.

Although the responding process we outline above implies knowledge (there is indeed abundant knowledge recorded in innate as well as experience-driven dispositional representations throughout the brain), it certainly does not imply, *per se*, that any brain component "knows" that responses are being generated to the presence of an entity. In other words, when an organism's brain generates a set of responses to an entity, the existence of a representation of self does not make that self *know* that its corresponding organism is responding. The self as described above cannot *know*. And here we arrive at the critical question in this discussion. How can the current image of an entity, on the one hand, and a set of images of the organism's state, on the other, both of which exist as momentary activations of topographically-organized representations, generate subjectivity? Our current answer to this question is in the form of a hypothesis. It consists of

1 having the brain create some kind of *description of the perturbation of the state of the organism* that resulted from the brain's responses to the presence of an image;
2 having the description *generate an image of the process of perturbation*;
3 displaying the image of the *self perturbed* together or in rapid interpolation with the image that triggered the perturbation.

Does the brain have the structures required for this proposed mechanism to operate? Indeed it does. Firstly, the brain possesses neural structures that support the image of an object and neural structures that support the images of the self, but it also has neural structures that support neither yet are reciprocally interconnected with both. In other words, the brain has available the kind of third-party neuron ensemble, which we have called a convergence zone, and which we have invoked as the neural substrate for building dispositional representations all over the brain, in cortical regions as well as in subcortical nuclei.

Secondly, such a third-party ensemble receives signals from both the representation of an object and the representations of the self, *as the latter are perturbed by the reaction to the object.* In other words, the third-party ensemble can build a *dispositional representation of the self in the process of changing, while the organism responds to an object.* This dispositional representation would be of precisely the same kind as the one the brain continuously holds, makes, and remodels. The information necessary to build such a dispositional representation is readily available (shortly after we see an object and hold a representation of it in early visual cortices, we also hold many representations of the organism reacting to the object in varied somatosensory regions).

As is the case with all dispositions, the dispositional construction we envision has the potential, once formed, to reactivate an image in any early sensory cortex to which it is connected. The basic image in the description would be that of the organism's body in the process of responding to a particular object, i.e., a somatosensory image.

We propose that all the ingredients described above – an object that is being represented, an organism responding to the object of representation, and a description of the organism in the process of changing in response to the object – are held simultaneously in working memory and are placed, side by side or in rapid interpolation, in early sensory cortices. Subjectivity would emerge during this latter step, when the brain is simultaneously producing not just images of an entity, of self, and of the organism's responses, but also another kind of image: *that of an organism in the act of perceiving and responding to an entity*. The latter kind of image (one might call it the metaself) would be the source of subjectivity incarnate (see A. Damasio, 1994, for details).

The description we have in mind is neither created nor perceived by a homunculus, and it does not require language. The third-party disposition provides a schematic view of the main protagonists from a perspective external to both, a nonverbal narrative document of what is happening to those protagonists, accomplished with the elementary representational tools of the sensory and motor systems.

We cannot think of any reason why the brains of birds and mammals would not be able to make such narratives. In effect, subjectivity would emerge in any brain equipped with some representation of self, with the capacity to form images and respond to them, and with the capacity to generate some kind of dispositional description in a third-party neuron ensemble.

The second-order narrative capacities provided by language would allow humans to engender verbal narratives out of nonverbal ones, and the refined form of subjectivity that is ours would emerge from this process. The virtual serial machine mechanism proposed by Dennett would operate at that high level rather than at the basic level we postulate here. It would not be the source of subjectivity, although it might contribute to important aspects of thinking and reasoning. In short, as we have noted elsewhere, language would not be the source of the self but it certainly would be the source of the "I."

Would a machine equipped with image-making devices, the ability to represent its physical structure and physical states imagetically, and dispositional knowledge about its past be capable of generating subjectivity if it were to construct images of itself perturbed, as described above? Probably it would not, unless the machine's body were a living body, with properties derived from its precarious homeostatic balance, from its need for survival, and from its inherent sense that what promotes survival is valuable. In the end, the neural device we propose for generating subjectivity serves to connect images with the process of life, and that may well be what consciousness is most about.

References

Churchland, P. M. (1984). *Matter and Consciousness*. MIT Press. Cambridge.

Churchland, P. S. (1986). *Neurophilosophy: Toward a Unified Science of the Mind-Brain*. MIT Press: Cambridge.

Churchland, P. S. and Sejnowski, T. J. (1992). *The Computational Brain: Models and Methods on the Frontiers of Computational Neuroscience*. MIT Press: Cambridge.

Churchland, P. S., Sejnowski, T. J., and Ramachandran, V. S. (1994). The critique of pure vision. In *Large-Scale Neuronal Theories of the Brain*, C. Koch (ed.). MIT Press: Cambridge.

Crick, F. (1994). *The Astonishing Hypothesis: The Scientific Search for the Soul*. Charles Scribners: New York.

Damasio, A. R. (1989a). Time-locked multiregional retroactivation: a systems level proposal for the neural substrates of recall and recognition. *Cognition*, **33**: 25–62.

Damasio, A. R. (1989b). The brain binds entities and events by multiregional activation from convergence zones. *Neural Computation*, **1**: 123–32.

Damasio, A. R. (1994). *Descartes' Error: Emotion and Reason in the Human Brain*. Putnam: New York.

Damasio, A. R. and Damasio, H. (1993). Cortical systems underlying knowledge retrieval: evidence from human lesion studies. In *Exploring Brain Functions: Models in Neuroscience*, P. Poggio and D. Glaser (eds). 233–48. Wiley: New York.

Damasio, A. R. and Damasio, H. (1994). Cortical systems for retrieval of concrete knowledge: the convergence zone framework. In *Large-Scale Neuronal Theories of the Brain*. C. Koch (ed.). MIT Press: Cambridge.

Damasio, H. and Frank, R. (1992). Three-dimensional *in vivo* mapping of brain lesions in humans. *Archives of Neurology*, **49**: 137–43.

Damasio, H., Grabowski, T. J., Damasio, A. R., Tranel, D., Boles-Ponto, L. L., Watkins, G. L., and Hichwa, R. D. (1993a). Visual recall with eyes closed and covered activates early visual cortices. *Society for Neuroscience*, **19**: 1604.

Damasio, H., Grabowski, T. J., Frank, R. J., Knosp, B., Hichwa, R. D., Watkins, G. L., and Boles-Ponto, L. L. (1993b). PET-Brainvox, a technique for neuroanatomical analysis of positron emission tomography images. *Quantification of Brain Function: Tracer Kinetics and Image Analysis in Brain PET. Proceedings of PET '93 Akita*, K. Uemura (ed.). 465–73. Elsevier: Amsterdam.

Dennett, D. C. (1991). *Consciousness Explained*. Little, Brown: Boston.

Kagan, J. (1989). *Unstable Ideas: Temperament, Cognition, and Self*. Harvard University Press: Cambridge.

Tononi, G., Sporns, O., and Edelman, G. (1992). Reentry and the problem of integrating multiple cortical areas: simulation of dynamic integration in the visual system. *Cerebral Cortex*, **2**: 310–35.

Tootell, R. B. H., Switkes, E., Silverman, M. S., and Hamilton, S. L. (1988). Functional anatomy of macaque striate cortex. II. Retinotopic organization. *The Journal of Neuroscience*, **8**: 1531–68.

Zeki, S. (1993). *A Vision of the Brain*. Blackwell Scientific Publications: Oxford.

8

The Furniture of Mind:
A Yard of Hope, a Ton of Terror?

John C. Marshall and Jennifer M. Gurd

Without a Hyphen Already

*Neuro*philosophy (Churchland, 1986)! A book by a professor of philosophy (at the University of California, San Diego) in which the first 235 pages are devoted to laying out, in considerable detail, what is known about the functional anatomy of the central nervous system; diagrams, even, of the biochemical steps in synaptic transmission and of the distribution of cerebral blood flow in organic dementia! This surely cannot be philosophy. How could such information be of any interest to the disciples of George Moore and Ludwig Wittgenstein? In his autobiography, Moore wrote: "I do not think that the world or the sciences would ever have suggested to me any philosophical problems" (Moore, 1942, 14). Likewise, Wittgenstein: "At bottom I am indifferent to the solution of scientific problems" (Wittgenstein, 1980, 79). One fears for Patricia Churchland's safety. Will not the serried ranks of linguistic philosophers rise up in arms against her, chanting in unison "Category-mistake, category-mistake ..."? Well, in certain benighted corners of the globe (sic) they probably will, but, happily, it was not always so (and will not for ever be so). Lovers of wisdom did not always equate wisdom with ignorance, even in the twentieth century.

During the 1920s, one of the most original and insightful German neurologists used to take his cousin, an equally distinguished philosopher, on ward rounds at the Frankfurt Neurological Institute. The first fruits of this highly productive collaboration appeared in 1929 when Ernst Cassirer published the third volume of his *Philosophie der symbolischen Formen* (*The Philosophy of Symbolic Forms*). As a latter-day Kantian, Cassirer had been concerned with the tangled relationship between the objective world ("out there") and the subjective knowledge that we, as limited biological creatures, can have of that world. In particular, Cassirer took over two of Kant's essential insights: that "sensory" experience is only interpretable within a framework of space and time that is not itself given by experience, and that our thinking about objects perceived in space and time is governed by concepts, such as number, affirmation and negation, substance and attribute, and necessity and contingency, that are again presupposed, rather than provided, by experience. In recognizing explicitly that perception and thought are constrained by constitutional factors not given in sensation, Kant hoped to rescue philosophy from anarchy and scepticism and to place metaphysics on foundations no less secure than those of physics. If there is a "reality" apart from or *behind* whatever the higher centres of our nervous system allow us to conceive, then it is precisely that – unknowable. For the rest, whatever is knowable, one could sum up Kant's position by saying: if you can't beat theoretical biology, you may as well join it. Kant's psychology may have been transcendental (Kitcher, 1990) but it was nowhere near as transcendental as the supposedly "common-sense" psychology of those who today claim to be engaging in "conceptual analysis" (Hyman, 1991). True, there may come a point at which "whereof one cannot speak, thereof one must remain silent", but there is little to gain in stipulating that point from the superficial depths of an armchair (or from the pages of the Oxford English Dictionary).

Cassirer met the world of medical science at the front line. It was there, on ward rounds, that he saw a way of exploring further the structure and functions of the categories postulated by Kant (and, if necessary, modifying these hypotheses in the light of empirical evidence). The way forward was to study how concepts of space, time, form, colour, number, language, causality and purposive action, and their manifold interactions break down when the organ of mind is partially incapacitated by disease or insult. Careful investigation of the overt manifestations of such impairment in the behaviour of patients with acquired brain damage thus came to play an important role in the development of Cassirer's philosophy. As he writes in chapter 6 (Toward a Pathology of the Symbolic Consciousness) of the third volume of his *magnum opus*: "It seems that the true inner connection between the language world on the one hand and the world of perception and intuition on the other can only be apprehended clearly when, because of special conditions, the bond between the two begins to slacken" (Cassirer, 1929/1957). Pure reason, as exercised from the philosopher's study, would no longer suffice to discover the underlying forms of human cognition. Rather,

the observation and exact description of pathological cases proved directly of value to phenomenological analysis. Here, as it were, a natural analytic comes to the help of our intellectual analytic; for in pathological cases the factors that in normal consciousness are given only in close combinations, in a kind of concrescence, begin to separate, so to speak, and their different significations begin to be set off from one another (Cassirer, 1929/1957).

Many of the neurological patients that his cousin, Kurt Goldstein, demonstrated to Cassirer were German ex-servicemen, injured by shrapnel and high-velocity missiles in the First World War. Such are the ironies of history that, when Goldstein came to repay his final intellectual debt to Cassirer, both men were working in America, in exile from the Third Reich. And Goldstein was now deeply involved in the care and rehabilitation of American servicemen, similarly injured in the Second World War. In his *Aftereffects of Brain Injuries in War* (1942) and *Language and Language Disturbances* (1948), Goldstein summed up a lifetime's experience of trying to understand how the organism as a whole (Goldstein, 1939) attempts to adapt to the loss of specific, innate capacities of mind.

Although Patricia Churchland nowhere mentions the work of either Goldstein or Cassirer, we were reminded of their collaboration by her account (1986) of some formative influences upon her own philosophical development: "A number of years ago I began going regularly to neurology rounds at the Health Sciences Centre in Winnipeg, and these Thursday mornings became the focus of extended perplexity and wonder." The first patient she saw on those rounds was a professor emeritus at a medical college, who had sustained a stroke in the deep subcortical regions of the brain's limbic system. Without provocation or any apparent cause, he would frequently cry uncontrollably, his body shaken by sobs. Yet, when questioned during these episodes, he would firmly and persistently deny any feelings of sadness or grief. The total dissociation between behaviour and emotion was as bewildering to the patient himself as it was to the visiting philosopher.

Everyday experience and reasoning tell us that such a dissociation between "feelings of sadness and sadness behaviour" should not exist "unless the subject was attempting to deceive, which this patient plainly was not." Churchland's response to this and subsequent case presentations partly resembles that of Ernst Cassirer:

... each Thursday brought a fresh assault on the commonsense framework within which we standardly comprehend the behavior of normal brains – the framework within which we think about awareness, reasoning, unity of self, connectedness of cognitive capacities, connectedness of concepts and beliefs, and so forth. So long as the brain functions normally, the inadequacies of the commonsense framework can be hidden from view, but with a damaged brain the inadequacies of theory are unmasked. (Churchland, 1986.)

The contemplation of illness, like death, concentrates the mind wonderfully. Her overall reaction, however, has clearly led Churchland to a much more radical rejection of folk psychology (what everyone's grandmother knows about people) than even Cassirer contemplated. More surprisingly (and less cogently), it also seems to have led her into a form of reductionism that Goldstein's "whole organism" approach firmly avoided.

From Form to Function (in One Bound)

To begin with, there's the matter of all those pages about cells and synapses, neurotransmitters and other chemicals in the brain, the layered structure of different cell types in different cortical areas and the mapping of those cells' properties by electrical stimulation and recording. These chapters provide an excellent introduction to molecular neuroscience, but at a level of nitty-gritty detail that Cassirer, and many more recent neuropsychologists (Mehler, Morton and Jusczyk, 1984) would have eschewed. Churchland is convinced that structure provides, if not *the*, at least *a* clue to function. And she has distinguished support for her belief from many eminent neurobiologists, including Francis Crick, whose pithy summary of the position she quotes: "I doubt if we can even guess what Natural Selection has achieved, without some help from the way function has been embodied in actual structures. The reason is simple. Natural selection is more ingenious that we are."

In the long run, Churchland and Crick may well be right – the physical construction of any material object, the brain included, clearly constrains what that object can do. Form and function *are* related, such that form may give clues to possible behaviour. Yet form can be misleading. It is not, after all, many centuries since neurobiologists informed us that the third ventricle of the brain (a cavity containing cerebrospinal fluid) was sacred to memory because it had the structure of a large, capacious warehouse eminently suited to the storage of events past but not forgotten (Marshall and Fryer, 1978). We, of course, do not make mistakes like that, and Churchland herself is a good deal more circumspect in her claims than were the ancients. For example, she provides a lucid and compelling account of the basic structure of the visual, auditory, and somatosensory systems. Receptors in the retina, the cochlea, and the skin may map in a very orderly fashion onto distinct areas of cortical cells in the horizontal dimension, providing thereby internal representations (or "maps") of the spatial positions of visual stimulation, the different frequencies that make up auditory stimulation, and of the parts of the body that are being subjected to touch, pressure, or vibration. In the vertical dimension (at right angles to the surface of the brain) there are linked columns of cells that, in the visual system for example, respond preferentially to stimuli at different orientations (horizontal, vertical, 45 degrees, etc.) in the world "out there". There seem then to be coherent relationships between the sensory surface of the body and cells in the brain that respond to the stimulation of sensory receptors. Churchland sums up our current picture of the brain as follows: ". . .we can think of the cortex as a *stack* of sheets, then as a stack of *sheets with methodical vertical connections*, then as a stack of sheets, *some of which are topographically mapped*, with methodical vertical connections, and finally, as *containing cells with highly specific origins and projections*" (Churchland, 1986).

So far, so good. But now the argument from design suddenly rears its head. Not, of course, the argument from God's design, but rather its modern reincarnation in the guise of neo-Darwinism and natural selection. Churchland concludes her description of the anatomy of the nervous system with a remark that goes well beyond anatomy *per se*: "Seeing so much architectural purpose, one is virtually driven to conclude that the secret of the brain's computational and representational capacities cannot be understood independently of understanding its functional architecture." It is some considerable number of pages later that one fully realizes why this particular vision of purpose seems so compelling to Churchland. She is, it turns out, a real reductionist. The title of her book is to be taken literally – no hyphen between the *neuro* and the *philosophy*; a unified science of the mind/brain is indeed the aim. Even if we do not yet comprehend the "architectural purpose" of the brain's design, a point Churchland willingly concedes ("The functional role of these columns is by no means fully understood", she writes), any, even partial, understanding of the mind will be no more (and no less) than an understanding of the brain.

Alternatives

Such full-blooded reduction to a pre-modern physicalism as Churchland espouses is, we suspect, not too popular, either in the world at large or in the more restricted circles of professional philosophers and neuro-psychologists. For present purposes, we can contrast reductionism with three rival ideologies, dualism, linguistic philosophy, and functionalism, the first two of which can be dismissed fairly speedily. Classical dualism is the belief that body and mind are distinct substances, the one consisting of physical matter, the other of spooky soul-stuff. But in order to be even minimally consistent with empirical evidence, these two domains must communicate with each other. When the soul is embarrassed the body blushes; when the body is injured the soul feels pain. The two most notorious accounts of such interaction between mind and body are due to René Descartes and John Eccles. Descartes proposed that the non-physical mind controls the physical brain via the pineal gland, and Eccles, more recently, transferred the locus of interaction to the supplementary motor cortex. As Churchland points out, both theories consist essentially of little arrows that connect mind and body, but the nature of mind and of the "force" whereby it affects the functioning of nerve cells remains as mysterious as ever.

Dualism has always been self-defeating. It is a straightforward confession of ignorance in the sense that extra-sensory perception, for example, implies either fraud or sensory perception involving the transmission of information in a medium of as yet unknown character. Once understood, however crudely, newly discovered forms of energy are simply assimilated into our concept of the physical; "action at a distance" was an occult phenomenon until Newton described its properties sufficiently well to make the force of gravity seem no less "physical" than hitting a billiard ball. Dualism, if true, would thus cease to be dualism at the moment we gained any insight into the nature of the "force" that flowed through the pineal gland. Dualism (and all standard formulations of the mind-body problem) fails not so much because of our limited knowledge of mind but rather because modern physics has dissolved the concept of the body (see Chomsky, 1988; 1993).

Traditional dualism did at least recognize that the two domains, if such there be, must interact. Linguistic philosophy, by contrast, sought to remove any link between mind and body by the curious stratagem of an appeal to how we usually *talk* about the mental and the physical. George Henry Lewes, the greatest of all English philosophers and good friend of the greatest English novelist, George Eliot, provided, in 1877, the most succinct summary of the linguistic philosophers' position: "To ask if Matter could think, or Mind move Matter, was a confusion of symbols equivalent to speaking of a yard of Hope, and a ton of Terror" (Lewes, 1877). Every 50 years or so, someone attempts to revive this non-argument. The mental, such intrepid souls avow, is described in one vocabulary: a pain is searing, a thought is original, a belief is false. But the physical is described by a quite distinct vocabulary: a neuron is spherical, a nerve fibre is a centimeter long, a neurotransmitter substance is found in the frontal lobes. Woe betide anyone who would dare to report a spherical thought or a spatio-temporal configuration of the brain that was a belief! Because of this incompatibility of vocabulary, anyone who seeks to identify mind-states with brain-states is alleged to be suffering from "conceptual confusion", a disease that (unlike such paradigm examples as scurvy or bronchitis) can only be cured by a course of tutorials in the later philosophy of Ludwig Wittgenstein (Gellner, 1959). It is as if the Inquisition had sought to remove the confusion in Galileo's mind by pointing out to him not the rack, but rather the sentence "The sun rises in the east and sets in the west."

Those of us who have no privileged access to ultimate truth, no stake in the validity of the common philosopher's turn of phrase, will perhaps be content to let the chips fall as they may. If well-supported theories can be devised in which the mental reduces to brain-states in anything like the sense that water reduces to H_2O or light to electromagnetic radiation, so be it. "The facts are the same", Lewes writes (1877), "whether we express them in physiological or in psychological terms." If folk psychology, with its belief in autonomous minds, should eventually go the way of folk physics, we shall not *necessarily* be the poorer thereby, although the dangers of pursuing science without regard to moral science are only too apparent (Anshen, 1992). Popular idiom may change less rapidly than scientific theory, but this in itself does not cast doubt upon the validity of the latter. As Churchland remarks, ". . . one person's category error is another person's deep theory about the nature of the universe." And eventually, of course, folk talk catches up with the conceptual revisions brought about by scientific advance; even linguistic philosophers no longer speak "vitalese" when embryonic growth is at issue. But the notion that cognitive psychology will "reduce" to (current day) neurophysiology is a belief for which we have seen no evidence. Even the notion that neurophysiology as presently understood is a more basic science than psychology seems to rest on a "mechanical philosophy" that has played no role in the truly physical sciences since the time of Newton.

Functions First

Churchland's reductionism and her commitment to traditional psychophysical identity theory already have one serious competitor: functionalism. Functionalist theories of the mind draw their inspiration from the fact that engineering will not *reduce* to physics. Consider, with Churchland, the notion of a humble mousetrap. This "functional kind" can be implemented "in all manner of physically different devices: spring traps, assorted cage traps, a sack of grain falling when a trip line is wriggled ...". Now, no one would deny that each of these distinct pieces of machinery is a purely physical object, each obeying all relevant laws of physics (whatever they may turn out to be); there is no temptation to impute a non-material soul (or essence of mousetraphood) over and above their material constitution. None the less, each device has a different physical embodiment and falls under different physical laws. A device that could *not* function as a mousetrap (a spring-loaded weighing machine, for example) may have more in common physically with a spring trap than does a cage trap that will catch mice. It is in this sense that functionalists (who remain nevertheless *token* materialists, in both senses of "token") claim that the natural kinds of one science cross-classify with the natural kinds of other sciences. There is no principled, unique reduction of "mousetrap" to physics; at best, it may be possible to enumerate by brute force a *finite* set of physical objects that meet the functional constraints of mousetraphood. One would not, however, bet too heavily on even this latter possibility, given our proclivity for devising not merely better but rather qualitatively different mousetraps. We could, perhaps, stun the little beasties by directing ultra-high-frequency sound onto particularly tasty morsels of brie (Fodor, 1975).

When applied to the neurosciences, the argument for functionalism runs as follows. The psychologist is concerned to discover how we, for example, recognize friends' faces, find our way from home to work, speak English (or Japanese), organize our actions in order to make a cup of coffee or remember what we had for breakfast yesterday. Some of the evidence that bears upon the so-called "functional architecture" that underwrites these capacities and skills may come from the study of patients with relatively focal brain lesions who have lost such abilities, either in whole or in part. These patterns of impaired and preserved performance provide a basic fractionation of the mind/brain into cognitive domains that are grounded in biology and observation, not speculation. To the claim that general intelligence can only be exercised through the medium of language, one counterposes the severely aphasic patient who remains highly skilled in visuo-spatial learning and problem-solving tasks (Marin, Glenn and Rafal, 1983); to the claim that learning requires conscious awareness and recall, one counterposes the amnesic patient who puts together the same jigsaw puzzle a little faster each day whilst resolutely denying that he has ever seen the puzzle before (Squire, 1987). Further fractionations within a cognitive domain provide more constraints on information-processing accounts of how an ability is organized functionally.

For example: current theories of normal reading postulate three distinct routes from print to pronunciation, routes that in the intact brain operate in parallel, but each of which can be selectively impaired by neurological disease (Marshall, 1987). One route links sight-vocabulary to the meaning of words, which in turn calls up the pronunciation; another route associates sight-vocabulary directly with pronunciation; and a third route derives pronunciation by general rule from regular spelling – sound correspondences over letter-sequences shorter than words. When, after brain damage, patients must rely on one of these routes to the exclusion of the other two, different patterns of impaired reading will be revealed. The patient using only the first route will be unable to read aloud even the simplest of neologisms (*mip*, for example), and he will make copious semantic errors, reading "ill" for *sick*, or "big" for *large* (Marshall and Newcombe, 1966); the patient with only the second route intact will likewise be unable to read neologisms but will read words aloud correctly in the absence of any comprehension of what they mean (Lytton and Brust, 1989); the patient with only the third route available will read neologisms and regularly spelt words correctly, but will regularize the pronunciation of words that are exceptions to the rule, reading *pint*, for example, to rhyme with *hint*, or reading *mown* to rhyme with *town* (Patterson, Marshall and Coltheart, 1985).

This kind of information-processing neuropsychology has to a large extent proceeded independently of a concern with the physical nature of the injuries that provoked the cognitive impairment. There are two primary reasons for this state of affairs. One reason is that many of the same types of functional disorder can be seen across different types of neurological damage. The same behavioural impairment may be found irrespective of whether the damage is due to stroke (cerebro-vascular accident), space-occupying lesion (neoplasm), penetrating missile injury or central nervous system infection, for example. For the neurologist or neurosurgeon these distinct pathologies are important "natural kinds"; the nature of the pathology determines the nature of the treatment. For the cognitive neuropsychologist, however, the relevant natural kinds are functional categories of behavioural disorder. These categories do not map uniquely onto neurological kinds in the principled way that would be required to *reduce* cognitive neuropsychology to neurology.

Second, the reductionist argument fares no better if we consider not the nature of the lesion but rather its location. Although there are some reliable correlations between high-level functional impairments and the locus of the responsible brain damage, these correlations are far from perfect. Thus the same cognitive disorder may be seen in one patient after left hemisphere damage, and in another after right hemisphere damage, or in one after temporal lobe damage and in another after parietal damage. It is in this sense that the analysis of function takes priority over the analysis of the means whereby function is realized. It is by no means impossible that the same function could be computed by two (or more) distinct areas of the brain, containing different cell types and neurotransmitter substances. In such cases, psychology would be no more *reducible* to anatomy or physiology than the mousetrap is to physics. The natural kinds in the one discipline would cross-classify with the natural kinds in the other. The argument does not deny that in all instances the behavioural impairment is dependent upon the neurological impairment. Neither does it deny that there are constraints that physiology imposes upon function. Rather, the claim is that form and function are not *so* intimately related that the latter can be reduced to the former.

Churchland (1986) does discuss the arguments for functionalism quite thoroughly, but, for our money at least, she does not succeed in countering fully the antireductionist stance of much modern cognitive theory; nor, from our admittedly prejudiced perspective, does she devote enough space simply to telling the story of functionalist neuro-psychology. Churchland mentions some of the counter-intuitive dissociations of function observed in neurological patients but never shows how psychologists have tried to put these observations together into (relatively) coherent information-processing theories of object recognition, spatial cognition, autobiographical memory and language. It is crucial to realize that the evidence for some functional decompositions is already sufficiently strong to constrain the interpretation of neurophysiological results; and that in those domains where cognitive theory cannot (yet) do so, it is unclear whether the neurophysiologist is studying signal or noise, phenomena or epiphenomena. Current work on *in vivo* brain imaging (briefly summarized in Churchland and Sejnowski, 1992) is totally meaningless in the absence of functional theory drawn from data-sources that are independent of neurophysiology; the number of degrees of freedom in the interpretation of rates of cerebral metabolism *per se* is little short of scandalous.

Multifarious Computations

Thus far, we have tried to support functionalism solely by arguments drawn from the neurosciences. Many cognitive scientists have, however, attempted to push functionalist claims much further by drawing attention to analogies between computation within the brain and computation within computers (Pylyshyn, 1984; Churchland and Sejnowski, 1992). The computer metaphor is almost ubiquitous now as the preferred way of talking about cognition by those who work in the area. And talk of hardware versus software, of machine code versus higher-level programming languages, and of running the same program on structurally very different machines does indeed seem to point one rather firmly in the direction of functionalism. The operating computer can be characterized on three levels: semantics, syntax, and mechanism. Churchland (1986) writes,

> At the semantic level, the machine can be described as (for example) having certain goals, computing a square root, sacrificing a rook, or inferring a conclusion from premises. At the syntactic level the nature of its code, its symbolic system, its access principles, and so forth, are described. The mechanism level concerns the nature of the machine's architecture and hence its physical constraints and capacities.

Psychological theory in these terms is concerned with "the dynamics of the semantical level as governed by the logical rules and control principles at the syntactic level"; neurobiology, on the other hand, is "focussed on the architecture – that is, on the level of the mechanism." Antireductionists now contrast "the cognitive relevant *logical* operations on symbols with the cognitively irrelevant *causal* relations among physical states of the implementing mechanism." And they may, in their more extreme moments, assert that knowledge of the latter can have no bearing whatsoever upon the truth or falsity of claims about the former, functional level. Marr (1980) is not as extreme as that, but he does none the less argue convincingly that his four levels of explanation (computational theory, representation and algorithm, mechanism, and hardware implementation) "are only rather loosely related".

Churchland's response to the "abstract functionalists" is basically twofold. In the first place, she denies that a successful reduction implies that "the properties in the reduced theory" must have "a *unique* realization in physical stuff". She is well aware that, with respect to the brain, "different neuronal events" may "on different occasions ... realize *my* adding 29 and 45". She likewise knows that, in electronic computation, "two computers can be executing the same program written in BASIC, though their hardware and even their assembly language may be quite different." Hence, for Churchland, reductionism seems to mean solely that each psychological state can be reduced, without residue, to some physical instantiation or other, including multiple instantiation in different physical forms for any one functionally characterized state. We leave it to others to decide whether or not this so weakens the concept of reductionism as to leave it indistinguishable from the "token" physicalism that all rational functionalists take for granted.

Churchland's second argument is more interesting. The characterization of computation on three levels of description – semantic, syntactic, and (purely) physical – evokes the image of a now somewhat old-fashioned digital computer with the original Von Neumann architecture. Interpreted as a model of human cognition, such an architecture suggests that "the mind is essentially a serial machine governed by rules of logic that operate on sentence-like representations." Yet, as John Von Neumann himself pointed out in the first systematic comparison of computer and brain (1958), the nature of the brain's physiology conclusively rules out any possibility that its organizational principles could be at all similar to those of a standard digital computer. Complex, accurate computation in a serial machine presupposes fast-acting components, each one of which is highly reliable. If these constraints are not met, errors rapidly propagate throughout the system, each step compounding the mistakes made previously. (Think of making a mistake in applying the algorithm for long multiplication.) Yet in the nervous system, as Sutherland (1986) points out, "synaptic delays and transmission time along axons restrict the brain to taking at most 50 serial steps in a quarter of a second." Each individual neuron is moreover a highly sloppy device, responding maximally to the particular stimulus to which it is tuned, but also responding, albeit less strongly, to similar stimuli. Despite these apparent drawbacks, the brain does, of course, work! The brain outperforms any digital computer on those tasks for which it has evolved, recognizing, for example, faces, objects, and complex scenes in less than half a second, a feat well beyond any conventional machine.

The fashionable solution to the problem of reliable, intelligent computation is parallel distributed processing. For both computer scientists and neurobiologists, the construction of giant networks of layered computing elements, multiply-interconnected with varying strengths, remains the hottest game in town. In these systems, the overall pattern of activation in the net is the functional state of the device, with individual elements entering into many different computations in parallel. Particular processes or states are represented in the distributed activation pattern of large sets of elements. The parallel nature of processing overcomes the temporal problem of serial computation (serial is too slow to match human performance); the statistical properties of large networks ensure that reliable outcomes are computed despite the sloppy response of any individual element; and the distributed nature of processing (in combination with the previous two design features) overcomes the problem of errors propagating when malfunction occurs within a limited part of the network. Here then we may have more adequate models of biological computation and the adaptive response of the brain to injury. Sutherland (1986) thus summarizes: ". . . because a single concept is not represented by a single unit, the system may continue to function after the loss of some units; in an analogous way, human memory often survives local damage to the brain tolerably well."

Churchland is particularly impressed by the undoubted fact that within such parallel distributed processing systems, it is difficult, if not impossible, to draw many of the conceptual distinctions that are prerequisites for the description of a Von Neumann computer. Hardware/software, machine code/programming language, control unit/ memory unit, these demarcations simply go by the board. The network is the network, it does what it does. And this, needless to say, seems good grist to the reductionism mill. Churchland (1986) accordingly devotes the last section of her book to a lucid account of recent results in neurobiological computation where the psychology is the physiology. These case-studies include discussion of how the cerebellum may act to direct movement toward a given point in space (the fly-swatting problem), how the cerebral cortex may compute three-dimensional visual forms from two-dimensional retinal stimulation, and how the thalamus may function as an attentional "searchlight", selectively activating areas within topographically organized cortical maps where something of importance to the organism is going on. The latter section does, however, raise an issue that might have merited further discussion. What if (as many cognitive psychologists have argued) the *functional* theory of an "attentional spotlight" is false? If this were so, "attention" would not reduce to the activity of the thalamus; rather, the neurophysiological data would require radical revision. Churchland does, of course, recognize such possibilities in her notion of a "co-evolutionary research ideology". Like love and wholemeal bread, we too are all in favour of unification, but much current connectionism (and neurophysiology) may need to be consigned to the dustbin of scientific history before the walls can be torn down.

No Conclusion

Will it all turn out right in the end? It is far too early to know. Serious work of the nature Churchland describes is only a decade or two old. For the moment, we remain agnostic. Information-processing models of language and visual perception that postulate well-defined operations upon highly structured internal representations are now fairly well developed. Whether or not the rules and representations at the heart of such theories (Chomsky, 1982) can be shown to emerge implicitly from the intrinsic structure of synaptic learning in diffusely interconnected nerve-nets only time (and hard work) will tell. What is the application to understanding the effects of brain damage? Here also scepticism is in order. Those of us who see clinical patients cannot escape the observation that small, focal lesions can, sadly and permanently, disrupt discrete domains of human cognition. If parallel distributed processing is the key to comprehending the mind/brain, cognitive neuropsychology provides crucial evidence that must severely constrain the rules of synaptic connectivity.

None of this detracts from the outstanding merits of Patricia Churchland's book. We are, after all, talking about the development of a science in which new ideas and empirical evidence come to light daily. And Churchland is certainly correct to see no firm demarcation line between philosophy and science. Her reductionism is simultaneously an ontological position and a methodological strategy for the discovery of empirical evidence that bears upon our theories of cognition. That we have made *some* progress can perhaps best be seen by comparing Churchland's *Neurophilosophy* with Descartes' *Treatise of Man* (1662). From understanding how reflex movement pulls the foot from the fire to understanding how a frog captures a fly is no small step. Although Descartes was a dualist with respect to higher mental functions, he knew that philosophically informed science was the way to understand what is understandable. In this sense too, Patricia Churchland's work brings the good news that philosophy has finally recovered from the time when a Viennese mystic and various schoolmasters *manqués* attempted to pervert the discipline into a commentary on the Oxford English Dictionary. And there remains at least a yard of Hope that the next few years will bring a yet more unified neuroscience. We only doubt that the shape of that unification will look much like the current picture (see Kitcher, 1992). If Spinoza could devise a naturalistic (but non-reductionist) philosophy for the seventeenth century (Donagan, 1988), some future Spinoza might yet emulate that achievement for the twenty-first century.

References

Anshen, R. A. (1992). *Morals Equals Manners*. London: Moyer Bell.

Cassirer, E. (1929/1957). *The Philosophy of Symbolic Forms* (vol. 3). New Haven: Yale University Press.

Chomsky, N. (1982). *Some Concepts and Consequences of the Theory of Government and Binding*. Cambridge, Mass.: MIT Press.

Chomsky, N. (1988). *Language and Problems of Knowledge*. Cambridge, Mass.: MIT Press.

Chomsky, N. (1993). *Language and Thought*. London: Moyer Bell.

Churchland, P. S. (1986). *Neurophilosophy: Toward a Unified Science of the*

Mind-Brain. Cambridge, Mass.: MIT Press.

Churchland, P. S. and Sejnowski, T. J. (1992). *The Computational Brain*. Cambridge, Mass.: MIT Press.

Descartes, R. (1662). *De Homine Figuris et Latinitate Donatus a Florentio Schuyl*. Leyden: Moyardum et Leffen.

Donagan, A. (1988). *Spinoza*. New York: Harvester Wheatsheaf.

Fodor, J. A. (1975). *The Language of Thought*. New York: Crowell.

Gellner, E. (1959). *Words and Things*. London: Gollancz.

Goldstein, K. (1939). *The Organism: A Holistic Approach to Biology Derived from Pathological Data in Man*. New York: American Book Company.

Goldstein, K. (1942). *Aftereffects of Brain Injuries in War, Their Evaluation and Treatment*. New York: Grune.

Goldstein, K. (1948). *Language and Language Disturbances*. New York: Grune.

Hyman, J., ed. (1991). *Investigating Psychology: Sciences of the Mind after Wittgenstein*. London: Routledge.

Kitcher, P. (1990). *Kant's Transcendental Psychology*. New York: Oxford University Press.

Kitcher, P. (1992). *Freud's Dream: A Complete, Interdisciplinary Science of Mind*. Cambridge, Mass.: MIT Press.

Lewes, G. H. (1877). *The Physical Basis of Mind*. London: Trubner.

Lytton, W. W. and Brust, J. C. M. (1989). Direct dyslexia: preserved oral reading of real words in Wernicke's aphasia. *Brain*, **112**, 583–94.

Marin, O. S. M., Glenn, C. G. and Rafal, R. D. (1983). Visual problem solving in the absence of lexical semantics: evidence from dementia. *Brain and Cognition*, **2**, 285–311.

Marr, D. (1980). Visual information processing: the structure and creation of visual representations. *Philosophical Transactions of the Royal Society*, **B290**, 199–218.

Marshall, J. C. (1987). Routes and representations in the processing of written language. In E. Keller and M. Gopnik (eds), *Motor and Sensory Processes of Language*. London: Erlbaum.

Marshall, J. C. and Fryer, D. (1978). Speak, memory! An introduction to some historic studies of remembering and forgetting. In M. Gruneberg and P. Morris (eds), *Aspects of Memory*. London: Methuen.

Marshall, J. C. and Newcombe, F. (1966). Syntactic and semantic errors in paralexia. *Neuropsychologia*, **4**, 169–76.

Mehler, J., Morton, J. and Jusczyk, P. W. (1984). On reducing language to biology. *Cognitive Neuropsychology*, **1**, 83–116.

Moore, G. E. (1942). An autobiography. In P. A. Schilpp (ed.), *The Philosophy of G. E. Moore*. Evanston, Ill.: The Library of Living Philosophers.

Patterson, K. E., Marshall, J. C. and Coltheart, M., eds (1985). *Surface Dyslexia: Neuropsychological and Cognitive Studies in Phonological Reading*. London: Erlbaum.

Pylyshyn, Z. W. (1984). *Computation and Cognition: Toward a Foundation for Cognitive Science*. Cambridge, Mass.: MIT Press.

Squire, L. R. (1987). *Memory and Brain*. New York: Oxford University Press.
Sutherland, S. (1986). Parallel distributed processing. *Nature*, **323**, 486.
Von Neumann, J. (1958). *The Computer and the Brain*. New Haven: Yale University Press.
Wittgenstein, L. (1980). *Culture and Value*. Oxford: Blackwell.

9

The Moral Network

Owen Flanagan

For practical purposes morals means customs, folkways, established collective habits. This is a commonplace of the anthropologist, though the moral theorist generally suffers from an illusion that his own place and day is, or ought to be, an exception.

John Dewey, 1922, 55

Moral science is not something with a separate province. It is physical, biological, and historic knowledge placed in a humane context where it will illuminate and guide the activities of men.

John Dewey, 1922, 204–5

1 Ethics and Cognitive Neuroscience?

What, God forbid, might a cognitive scientist or even, worse, a cognitive neuroscientist have to say about the nature of human morality? Paul Churchland (1989, chapter 14, "Moral Facts and Moral Knowledge") has recently provided a short meditation on morals from just such a perspective, and as far as I can see, no demons of deflation lurk in the vicinity. I call the view he sketches "moral network theory." My aim in this chapter is to defend this theory (or perhaps better, this model) by extending some of the insights Churchland makes and by showing how moral network theory can account for certain significant features of moral psychology that stand in need of explanation. It will then be for Paul Churchland to say if my elaboration of his view is one he finds acceptable. My two significant reservations have to do not so much with the theory itself but with Churchland's way of conceiving of the normative side of a naturalistic ethics. It seems to me

1 that Churchland is overly optimistic about the capacities of the moral community to arrive at high-quality moral knowledge;[1]
2 that he fails to emphasize sufficiently the local nature of much moral knowledge.

Both problems are rooted, I believe, in excessive dependence on the analogy between scientific and moral knowledge. One needs to press the ways that science and ethics are alike to win the case for moral knowledge. But things that are alike are not alike in all respects – all sciences are not even like all other sciences. And one needs to mark certain unique aspects of the ends of moral life to understand some of the special features of moral knowledge.

* * * *

There are two aspects of Churchland's view that I find particularly compelling and fecund. The first is the idea that moral responsiveness does not (normally) involve deployment of a set of special-purpose rules or algorithms that are individually applied to all, and only, the problems for which they are specifically designed. Nor does moral responsiveness normally involve deployment of a single general-purpose rule or algorithm, such as the principle of utility or the categorical imperative, designed to deal with each and every moral problem. Moral issues are heterogeneous in kind, and the moral community wisely trains us to possess a vast array of moral competencies suited – often in complex combinations and configurations – to multifarious domains, competencies which, in fact and in theory, resist unification under either a set of special-purpose rules or a single general-purpose rule or principle.

The second feature of Churchland's view that I like is this. The theory is a moral network theory, but the total network comprises more than the neural nets that, so to speak, contain the moral knowledge a particular individual possesses. Whatever neural net instantiates (or is disposed to express) some segment of moral knowledge, it does so only because it is "trained" by a community. The community itself is a network providing constant feedback to the human agent.

The neural network that underpins moral perception, thought, and action is created, maintained, and modified in relation to a particular natural and social environment. The moral network includes but is not exhausted by the dispositional states laid down in the neural nets of particular individuals.

2 Ethics Naturalized

Moral network theory is a contribution to the project of naturalizing ethics. Naturalizing ethics is in certain views a dangerous or impossible thing. It will be wise to start by saying what the project consists in. It is, both Churchland and I agree, the only show in town.

A naturalistic ethical theory will, like a naturalistic epistemology, have two components: a descriptive-genealogical component and a normative component. The descriptive-genealogical part will specify certain basic capacities and propensities of *Homo sapiens*, e.g., sympathy, empathy, and egoism, that are relevant to moral life. It will explain how people come to feel, think, and act about moral matters in the ways they do. It will explain how and in what ways moral learning, engagement, and response involve the emotions. It will explain what moral disagreement consists in and why it occurs; and it will explain why people sometimes resolve conflict by recourse to agreements to tolerate each other without, however, approving of each other's beliefs, actions, etc. It will tell us what people are doing when they make normative judgments. And finally, or as a consequence of all this, it will try to explain what goes on when people try to educate the young, improve the moral climate, propose moral theories, and so on.

The distinctively normative component extends the last aspect of the descriptive-genealogical agenda: It will explain why some norms (including norms governing choosing norms), values, and virtues are good or better than others. And it may try to systematize at some abstract level the ways of feeling, living, and being that we, as moral creatures, should aspire to (for a debate about the prospects for naturalistic ethics on a par with naturalistic epistemology, see Quine, 1979; 1986; Flanagan, 1982; 1988; 1991; White, 1986; Gibson, 1988).

In sum, the descriptive-genealogical agenda consists of explaining innate moral tendencies, moral learning, moral conflict and conflict resolution, what moral thought and judgment have as their subject matter, and what is involved in moral education and moral theorizing. The normative agenda involves saying (possibly by way of abstract criteria gleaned from some underlying unity the class of good practices displays) what is right, wrong, good, bad – saying what modes of moral perception, feeling, and action are good or at least better than the alternatives.

The standard view is that descriptive-genealogical ethics can be naturalized, but that normative ethics cannot. The claim is that naturalism is deflationary and/or morally naive. It makes normativity a matter of power: either the power of benign but less-than-enlightened socialization forces or the power of those in charge of the normative order, possibly fascists or Nazis or moral dunces.

Both the standard view and the complaint about naturalistic normative ethics turn on certain genuine difficulties with discovering how to live well, and with a certain fantastical way of conceiving of what's "*really* right" or "*really* good." But these difficulties have everything to do with the complexities of moral life and have no bearing whatsoever on the truth of ethical naturalism. It is an illusion to which the moral theorist is historically but perhaps not inevitably prone that his pronouncements can move outside the space of human nature, conduct, and history and judge *from the point of view of reason alone* what is right and good. This is a silly idea.

The key to a successful normative naturalism is to conceive of "reasoning" in the cognitive loop, as a natural capacity of a socially-situated mind/brain, and to argue for the superiority of certain methods of achieving moral knowledge and improving the moral climate. Arguments for the superiority of some methods and norms over others need to be based on evidence from any source that has relevance to claims about human flourishing. Sometimes naturalists take the refinement and growth of moral knowledge over time too much for granted. Some naturalistic approaches emphasize the invisible hand of some sort of socio-moral assimilation-accommodation mechanism in accounting for the refinement of moral knowledge over time; or they emphasize the visible processes of aggregation of precedent, constraint by precedents, and collective discussion and argument that mark socio-moral life. One can believe that moral knowledge exists without thinking that it grows naturally over time, that it has increased in quality and quantity in the course of human history. I'll say more about this issue in the final section of the paper.

3   Moral Network Theory: The Descriptive-Genealogical Component

In this section I offer a reconstruction of the descriptive-genealogical component of moral network theory. In the next two sections I'll develop an example, the example of learning about lying and honesty, to exemplify the view. Then in the final section I'll address the issue of whether, and if so how, the theory can respond to the worry that no naturalistic theory has a right to say anything about what is really good and right.

I'll lay out Churchland's view in a series of propositions and largely in his own words (all from Churchland, 1989), which, suitably elaborated, constitute the core of his argument for moral network theory. It should be noted that his theory has much in common with the view recently advanced by Mark Johnson (1993).

1   "Moral knowledge has long suffered from what seems an unflattering contrast with scientific or other genuinely 'factual' forms of knowledge. It is not hard to appreciate the appearance. One has no obvious sense organ for moral facts, as one does for so many of the facts displayed in the material

world, and so there is an immediate epistemological problem about moral facts. How does one apprehend them?" (p. 297)

2 "My own inclination is to resist the appearance [that science is the repository of facts and facts correspond to the way things are] that tends to produce these two reactions, and thus to avoid the motivation for both pathologies. Moral truths ... are roughly as robust and objective as other instances of truth, but this objectivity is not secured by their being grounded in pure reason or in some other nonempirical support. It is secured in something very like the way in which the objectivity of scientific fact is secured." (p. 297)

3 "What motivates this suggestion is the novel account of knowledge and conceptual development emerging from neural-network models of cognitive function ... On these neurocomputational models, knowledge acquisition is primarily a process of learning *how*: how to recognize a wide variety of complex situations and how to respond to them appropriately. *The quality of one's knowledge is measured not by any uniform correspondence between internal sentences and external facts, but by the quality of one's continuing performance.* From this perspective, moral knowledge does not automatically suffer by contrast with other forms of knowledge." (p. 298, my italics)

4 Consider the sorts of empirical observations that are thought to contrast dramatically with moral perception and observation: "It has become evident that very few, if any, of the properties we commonly regard as observational are distinguished by the peripheral cells alone. Most of them involve the activity of several subsequent layers in the processing hierarchy. And this is certainly true of relatively subtle properties. Consider your observing that the sky is threatening, that a banana is ideally ripe, that the car's engine is still cold, that Mary is embarrassed, that the lamb chops on the grill are ready, that the class is bored, that an infant is overtired, and so forth. These are the sorts of immediate and automatic discriminations that one learns to make, and on which one's practical life depends. To be sure, they are ampliative discriminations relative to the often meager peripheral stimulation that triggers them, and they are highly corrigible for that very reason. *But they are not the result of applying abstract general principles, nor the result of drawing covert discursive inferences, at least in a well-trained individual. They represent the normal and almost instantaneous operation of a massively parallel network that has been trained over time to be sensitive to a specific range of environmental features.*" (p. 299, my italics)

5 "The discrimination of social and moral features is surely an instance of the same process, and it is made possible by training of a similar kind. Children learn to recognize certain prototypical kinds of social situations, and they learn to produce or avoid the behaviors prototypically required or prohibited in each. Young children learn to recognize a distribution of scarce resources such as cookies or candies as a *fair* or *unfair distribution*. They learn to voice complaint in the latter case, and to withhold complaint

in the former. They learn to recognize that a found object may be *someone's property*, and that access is limited as a result. They learn to discriminate *unprovoked cruelty*, and to demand or expect punishment for the transgressor and comfort for the victim. They learn to recognize a *breach of promise*, and to howl in protest. They learn to recognize these and a hundred other prototypical social/moral situations, and the ways in which the embedding society generally reacts to those situations and expects them to react." (p. 299)

6 "How the learning child subsequently reacts to a novel social situation will be a function of which of her many prototypes that situation activates, and this will be a matter of the relative similarity of the new situation to the various prototypes on which she was trained. This means that situations will occasionally be ambiguous. One and the same situation can activate distinct prototypes in distinct observers. What seems a case of unprovoked cruelty to one child can seem a case of just retribution to another. *Moral argument then consists in trying to reduce the exaggerated salience of certain features of the situation, and to enhance the salience of certain others, in order to change which prototype gets activated. The stored prototypes themselves regularly undergo change, of course, as experience brings ever new examples and the child's social/moral consciousness continues to develop.*" (p. 300, my italics)

7 "What the child is learning in this process is the *structure of social space* and *how best to navigate one's way through it*. What the child is learning is practical wisdom: the wise administration of her practical affairs in a complex social environment. This is as genuine a case of learning about objective reality as one finds anywhere. It is also of fundamental importance for the character and quality of any individual's life, and not everyone succeeds equally in mastering the relevant intricacies." (p. 300)

❄ ❄ ❄ ❄

Two comments are in order before we proceed further. First, it should be emphasized, in case it is not obvious, that Churchland is using the concept of *prototype* in a broad but principled sense. Indeed, earlier in the book, he argues that the prototype activation model is general enough to account for perceptual recognition *and* scientific explanation. For example, inference to the best explanation is (roughly) activation of "the most appropriate prototype vector" given the evidence (Churchland, 1989, 218). And what Churchland calls "*social-interaction* prototypes underwrite *ethical, legal*, and *social-etiquette* explanations" (216). So we explain why the Czech driver stops to help the man with the flat tire by explaining that there are "good samaritan" laws in the Czech Republic. Conversely, the existence of the relevant social expectations expressed in such laws explains why the Czech driver sees a person with a flat as a person in need of his help and sees helping as something he ought to do – perhaps for prudential reasons, or perhaps because samaritanism is deeply engrained. The sort of socio-moral learning that takes place in the Czech Republic but not in (most parts of) America means that Czech drivers just stop to help people stuck on the side of the road and that seeing drivers stuck on the side of the road engages certain feelings, either fear of the law, if one is observed not stopping, or a moral pull to help, if the engrained disposition involves some sort of genuine compassion or fellow-feeling.

The second comment is that the prototype activation model designed to explain moral learning must explain our notion of morality itself. Morality does not pick out a natural kind. What is considered moral, conventional, personal, and so on depends on the complex set of practices, including practices involving the use of certain terms, that have evolved over time in different communities. If one asks for a *definition* of "moral" in our culture, it will, I suspect, be framed in terms of rules designed to keep humans from harming other humans. If, however, one looks to the meanings that reveal themselves in ascriptive practices and in response to verbal probes of a more complex sort, one will also find that we think of the moral as having an intrapersonal component. That is, there are norms governing personal goodness, improvement, and perfection, as well as norms governing self-respect and self-esteem, that are not reducible to conformity to interpersonal moral norms (Flanagan, 1991). This point will matter for what I say in the final section.[2]

4   An Illustration: The Prototypical Structure of *Lie*

It will be useful to consider the process of learning about lying and truth-telling as an illustration of moral network theory. One standard way of thinking about the issue is that children must learn both what the word "lie" means and also a rule to the effect that lying is wrong. When confronted with a temptation to lie, the rule is activated and leads to the inference that the truth ought to be told, which leads, in a suitably motivated system, to truth-telling. It is also standardly thought that children are taught that lying is wrong *simpliciter*. Neither view is plausible.

To put things in the most contentious way, it would be better to say that children are taught (are exposed to) norms of honesty, politeness, privacy, reticence, and loyalty, which taken together – and they are – teach them that there is no categorical obligation to tell the truth. We hear that honesty is the best policy. But honesty has a complex meaning for us. And the policy is by no means set forth as a categorical one.

Rational self-interest, the need for privacy, self-esteem, and self-respect compete with honesty and are thought, in some cases, to override the requirement to be honest. Kindness, politeness, tact, loyalty, and the demands of friendship also compete with honesty, and they too, in certain cases, override the requirement to be honest. Socialization in honesty involves the acquisition of what Aristotle called *phronesis*, practical wisdom; it does not involve the acquisition of definitions, nor (except in rare cases) special-purpose or general-purpose rules. The honest person is the person who knows when to tell the truth and does so in the right circumstances, in the right way, and to the right persons. There is no known rule or algorithm that can be taught and that will produce the requisite set of moral sensitivities.

On moral network theory, it is a mistake to think that in order to lie either the child or the moral community needs to know the definition of "lie." The classical view is that the extension of a concept consists of a set of conditions that are jointly necessary and sufficient for the correct application of the concept. The main problem with this idea is that, like most concepts, the concept of "lie" does not admit of characterization in terms of jointly necessary and sufficient conditions. Since there is no definition of "lie," it is good that no one needs to know one in order to lie or ascribe lies. The idea that conceptual structure is normally rooted in family resemblance, and thus in prototypes, frames, scripts, cluster concepts, and the like, rather than in necessary and sufficient conditions, helps explain why exceptionless definitions for nontechnical terms almost never exist.

One might think that expressing a falsehood, knowing it is false, and intending to mislead by expressing this known falsehood are jointly necessary and sufficient conditions for lying. The trouble is that a speech act can express a falsehood, be known by the speaker to express a falsehood, be intended to deceive and not be a bona fide lie. Practical jokes are examples.

Even the assumption that a lie must involve a speech act is problematic if one sticks to the straight and narrow in characterizing speech acts. Sissela Bok, for example, defines a lie as "an intentionally deceptive message in the form of a statement" (Bok, 1978, 15). But surely pointing someone in the wrong direction can count as a lie even though no statement is involved at all.

All the putative necessary conditions – saying something false, knowing that it is false, and intending by one's utterance to deceive – matter in our determination of some act to be a lie. But these conditions can be satisfied and a lie not be told because of subtle features in the context or the speaker's overall intentional state. Again, certain jokes fit this mold straightforwardly. More counterintuitively, one can tell a lie by telling the truth. Indeed, one lying strategy is to tell an abridged version of the truth knowing that one's audience will elaborate its meaning in exactly the wrong direction. If one's concept of "lie" has as a necessary condition the requirement that one says what is false, then such lies are not real lies.

So-called "benevolent lies" will be thought by some not to be real lies at all. The best explanation for this is that for some individuals, bad moral intent is the most important determinant of a lie. Since a benevolent lie is a false utterance intended to mislead but with good moral intent, it is not really a lie. But our intuitions pull in both directions here. We might be tempted to say of a speech act intended to save a life that it is not a real lie or, equally sensibly, that it is a lie but excusable.

The upshot is this: knowing what counts as a lie is no simple matter of knowing a definition. Lies have a prototypical structure (Burton and Strichartz, 1992). Almost all the research shows that objective falsity has greatest saliency in determining whether something is a lie for very young children; thus, for them, mistakes are considered lies (Piaget, 1932; Peterson, Peterson, and Seeto, 1983; Wimmer, Gruber, and Perner, 1985).

A different way to make some of the same points is to say that *using* words and saying what we *mean* by those words do not always end us up in the same place. Definitions, even loosely understood, and ascriptions come apart in important ways. Although Coleman and Kay (1981) found that objective falsehood was the main feature given by adults when asked to define "lie," it "turned out consistently to be the least important element by far in the cluster of conditions" in determining whether a lie is ascribed (Lakoff, 1987, 72). Other important elements in the cluster of conditions relevant to the determination of whether some act is a lie include believing the opposite of what one says and intending to deceive. All the research shows that both these factors increase in salience over time in determining whether a lie is attributed, despite the fact that they do not display similar salience in attempts to give definitions of the word "lie." For many adults, objective falsehood reigns supreme for the definitional task, even as its power wanes in determining ascriptions.[3]

An individual can possess first-order competence at lying and even attribute lies correctly (especially to others) without being able to provide a definition, either in terms of jointly necessary and sufficient conditions (there are none) or even in terms of the properties that the individual herself thinks constitute the most important practical factors in determining whether some act is a lie. Competent use of the term "lie" is best measured against the preferred prototype in the linguistic community in contexts where ascription, rather than definition, is called for. Ability to define the term is a bad test for adults as well as for children (Coleman and Kay, 1981). That said, the evidence indicates that the preferred prototype, in which belief in something other than what is conveyed and intent to deceive have greater weight than objective falsehood, is not fully acquired until the teenage years – and even then it is somewhat unstable (Burton and Strichartz, 1992).

Why does intent eventually take top billing in our conception of a lie? It has to do, I think, with the distinctively moral character of lying. Lying is asymmetrical with truth-telling in this respect. That is, even though we are taught that it is right to tell the truth and wrong to lie, almost all lies are moral violations, whereas most truthful utterances have nothing to do with morality. To inform another truly about the weather, one's health, what's on TV, or the latest finding about neurotransmitters is not conceived of as doing something that falls within the domain of the moral. If you lie about these things, you do what is morally wrong, but when you say what is true in these domains, you do not do something morally good or praiseworthy. You simply do what is expected.

Focusing on the moral component of our prototype helps explain one respect in which practical jokes differ from lies. When you say something false with the intention of deceiving me in order to get me to open a door with a bucket of water on top of it, you satisfy the conditions of intent, belief, and falsehood. The temptation to say that you have not really lied comes from the fact that you intended fun, not harm.

5 Socialization for Honesty

Assuming the case of honesty is typical, the question arises, how is it that we respond to, think about, and debate moral matters without having, as Socrates thought we must, definitions of the relevant terms clearly in mind? How can fuzzy prototypes acquired in fuzzy, indeterminate social settings, give rise to morally competent agency? How must moral socialization work such that moral network theory is true? The answers to these questions are implicit in much of what has been said in the previous sections, but let me develop the relevant points more explicitly, sticking with the example of socialization for honesty as illustrative.

First, when should a child begin to receive instruction about the morality of lying? Second, what sort of prominence should be given in the overall structure of the socio-moral understanding that is being constructed in the mind/brain of the child? Observations of normative interactions between mothers and children in their second year indicate that transgressions discussed involve the following issues, in order of

frequency: destruction/dirt, place/order, teasing/hurting others, politeness, and sharing (Dunn, 1987). Lying itself is not a major issue before a
child's second birthday. It is unlikely that parents engage in instruction
about the wrongness of lying before children begin trying to lie. When
does this occur? I'm not sure. But it seems plausible that the first
"ecologically valid" lies are ones about misdeeds (Bussey, 1992), and
that they start to occur with enough frequency to be noticed after the
second birthday. Children who already understand that certain actions
constitute misdeeds, and who know that these misdeeds are disapproved
of, begin to be taught that lying about misdeeds is also disapproved of.

How disapproved-of is it? There is no simple and clear-cut answer to
this question. We teach children that it is wrong to lie about a misdeed.
But we understand – and convey this understanding – that it is among
the most natural things to try to cover up a misdeed. Furthermore, even
as children are learning that lying about misdeeds is wrong, they are still
in the process of learning what misdeeds are. Bunglings and accidents
are sometimes discounted by adults (try giving definitions of "bunglings" and "accidents"), but not always – at least not in the rush to
anger. Thus children are rightfully wary about underestimating what the
adult theory of misdeeds includes and excludes. Overgeneralizing is not
a bad strategy.

Although many parents try to teach that the lie is worse than the
misdeed, children also realize that certain misdeeds are bad enough to
be worth trying to cover up. The added marginal cost of being caught in
the lie, as well as in the misdeed, is not so significant as to constitute a
genuine disincentive to lying.

The first set of points can be summarized this way. Initial learning
about the wrongness of lying is almost certainly tied to a certain class of
lies – lies about misdeeds. Children are not exposed, at least at first, to
anything like a general theory of lies and lying. Learning about the
wrongness of lies about misdeeds comes after there has been prior
instruction in the wrongness of misdeeds. How wrong the child thinks
lying about misdeeds is depends on how wrong adults convey that it is.
But this is variable; it depends on how parents, caretakers, and
preschool teachers treat lies. Do children learn that they are under an
obligation to tell the truth at this stage? I doubt it. Certainly talk of
"obligation" or "duty" is not normally introduced to youngsters. Do
children learn that it is unconditionally wrong to lie about misdeeds?
Again, I think not. Sensitive adults convey to the child an understanding
of why she has lied. In this way they convey the impression that they
understand that there are certain conditions that make it hard not to lie
and that ameliorate, and possibly even dissolve, judgments of wrongness.[4]

The second point relates to the development of the child's general understanding of the virtue of honesty and the vice of dishonesty. Most (but not all) lies involve speech acts. It follows that both the nature and wrongness of lies need to be considered in relation to the norms governing speech acts more generally. Thinking of lies in this way imperils thinking about lies as a simple class to pick out, or as a class with simple norms governing rightness and wrongness. Annette Baier puts the central point eloquently when she writes (1990, 262):

> Talk, as we teach and learn it, has many uses. It is not unrelievedly serious – it is often an extension of play and fun, of games of hide and seek, of peekaboo, where deceit is expected and enjoyed, of games of Simon says, where orders are given to be disobeyed, of games of tag, where words have magic power, of skipping games, where words are an incantation. Speech, as we teach and learn it, is not just the vehicle of cool rational thought and practical reason but also of fun and games of anger, mutual attack, domination, coercion, and bullying. It gives us a voice for our many moods, for deceit and sly strategy, as well as for love and tenderness, humor, play and frolic, mystery and magic. The child is initiated into all of this and gradually learns all the arts and moods of speech. Among these are the arts of misleading others, either briefly and with intent soon to put them straight ("I fooled you, didn't I!") or more lastingly to keep deceit going for more questionably acceptable purposes.

Exaggeration, politeness, tact, reserve in self-expression, omitting to say certain things, joking, and so on all have to do with honest expression. Children are decidedly not taught that it is right, or even good, to be honest in the expression of all the matters that one could be honest about. Insofar as children are taught that there is an obligation to be honest, and thus not to lie, it is a complex, conditional, and culturally-circumscribed obligation.

Consider in this regard the norms governing answers to polite queries about one's well-being. "If you ask me 'How are you?' and I reply 'Fine thanks, and you?' although I take myself to be far from fine, I have not lied" (Baier, 1990, 268). Such speech acts are "a form of consideration for others, a protection of them from undue embarrassment, boredom, or occasion for pity. Truth, let alone 'the whole truth,' is something we very rarely want told to us . . . veracity is knowing *when* one is bound to speak one's mind and then speaking it as best one can" (Baier, 1990, 268).

Most children, in our culture at least, are not raised to think of the obligation to tell the truth as a duty (notice the word itself has an almost archaic quality), or as a categorical obligation. This is not necessarily due to defects in our moral educational practices. It may be, given what has just been said, an accession to the complexity of moral life and motivated by a recognition that it is sometimes good, and not merely permissible, to lie or at least not to tell the whole truth.

Close attention to socialization for honesty makes credible the idea that, far from being taught explicit rules and definitions, children are exposed to complex situations, attuned in multifarious ways (by observing behavior, body language, emotional expression, what is said, and so on) to certain saliencies in these situations, and gradually learn how to perceive social situations in appropriate ways, make wise choices, and have apt feelings (Gibbard, 1990).

Although I have been focusing on socialization for honesty, the main point I have been trying to draw out is that we learn about honesty, about prototypical honest and dishonest acts, at the same time we are learning about kindness, tact, politeness, and how to save our own skins. A child who is acquiring the psychoneural structures that enable him to identify a situation as calling on him to speak the truth had better also be learning the dispositional structures governing kindness, tact, and politeness or, if these latter are already in place, had better have the relevant nets knit together. A situation rarely calls on us to be honest *simpliciter*. There is often the matter of how (sensitively) to convey the truth (if it is painful). The point is that nests of nets, bunches of prototypes, scenes with multiple scripts – call them what you will – normally need to be activated if a person is to respond adequately to complex socio-moral issues. Assuming there is a prototype for simple cases of honesty, it had better activate the nets disposed to kindness, politeness, and tact, if these have bearing. Otherwise, we have an honest boor – someone who always (and therefore insensitively) speaks the truth. So the moral network needs to have the right structures activated. Issues of honesty should normally spread some activation from nets that know about honesty to nets and nodes that know about politeness and tact and kindness. It would be idle (possibly even destructive) labor were scripts about restaurant etiquette and catching groundballs also activated. The brain is very smart and picks up from the moral community's nonroutinized socialization practices what is relevant to what, and it eventually represents standards of relevance in its patterns of spreading activation in the neuronal network. "Character," John Dewey said, "is the interpenetration of habits," adding that "interpenetration is never total" (1922, 30). This, we have seen, is the way things should be – a particular situation should activate habits of perception, feeling, and response that are relevant to it. The spread of activation should decline as relevance does.[5]

The discussion of socialization for honesty is designed to illustrate the sort of descriptive-genealogical account moral network theory will give for the acquisition, modification, and activation of moral knowledge. The theory is a theory of how, in varied and sundry interactions, the child learns about "the *structure of social space* and *how best to navigate one's way through it*." Although I haven't done so here, I am prepared to argue that the theory explains moral complexity, moral ambiguity, and moral conflict as well as any competitor theory that has been put forward. And it rids us of the implausible ideas that moral cognition and response are routed standardly through either domain-specific rules ("tell the truth") or general-purpose moral principles such as the principle of utility or the categorical imperative. Moral response is more domain-specific than any general-purpose model would have us think, but it cannot be completely domain- or problem-specific in the way some pre-established rule could accommodate. The reason is simple: The domains and problems are messy and interconnected. The mind/brain of the child does not acquire rules for each domain. The child acquires knowledge structures, disposed to interact with each other and to modify and adjust each other's level of activation, as particular circumstances require.

6 Normative Networks

So far I have concentrated on the merits of moral network theory as a descriptive-genealogical theory. The time has come to see how moral network theory can handle the normative issue. Churchland himself raises the worry, the objection that every naturalist is familiar with. He puts it this way (1989, 300):

> What is problematic is whether this process amounts to the learning of genuine Moral Truth, or to mere socialization. We can hardly collapse the distinction, lest we make moral criticism of diverse forms of social organization impossible. We want to defend this possibility, since ... the socialization described above can occasionally amount to a cowardly acquiescence in an arbitrary and stultifying form of life. Can we specify under what circumstances it will amount to something more than this?

Churchland claims that "an exactly parallel problem arises with regard to the learning of Scientific Truth" since almost no scientific learning is first hand, and even that which is occurs within a research tradition with a particular orientation, set of methods, and so on. Nonetheless, despite overblown views of *scientific truth* and the *correspondence to the real* held by certain scientistic thinkers and hard-core metaphysical realists, Churchland insists that "there remains every reason to think that the normal learning process, as instanced both in individuals and in the collective enterprise of institutional science, involves a reliable and dramatic increase in the amount and the quality of the information we have about the world" (1989, 301). And, he claims (301–2), the same is true of moral knowledge.

> When such powerful learning networks as humans are confronted with the problem of how best to perceive the social world, and how best to conduct one's affairs within it, we have equally good reason to expect that the learning process will show an integrity comparable to that shown on other learning tasks, and will produce cognitive achievements as robust as those produced anywhere else. This expectation will be especially apt if, as in the case of "scientific" knowledge, the learning process is collective and the results are transmitted from generation to generation. In that case we have a continuing society under constant pressure to refine its categories of social and moral perception, and to modify its typical responses and expectations. Successful societies do this on a systematic basis.[6]

Churchland then asks (302):

> Just what are the members of the society learning? They are learning how best to organize and administer their collective and individual affairs. What factors provoke change and improvement in their typical categories of moral perception and their typical forms of behavioral response? That is, what factors drive moral learning? They are many and various, but in general they arise from the continuing social experience of conducting a life under the existing moral framework. That is, moral learning is driven by social experience, often a long and painful social experience, just as theoretical science is driven by experiment. Moral knowledge thus has just as genuine a claim to objectivity as any other kind of empirical knowledge. What are the principles by which rational people adjust their moral conceptions in the face of unwelcome social experience? They are likely to be exactly the same "principles" that drive conceptual readjustment in science or anywhere else, and they are likely to be revealed as we come to understand how empirical brains actually do learn.

The core argument is this. Moral knowledge is the result of complex socialization processes. What keeps moral socialization from being "mere" socialization has to do with several features of socio-moral (and scientific) life. "Mere" socialization is socialization toward which no critical attitude is taken, for which there are no mechanisms that drive adjustment, modification, and refinement. The reason moral social-ization is not (or need not be) "mere" socialization has to do with the fact that there are constraints that govern the assessment and adjust-ment of moral learning. We are trying to learn "how best to organize and administer [our] collective and individual affairs." Social experience provides feedback about how we are doing, and rational mechanisms come into play in evaluating and assessing this feedback. So there is an aim, activity to achieve this aim, feedback about success in achieving the aim, and rational mechanisms designed to assess the meaning of the feedback and to make modifications to the activity.

What are these rational mechanisms? They include individual reflection as well as collective reflection and conversation. Now it is important to understand what our reflective practices are, ontologically. They do not involve the deployment of some rarefied culture-free faculty of reason. Dewey puts it best (1922, 56): "The reflective disposition is not self-made nor a gift of the gods. It arises in some exceptional circumstances out of social customs ... when it has been generated it establishes a new custom." According to Dewey, Plato made the mistake of thinking of our rational capacities as metaphysical or transcendental. This mistake is preserved among those who treat some special custom or set of customs (invariably their own) as "eternal, immutable, outside criticism and revision" (1922, 58). How much better things would go (and would have gone) if we had been able to see that our practices of reflection are themselves natural developments that emerged partly because they were useful. Our reflective practices, from individual reflection to collective conversation and debate, are themselves customs that permit "experimental initiative and creative invention in remaking custom" (1922, 56). The choice "is not between a moral authority outside custom and one within it. It is between adopting more or less intelligent and significant customs" (1922, 58).

I think of these Deweyan points as extensions of Churchland's general line about moral knowledge.[7] But this idea – that to be rational, self-conscious, and critical are developments of natural capacities, that they are things we learn to be and to do, rather than transcendental capacities we simply have – is still not well understood, nor is it widely accepted.[8] But it is true. Critical rationality is a perfectly natural capacity displayed by *Homo sapiens* socialized in certain ways. Fancy, yes. But nothing mysterious metaphysically.

So far I have tried to extend the picture of moral learning Churchland favors, explaining how moral network theory can account for complex prototype activation and how it can account for our rational practices themselves as socially acquired and communally circumscribed in structure and content. In closing, I want to speak about my two concerns with the picture as Paul Churchland puts it forth. I said at the start that my reservations had to do with Churchland's over-optimistic attitude about the capacities of the moral community to arrive at high-quality moral knowledge and with his failure to emphasize sufficiently the local nature of much of our moral knowledge. To be fair, Churchland doesn't say a whole lot about these issues, and it is possible I have misunderstood him. But in either case, it will be good to draw him out and have him say some more.

First, there is the over-optimistic attitude about moral progress. Now, both Paul Churchland and I are pragmatists, so I agree with him completely when he says that "the quality of one's knowledge is measured not by any uniform correspondence between internal sentences and external facts, but by the quality of one's continuing performance" (1989, 298). I also agree with him when he writes (300) of socio-moral knowledge acquisition that "what the child is learning is practical wisdom: the wise administration of her practical affairs in a complex social environment. This is as genuine a case of learning about objective reality as one finds anywhere."

Here's the rub: What the child learns about "the wise administration of her practical affairs" is a complex mixture of moral knowledge, social savvy, and prudential wisdom. These things overlap in important ways but not in all respects, and they are worth distinguishing. Once they are separated, it is easy to see that these things are typically in some tension with one other. The demands of social success and prudence can compete with each other and with the demands of morality. If most knowing is knowing how, then what the socio-moral community must do is teach people how to resolve such conflicts. Communities of possessive individualists learn one form of resolution, while Mother Teresa's nuns learn a different one. Practical success may come to both communities as they see it, but one might argue that moral considerations are hardly improved or developed equally in both communities. This may be fine and the way things should go, all things considered. But it is important not to think that when Churchland writes that "we have a continuing society under constant pressure to refine its categories of social and moral perception, and to modify its typical responses and expectations," the constant pressure to refine is primarily working on the moral climate. The reason we shouldn't think this is simply that there are too many interests besides moral ones vying for control of our socio-moral responses: There is simple self-interest, prudence, concern with economic, social, and sexual success, and much else besides. Furthermore, it really is in the interest of different individuals and social groups to train others to believe (and even to make it true, up to a point) that their being well and doing well involves conforming to norms that produce disproportionate good for the trainers.

A different but related point comes from reflecting on the ends of ethics. I certainly don't think that the ends of science are simple or unambiguous, but I suspect that they do not display the inherent tension that the ends of ethics do. What I have in mind here goes back to what I said earlier about the two sides of ethics: on the one side, the interpersonal, concerned with social stability, coordination, prevention of harms, and so on; and, on the other side, the intrapersonal, concerned with individual flourishing, personal goodness, and the like. The tension between impartial moral demands and what conduces to individual flourishing is ubiquitous. Moral ambiguity is endemic to the first steps of ordinary moral life. We wonder how spending so much on luxuries that we can afford could possibly be justified, given the absolute poverty that exists in many places in the world. Much recent philosophical attention has been given to this tension between the more impartial demands of morality as we are exposed to it and the goods of personal freedom, choice, and integrity that we also learn. (Rawls, 1993, sees the tension as one between the ends of politics and ethics, but the basic point is the same.) There are conceivable ways to remove the tension – just remove one of the dual ends of moral life from the way we construct our conception of it. But this seems an unappealing idea. It seems best to leave the tension as it is; it is real, and more good comes from having to confront it again and again than could come from simply stipulating it away. But one consequence of leaving the causes of moral ambiguity in place is that we will often rightly feel a certain lack of confidence that we have done the right thing. This suggests that we are often, at least in the moral sphere, in situations where we have no firm knowledge to go on.

A related consequence of the fact that the very aims of ethics are in tension is this: Interpersonal ethics requires that we cast the normative net widely and seek agreement about mechanisms of coordination and what constitutes harm. Intrapersonal ethics creates pressures to cast the net narrowly. We think it is good that different people find their good in different ways; it is good that the Amish construct virtue the way they do, and it is good that some communities think benevolence is the most important individual virtue while others think humility or peace of mind is. One problem that often occurs, which this picture helps us understand, is that wide-net policies, e.g., US abortion laws, can not only conflict with the ways some individuals and groups find ethical meaning but also undermine their sense of their own integrity by virtue of their complex commitment to both the larger culture and the values of their group.

In casting its net more widely, the interpersonal side may well yield relatively global moral knowledge: It is just wrong to kill someone, except in self-defense. But the idea that different persons find their good in different ways will require acknowledgement that much ethical knowledge is local knowledge. It is knowledge possessed by a particular group – Catholics, Amish, secular humanists, Hindus, and Muslims –

and it is hugely relevant to the quality of the lives of the members of the group that they live virtuously as they see it.

❊ ❊ ❊ ❊

In closing, I return to the second of the two quotes from Dewey that mark the beginning of this paper: "Moral science is not something with a separate province. It is physical, biological, and historic knowledge placed in a humane context where it will illuminate and guide the activities of men" (1922, 204–5). What is relevant to ethical reflection is everything we know, everything we can bring to ethical conversation – from the human sciences, from history, and from literature – that merits attention. One lesson such reflection teaches, it seems to me, is that if ethics is like any science or is part of any science, it is part of *human ecology*, concerned with saying what contributes to the flourishing of human groups and human individuals in particular natural and social environments. Thinking of normative ethical knowledge as something to be gleaned from thinking about human good relative to particular ecological niches will, it seems to me, make it easier for us to see that there are forces of many kinds operating at many levels, as humans seek their good; that individual human good can compete with the good of human groups and of nonhuman systems; and finally that only some ethical knowledge is global – most is local, and appropriately so. It might also make it seem less compelling to find ethical agreement where none is needed.

Notes

I thank Bob McCauley and members of the Triangle Ethics Group, especially Simon Blackburn, Gerry Postema, Dorit Bar-On, Jay Rosenberg, and Andrews Reath for extremely helpful comments.
1 Churchland's views remind me somewhat of Piagetian views where there is an assimilation-accommodation dialectic occurring between the organism and the world as the organism tries to figure out how space, time, causality, and so on work. Kohlberg appropriated the Piagetian model to ethics (a project Piaget had himself begun in 1932), but the crucial point Kohlberg and Kohlbergians pay insufficient attention to is that the moral world isn't fixed in remotely the same way the spatial, temporal, or causal structure of the world is fixed. When the moral universe is in need of repair, it is neither good nor required that we accommodate ourselves to it. Changing it is a better idea.
2 One issue I haven't emphasized here but discuss as length in *Varieties of Moral Personality* (1991) is the way personality develops. One might think that it is a problem for a network theory that it will explain the acquisition of

moral prototypes in such a way that character is just a hodgepodge of prototypes. I don't think this is a consequence of moral network theory. One idea is to emphasize the fact that the human organism is having its natural sense of its own continuity and connectedness reinforced by the social community. A self, a person, is being built. The community counts on the individual to develop a sense of his own integrity, of seeing himself as an originator of agency, capable of carrying through on intentions and plans, and of being held accountable for his actions. The community, in effect, encourages a certain complex picture of what it means to be a person, and it typically ties satisfaction of moral norms to this picture. Identity involves norms, and the self is oriented towards satisfying these norms. This helps explain the powerful connections shame, guilt, self-esteem, and self-respect have with morality. Morality is acquired by a person with a continuing identity who cares about norm satisfaction and about living well and good.

3 What about self-ascription of lies? Attribution theory provides good evidence of a self-serving bias. This bias warrants the prediction that third-person attributions of lies and self-attributions will diverge in identical circumstances. Not surprisingly, children powerfully tempted to transgress some rule will do so, but will deny that they have done so. Children who peek at a toy will lie when asked if they did (Lewis, Stanger and Sullivan, 1989). It is unlikely that the children think that they did not peek. In fact, it is well known that both children and grown-ups often construe certain circumstances as mitigating in their own case (which would not be mitigating for others), and thus offer self-serving construals of their own lies as not *real* lies. The child who is caught in a lie and says sheepishly, "I was only kidding," may well believe her own, after-the-fact, self-attribution to a far greater extent than perfect memory of her actual prior intent would permit.

4 Of course, these matters are variable. Some adults do convey that it is absolutely wrong to lie and try to evoke the fear of God in youngsters.

5 There is a problem with the individuation of both prototypes and neural nets and thus questions of how simple or complex we ought to think prototypes are, how we should conceive the realizations of prototypes in neural nets, and how we should conceive what exactly is activated when a person is confronted with a complex situation. Churchland writes (1989, 300),

> How the learning child subsequently reacts to a novel social situation will be a function of which of her many prototypes that situation activates, and this will be a matter of the relative similarity of the new situation to the various prototypes on which she was trained. This means that situations will occasionally be ambiguous. One and the same situation can activate distinct prototypes in distinct observers. What seems a case of unprovoked cruelty to one child can seem a case of just retribution to another.

Although I doubt that Churchland is committed to it, the picture here could be read as assuming that each child has, say, her prototype of cruelty and her prototype of just retribution. Response depends on the saliencies in the situation which activate the relevant prototype for that individual. An alternative picture, one I am inclined to think is more plausible, is that any situation will spread activation through a complex array of prototype structures, which will then determine response.

6   Churchland continues the quoted passage this way: "A body of legislation accumulates, with successive additions, deletions, and modifications. A body of case law accumulates, and the technique of finding and citing relevant precedents (which are, of course, *prototypes*) becomes a central feature of adjudicating legal disputes." The law is a good example of a well-controlled normative domain where previous decisions produce weighty constraints and norms accumulate. But it is not obvious that the law and morality, despite both being normative, are alike in these respects. In the law, publicity, precedent, and stability are highly valued – indeed they are partly constitutive of the law. Public, stable norms, with precedents, are thought to be good, and essential to successful and reliable negotiation of the parts of life covered by the law. But it is also recognized that the goods of stability, publicity, and so on are perfectly compatible with irrational or immoral laws. So one point is that the aims of the law are not the same as those of ethics (ignorance of the law is no defense, but ethical ignorance can be). Another issue arises in the first part of the quoted passage where Churchland frames the issue as one of humans confronting "the problem of how best to perceive the social world, and how best to conduct one's affairs within it." This is, I think, just the right way to see the problem. But I want to insist that there is a telling difference between, for example, learning about legal reality, or how best to perceive the causal, temporal, spatial structure of the world, and how to conduct one's affairs in this (these) world(s). The difference is simply this: These latter structures are more stable and more global than the moral structure of the world. This is one reason that Piagetian developmental-stage theories have had some success with space, time, causality, conservation, and number, while Kohlberg's extension of Piaget's model to the moral sphere has turned out to be a dismal failure, an utterly degenerate research program, despite many true believers.

7   We might also compare the view being floated to Allan Gibbard's norm expressivist view (1990). For Gibbard, norms express judgments about *what it makes sense to feel, think, and do*. Norm expression involves endorsement, as it does in classical emotivism. But it is endorsement that can be rationally discussed among conversants – endorsement that can be "discursively redeemed" to give it a Habermasian twist (p. 195). Pushing all talk of the literal truth or falsehood of normative utterances generally – and normative moral utterances specifically – to one side, there is still plenty to be said on behalf of the rationality or sensibility of particular normative claims. There are conversational challenges to be met, facts to call attention to, consistency and relevance to be displayed, and higher-level norms that govern the acceptance of other norms to be brought on the scene. We will need to explain whether the norms we endorse forbid a particular act, require it, or

simply allow it. And we may be called upon to explain the point behind any of our norms.

For Gibbard, morality is first and foremost concerned with interpersonal *coordination* and *social stability*. Given linguistic capacity it is natural that the need for coordination will lead eventually to norms of conversation that govern normative influence, to the vindication of specific normative judgments, and so on. It makes sense to develop such norms if our aim is coordination. We expect our fellow discussants to be consistent in their beliefs and attitudes, and thus we can reasonably ask them to show us how it is that their normative system is consistent. We can ask them to say more about some normative judgment to help us to see its rationale. We can ask them to provide a deeper rationale or to provide us with reasons for taking them seriously as reliable normative judges, and so on. A reason is anything that can be said in favor of some belief, value, or norm – any consideration that weighs in favor of it. Since the things that can be said on behalf of almost anything constitute an infinitely large class, reasons abound in normative life. No set of reasons may yield conviction in the skeptic or in someone whose life form lies too far from our own, but this in no way distinguishes normative life from the rest of life.

8   We find Stanley Fish, more than a half-century after Dewey, making very much the same point (1993, 14), albeit in a more contentious manner.

> Critical self-consciousness, conceived of as a mental action independent of the setting in which it occurs, is the last infirmity of the mind that would deny its own limits by positioning itself in two places at the same time, in the place of local embodiment and in the disembodied place (really no place) of reflection. Reflection, however, is not a higher and relatively detached level of a particular practice; it is a practice and when one is engaged in it, one is obeying its constitutive rules rather than relaxing the constitutive rules of another practice ... What this means is that there is no such thing as critical self-consciousness, no separate 'muscle of the mind' that can be flexed in any situation, no capacity either innate or socially nurtured for abstracting oneself from everyday routines in the very act of performing them.

References

Baier, Annette C. (1990). Why honesty is a hard virtue. In O. Flanagan and A. O. Rorty (eds), *Identity, Character, and Morality: Essays in Moral Psychology*. Cambridge: MIT Press.

Bok, Sissela (1978). *Lying: Moral Choice in Public and Private Life*. New York: Random House.

Burton, R. V. and Strichartz A. F. (1992). Liar, liar! Pants afire. In S. J. Ceci et al. (eds), 11–28.

Bussey, Kay (1992). Children's lying and truthfulness: implications for children's testimony. In S. J. Ceci et al. (eds), 89–110.

Ceci, Stephen J., Leichtman M. D., and Putnick, M. E. (eds) (1992). *Cognitive and Social Factors in Early Deception*. Hillsdale, N. J.: Erlbaum.

Coleman, L. and Kay, P. (1981). Prototype semantics: the English verb *lie*. *Language*, **57**, 26–44.

Chandler, M., Fritz, A. S. and Hala, S. (1989). Small-scale deceit: deception as a marker of two-, three-, and four-year-olds' early theories of mind. *Child Development*, **60**, 1263–77.

Churchland, Paul M. (1989). *A Neurocomputational Perspective: The Nature of Mind and the Structure of Science*. Cambridge: MIT Press.

Dewey, John (1922/1988). *Human Nature and Conduct*. Carbondale: Southern Illinois University Press.

Dunn, J. (1987). The beginnings of moral understanding: development in the second year. In J. Kagan and S. Lamb (eds), *The Emergence of Morality in Young Children*. Chicago: Chicago University Press.

Fish, Stanley (1993). Why literary criticism is like virtue. *London Review of Books*, 10 June, 11–16.

Flanagan, Owen (1982). Quinean ethics. *Ethics*, **93**, 56–74.

Flanagan, Owen (1988). Pragmatism, ethics, and correspondence truth: response to Gibson and Quine. *Ethics*, **98**: 541–49.

Flanagan, Owen (1991). *Varieties of Moral Personality: Ethics and Psychological Realism*. Cambridge: Harvard University Press.

Flanagan, Owen (1992). Other minds, obligation, and honesty. In S. J. Ceci et al. (eds), 111–24.

Gibbard, Allan (1990). *Wise Choices, Apt Feelings: A Theory of Normative Judgment*. Cambridge: Harvard University Press.

Gibson, Roger (1988). Flanagan on Quinean ethics. *Ethics*, **98**: 534–40.

Johnson, Mark (1993). *Moral Imagination: Implications of Cognitive Science for Ethics*. Chicago: Chicago University Press.

Lakoff, G. (1987). *Women, Fire, and Dangerous Things: What Categories Reveal About the Mind*. Chicago: Chicago University Press.

Lewis, M., Stanger, C. and Sullivan, M. W. (1989). Deception in three-year-olds. *Developmental Psychology*, **25**, 439–43.

Peterson, C. C., Peterson, J. L. and Seeto, D. (1983). Developmental changes in ideas about lying. *Child Development*, **54**, 1529–35.

Piaget, J. (1932). *The Moral Judgment of the Child*. London: Kegan Paul.

Quine, W. V. O. (1979). On the nature of moral values. *Critical Inquiry*, **5**, 471–80.

Quine, W. V. O. (1986). Reply to Morton White in L. E. Hahn and P. A. Schilpp (eds), *The Philosophy of W. V. Quine*. LaSalle, Ill.: Open Court.

Rawls, John (1993). *Political Liberalism*. New York: Columbia University Press.

Sodian, B. (1991). The development of deception in young children. *British Journal of Developmental Psychology*, **9**, 1, 173–88.

Wellman, H. M. (1990). *The Child's Theory of Mind*. Cambridge: MIT Press.

White, Morton (1986). Normative ethics, normative epistemology, and Quine's holism. In L. E. Hahn and P. A. Schilpp (eds), *The Philosophy of W. V. Quine*. LaSalle, Ill.: Open Court.

Wimmer, H., Gruber, S. and Perner, J. (1985). Young children's conception of lying: moral intuition and the denotation and connotation of "to lie." *Developmental Psychology*, **21**, 993–5.

Part II

Replies from the Churchlands

We begin by expressing our heartfelt thanks to the distinguished contributors to this volume, and especially to its wise and patient editor, Robert McCauley. We are honored to be the focus of their collected criticisms. These arrive from many different points on the ideological compass, but, even so, there are unifying themes among them and structure to the issues behind them. Accordingly, our replies to the twelve critics at hand, and to other critics whose voices sound elsewhere, are organized around five major topics. This buys us some welcome simplicity in formulating our responses and will make it easier for others to profit from our collective theoretical encounter.

A

The Future of Psychology, Folk and Scientific

There is an arresting consistency to the critical essays of the authors addressed in the present subtitle. Their differences, while worthy in their own right, pale next to their convergence on a specific set of criticisms. The convergence is the more compelling since the criticisms stem, independently, both from overt connectionist sympathizers (Clark and McCauley) and from declared I'm-from-Missouri skeptics about connectionist models (Kitcher). Fodor, Lepore, and Lycan, while they happen to be focused on other topics in the present volume, should also be included in this list of *amici psychologiae*. To a first approximation, the principal conviction shared by all of them is that psychological descriptions and explanations comprehend an objective level of organization in nature, a level that demands a vocabulary and system of laws appropriate to its high-level structures, a vocabulary and system of laws that should not be eliminated in favor of, and need not be reducible to, the vocabulary and system of laws appropriate to any lower level of natural phenomena – to the level of the brain's neural microstructure and neurophysiology, for example.

Our iconoclastic reputations aside, we count ourselves among the most fervent of the Friends of Psychology, at least in the following respects. As we see it, the development of psychological theories adequate to human and animal phenomena is and should be among the highest priorities of modern science. Moreover, the existence of psychological phenomena and of some level-appropriate concepts with which to comprehend them are not in the least threatened by the emergence of systematic neuroscience. The history of science contains several obvious parallels. Biological phenomena and the propriety of biological-level concepts are not threatened by the emergence of a systematic chemistry. Chemical phenomena and the propriety of chemical-level concepts are not threatened by the emergence of atomic and subatomic physics. Astronomical phenomena, and the propriety of astronomical-level concepts, are not threatened by the emergence of mechanics, optics, and electromagnetic theory. So it is with psychology and the neurosciences.

The discipline of psychology will still be with us a hundred years from now, and five hundred, and a thousand. Practically speaking, it may well emerge as the most important to us of all the sciences. Its existence is unthreatened. What is *occasionally* threatened, here, as in the other examples, is the propriety of specific concepts and theories *within* the "higher-level" discipline. (For example, astronomy no longer speaks of rotating crystal spheres; chemistry no longer speaks of phlogiston and caloric fluid; biology no longer speaks of animal spirits and the archeus; and so on.) Such concepts and theories are ever hostage to epistemic fate and to new evaluation in the light of goodness-knows-what sorts of new information. Any attempt to spare them the measure of such evaluation is a corruption of scientific integrity. Further, what is *regularly* threatened, here as in the other examples, is the *autonomy* of the "higher-level" discipline. As the disciplines at every "level" slowly mature, it becomes increasingly impossible (and increasingly benighted) to try to conduct the affairs of any one discipline independently of the affairs of its immediate neighbors, both upward and downward in level.

For example, the true nature of biological metabolism was a mystery until chemistry allowed us to reconstruct, in molecular terms, the many transformations that turn any animal's input nutrition into heat, growth, locomotion, and waste. For a second example, at this lower level of organization in turn, the structure of chemistry's periodic table, though well mapped by Mendeleev and his followers, was a profound mystery until the wave mechanics of stable electron shells allowed us to reconstruct the valences and other bonding behaviors of the 96 natural elements.

Moreover, such interlevel illumination occasionally comes not from one but from *two* levels down. Recall the biological mystery of how living things manage to reproduce themselves. As the Watson–Crick story has made familiar, here one had to reach down not just to the level of organic chemistry, but all the way down to the level of x-ray crystallography (to reveal experimentally a helical structure of some kind) and to the level of atomic physics (to determine the allowable bonding angles consistent with any structural model of the DNA molecule). It is at this same *sub*-basement level of quantum-atomic physics that one finally finds the explanation for the *genetic variation* so essential to evolutionary biology, namely quantum-statistical copying errors and the occasional revisions in native DNA coding produced by the impact of subatomic cosmic rays.

We therefore regard it as completely unproblematic both that a hierarchy of independently worthy sciences should exist and that major illumination should often flow from the lower-level sciences upwards. Also, we have argued (especially PSC, 1986a) that illumination often flows from the high-level sciences *down*wards. The structural information that Lavoisierian chemistry imposed on the development of modern atomic theory is a shining example, and there are many others. More generally, theories at different levels quite properly function as ongoing checks, balances, and inspirations for theories at adjacent levels, both up and down. All of this is part of what PSC has called the "co-evolutionary strategy" for constructing a coherent story of reality at all of its organizational levels. Finally, and to close the circle, we agree that molar-level psychological theory has as much a priori right to exert critical and integrative pressures on neuroscientific theorizing as the latter has on the former.

Wherefore, then, the conflict with our critics? It is slightly different for each, but the major sticking point is still our well-known prediction that the propositional attitudes displayed in folk psychology, and in some scientific psychological theories as well (Fodor, 1975, for example), are fated to be swept away in favor of a new set of theoretical notions, notions inspired by our emerging understanding of the brain.

For us, this is an empirical claim, based on our reading of a broad range of overlapping evidence. Certainly there is ample room for reasonable people to disagree in their reading of it. We welcome the opportunity to reweigh the evidence, since it has matured considerably since PMC's 1981 and PSC's 1986a. We welcome also the form of the criticisms here urged upon us, for they are entirely free of any a priori arguments designed to make propositional-attitude psychology forever invulnerable to empirical criticism. (Our responses to various objections of this latter kind can be found in PMC, 1988; 1989b; 1993; and PSC, 1986b.)

10
McCauley's Demand for a Co-level Competitor

McCauley's is perhaps the most straightforward of the criticisms. He sees some form of *reductive* accommodation as the relation most likely to develop between propositional-attitude psychology, on the one hand, and the underlying neurosciences, on the other. In support of this expectation, he cites the typical co-evolutionary process described by PSC, wherein theories at adjacent levels gradually knit themselves into some appropriate reductive relation or other. McCauley's crucial move is then to claim that *eliminative* adjustments of theory are never (almost never?) motivated by considerations of cross-level conflict; rather, they are typically or properly motivated only by conflicts of theory at or within the *same* level of organization. In the absence of some compelling and comparably high-level alternative to folk psychology, then, we need not see folk psychology (FP) as facing any real threat of elimination. Accordingly, says McCauley, we should stand back and let the gradual interlevel knitting of theory proceed.

McCauley's portrait of FP's future may be correct. His guess is as good as ours, and a largely retentive reduction remains a live possibility. But the historical pattern he leans on is not so uniform as he suggests, and any probative classification of reality into distinct "levels" is something that is itself hostage to changeable theory. Consider the highly instructive example of astronomy.

For at least two thousand years (roughly from Aristotle to Galileo), the realm of the heavens was regarded as a distinct and wholly different level within the natural order. It was distinguished from the terrestrial, or sublunary, realm in several mutually-reinforcing ways. Sheer scale was the first difference, then as now. Thanks to Aristotle, Aristarchos, and Eratosthenes, even the geocentric ancients were aware that the moon was 240,000 miles away, that the sun was at least 5,000,000 miles away, and that the planets and the stars were more distant still.

Astronomical phenomena evidently took place on a spatial scale at least four or five orders of magnitude beyond the scale of any human practical experience.

Second, the laws that governed our small-scale sublunary realm had neither place among nor grip upon the obviously special superlunary objects. They moved in their (almost) perfectly circular paths, according to their own laws, in a fashion that had no parallel within the terrestrial domain. Third, the realm of the heavens was immutable and incorruptible, in contrast to our own sorry domain. Centuries may flow by, but the heavens remain unaltered. Fourth and finally, the realm of the heavens was evidently the realm of the divine, the home or doorstep of the gods.

Accordingly, even the most casual of observers could appreciate that the discipline of astronomy was attempting to grasp a level of the natural order far beyond what the Lilliputian mechanics of falling stones, taut ropes, and rolling wagons could ever hope to address. Ptolemy was explicit in rejecting the aspirations of "physics" to explain astronomical phenomena, and his voice reflected an almost universal opinion. Astronomy was an autonomous science attempting to grasp the autonomous laws appropriate to the phenomena at a dramatically distinct level of the natural order.

Further, the ancient astronomical theories actually made good on this conviction. Aristotle's account had a nest of 57 concentric earth-centered spheres, spheres made of the transparent and exclusively superlunary "fifth essence" (Plato's cosmium), each moving at the behest of its own perfectly circular, perfectly uniform *telos*. Ptolemy's different but similarly geocentric account had the familiar nest of perfectly circular deferent circles with eccentrically-placed centers, moving epicycles, and artfully placed "equant" points with which to cheat a bit on the issue of the perfect uniformity of astronomical motions.

We all know what finally happened to these ancient, "high-level" theories. They turned out to be radically false theories, so fundamentally defective that both their principles and their ontologies were eventually displaced, rather than smoothly reduced, by Newton's completed mechanics of motion (cf. the opening sentence of PMC's 1981). Astronomy as a discipline is still with us, of course, and is more vigorous than ever, but it no longer speaks of crystalline spheres, fifth essences, moving epicycles, and phantom equants. An anisotropic, geocentric, rotating, finite spherical universe was displaced wholesale in favor of an isotropic, earth-indifferent, nonrotating, possibly infinite space. And the laws that govern the heavens turned out to be the very same laws that govern phenomena at the terrestrial level. They are the laws of Newtonian mechanics.

We present this as a presumptive counterexample to McCauley's claim that theories suffer radical displacement only at the hands of co-level competitors, and never at the hands of theories whose primary home is at a different level of scale or organization. Since the Newtonian revolution, modern astronomy has simply *become* the Physics of the Heavens. What remains, then, among the patterns of history, that would preclude modern psychology from simply *becoming* the Neuroscience of very Large and Intricate Brains? Perhaps brains differ from sea-slug ganglia only in the scale of neuronal interactions they involve.

We anticipate the reply, from McCauley, that this historical elimination of an ancient astronomical theory was not a cross-level displacement at all, but rather a displacement by a theory (Newtonian mechanics) that encompassed phenomena at the *same* dynamical level as the old theory. It is just that astronomical phenomena turned out not to be unique or special after all: They are distinguished only by their vast scale.

The reply has a point, and McCauley may succeed in pressing this interpretation upon us. But this reply entails what should have been clear anyway: that science can be profoundly wrong about what counts as a nomically-distinct level of phenomena, and profoundly wrong in its estimation of which theories do and do not count as genuinely "co-level" theoretical competitors. And if McCauley accepts this point, as we think it clear he must, then he is in no position to insist that the psychology/neuroscience case must turn out differently from the astronomy/physics case. Psychological phenomena, perhaps, are distinguished only by the unusual scale of the networks that display them.

Our conclusion, then, is as follows. The claim that psychology comprehends a distinct level of phenomena comprehended by a distinct set of laws uniquely appropriate to that level *is not an assumption that our opposition can have for free*. It is part of what is at issue – *empirically at issue* – in this broad debate, and the historical fate of ancient astronomy should caution against any premature convictions in its favor.

Astronomy aside, there are other historical examples that contradict McCauley's generalization about the agents of ontological displacement.[1] Eliminative cross-level impacts on conceptual structure, both upward and downward, seem to us to be historically familiar, not rare or nonexistent. But we need not explore further examples here. Instead, let us explore directly the popular conviction that psychological phenomena really do belong to a more abstract level of analysis. If they do, would that really serve to insulate FP or other propositional-attitude theories from the threat of wholesale displacement?

Not in the least. Even if an abstract or higher-level explanatory framework were somehow essential to grasping psychological phenomena, it would remain an open question whether our current FP is the *correct* framework with which to meet this challenge. Legitimating the office need not legitimate the current office holder. This point is important because a priori there are infinitely many comparably high-level alternatives to FP; and because it is arguable that the conceptual framework of neo-connectionism is one of them.

As we sketched the fate of ancient astronomy a few paragraphs ago, it turned out that astronomical phenomena were not distinctly higher-in-level after all. But we might just as well have expressed the outcome by saying that the assembled laws of Newtonian mechanics turned out to be, when suitably articulated to fit the astronomical context, exactly the high-level theory that was needed to do the relevant high-level job. The analog of this latter stance, within psychology, will now be explored.

The claim on the table is that a psychological-level competitor for FP is already here and is already staring us in the face. It is the framework in which the occurrent *representations* are patterns of activation (or sequences of such patterns) across millions of neurons. It is the framework in which the *computations* are synapse-driven transformations of such patterns (or sequences thereof) into further such patterns across further neuronal populations. It is the framework in which such transformations are dictated by the *learned* patterns of synaptic connection strengths that connect one population of neurons with another. It is the framework, in short, of contemporary connectionist theory.

A frequent judgment about connectionist models of cognition is that they constitute at most an account of how classically conceived cognitive processes might be *implemented* in an underlying neural hardware. A quarter-century from now, we predict, this dismissal will be celebrated as one of the great head-in-the-sand episodes of twentieth-century science. Our confidence here is born not primarily of confidence in the ultimate correctness of connectionist models of cognition. (They must chance their hand to fate along with every other approach.) Rather, it is born of the recognition that the kinematics and dynamics of current connectionism already constitute an account of cognition at a decidedly abstract level. Allow us to explain.

When one sees a standard introduction to the connectionist modeling of cognitive processes, one is typically presented with a diagram of several layers of neuron-like units connected to one another by way of axon-like projections ending in synapse-like contacts (see figure 10.1, for example). One is then told about the variable nature of the weights of such contacts, about the multiplication of each axonal activation level by the synaptic weight it encounters, about the summation of all such products within the contacted neuron, and finally about the great variety of real-world discriminations such networks can be trained to make. We have given such accounts ourselves, and any audience can be forgiven for thinking that they are witness to an account of the underlying wheels and gears that might or might not *realize* the many abstract cognitive faculties that psychology presumes to study.

And so witness they are. But the real story only begins there, and strictly speaking that beginning is inessential. Neuronal details are no more essential to connectionist conceptions of cognition than vacuum-tube or transistor details are essential to the classical conception of cognition embodied in orthodox AI, Fodorean psychology, and FP itself. What is essential is the idea of fleeting high-dimensional patterns

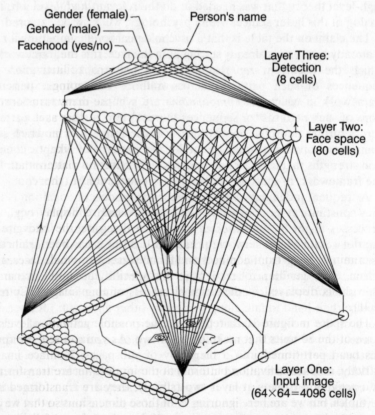

Figure 10.1 A feedforward network for discriminating facehood, gender, and personal identity as displayed in photographic images (adapted from Cottrell, 1991)

being transformed into other such patterns by virtue of their distributed interaction with an even higher-dimensional matrix of relatively stable transforming elements. The fleeting patterns constitute a creature's specific representations of important aspects of its changing environment. And the relatively stable matrix of transforming elements constitutes the creature's background knowledge of the general or chronic features of the world.

The abstract nature of this new conception of cognitive activity is revealed immediately by the fact that such activity can be physically realized in a wide variety of ways: in sundry biological wetwares, in silicon chips etched with parallel architectures, and even in a suitably programmed serial/digital machine, although this third incarnation exacts an absurdly high price in lost speed.

Its abstract or high-level nature is further revealed when we explore its kinematical and dynamical properties. Each *population* of elements (such as the neurons at the retina, or at the LGN, or at the primary visual cortex, and so on) defines a high-dimensional *space* of possible activation patterns across that population, patterns that are roughly equiprobable to begin with. But their relative probabilities gradually change over time as the system learns from its ongoing experience. Learning consists in the gradual modification of the many transforming matrices through which each activation pattern must pass as it filters its way through the system's many layers. Each matrix is so modified as to make certain activation patterns at the next layer more likely and other patterns less likely. The space of possible activation patterns at each layer thus acquires an intricate internal structure in the course of training.

Visual models are helpful here, and two standard display types are shown in figure 10.2. Their purpose is to illustrate the background cognitive state of the network of figure 10.1 after it has been trained to discriminate faces from nonfaces and female faces from male faces, and, within each gender, to recognize the specific faces of 11 named individuals displayed in the original set of training images (Cottrell, 1991).

The space in figure 10.2a represents the possible activation levels of three of the 80 units that make up layer two. As you can see, the space has been partitioned into a hierarchy of subspaces. Nonface images (strictly, nonface activation patterns) at the input layer are transformed into activation triplets at layer two (strictly, they are transformed into 80-tuples, but we are here ignoring 77 of those dimensions so that we can have a coherent picture to examine), triplets that always fall into the smallish subvolume near the origin of this 3-space. Evidently, most of the dynamic range of the units at layer two has been given over to the representation of faces. For all face images at the input layer get transformed into triplets that fall into the much larger subvolume to the right of the small triangular partition.

Within that larger subvolume is a second partition, this time dividing the range of activation triplets that represent female faces from the range of activation triplets for male faces. Activation triplets that fall anywhere on that speckled vertical partition are the network's mature

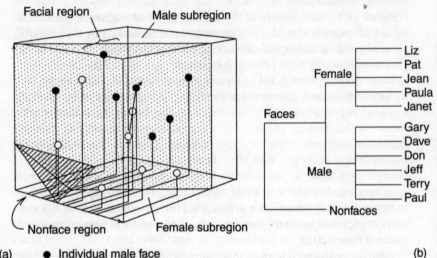

(a)
● Individual male face
○ Individual female face
♂ Prototypical male face
♀ Prototypical female face
⊕ Gender-ambiguous face

(b)

Figure 10.2 (a) An activation state space whose three axes represent three of the 80 units at the middle layer of Cottrell's face-discrimination network. The partitions into subcategories are visible, as are the small volumes that code input images for each of the eleven individuals variously portrayed in the training set. This 3-space is frankly a cartoon, in that the distinctions displayed cannot effectively be drawn within only three of the 80 dimensions available at Layer Two. If they could, the network would need only three units at that layer. In fact, only the bulk of those 80 units working together will draw all of those distinctions reliably. However, the 3-space does represent fairly the kind of partitioning that training produces, except that the true partitions are high-dimensional hypersurfaces rather than 2-D planes.

(b) A dendogram representing the same set of hierarchically organized categories. Since they make no attempt to portray partition surfaces and hypersurfaces, dendograms are indifferent to the dimensionality of the activation space at issue.

responses to input-layer face images that are highly *ambiguous* as to gender. Activation triplets within each of the 11 small volumes scattered on either side of that partition represent slightly different photographs of the 11 different individuals represented in the training set. The network has thus developed six further subcategories within the male subvolume and five subcategories within the female subvolume. The relevant partitions have been left out of figure 10.2a so as to avoid visual clutter, but the 11 prototypical "hot spots" within each final partition are saliently represented.

Figure 10.2a indicates how the regularities and variances implicit in the set of training images have come to be represented by an acquired set of structures within the activation space of layer two. The job of the network's Layer Three is now the relatively easy one of the discriminating just where, within this hierarchy of Layer Two subspaces, any fleeting activation pattern happens to fall. This it does well. Overall, Cottrell's network achieved 100 percent reliability on the (roughly 100) images in the training set, in facehood, gender, and individual identity. More importantly, its acquired perceptual skills generalized robustly to images it had never seen before. It remains 100 percent accurate on faces vs. nonfaces; it remains almost 90 percent accurate on arbitrary male and female faces; and to any novel face, it tends to apply the name of the individual among the original eleven to whom that novel face bears the closest resemblance, as judged by relevant proximity in the space of figure 10.2a.

What we are looking at in this figure is the *conceptual space* of the trained network. (Or, rather, *one* of its conceptual spaces. The fact is, a network with many layers has many distinct conceptual spaces, one for each layer or distinct population of units. These spaces interact with each other in complex ways.) We are looking at the categorial framework with which the network apprehends its perceptual world.

Here it is important to appreciate, once more, that it is the overall activation pattern across all or most of layer two that is important for the network's cognitive activities. Because each element of the network contributes such a tiny amount to the overall process, no single unit is crucial and no single synapse is crucial. If any randomly chosen small subset of the units and synapses in the network is made inactive, then the quality of the network's responses will be degraded slightly, but its behavioral profile will be little changed. It is the *molar-level* properties of the network – its global activation patterns and its global matrix configurations – that are decisive for reckoning the major features of its ongoing input-output behavior. A single unit is no more crucial than is a single pixel on your TV screen: its failure is unlikely even to be noticed.

Evidently, this "vector/matrix" or "pattern/transformer" conception of cognition comprehends a level of abstraction beyond any of its possible implementation-level counterparts. It is not itself an implementation-level theory. The fact is, we have long been in possession of the relevant implementation-level science: It is neuroscience. Connectionism is something else again. What connectionism brings is a new and revealing way of comprehending the molar-level behavior of cognitive creatures, a way that coheres smoothly with at least two implementational stories: the theory of biological neural networks, and the theory of massively parallel silicon architectures. If McCauley insists upon a suitably high-level competitor for FP, fate has already delivered what he deems necessary. FP is already being tested against a new and quite different conception of cognition.

Let us now return to the examination of that new conception. Before addressing Kitcher's worries, we wish to draw out a little more of its molar-level potential.

Note

1 First, the rather feeble conceptual framework of early biology – sporting notions such as *telos, animal spirits, archeus,* and *essential form* – was eventually displaced by an entirely new framework of biological notions (such as *enzyme, vitamin, metabolic pathway,* and *genetic code*), notions regularly inspired by the emerging categories of structural and dynamical chemistry, a science that addressed a lower level of natural organization.

Second, the molar-level theory of classical thermodynamics, which identified heat with a macroscopic fluid substance called "caloric," was displaced by the molecular/kinetic account of statistical thermodynamics, a theory that addressed the dynamical behavior of corpuscles at a submicroscopic level.

Third, the well-established conceptual framework of geometrical optics, while a useful tool for understanding many macro-level effects, was shown to be a false model of reality when it turned out that all optical phenomena could be reduced to (i.e., reconstructed in terms of) the propagation of oscillating electromagnetic fields. In particular, it turned out that there is no such thing as a literal *light ray*. Geometrical optics had long been inadequate to diffraction, interference, and polarization effects anyway, but it took Maxwell's much more general electromagnetic theory to retire it permanently as anything more than an occasionally convenient tool.

Fourth, the old Aristotelian/alchemical conception of physical substance (as consisting of a continuous but otherwise fairly featureless base matter that gets variously informed by sundry insubstantial spirits) was gradually displaced in the nineteenth century by Dalton's atomic/structural conception of matter. Once again, we may count this an intralevel displacement if you wish, but it is clear that most of the details of Dalton's atomism – in particular, the relative atomic weight and the valence of each elemental atom – were inspired by higher-level chemical data concerning the intricate web of constant *weight ratios* experimentally revealed in chemical combinations and dissociations. Bluntly, a maturing chemistry had an enormous and continuing impact on the shape of a still-infantile atomism. In this case, note well, it was a higher-level science that was dictating our theoretical convictions at a lower level of natural organization.

11
Connectionism as Psychology

Our sketch to this point is missing any account of time, and of structures unfolding in time. These are important, since the ultimate function of cognition is to guide temporally organized behavior, and because its fruitful guidance requires in turn the perceptual recognition of temporally structured processes. Neural networks offer an unexpectedly powerful way of addressing both domains.

If a feedforward network is augmented by the addition of recurrent or descending pathways, as shown in figure 11.1a, it becomes capable of a continuous and cyclical mode of activity. A fleeting input pattern may initiate an extended sequence of activation patterns at the middle layer, a sequence sustained by the returning activation and dictated by the character of the several synaptic matrices that transform the patterns now circling within the neuronal loop. These *recurrent* networks can be trained to realize a family or hierarchy of prototypical *trajectories* in activation space (figure 11.1b), as opposed to the prototypical *positions* achieved by purely feedforward networks.

Such trajectories can take the form of closed loops in activation space, or open lengths with starting and stopping points. In both cases, they constitute ideal vehicles for the representation and production of complex *motor* behaviors. An animal's body contains literally thousands of distinct muscles, and these must somehow be collectively and coherently controlled. A 1,000-dimensional activation pattern conveyed by 1,000 motor axons to each of those 1,000 muscles gives the animal's central network simultaneous control over every one of them. And an appropriate sequence of such patterns can produce any gross motor behavior that is mechanically possible for the animal in question. Closed trajectories in activation space will produce periodic motor behaviors, such as chewing, walking, and running. Open trajectories will produce one-shot behaviors, such as redirecting one's gaze, biting an intruder, or reaching for an apple.

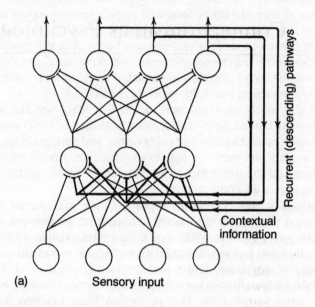

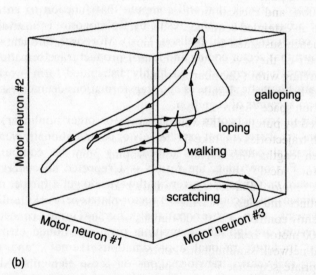

Figure 11.1 (a) A simple recurrent network. Such networks learn to produce not patterns but appropriate pattern sequences.

(b) The activation space of the recurrent network's middle layer. Each trajectory denotes a temporal sequence of activation patterns across those units.

Altogether, vector-transforming networks are just as remarkably appropriate for producing complex motor outputs at one end of the system as they are for processing complex sensory inputs at the other. Given that one and the same network can do both, and given that highly-processed sensory patterns can be synaptically transformed into muscle-controlling motor patterns, we have here the outlines of a general theory of cognitively-mediated sensorimotor coordination. A theory, moreover, that is biologically realistic.

To this much, everyone will agree. But many see the account just outlined as limited, in its explanatory potential, to the cognitive powers of simple creatures such as sea-slugs, ants, and perhaps frogs and lizards; and to only the simplest and most primitive aspects of cognition in humans and the other higher animals. High-level cognition, some say, will require a different account.

Perhaps it will. We won't know until we push it, for the issue is empirical. Despite some recent attempts at preemptive indictments (Fodor and Pylyshyn, 1988; Fodor and McLaughlin, 1990), it is now plain that no a priori limitations preclude a successful connectionist account of cognition. Quite the reverse. Hornick et al. (1989) have established that three-layer networks with sigmoid transfer functions are *universal approximators*. That is, for any finite function there exists a feedforward network that will compute that function to an arbitrary level of accuracy. An earlier result by Kolmogorov is equivalent to a similar conclusion (Hecht-Neilson, 1990). Moreover, Smolensky (1990) has shown that vector coding and tensor-product transformations are at least adequate to embody – in highly distributed form – exactly the systematic linguistic structures and transformations deemed essential by Fodorean accounts of cognition.

Vector-matrix networks with sigmoid (or other nonlinear) transfer functions are therefore not expressively or computationally weaker than their classical counterparts. Indeed, they may be computationally stronger. For one thing, the results just reported all concern purely feed*forward* networks: Recurrent pathways add yet a further computational dimension. Second, physical vector-matrix networks, unlike physical systems that answer to the Church–Turing conception of computation, are typically computing over real-valued elements (as opposed to finite, rational approximations thereof), and they are imposing real-valued transformations on those elements. All of this takes us into a domain of computation strictly unaddressed by the classical Church–Turing account. In sum, we reject the familiar complaints about the a priori limitations of connectionist architectures. They are unfounded.

None of this means that real creatures must be using connectionist architectures. It means only that, a priori, they might be. What indicates that they actually are using those representational and computational techniques is, first of all, the empirical evidence from microanatomy and neurophysiology. Crack open the skull of any real creature and what you find is an integrated committee of massively parallel and highly recurrent neural networks. That much, to use an expression of Fodor's, is nonnegotiable. It remains possible, to be sure, that they do the job of sustaining our conceptual and linguistic abilities only because they somehow *implement* exactly the systematic, compositional, rule-governed processes favored by the classical approaches to cognition. Testing this fallback hypothesis requires a closer look at how real networks, both biological and artificial, embody and execute their acquired skills.

Grammatical skills are an appropriate target for experiments in network learning, since they are the epitome of the cognitive skills for which the classical theories were developed. If networks can acquire such skills by repeated exposure to grammatical sentences, and do so without generating and subsequently applying any structure-sensitive rules, then the classical approach is in trouble.

Here there is an important sequence of results. Jeff Elman (1989; 1992) trained a recurrent network (figure 11.2a) to discriminate all and only the grammatical sentences generated by a simple but genuinely productive grammar over a lexicon of 21 words. The grammar permits considerable complexity in the form of embedded relative clauses, as in the sentence "Boys who kiss girl who feeds dog chase cats." The grammar demands, as does the trained network, that the plural verb "chase" agrees with the plural subject "Boys" despite being separated from it by six words, two nested relative clauses, and two distracting *singular* nouns.

The trained network is presented with a candidate sentence one word at a time, and it yields as output (for that word) a list of the grammatical categories permissible, at that point, for the next word in the sentence. In order to do that, it regularly needs to know not just what the current input word is but also what the preceding word was, and perhaps even the two or three words before that.

It is the recurrent loop, from the middle layer to the "auxiliary" input layer, that gives the network this continuous access to its own recent past. As you can see from figure 11.2a, what the network returns to the middle layer, along with each new input word, is not just the previous word, but rather its subsequent "digest" at the middle layer, a digest that places the previous word into the context of *its* preceding word, and so on. Evidently, information about earlier words can survive repeated cyclings through that recurrent loop, and thus exercise an influence on

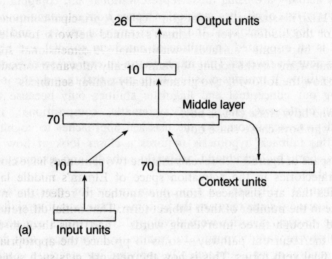

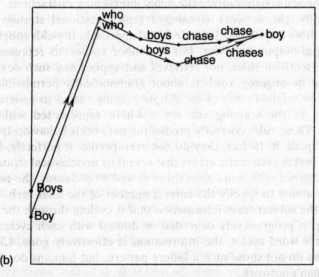

Figure 11.2 (a) The basic architecture of Elman's grammatically competent network.

(b) One surface within the hyperspace of the 70-unit middle or hidden layer. It reveals the distinct trajectories of two sentences differing only in the number of their subject terms and in the corresponding number of their final verbs. Note that the grammatically relevant subject difference is preserved in a distinct trajectory until it is finally discharged at the final verb, whereafter it disappears.

the network's response to an input word even at the end of a long sentence.

Figure 11.2b illustrates the point graphically. A principal-components analysis of the hidden layer of Elman's trained network revealed a number of important "surfaces" within that 70-dimensional space, surfaces important for the coding of grammatically relevant information. Consider now the following two grammatically similar sentences.

1   Boy who boys chase chases boy.
2   Boys who boys chase chase boy.

The 2-D space of figure 11.2b reveals that the two sentences have closely similar trajectories in the activation space of Elman's middle layer, trajectories that are displaced from one another to reflect the initial difference in the number of their subject term. That initial difference is preserved through three intervening words – and thus through four cycles of the recurrent pathway – so as to produce the appropriately different final verb forms. This is how the network gets such subject–verb agreements right despite the many intervening distractions.

Evidently, the network is using a representational strategy quite different from any classical or rule-based approach. It yields roughly the same input-output behavior, but it neither comes to represent any structure-sensitive rules, nor retrieves and applies any such devices in rendering its ongoing verdicts about grammatically permissible next words. The original rules of the simple grammar used to generate the sentences in the training set are nowhere represented within the network. Those rules correctly predict the network's behavior, but they do not explain it. In fact, they do not even predict it perfectly, for the network makes systematic errors that reveal its nonclassical strategy. In a long sentence with more than three nested who-clauses, the network loses the ability to specify the correct number of the final verb. This is because the subject-term information that is cycling through the recurrent loop is progressively degraded or diluted with each cycle: After three three-word cycles, the information is effectively gone. Classical algorithms do not show such a failure pattern, but humans do. And so does Elman's network.

A more recent experiment along these lines (Christiansen and Chater, 1994) uses a more complex and slightly more realistic grammar to generate a training set of 10,000 sentences. Three examples follow.

3   Mary knows that John's boy's cats eat mice.
4   Man who girls in town love thinks that Mary jumps.
5   Mary who loves John thinks that men say that girls chase boys.

Once again, the network learns to make these more complex grammatical discriminations almost perfectly for the sentences in the training set. And, like Elman's network, it generalizes well to novel sentences – that is to sentences generated by the initial grammar but not included in the training set.

The question addressed by Christiansen and Chater is, *How* well does it generalize? In particular, will the network parse correctly a sentence that is novel by reason of having a term in a type of syntactic position unoccupied by that term anywhere in the training set? Roughly, the issue is whether the network can get enough of a grip on the grammatical type of a given word – when the training set shows only a subset of the full range of its syntactic possibilities – to project that word into the rest of the relevant range. This ability is called "strong generalization" and their network failed to achieve it. Or, rather, it achieved it only very weakly, for noun-phrase conjunctions involving exactly two of the ten nouns in the lexicon. Humans, on the other hand, often do make such generalizations.

The authors express optimism that the network's marginal performance here can be improved, and they point out that strong generalization is also a problem for classical approaches to grammar. Humans do it better than either kind of model. Perhaps this is not surprising. Humans have a great deal of *semantic* information about the words they use, information useful for making the syntactic projections at issue. It may be that a purely syntactic approach to strong generalization is a mistake.

Only the classical approach, note well, is committed to a sharp distinction between syntax and semantics. Connectionist approaches are free to treat them, as the cognitivist tradition in linguistics (Lakoff, Langacker, Bates, Fauconnier) has always treated them, as being inseparable.

In any case, it is clear that connectionist cognitive architectures can handle grammatical structures of considerable complexity, not just in principle but in fact. Functioning networks already exist. It is also clear that they do it rather easily, for the networks we have been discussing are ridiculously small (< 500 units) compared with biological brains, and they have only the simplest of recurrent architectures. Larger and more complex networks may do much more. It would frankly be puzzling if, in real creatures, such a powerful resource was limited in its exploitation to sensorimotor coordination at the level of frogs and lizards.

12

Kitcher's Empirical Challenge: Has There Been Progress in Neurophilosophy?

This is the question raised by Patricia Kitcher. Although she fails to see significant progress in that domain, she does see considerable progress in psychology. This prompts her to propose that the "neuro" part of the project is, at best, premature and should wait upon further developments in psychology, which she thinks I (PSC) shun. Her proposal is that we shelve "neurophilosophy" in favor of what one might call "psychophilosophy." My reply has three parts:

1   the co-evolutionary vision of research proceeding on many levels simultaneously was an essential theme of the book, *Neurophilosophy*. I have been unwaveringly committed to the idea that neuroscience cannot do it alone, and that experimental psychology is indispensable if we are to have a prayer of understanding the nature of the mind/brain.
2   There has in fact been a tremendous flowering of activity and results in cognitive neuroscience. Research in that field focuses on the overlap between psychology and neuroscience and is centrally located in the wider program of understanding the neurobiological basis for psychological functions.
3   We can cite many examples of neuroscience relevant to current issues in philosophy.

Did Scientific Psychology Get Scrubbed in Neurophilosophy?

The principal aim of the book was to argue that neuroscience is relevant as we try to understand the nature of the mind. I took it to be obvious that scientific psychology is relevant, or at least obvious, once the purity of the armchair is abandoned and empirical data are considered relevant at all.

And I said at the time that psychology was not just relevant but essential.

Why was it necessary to argue for the relevance of neuroscience in particular? Because a number of psychologists, Fodor and Pylyshyn most notoriously, had gone to considerable lengths to explain why neuroscience was *irrelevant*, and because the existence of a "neurophobia" in linguistics and some areas of psychology was a brute fact in 1986. Many philosophers thought of themselves as functionalists in the Dennettian vein, meaning that they saw cognition as analogous to the software, and the brain as analogous to the hardware. As they saw it, it is no more necessary to look at the brain to understand the nature of, say, learning than it is necessary to understand my computer's microchips in order to understand how Microsoft Word constitutes a word processor.

As an autobiographical comment, I should mention that my early days studying brains at the medical school were often greeted with hilarity and disbelief by philosophers. How could I waste my time on something that would teach us nothing significant for understanding perception, reasoning, and so forth? It was not unusual for a concerned philosopher to sit me down patiently and try to explain functionalism to me, since I must obviously have missed its point.

Incidentally, the criticism of folk psychology should not be mistaken for an attack on scientific psychology generally, and I was at pains in *Neurophilosophy* to keep the two issues separate (see also earlier, p. 225). Indeed, many psychologists readily agree that scientific psychology will produce major changes to old ways of thinking about the mind and mental processes.

Was psychology an afterthought? Quite the contrary. In the introduction to *Neurophilosophy* I stated as the crux of my point that we needed an ". . . interanimation of philosophy, psychology and neuroscience, or, more generally, of top–down and bottom–up research" (3–4). "Thus, the co-evolution of microtheory and macrotheory – broadly, of neuroscience and psychology – is a major methodological theme throughout" (6). The same theme was sounded in almost every chapter. Some psychologists (e.g., Corballis, 1987) did indeed feel that the book would have been better had it included psychology chapters comparable in depth and detail to the neuroscience chapters. In principle the criticism is certainly right, but in practice it was impossible to avert, given that the book should be movable by something smaller than a wheelbarrow.

Undoubtedly psychologists comforted by functionalism's dismissal of the brain as "mere implementation" did find my arguments for the importance of neuroscientific constraints annoying. On the other hand, psychologists such as Richard Gregory and Elizabeth Bates, who had long been stressing the importance of neuroscientific findings for theories of perception and language respectively, found the slant positively congenial. Some psychologists, such as Steve Kosslyn, who initially felt psychology had been slighted in *Neurophilosophy*, are now energetically doing research at the psycho-neural interface.

My recent work with Ramachandran on the perceptual phenomenon of "filling in" (Churchland and Ramachandran, 1993) exemplifies my opportunistic naturalism. In that work, we made use of whatever data were available – from psychology and from neuroscience – to help understand the phenomenon that goes by the name of "filling in." Is it, as Dennett thought, just the brain ignoring something, or is it at least sometimes an active process in which a sensory representation is more complete afterwards? Our answer, after examining the available empirical data, was that in some cases visual filling in is quite evidently an active process of the brain. In fact, filling in at many levels can be understood as vector completion and is one of the things brains and nets do best (PMC, 1995). In *The Computational Brain*, with Terry Sejnowski (1992), we gave prominence to neural network research that uses both top–down and bottom–up constraints. Hence the discussion on stereo vision (chapter 4), learning and memory modeling (chapter 5), and locomotion (chapter 6), not to mention the overview of levels of organization in chapter 2.

Did I Harbor Misgivings about the PDP Approach in Neurophilosophy?

Kitcher wonders on p. 68 why PDP modeling got so little attention in *Neurophilosophy*, relative to the work by Llinas and Pellionisz (and, she should have added, relative to the Boltzmann machine work by Sejnowski and Hinton). There are a number of basic confusions behind her question. First, let us start with what is meant by PDP. It is an acronym for "parallel distributed processing." More specifically, it means that input-output functions are executed by configurations called "nets" that consist of many *units* that admit of varying levels of *activation*, and many activation-transforming *connections*, between those units, with stable but modifiable *weights*. The basic contrast with PDP (also known as connectionist modeling or neural network modeling) is of course classical AI, where the prototypical machine is serial, not parallel; digital, not analog; and where the transitions are accomplished according to the specifications of an explicit algorithm. Nets are not programmed, there is processing in multiple channels simultaneously, and values are typically analog.

Now the Llinas–Pellionisz work is indeed a PDP approach. Their models are nets with variable weights and connections. The Llinas–Pellionisz work shares with later neural nets the conceptual framework of vector coding and vector–vector transformations. Arguably, it was one of the first to make the full utility of this framework clear. It shares the highly general idea of a state space as a way of characterizing the geometry of the relationships between patterns of neural activity. The highly general notion of a *tensor* was used primarily because Pellionisz thought that neuronal state spaces were probably non-Euclidean, as well they might be, and the tensor calculus is ideally suited to represent such subtleties. Recently, others, notably Smolensky (1990), have also exploited the tensor vocabulary, though for other reasons. In my discussion of the Llinas–Pellionisz work I stuck mainly with the more specific vocabulary of vector codings and matrix transformations. (The Hinton–Sejnowski Boltzmann machine is of course also an instance of PDP, although it is a "relaxation" rather than a feedforward network.) In failing to see the robust continuities that connect the Llinas–Pellionisz cerebellar networks with later prototypes, Kitcher is the victim of a change in nothing more than preferred vocabulary. The prototypical two-layer feedforward network is uniquely specified by the matrix of its synaptic connection coefficients (see, for example, PMC, 1989a, 183). And a matrix remains the prototypical instance of a second-rank tensor.

> A zero-rank tensor is a scalar.
> A one-rank tensor is a vector.
> Next – Oh, please! – do not forget:
> A two-rank tensor is a *net*!
>
> (with apologies to Ogden Nash)

Because the Pellionisz and Llinas models and the Hinton and Sejnowski models were all examples of parallel distributed processing (PDP), my answer to Kitcher's query is straightforward: Far from shunning PDP in *Neurophilosophy*, I was wholeheartedly embracing it. Perhaps, therefore, Kitcher was really asking a different question. I suspect what she really meant was this: "Why was there no discussion of the kind of network models using the Hinton–Rumelhart–Williams weight-modification rule (the generalized delta rule for the back-propagation of error) that has since become so famous?" Crudely, why no "back prop" nets?

The answer to this very different question lies, appropriately enough, in the history. *Neurophilosophy* was in press during the summer of 1985, and it was during that summer, in the cognitive science seminar at UCSD, that Rumelhart announced that it looked like he, Williams, and Hinton had found a fast and efficient weight-updating rule for multi-layer nets, so that weight-setting need no longer be done by hand. Now there are many different ways of modifying the weights between connections so that the right function comes to be embodied in the network at issue. Such modification can be done by hand, but it is a very tedious and time-consuming procedure when it is possible at all. Boltzmann machines do have an automated method of adjusting weights so that the net "learns" according to a process that simulates the process of annealing in metals, as I discussed in *Neurophilosophy*. This method is rather more powerful, but exceedingly slow. For neural network approaches to be really powerful, what was needed was a method of fast, automated updating of weights so that a system could learn swiftly from repeated feedback on a very large population of training examples.

The discovery by Hinton, Rumelhart and Williams (1986) of the generalized delta rule meant that artificial networks could now learn functions of unprecedented complexity and sophistication. In particular, nets could learn, from examples, to solve nonlinear problems that Minsky and Papert (1969) had claimed were beyond the capacities of nets. Needless to say, "back prop" was a very exciting and important technical discovery, and much of the summer and fall of 1985 was spent trying to understand the significance of the discovery for network modeling. So far as *Neurophilosophy* was concerned, however, the discovery (actually *re*discovery) of the delta rule had come too late to be included in my discussion. In truth, it came almost too late even for the watershed Rumelhart and McClelland (1986) PDP collection: the Hinton, Rumelhart, and Williams paper explaining the generalized delta rule was slipped in at the very last moment. Since that time, neural network research and computational neuroscience have enjoyed spectacular development.

Kitcher's speculations on why more PDP work was not included are, therefore, ill motivated and quite inaccurate. The fact is, large-scale neural net modeling as we know it today did not really take off until after the discoveries concerning automated and efficient update rules, free-floating hidden units, and nonlinear squashing functions. After 1986 came the flowering of meetings, grant support, journals, and books. Consequently, when in 1990 I considered rewriting chapter 10 of *Neurophilosophy*, what happened instead was *The Computational Brain*, an entirely new book (Churchland and Sejnowski, 1992). In that volume we discussed a variety of kinds of model, some of which use "back prop," some of which are Hopfield nets, some of which are Kohonen nets, some of which use Hebbian learning, and some of which still have hand-set weights.

Finally, in response to Kitcher's query about the biological realism of PDP models, I repeat my prejudice as expressed in *The Computational Brain*. Sejnowski and I there stated that we prefer to spend time on

network models that are highly constrained by neurobiology, rather than on high-level psychological models, because network models are more straightforwardly testable against the independent reality being modeled. At the same time we prefer models of capacities that are well-studied in psychology [*sic*] and neuropsychology, so that we can take advantage of economizing constraints from top-down research (12).

Although "neurally close" models of "psychophysically dissectible" capacities are our preference, we hasten to say that we recognize that other scientists have quite different preferences, and that ideas useful for the science of the mind-brain may come from widely diverse locations in the research spectrum (13).

But Is Computational Neuroscience Relevant to Philosophy?

Kitcher sees no significant progress in neuroscience since 1986 that might suggest a positive answer to this question. Insofar as there has been demonstrable progress, I take her forthright skepticism as an invitation to point to some poignant examples.

To begin, I cite a number of presumptive neuromodeling results that have their first impact on psychology, since we both agree that a salient route for philosophical implications is through the science of psychology.

1   The grammatically competent networks of Elman (1989; 1992), and Christiansen and Chater (1994) show that even plain-vanilla recurrent networks can master the systematic and productive character of nontrivial *generative grammars* and show human-like limitations in their performance. (A recurrent network, recall, has axonal pathways that project back toward earlier neuronal layers in its processing hierarchy. This allows information present at higher levels to influence the processing of information at earlier or lower layers of the network. See again figure 11.1a.)

2   The training history of Elman's grammatical network revealed that effective learning of the target grammar required some initial *baby steps*, in the form of an "introductory" training confined to the simpler cases of the hierarchy to be mastered (Elman, 1991).

3   O'Toole's face-recognition network (1995) showed that the well-known *familiarity effects* in face discrimination (as in "all Oriental faces look pretty much alike to Fred") are automatically recreated when the set of face images on which a network is trained contains a statistical preponderance of one style of face over another.

4   Hinton and Shallice's crude semantic network (1991), when artificially "lesioned," displayed systematic output errors intriguingly similar to the *dysphasia* of brain-damaged human speakers.

5   Cottrell's (1991) face-recognition network (and almost every other

trained network, for that matter) displays a capacity for accurately "completing the hidden-unit vector" when confronted with partial or degraded signals at the input layer. Such behavior constitutes a sort of *ampliative "inference"* that draws on the network's past experience.

6   As Elman's grammar network illustrates, networks with recurrent pathways display a dynamical form of *short-term memory*, a memory, moreover, with a variable and *information-selective decay time*. In this way, task-relevant information can be preserved and automatically exploited through many cycles of network operation.

7   As PMC has explained (1989a; 1995), recurrent networks also embody a simple and plausible account of *expectation effects in perception* generally, since recurrent information typically serves to modulate the network's recognitional response, at the level of its hidden units, to its current perceptual input. One and the same input, accordingly, can be cognitively processed in two or more very different ways, depending on the *dynamical* state of the network at the time.

8   A network's acquisition of discriminative skills (as in the face-recognition net or in Sejnowski and Rosenberg's NETtalk) typically involves the spontaneous generation, across the network's activation space, of a conceptual framework in the form of an organized hierarchy of *superordinate and subordinate categories*.

9   Those learned categories typically display a variety of *prototype phenomena* in their high-dimensional and smoothly graded representations of category membership, and in their freedom from necessary and sufficient membership conditions.

10   Mead and Mahowald's silicon/VLSI reconstruction of the massively parallel network of the human retina (1991) displayed the expected capacity for effective visual imaging and also the capacity for *negative after-images, highly-sensitive motion detection, and still-image fadeout*. (If an image is projected onto a human retina that is held completely motionless, the image fades from consciousness in a matter of seconds.)

11   Shawn Lockery's biologically-inspired recurrent network (Lockery et al., 1990) successfully reproduced the *sinuous motor behavior* of the swimming leech. More generally, recurrent nets constitute an extraordinarily fertile resource for explaining (and recreating!) the complex motor behaviors of any creature whatsoever. (See again figure 11.1.)

12   PMC's binocular network (1995) recreated the human capacity for *stereoscopic perception* of 3-D structures, including several of its familiar illusions (the wallpaper illusion, the Lilliputian effect, and failure under isoluminent contrasts). It also recovers 3-D structure,

as we do, from random-dot stereograms and from the recently popular "autostereograms."

13   Somewhat surprisingly, the shape-from-shading network of Lehky and Sejnowski (1990) learned to recover 3-D information reliably from 2-D grey-scale pictures of smoothly curved surfaces. Quite unexpectedly, it also recreated, at its hidden units, the "preferred stimulus" or *receptive field behavior* of the neurons in the primary visual cortex of visually active cats, as earlier discovered by Hubel and Wiesel. Ironically, the net also upset the standard interpretation of the "function" or "semantics" of those receptive-field patterns in cats (they were thought to be detectors of dots, edges, and oriented lines) because the artificial net had never once seen any dots,edges, or lines, only smoothly curved and unbroken surfaces.

Thus I offer a baker's dozen of psychologically relevant results. The list is arresting not just because of the broad range of the results achieved but because they all flow from a single unitary approach, vector coding and parallel distributed processing, which are the presumptively basic cognitive mechanisms of any terrestrial brain.

These results, and others, set the stage for addressing Kitcher's real concern: *philosophically* relevant results. I share Kitcher's approbation for almost all the philosophically relevant psychological results that she herself lists. Empirical data is empirical data and, when relevant, is welcome from any quarter. But I also have data to urge on the reader's attention, and philosophical lessons to be drawn from them. Kitcher asks if connectionist/neurobiological research really contains any such lessons. For the reader's evaluation, I here propose a lucky seven of them.

1   The empirical behavior of neural networks, both real and artificial, illustrates that *the structure of thought* need not be the structure of language, as so many approaches, both historical and contemporary, have assumed. Classical (rule-based) cognitive architectures are not necessary for sophisticated cognition. As it happens, they are not necessary even for specifically linguistic phenomena, as Elman's grammatical net, Hinton and Shallice's semantic net, and Sejnowski and Rosenberg's phonetic net so clearly attest. Where the structure of cognition is concerned, we now have a systematic alternative to explore.

2   The discriminative behavior of nets gives us a new and powerful model of *the nature of the perceptual process* and of the achievement of perceptual recognition. The philosophy of perception need no longer be imprisoned by the picture of a peripheral irritation causing a conscious sensation that causes in turn some linguaformal judgment. Instead, we are presented with a picture of a many-layered hierarchy of learned partitions across native neuronal activation

spaces, with prototypical hot spots within them and recurrent pathways connecting them to permit self-modulation of the perceptual process. Questions about the foundations of empirical knowledge will never be the same.

3   The vector-coding/matrix-processing approach floats a novel account of what *universals* might be, how they are "grasped" by the mind, and how they are put to work in particular circumstances. In brief, they are dynamically "preferred" neuronal activation patterns of high dimensionality (or sequences thereof). Once learned, they allow their embedding network to see past its imperfect, incomplete, and ephemeral sensory inputs so as to represent the stable and objective reality beyond. Plato would, and Aristotle wouldn't, be surprised to find them inside the head, but both would recognize them for what they are.

4   The process of prototype activation, especially where it involves significant degrees of vector completion, floats a novel account of the nature and production of *explanatory understanding* (see PMC, 1989a, chapter 10), and, as there explained, it sustains a novel approach to the normative question of how presumptive explanations should be evaluated.

5   The vector/matrix approach floats a novel theory of *learning from experience*, a unified theory of both "inductive" and "abductive" learning. To a first approximation, the former involves structural change to the brain in the form of a gradual modification in the values of its trillions of synaptic connections. And the latter involves a relatively sudden dynamical (i.e., nonstructural) change in the brain's modulation of its own cognitive activity (PMC 1989a, chapter 11; 1995, chapter 10).

6   The vector/matrix approach sustains a detailed and experimentally successful approach to the nature of *sensory qualia*, a philosophical problem much on the contemporary mind. For taste qualia and color qualia, we already possess neurally-grounded accounts that smoothly reconstruct all or most of the familiar phenomenological data – (see Austen Clark's excellent *Sensory Qualities*, 1993) – and the same approach is clearly extendible to the other modalities. Given the nature of neural coding, it turns out that inarticulable qualia are precisely what you would *expect* to find at the early stages of the perceptual process.

7   The vector/matrix approach sustains several novel approaches to the problem of *consciousness itself*. Neurologists have long known that the intralaminar nuclei of the thalamus are crucially important for conscious cognitive activity, and the recent empirical discoveries by Llinas and Ribary (1993) are beginning to reveal why. Those nuclei

are the source of a radiating set of axonal projections to the basal ganglia and to almost every area of the cerebral cortex. And they are the focus in turn of a descending set of axonal projections from all of those same areas. That brain-encompassing recurrent system is active at about 40 Hz during the brain's waking state, almost completely inactive during deep sleep, and active again at 40 Hz during REM or dreaming sleep, although in that condition the changing amplitude of that neuronal activity is no longer keyed to external sensory stimuli, as it is during the waking state.

Perhaps consciousness arises from the brain-wide *temporal coordination* of diverse cognitive activities, at the hands of this central 40 Hz "conductor," as Llinas himself, Crick (1994), and I are inclined to suggest. Or perhaps it resides in the *critical mix* of cognitive properties displayed in that uniquely encompassing recurrent system, as PMC has suggested (1995, 208–26). Perhaps neither, of course. But relevance was all that was asked for, and the philosophical relevance of these empirical findings and theoretical conjectures is patent. There has, quite evidently, been progress in neurophilosophy since 1986.

I close by briefly addressing Kitcher's own closing criticisms. The first concerns the virtues or vices of geometrical models of "similarity," and the second concerns the significance of the hidden-unit coding-strategies that networks discover during the course of their training.

Kitcher is quite right to object to a simple, single-space modeling of similarity relations. In general, they cannot be adequate to the phenomena. True similarities, as revealed in the complex judgments of humans and other creatures, are seldom captured by geometrical proximities in a peripheral activation space. Some axes are far more important than others. Some axes have dramatically nonlinear metrics along their extent. Some axes are relevant only severally – in conjunction, in opposition, or in proprietary interaction with other axes. All of this is true.

And all of this is precisely what multilayer networks (with massively distributed connections across successive layers, and nonlinear transfer functions between them) were designed to capture. It is precisely these distinguishing features of recent connectionist models that allow them to embody and to explain the very complexities to which Kitcher so rightly points. By these means, a geometrical "similarity" relation, which has, at the input layer, all of the defects she points to, can be transformed into a very different geometrical similarity relation (= proximity relation), within the activation space of a higher layer in the processing hierarchy, a similarity relation that has none of those defects. In fact, Kitcher is pointing not to an incidental failure of modern connectionist models but to one of its most deliberate and salient successes. Her generalization from the legitimate results of Clement and Gentner was "hasty" for exactly the connectionist models at issue. Part of their purpose was to solve the very problems she points to. And they have succeeded to a depth that is still not fully plumbed.

Not grasping this point, Kitcher then turns to the case of NETtalk, and she questions the significance of the distributed representations that training has produced across the network's hidden units. The burden of her argument, drawn partly from Vershure, is that the allegedly surprising structures among those representations are foreordained by various antecedent regularities implicit in the data on which the network was trained. So they are not surprising after all.

Well, they are and they aren't. For functional problems with a small and closely similar class of computational solutions, any successful network can be expected to settle on a solution within that class. But not all problems have such unique solutions. In fact, most do not. (Indeed, it is not clear to me that NETtalk's problem has such a unique solution: different training trials yield grossly similar but still interestingly diverse coding strategies at the hidden units. These different results reflect the random initial settings of the network's weights, the idiosyncratic contents of alternative training sets, and even differences in the order of presentation of the training examples.) Finally, there is no guarantee that a given net will succeed in finding such an "obligatory" solution, even where it does exist. For various reasons, many nets simply fail.

So it is always at least moderately gratifying when a network does manage to filter out the antecedent regularities that are, after all, only *implicit* in the global corpus of the training data. In some cases it may become clear, after informed reflection, that a successful network would *have* to find something close to *those* representational factors. And in some of those cases it may also become clear, after deeply informed reflection, that the network was further doomed to *find* those factors, given the learning rule employed and the rich training data presented. But this just means that artificial nets, while complex, are still deterministic systems. It does nothing to minimize the significance of what they manage to achieve, even when we are occasionally able to predict it. And it does nothing to indicate that biological creatures might not be making similar sorts of achievement. In all, the point of Kitcher's closing objection is rather opaque to us, but on its most straightforward interpretation, it seems to set the hurdle for connectionist success at an absurd height. It seems to require that learned coding strategies at the hidden-unit layer are interesting only if they are inexplicable. On the contrary, they must always be *explicable*, at least in principle. But they will regularly be surprising – to us, if not to God.

13
Clark's Connectionist Defense of Folk Psychology

Andy Clark needs no instruction from us or anyone else on the reasons why a *scientific* cognitive psychology is likely to settle on a radically new conception of how the brain represents and computes, one that bears no resemblance to the propositional-attitude framework that constitutes the descriptive and explanatory core of FP. His earlier writings give powerful arguments to that effect (Andy Clark, 1989; 1993a), and his present paper provides yet another (*vide* his remarks on the "eater" networks explored by Nolfi and Parisi). Yet, upon leaving his philosophical study and upon reviewing the functions of our current FP in its original and natural setting, his apparently hardened heart quickly remelts in the warmth of that familiar context. FP, he argues, does not serve the same purposes as a scientific psychology. Hence, it should not generate the same expectations and should not be held to the same standards. Its legitimate survival as a continuing form of "social adhesive" is therefore quite consistent with the revolutionary scientific implications of connectionism.

Faced with such a wise critic, a pair of wise targets might be tempted to accept the welcome concession about the future form of a successful *scientific* psychology and simply write off the issue of *folk* psychology's future as a moot and comparatively uninteresting problem. That temptation will be resisted, however, because the latter issue is of profound importance – both for our social future, and for an accurate understanding of our social present. Clark sees this, and so do we. Let us, therefore, examine his exculpatory story more closely.

In fact, that story is ambiguous. Clark's positive case for FP variously appears, at different points in his essay, as

1 a pragmatic toleration of a strictly *false* but nevertheless highly useful causal/explanatory theory;
2 a generous version of the (reductive) identity theory;

3   a form of Dennettian intentional-stance instrumentalism;
4   an alternative portrayal of FP as an ontologically innocent form of pure social *practice* rather than a framework of corrigible factual suppositions.

These are all quite different and mutually incompatible alternatives. Each has its own modest appeal, perhaps, and Clark's exculpatory case for FP derives at least some of its broad appeal from the fact that he does not distinguish very forcefully between them.

We shall. Let us address them in decreasing order of plausibility. The very real possibility voiced in (1) has many historical precedents. For example, Newton's simple mechanics (the three laws of motion plus the gravitation law) is strictly false as judged from the perspective of Einstein's more penetrating mechanics. But it would be entirely too precious and puritanical to insist that the former be eliminated in favor of the latter in all practical contexts. Other examples will illustrate the same point: False theories can still be indispensable approximations.

Just so. The additional factors encompassed by Einstein's mechanics (near-luminous velocities, strong gravitational fields) intrude negligibly into the domain of human practical experience. Within that domain, there is neither demand nor reward for adopting a conceptual framework that systematically tracks them. Perhaps something similar is true of FP.

Perhaps indeed. This is not a possibility we feel any confidence in ruling out. Yet, the analogy just drawn is clearly flawed and importantly question-begging. Specifically, we can formally *demonstrate* that Newtonian and Einsteinian mechanics are empirically indistinguishable within the domain of mundane human experience. Given that $v << c$, and that the masses involved are small, the relevant equations collapse into the same form. Within that envelope, their "empirical contents" are the same. Systematic attention to Einsteinian factors thus buys one no practical or manipulative advantage within the realm of ordinary life.

But we have no such assurance concerning the respective empirical contents of folk psychology and a matured connectionist-psychology-cum-cognitive-neuroscience, even within the domain of common human experience. The complacent view is that vector coding, vector transformations, attractor landscapes, and chemical modulations thereof will remain similarly submerged below the level of practical attention and mundane manipulative advantage. But no intertheoretic reduction assures this; no consistency proofs guarantee it; beyond complacency, nothing even suggests it.

To the contrary, what little we do know suggests that a firm theoretical grasp of the true pulleys and levers of human cognition (including our emotions, perceptions, deliberations, moods, and basic character) will give us a much more penetrating expectation of how any person's daily mental life will unfold, and a much more effective practical grip on the manifold factors that influence it. Should it turn out this way, then the argument from "relevance to practical concerns" will weigh strongly in *favor* of a conceptual displacement, not against it.

Neurological and psychiatric medicine have already made real strides here, thanks to our growing appreciation of subtle structural damage and chemical and physiological anomalies in the brains of human patients and the various social/emotional/cognitive peculiarities that typically accompany them (cf. Damasio, 1994). The relevance of this new understanding is not confined to humans at the "deranged" end of the spectrum: it throws light across the entire spectrum of human mental activity and social behavior, if only because it begins to teach us what the structure of that polydimensional spectrum really is. Einsteinian mechanics may not touch our practical lives, but a successful neuro-psychology can hardly fail to do so. The process has already begun.

While these remarks are fair, they may not be fair to Clark. He has made it plain that he fully expects the new framework to "augment" our existing conceptual resources. And he has also made it plain that he regards the ascriptions of beliefs and desires to humans as literally *true* expressions of our global informational state, and not just as false-but-still-useful approximations, as claimed in (1). The complacent option (1), it would seem, is not Clark's real intention.

Let us try interpretation (2) then. This possibility, too, we are unwilling to rule out. Something answering to the propositional atti-tudes – roughly, but systematically, in at least some dimensions – may yet be constructible from within the resources of computational neuro-science. In an earlier paper (1993b), Clark cites with approval my gloss (PMC, 1981) of a sentential belief-content as a "one-dimensional projection" of a higher-dimensional neural reality. I (PMC) fully agree that this is a possible path of broadly reductive contact between the two frameworks.

However, Clark is trying to have it both ways. He hopes to preserve, not just a descriptive role for the propositional attitudes, but something like their current causal/explanatory role as well. (That, after all, is why such descriptions are so useful.) Yet it is modestly clear already that the propositional attitudes, even if they do survive in the way suggested, will no longer play the central causal/explanatory role they play in our current folk psychology. That central role, within the new framework, is played instead by high-dimensional activation vectors and synapse-mediated transformations thereof. And the internal structure of this new causal dynamics is strikingly alien to, rather than isomorphic with, the classical dynamics of the propositional attitudes. Any reduction of the propositional attitudes, then, is likely to be strained, local, and highly deflationary at best. Once again there is no clear and compelling case that the explanatory framework of the propositional attitudes will survive more or less intact – or, anyway, *deserve* such survival – within the updated folk psychology of the millennium.

Turning now to option (3), we must acknowledge that Clark himself briefly describes his position as following Dennett's, although he immediately dissociates himself from Dennett's early instrumentalism, as the more recent Dennett (1987) has also. This is welcome, because instrumentalism is strictly emasculatory rather than exculpatory, and its anti-realism is a poor home for claims of literal truth for the ascriptions of folk psychology.

On the other hand, while instrumentalism was clearly a weak position here, it was at least a clear position. (The virtue of propositional-attitude ascriptions was not truth, and the basis of such ascriptions was sheer usefulness, nothing more.) Dennett's and Clark's new position is rather more opaque. Both still make appeal to the allegedly *abstract* nature of propositional-attitude ascriptions, as if such a feature could buy them safety from the evaluatory demands that are binding on literally true causal/explanatory ascriptions generally. In his 1987 book, Dennett briefly explores option (1), the "useful, oversimplifying falsehood" construal (bottom of his p. 72). Curiously, he then rejects it in favor of the (different?) view that FP ascriptions have a kind of *veritas cum grano salis*, a status grounded in the "uses we find" for them (top of his p. 73).

This will sound like evasive double-talk to some – a case of claiming "not P (exactly), but still P (roughly)." So far as we can divine, Dennett has no clear position here. Talk of various "stances" avails us nothing, because a stance-toward-x is just a way-of-understanding-x, it is just another candidate theory-about-x. The original questions about literal truth and evidential grounding remain as pressing as ever.

Clark's position is only slightly less evasive. He wants a "coarse-grained" but *literal* truth for FP ascriptions, a truth grounded in the "global" state of the brain rather than in the isolated states of its various subsystems. Insofar as we understand him, and can distinguish him from Dennett, this sounds like the broadly reductive option voiced in (2) again. That, we repeat, is a live possibility (if a somewhat faint one), and we are puzzled that Clark does not just declare his broadly reductive hopes, proceed accordingly, and chance his program to fate. Where Dennett hovers unstably between options (1) and (3), Clark hovers unstably between options (2) and (3).

There is a perfectly respectable motive behind their struggles, i.e., the desire to give due credit to the polydimensional social practice that our current FP sustains, a practice essential to our individual and collective humanity as currently constituted. Thus, option (4) is a final point of the compass to which Clark and Dennett are occasionally drawn, a position that has been explicitly defended by Kathleen Wilkes (1984).

We share our critics' regard for the social practices at issue and, being philosophical pragmatists in the spirit of C. S. Peirce, have considerable sympathy with the claim that the cash value of FP-as-a-theory is ultimately the intricate social practice that it sustains. In fact, we think it is difficult to overstate the importance of this point.

Wilkes, however, succeeds. She evidently regards FP-as-a-theory and FP-as-a-form-of-practice as mutually exclusive alternatives, and she attempts (confusedly) to argue against the former by arguing (quite correctly) in favor of the latter. With FP thus freed of factual responsibilities, she concludes, it is thereby freed of any threat of empirical falsification, and thus FP-the-form-of-practice has nothing to fear from advances in neuropsychology.

In fact, theories *typically* sustain some intricate practice or other. Think of chemistry, electronics, metallurgy, acoustics, mechanics, cell-biology, and so on. Moreover, the content of those theories explains the form of the practice sustained. This was always the point of my attempts (PMC, 1970; 1979; 1981) to reconstruct the implicit "laws" of FP, i.e., to explain the form of our existing explanatory and predictive social practices, why certain prototypical factors are thought relevant to explanation, and why certain kinds of objections are thought effective. (Despite my growing skepticism of "sentential epistemologies," that early work was still formulated within the then-dominant framework of logical empiricism, the better to address my target audience.) In any case, theory and practice are intimately entwined, even on the classical view of theories.

More recent views of theories – following the lead of T. S. Kuhn (1962) for example – portray the acquisition of any theory as being *primarily* the acquisition of an interrelated set of skills: perceptual, inferential, manipulative, evaluative, calculative, etc. An account more recent still (PMC, 1989a; 1995) looks at the neural embodiment of both theories and skills and finds them to be fundamentally the same: a behavior-steering neuronal activation space with an acquired structure shaped by past experience. In all, Wilkes's presumed automatic contrast between theories and practices is just a mistake.

The effort was wasted in any case, because the eliminativist does not need an explicitly discursive sense of "theory," and the real issue is located elsewhere. The bottom-line claim of the eliminative materialist (see again PMC, 1981, section V, "Beyond Folk Psychology") is and always has been that *the content and the character of our social practices in the domain of mutual perception, explanation, anticipation, and behavioral interaction are going to change, and change substantially, with the dawning of a truly adequate neuropsychology.* Current practices will change because, with a transformed understanding of what we are and how we work, we are almost certain to develop different and much *better* practices. "Better" here means "serves more effectively the manifold practical needs that any normal human has." Most people care nothing about Mercury's orbit, stretched light, or the extended half-life of fast particles. But everyone cares about the emotions, affections, development, character, understanding, skills, pathologies, and social behavior of themselves and other people, especially the people they work with and the people they hold dear. The eliminativist will not need to push some antiseptic and alienating scheme on an unwilling public. Nothing of the sort. As the new framework and its more penetrating practices are made publicly available, it will spread through the population like wildfire. Clark, Dennett, and Wilkes are all defending a fort that will simply be bypassed and forgotten in the rush.

Clark, recall, began by remarking that FP does not serve the same purposes as a scientific psychology. That is not true, as our explanatory, predictive, and manipulative practices show. But that issue may be somewhat beside the present and precisely inverse point, which is this: *Can a scientific psychology serve the same purposes as our current folk psychology?* To this question the answer is almost certainly yes. And that new framework will open up for us a universe of new purposes into the bargain.

The prospect, I (PMC) concede, sends a *frisson* down my own spine. But we have successfully navigated this sort of transformation before, and more than once. We must have. Though they must have had some framework of personal and social conceptions, *Pithecanthropus erectus* did *not* use our current folk psychology. And yet a history of conceptual development connects us. The near future, I suggest, contains more of the same.

B

The Impact of Neural Network Models on the Philosophy of Science

14

On the Nature of Explanation:
William Lycan

Lycan's perceptive and penetrating paper has two main burdens. The first is to defend the Hempel–Oppenheim (1965), or deductive-nomological (DN), model of explanation from the specific criticisms I have leveled against it. The second is to probe the virtues and shortcomings of prototype activation as an account of what an individual's explanatory *understanding* really consists in.

Lycan is well aware of the fundamental shift in analytic focus represented by the prototype-activation model (hereafter PA model), and evidently he does not entirely disapprove of my emphasis on descriptive and theoretical matters. At the same time, he wishes to defend the traditional DN model, at least from my criticisms, on the grounds that the model has a primarily *normative* purpose. Let us take a deeper look into this matter.

We can find at least four faces for the notion of explanation, all of them familiar. It is illuminating to confront them in concert.

E_1 Explanation as *a way of understanding* (something one *has*, *uses*, *perfects*, and *redeploys*).

E_2 Explanation as *an object of discovery* (something one *searches for*, *finds*, or *stumbles across*).

E_3 Explanation as *a focus of evaluation* (something one *criticizes*, *rejects*, or *accepts*).

E_4 Explanation as *a set of sentences or statements* (something one *proposes*, *presents*, or *writes down*).

The DN model of Hempel and Oppenheim was, I believe, nontrivially concerned with all four of these aspects of explanation, but Lycan and I can agree that its primary focus lay with E_4 and, derivatively, with E_3. After all, an explanation is first and foremost a *set of sentences*, on their account. And its virtues and vices reside in the semantic features of those sentences and in the deductive relations that hold or fail to hold between them.

The PA model, by contrast, has E_1 (understanding) as its primary concern, and its account of both E_2 (discovery) and E_3 (evaluation) is based on its antecedent neurofunctional account of E_1. Explanation as E_4 (item of written or verbal exchange) emerges as the least of its concerns. On this, more in a moment.

What is the relation between these four faces of explanation? As I see it,

$$E_1 = E_2 = E_3 \neq E_4.$$

A way of understanding *is* something that one seeks, discovers, or develops, and it *is* something that one evaluates. But it is not itself a linguistic expression, although it may occasionally be the target of a successful *representation* by a linguistic expression, by an explicit DN argument, to give just one example. E_4 is thus the odd man out here. If humans neither spoke nor wrote, there would be no E_4s; but ways of understanding the world would still be discovered, used, and displaced on occasion by better ones.

Lycan finds a problem for me here. The more closely E_1 is explicated in terms of psychological or neurofunctional goings on, he claims, the more difficult it becomes to say when a *non*psychological thing or event counts as an explanation in the sense of E_4. As he points out, the relation of causal sufficiency ($E_4 \rightarrow E_1$) plainly will not do, for an electric shock or a blow to the head might produce explanatory understanding of something in some artfully primed human victim, but the shock or the blow would not thereby ascend to the status of an explanation.

Agreed. A causal account won't do. But there is an obvious alternative, untested by Lycan, that will serve to filter out electric shocks, sharp blows, and their ilk, namely a semantic account. What makes a DN argument, or a functional outline, or an analytical diagram an explanation in the sense of E_4 is that each is a *conventional representation* of a way of understanding the problematic phenomenon. Shocks and blows are not representations of anything, so they don't count. To be sure, conventional representations typically will be causally effective in producing explanatory understanding in their hearers, at least if the hearers command the representational framework in which they are expressed, but causal efficacy is neither necessary (the hearer might be a dimwit) nor sufficient (recall the shocks and blows). In all, I see no problem here. E_4 is related to $E_{1,2,3}$ exactly as it should be: E_4s *represent* $E_{1,2,3}$s.

Let me now return to Lycan's claim that the DN model is immune from all or most of my criticisms precisely because it was never intended by Hempel and Oppenheim, nor by its many advocates, to be an integral part of a descriptive cognitive psychology. It was and always has been intended as a *normative* account of explanation, says Lycan. There are two questions here. Were the DN model's ambitions so narrowly drawn? Does it escape my criticisms even if they were?

I cannot speak for the profession, but as many of us understood the orthodox logical empiricism of the 1960s and 1970s, to search for explanations was to search for the laws and conditions that sustained them; and to possess explanatory understanding was to have knowledge of the needed laws and conditions, and of their deductive relations to the explanandum at hand. Thus understood, the DN account was indeed tightly integrated with a general account of the nature of human knowledge, and it had the additional virtue that it, like the PA account, had no obvious Zaffron point (see Lycan, pp. 107–8). This was because it, too, offered a powerful account of what understanding consisted in: knowledge of a system of law-like statements. To repress or deny these compelling dimensions of the DN model is to emasculate it after the fact. Lycan is rewriting history if he suggests that the DN model was not widely understood in these descriptive and highly ambitious ways.

So understood, it is now evident that the model performs poorly. That is surely a point worth highlighting, since classical AI had ambitions along such lines, and Fodor's computational theory of mind still labors in their pursuit. Here it is worth listing some of the presumptive advantages that the PA model of explanation has over the DN model. In the left column are listed familiar problems. On the right, I cite the PA model's peculiar virtue.

DN problems	*PA virtues/solutions*
1 Slow access to relevant explanatory beliefs.	Access in milliseconds (no search at all).
2 Ignorance of laws.	We access prototypes (often inarticulate), not laws.
3 Deductive incompetence.	Deduction is rarely, if ever, involved.
4 Animals have explanatory understanding, but no discursive laws.	They access prototypes (always inarticulate), not laws.
5 "Flagpole" problem.	Etiological prototypes are temporally asymmetric.
6 Contraposed laws problem.	Etiological prototypes are temporally asymmetric.

7 "Hexed salt" problem.	No corresponding learned prototype.
8 Accidental universals.	No corresponding learned prototype.
9 Logical diversity in types of explanation.	Distinct major classes of explanatory prototypes.
10 Why is simplicity/unity a virtue of explanations?	Unified partitions generalize more successfully to novel cases.

The reader will note that the first four problems concern the DN model's inadequacies as a descriptive account of explanatory understanding. More important for the present dispute, however, is that the final six problems listed are all famous defects in the DN model construed as a *normative* account. Descriptive inadequacies aside, the DN account has long been up to its neck in normative difficulties, difficulties internal to the logical empiricist tradition. What is interesting in the present context is that for each of the familiar problems cited, the PA perspective offers an illuminating diagnosis of the failure, and an alternative account that is free from the defect at issue. (For the original details, see PMC, 1989a, chapter 10.)

Lycan's portrayal of the DN model as a normative account, while surely correct, buys it no proof against disaster. Normative convictions regularly have factual presuppositions, and these are always hostage to fresh empirical developments. The fact is that the DN model's normative story has shown defects for decades. In retrospect, we should not be surprised at those failures. That traditional model is focused on linguistic structures. But the basic virtues of a way-of-understanding are simply not to be found at the linguistic level of E_4. Instead, it would seem, they are to be found at the level of high-dimensional prototype vectors, that is to say at the level of learned activation patterns across large populations of neurons. It is these that constitute our ongoing representational activities. It is these that get repeatedly transformed by matrix multiplication at the hands of millions of synaptic coefficients. It is these that constitute our learned cognitive responses to perceptual inputs. And it is these that ultimately direct our motor behavior. Cognitive activity, contrary to a tradition with many strands, is not language-like in its structure and its computational behavior. Any account of explanation still burdened with this assumption can expect chronic difficulties in both the descriptive and the normative domains.

If we now turn to the PA model itself, Lycan has some friendly but pointed queries. My assertion that perceptual recognition is just a special case of explanatory understanding prompts a question about the location or the identity of the explanandum in such cases, and raises the issue of whether *explanatory* understanding is involved at all.

My first response is that the expectation of a canonical form of explanandum is itself an idiosyncratic legacy of the DN model and should be dropped along with the model that gave rise to it. However, this does not really address the puzzlement, expressed by Reid and seconded by Lycan, about "what is explained or (explanatorily) understood" in simple cases of perceptual recognition. Lycan explores an esoteric answer concerning the microfeatures present in one's activation vectors. This is a mistake. The correct and much simpler answer, I think, is just "the *world*," or "that part or aspect of the world that is the current focus of perception, attention, or concern." As to why the understanding should be described as explanatory, let me illustrate.

The character and magnitude of the achievement involved in any perceptual recognition is chronically obscured by the fact that the typical examples of such recognitions are so easy for us. The true picture emerges only as we begin to consider genuinely and deliberately difficult cases. We can produce suitable test cases at will by taking black-and-white photographs of a variety of familiar objects in natural settings and then *degrading* each image by a series of high-contrast xerox copyings. The idea is that each copy is made from the xerox copy preceding it, so that information is progressively lost with each copying. The typical result of this procedure is a chaotic pattern of black splotches on a white background, as displayed in figure 14.1.

If you were asked to predict what direction of motion is to be expected from the scene elements of the figure or what sounds might emanate from what parts, or how it might separate into distinct objects, or why there are two similar objects at the lower right, two pointy ones at the upper left, and a large blob at the extreme right, you would be unable to say anything useful. Initially, at least, you have no understanding of anything about this scene. It is a chaos. If you see anything at all, most likely it is a stupidly smiling face at the top center of the scene.

With the preceding sentence, I have just given you a false understanding of the scene. Its falsity is reflected in the fact that it fails to make any sense of the rest of the scene, the scene beyond the cartoon face. Compare that flawed way of understanding with an alternative take on things. The figure portrays a man on horseback. The pointy objects at the upper left are the horse's ears. From there, its face angles down to the left. The left border of the animal's neck lies underneath, broadening to a shadow across its chest. Its forelegs lie directly below the chest, and the right hoof is lifted. At this point, very likely the character of the entire scene has suddenly been transformed for you, and you may

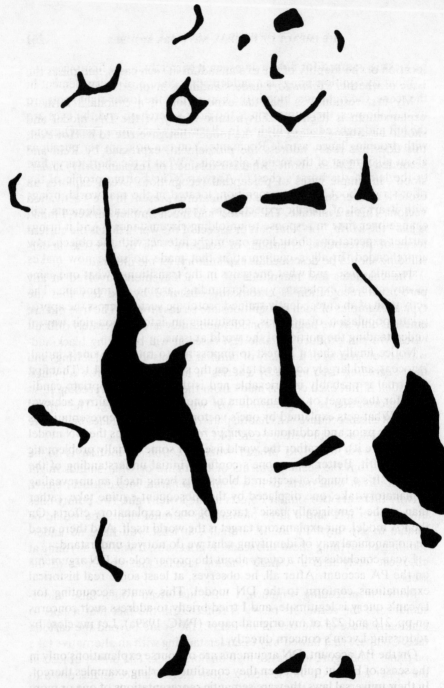

Figure 14.1 A degraded visual stimulus that resists recognition of what it is. Confusion when viewing this scene is the fate of most people, until additional information is provided so that comprehension of the various parts of the picture finally dawns. (Thanks to Irvin Rock, 1983.)

be kicking yourself for not having seen it correctly in the first place.

What recognition brings is a sudden appreciation of every element in the scene: the rightmost blob is the horse's tail, the lower right spots are its back hooves, the stupid grin is the rider's kerchief, and the eyes are the left and right edges of his hat. In all, we may recognize Don Quixote, with drooping lance, astride Rocinante. You can now answer questions about all or most of the scene's elements. "What is the short, curvy line to the left of the horse's chest?" Answer: "The bottom profile of the rider's right boot." Such recognition, located in the real world, brings with it a host of specific expectations about how scene elements will change over time in response to unfolding circumstances. And it brings further expectations about how one might interact with the objects now apprehended. In all, a configuration that made no sense now makes systematic sense, and what one gains in the transition is what one gains in any case of explanatory understanding, arcane or mundane. The activation of an antecedently-trained prototype vector, across the appropriate population of neurons, constitutes an information-rich way of understanding the portion of the world at issue.

Notice finally that it is next to impossible to return to one's initial, innocent, and largely confused take on the scene of figure 14.1. That first construal is probably irretrievable and is thus an inappropriate candidate for the target or explanandum of one's current cognitive achievement. What gets explained by one's vectorial cognitive representation is not some prior and additional *cognitive representation* (as the DN model would have it), but rather the world itself, or some initially problematic aspects of it. Better to see one's confused initial understanding of the figure ("It's a bunch of scattered blobs") as being itself an unrevealing explanatory take, one displaced by the subsequent equine take, rather than as the "empirically basic" target of one's explanatory efforts. On the PA model, our explanatory target is the world itself. And there need be no canonical way of identifying what we do not yet understand.

Lycan concludes with a query about the proper role of DN arguments on the PA account. After all, he observes, at least some real historical explanations conform to the DN model. This wants accounting for. Lycan's query is legitimate, and I tried briefly to address such concerns on pp. 216 and 224 of my original paper (PMC, 1989a). Let me close by addressing Lycan's concern directly.

On the PA account, DN arguments are of course explanations only in the sense of E_4, but quite often they constitute sterling examples thereof. In their universal laws, they are semantic representations of one or more general prototypes (e.g., of a force due to gravity, of a body moving under a net force, etc.). And in their initial conditions they are indications of just how those prototypes are to be applied to the case at hand. For people who possess those represented prototypes, DN arguments are also causally efficacious at activating those prototypes in a fashion appropriate to the local problem. They are thus five-star representations of certain kinds of ways of understanding.

But they are not themselves ways of understanding, and their peculiar form is not adequate to represent the full variety of cognitive prototypes actually deployed by humans. To understand these deeper matters, we have to look inside the human head, to the complex partitions and trajectories across the brain's overall neuronal *activation space* – to the many prototypes, that is, that prior training has sculpted. It is these multiform vectors and vector-sequences that are the true vehicles of explanatory understanding.

15
Bechtel on the Proper Form of a Connectionist Philosophy of Science

Bechtel urges me (PMC) to modify or expand my admittedly brain-centered accounts of what a theory is and what explanatory understanding is (PMC, 1989a), so as to embrace a range of factors that lie outside the heads of individuals – factors such as linguistic and other symbolic formulae, calculation techniques, figures and diagrams of various kinds, physical instruments, and experimental techniques. His advice can hardly be rejected, since these factors are indeed part of the warp and woof of modern, institutionalized science. Let me see what I can do.

Bechtel is himself a connectionist researcher and a reformist philosopher of science. His own emphasis on the search for and the application of suitable mechanisms and models (as opposed to universally quantified laws) is highly welcome to these ears, since it is exactly such mechanisms and models, in my view, that our neurally-embodied prototype vectors so frequently represent (see also Giere, 1994). His historical example of Buchner's reaction-path model of the fermentation process illustrates his point very forcefully. In future, I shall make illustrative use of it myself.

However, rather than celebrate the points of doctrine that we share, let me focus instead on what divides us. In fact, Bechtel's chapter evokes a specific role for connectionism in the philosophy of science, a role importantly different from the role that I expect it to play. In what follows I will try to highlight these differences, and the motivations that lie behind them.

Twenty years ago, in criticizing the bulk of this century's empiricist philosophical literature, I wrote (PMC, 1979, 1):

> Theoretical "knowledge" is there represented as an essentially peripheral superstructure erected on the body of human knowledge proper. ...This approach did offer some advantages. ...taking the non-theoretical as a temporary given, one could hope to provide a successful account of

theoretical understanding *short of* the larger business of constructing an account of human understanding in general.

This now appears to be impossible.

I still think it is impossible. And for the same reason. Specifically, "all knowledge (even perceptual knowledge) is theoretical ... there is no such thing as *non*-theoretical understanding" (PMC, 1979, 2). Human and animal understanding is theoretical in nature from its earliest stages and in even its simplest incarnations. By this I mean that it is *speculative, systematic*, and *corrigible*, and that it earns its keep to the degree that it enables its possessor to anticipate, explain, and manipulate its environment.

This commits me to the view that theoretical activity, most obviously in children and nonhuman animals, antedates linguistic activity, public calculation techniques, figures and diagrams, and artificial instruments by some years in the case of modern human children, and by millions of years in the case of the rest of the animal kingdom, early humans included. Here, then, is the first major conflict between Bechtel and me. Of these quite recent public devices and techniques, Bechtel says "these external representations ... are crucial to science" (130). And of the need to account for them he says "...this is not a task we can put off until we have worked out notions of theories and explanatory understanding. Scientific theorizing and explanation depend upon this external representational capacity" (130).

I disagree. *Institutionalized* science certainly depends on them, but individual theorizing and explanatory understanding need not. Those external, public factors extend and enhance our theoretical capacities quite dramatically, but they do not constitute them, especially not in their first instances. Those external factors are only contingently embedded in a much deeper and much older symphony, whose form already displays the essential elements of "scientific" activity: speculative theorizing, critical evaluation, conceptual evolution, and the payoffs of enhanced prediction and control.

My worry is that Bechtel's central focus on the traditionally obvious and public elements of human intellectual practice will repeat something close to this century's error of modeling cognitive activity on its public, linguistic manifestations. Bechtel's vision already embraces much more than language, to be sure, but my worry remains. As Bechtel seems to portray it, connectionist neuroscience is merely a more recent and accurate account of how our "manifest" cognitive activities are *implemented* in or *sustained* by the brain rather than, as I have urged earlier in these replies, a fundamentally novel molar-level account of the nature of cognition in its own right.

Quite possibly this worry is unfair to Bechtel. But others, I am sure, will read him as indicated. It is the reading, then, that I wish to resist. And the basic counterclaim is simply that (a) speculative attempts to understand the world have their primary, original, and still typical home within the brains of individual creatures, and (b) an adequate account of that original activity must precede and sustain the secondary account of its subsequent flowering within the social matrix of the occasional social animal such as *Homo sapiens*.

To say this is not to denigrate the extraordinary importance of that secondary account. Quite the contrary: Take away the social character of our cognitive history, and scattered humans would still be hunting for grubs under stones and lurking behind bushes at the edge of the savanna, hoping to snatch a scrap of some more powerful creature's kill. But it is clear that, even then, human brains and the brains of creatures both above and below them in the food chain were already engaged in complex theoretical activity and had been for many millions of years; for even the humblest of non-social creatures must construct and constantly fine-tune a conceptual framework with which to apprehend and navigate the world. And since there is no analytic/synthetic distinction, a conceptual framework is nothing other than a speculative theory.

With these points made, let me return to the business of the "secondary" account, on whose eventual existence Bechtel quite rightly insists. He is most obviously right about the importance of physical instruments and the novel techniques of observation or data capture that they permit. His illustrative example is the historical development of cell-fractionation techniques using the centrifuge. But he might just as easily have pointed to the gradual development of the telescope (through Galileo's tribulations to the development of compound, achromatic lenses and of Newton's aberration-free reflecting telescope), or to the development of the microscope, the Geiger counter, electrophoresis, the magnetometer, the radio telescope, or a thousand other extensions of the normal human battery of sensory organs. These cases all serve to make the same two points: that modern science would be unthinkable without such external sensory devices, and that their informational significance is not written on their sleeves but is itself a matter for experimental and theoretical determination, and occasional redetermination.

I welcome Bechtel's insistence here, because I have long argued that the very same thing is true of our *native* sensory devices – our eyes, our ears, and so forth. We can all agree that empirical cognition would be unthinkable without some devices/organs of discriminative response to the environment. But further, just as with voltmeters and thermometers, the informational significance of the activities of our native sense organs is not written on their sleeves either. Here, too, their significance is a matter of experimental and theoretical determination. And occasional redetermination (cf. PMC, 1979, sections 3–5).

In the case of our native sense organs, that determination is initially made in the course of assembling a framework of concepts – that is in the course of partitioning one's neuronal activation spaces into a hierarchy of observational prototypes – with which to apprehend and navigate the world of one's childhood. That concept-generating process is one that cognitive theorists have recently begun to understand (again see Clark), thanks to our recently acquired abilities to train up artificial neural networks to a variety of sophisticated discriminative and behavioral competences. The naive network, prior to training, has no fix on which aspects of its many sensory input vectors constitute signal and which noise, and no initial grasp of which categorial framework will most faithfully and most usefully represent the several dimensions of structure within whatever signal its inputs contain. Yet, as the network responds to the joint pressures of a synapse-adjusting learning algorithm and repeated encounters with its sensory environment, it gradually generates, *en deux*, both a specific categorial framework in which to express its cognitive responses and a specific strategy of selecting from its high-dimensional input vectors just those aspects it has discovered to be relevant to the reliable application of its emerging high-level categories.

This now-transparent process is a revealing analog of the gradual process by which all brains have to "sleuth out" the informational significance of their own sensory input states. And, to return to Bechtel, it is no different from the process by which one gradually masters the use of any new instrument invented for the purpose of augmenting our native sensory devices.

Think of it this way: one sticks a pair of high-power microscopes over someone's eyes and points him toward a tiny volume of living neural tissue; one gives the person some vernier control over a micro-thin electronic probe inserted into that volume; and one puts probe-connected earphones over the person's ears so that he can listen to the activity of whatever neurons or axons the probe may encounter. In effect, he has been launched into a new environment with a new set of sense organs and motor effectors, and he must learn to cope by exploring the structures that slowly emerge within each and the inter-actions that show up among all three. A systematic feel for the objects that this neural microworld contains, and for how they behave, is the eventual result of that exploration.

This highlights the parallel between the "native" and the "instrumental" cases by portraying several obvious instruments in the role of native systems. But research on how artificial neural networks learn has already given us a penetrating account of the cognitive process in question. Accordingly, we do not need a new and separate story to account for how humans come to master the use and significance of external sensory instruments. Bechtel is right to insist that an adequate philosophy of science must provide some account of that process. But it is at least arguable that we already have such an account, the one that modern connectionist theory provides for how *any* network comes to master the use and significance of the activational behavior of its sensory input layers, whatever the physical devices that may produce that behavior.

The parallel here drawn has a further dimension. Research on recurrent artificial networks (see again figure 11.1) has shown that a network can fall into alternative and competing modes of processing and categorial interpretation, alternatives that will make very different cognitive use of the very same sensory inputs. What steers the network between alternative interpretations of the same data is the network's prior dynamical state or "frame of mind." Elsewhere (PMC, 1989a, chapter 11; 1995, chapter 10), I have appealed to this model in order to illuminate shifts in human perceptual interpretation (as with the vase/ faces and other ambiguous figures), and also shifts in high-level theoretical or *scientific* interpretation (as in a particle vs. a wave interpretation of various optical phenomena). Such shifts represent the possibility of a kind of "fast learning," as opposed to the "slow learning" involved in the inevitably gradual adjustment of synaptic weights. That is to say, a network can stumble across, by the recurrent manipulation of some of its input information, a more successful mode of processing that information than it may have learned initially.

As indicated in those earlier essays, I now regard such recurrently-modulated reinterpretations of sensory data as providing the most realistic model for sudden changes in theoretical commitment in adult human scientists. I mention this because it is left out of Bechtel's otherwise excellent outline of my connectionist philosophy of science. Global synaptic-weight change is the only avenue to conceptual change mentioned in his essay. But there is a dynamical as well as a structural route to radical change in one's conceptual activities. The dynamical route does not destroy old categories, because it leaves one's synaptic weights unchanged. And it is much faster, as it occasionally happens on a time scale of fractions of a second, as when "the scales fall from one's eyes" and, like Archimedes in the bath, one cries "Eureka!" This can also happen, note, to one's interpretation of an opaque or problematic instrumental datum. Once again, a process in the head explains our changing use of external instruments.

In summary, I accede to Bechtel's point that a proper connectionist philosophy of science must embrace the social and instrumental surround. I hope I have illustrated, however, that the best place from which to embark on this larger account is an adequate theory of the cognitive processes taking place within individual human brains.

C
Semantics in a New Vein

16

Fodor and Lepore: State-Space Semantics and Meaning Holism

Fodor and Lepore recognize the state-space kinematics of neural networks for what it most assuredly is: a natural home for holistic accounts of meaning and of cognitive significance generally. Precisely what form such accounts should take is still to be worked out, but Fodor and Lepore (hereafter "F&L") see some early possibilities well enough to try for a preemptive attack on the entire approach. My aim here is to show that the state-space approach is both more resilient and more resourceful than their critique would suggest.

A typical neural network (see figure 16.1) consists in a population of input or "sensory" neurons $\{I_1, \ldots, I_n\}$, which project their axons forward to one or more populations of hidden or "processing" neurons $(H_1, \ldots, H_m)$ and $\{G_1, \ldots, G_j\}$, which project their axons forward to a final population of output or "motor" neurons $\{O_1, \ldots, O_k\}$. The network's occurrent representations consist in the several activation patterns across each of these distinct neuronal populations. For example, the network's input representation at any given moment will consist in some ordered set of activation levels, $<i_1, \ldots, i_n>$ across the input units $\{I_1, \ldots, I_n\}$. It is this particular pattern or vector, *qua* unique combination of values along each of the n axes, that carries the relevant information, that has the relevant "semantic content." A parallel point holds for each of the network's representations at each of the successive neuronal layers. The point of the *sequence* of distinct layers is to permit the *transformation* of input representations into a sequence of subsequent representations, and ultimately into an output vector $<o_1, \ldots, o_k>$ that drives a motor response of some kind. This transformational task is carried out at each stage by the configuration of synaptic "weights" that connect each layer of neurons to the next layer up.

F&L claim that sameness-of-content across distinct persons will require sameness of activation vectors across precisely parallel sets of n neurons, one set for each person, where the parallel consists in identical semantic significance for each of the corresponding elements or dimen-sions of the two *n*-tuples at issue. In short, one has the same meaning iff one has the same pattern over the same dimensions. This demand is easily met for simple cases such as taste coding, where all normal humans share a common system of four types of taste receptor on the tongue. Sameness of taste, whether across individuals or across times, consists in an identity of the candidate activation patterns across those four universal types of sensory neuron.

But sameness of content (thus reckoned) becomes exponentially more difficult to achieve when the dimensionality of the representations involved reaches into the millions, and where we do not have a universal one-to-one correspondence between neuronal populations across indi-viduals. There is enormous idiosyncrasy in the number and distribution

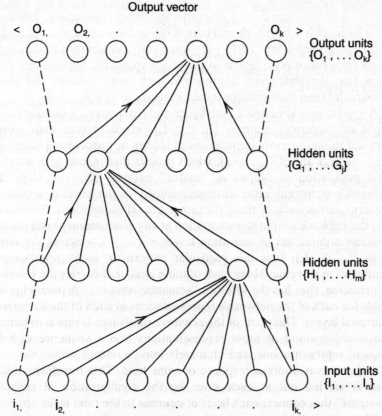

Figure 16.1 A typical feedforward network. Only some of its connections are shown, in order to highlight one chain of progressively more abstract "feature detectors."

of retinal cells, for example, or cochlear cells, or somatosensory cells. And the idiosyncrasy is at least as great as we ascend the processing hierarchy into the sensory cortex and beyond. How can we get sameness of vectors if we cannot even hope to get sameness of constituting dimensions?

A second formulation of this objection asks "Where do the constituting dimensions of the relevant activation-vector space get *their* semantic content?" Here F&L charge the network approach with being committed to an intolerably strict form of concept empiricism: all meaning arises from vectorial combinations of basic meanings, which basic meanings must be fixed by the causal sensitivities of the individual sensory neurons. This objection has an especial force as urged against me, since, as F&L observe, I have argued at length against such empiricist accounts of meaning (PMC, 1979, 7–41, 63–6). For me, the meaning of observation terms is typically *independent* of the sensory inputs that prompt their occasional application. In particular, I have argued that two creatures could share essentially the *same* conceptual framework even in the extreme case where they share *no* sensory organs in common. F&L's construal of state-space semantics would render this flatly impossible.

Thus the critique. We may begin the defense as follows. F&L persist in seeing network architectures as engaged in the classical business of assembling semantic simples into appropriate semantic complexes. But in actual brains, and in realistic networks, the functions performed are typically just the reverse of what F&L imagine. Rather than assembling complexes from simples by Boolean articulation, neural networks are struggling to recognize or to recover useful "simples" from enormous complexity, noise, and confusion at the sensory level.

Upon reflection, this fact is not hard to appreciate. When walking past a mewing kitten among the pillows on the couch, for example, one has active some 200 million retinal cells and some tens of millions of auditory cells. These cells are simultaneously responding to many millions of environmental features beyond those available from the kitten, in whose larger sensory surround its "possibly kittenish" features are thoroughly buried. The activation pattern across one's peripheral sensory neurons is changing continuously as one moves through the room, as the kitten uncoils its tail and yawns, as the children chatter, as the morning news drones from the radio, and as the mottled sunlight dances on the couch because of nodding tree branches outside the window. A second person, Patricia, standing behind the couch, brings a different set of sensory neurons to the situation, and confronts her own unique cacophony of neural stimulations.

And yet, despite the overwhelming sensory complexity within us and sensory diversity across us, both of us manage to recognize the presence of the kitten on the couch, swiftly and effortlessly. The marvelous features of vector coding and non-linear parallel processing allow us to explain how this is possible. Prior training has shaped the activational tendencies of one's higher populations of hidden units into a finite family of practically relevant prototype activation patterns: for couches and kittens, for voices and meows, for pillows and pets, and for all of the other categories that make up one's conceptual framework. The tendency to fall into just these categorial patterns has been created during the learned configuration of the myriad synaptic connections that allow activations at one neuronal level to produce different activation patterns at the next level up. This training process also turns the neurons at lower levels into detectors of subtle activation patterns or sub-patterns at still earlier levels, and ultimately at the sensory level.

Experience with artificial networks has taught us, however, that the many interlocking sub-features detected at lower levels – whose collective impact at higher levels ultimately produces the activation vector for "kitten" – are rarely the features that one would list in a definition of "kitten" (e.g., small, furry, four-legged, young, feline). More typically they will be diffuse, opaque, inarticulable features whose only obvious significance is that, in conjunction with hundreds of other similarly diffuse coding features passing through the labyrinth of the massively parallel network, they occasionally participate in the selective activation of the higher-level "kitten" vector. This comparative "semantic opacity" of the computational process reflects in part the difficulty of the processing task. But it also reflects the fact that multi-layered nonlinear neural networks are typically *not* computing mere Boolean combinations among their sensory inputs. The net's activity is abstractive rather than constructive, and statistical rather than Boolean. We have entered a different universe of computational activity. In fact, such networks can approximate the computation of any computable function, including highly esoteric functions. This feature is essential to their celebrated successes.

In the event, within both Patricia and me there is activated, at some fairly high-level population of hidden units, a vector that represents kittens, that has the content "kitten." What makes each vector, Patricia's and mine, a "kitten" vector is not the identity of our respective patterns of neuronal activation across the hidden layer (these are likely quite different), nor the semantic identity of the constituting dimensions in her hidden-unit population and in mine (their diffuse "contents" may well be quite idiosyncratic). What gives this vector the content "kitten" is the overall role that this vector plays in the larger cognitive and motor economy of which it is an interlocking part. Thanks to an almost magical process of sensory filtering and vector completion, that prototype vector is typically activated in me by any one of a wide range of possible sensory impacts on me by a kitten. But much more importantly, that prototype vector has rich causal and computational *sequelae* of its own. Because of its own transformational significance to the extensive and well-trained network *downstream* from that prototype vector, it prompts a family of kitten-specific perceptual expectations and prepares one to engage in a family of kitten-specific behaviors.

It is this downstream aspect of the vector's computational role that is so vitally important for reckoning sameness of cognitive content across individuals, or across cultures. A person or culture that discriminated kittens reliably enough from the environment, but treated them in absolutely every respect as a variant form of *wharf-rat*, must be ascribed some conception of "kitten" importantly different from our own. On the other hand, an alien person or species whose expectations of and behavior towards kittens precisely mirror our own must be ascribed the same concept "kitten," even though they might discriminate kittens principally by means of alien olfaction and high-frequency sonars beamed from their foreheads.

One of the great virtues of neural networks is that they can overcome the inevitable chaos, complexity, noise, and perspectival variety at the sensory periphery in such a way as to activate comparatively well-behaved and dynamically salient categories at higher levels of processing. If we wish to understand the significance – the meaning, the content – of those prototypical categories, the most revealing place to look is at their computational role within the overall cognitive economy and motor behavior of the creature at issue. This is why neural network researchers so often find it useful, in sleuthing out the cognitive strategy of some successful network, to examine the set of partitions that training has produced across the activation space of each of its distinct hidden layers, to examine their relations with adjacent partitions, to explore their causal interactions with the partitions across earlier and later layers, to examine the "receptive fields" of individual neurons, and their "projective fields" as well. We do this with artificial networks and real neural networks alike, and with increasing success. (See also Rosenberg and Sejnowski, 1987; Lehky and Sejnowski, 1988; 1990; Gorman and Sejnowski, 1988.)

This returns us to a robust and recognizable form of meaning holism: it is conceptual role that counts. What is novel in the state-space or vector-coding approach is the fresh account it provides of what our cognitive economy actually consists in. Instead of a rule-governed dance of propositional attitudes, we are presented with high-dimensional activation vectors being transformed into new vectors by virtue of passing through a series of well-trained matrices of synaptic connections.

If we hope to solve the problem of sameness-of-meaning by exploring relevant structural and dynamical similarities across distinct cognitive economies, as holists typically do, we now have a new universe of possibilities to explore. We know also that the vector-processing approach addresses the actual microstructure of the brain. We know further that artificial networks display some intriguing cognitive properties, including the spontaneous development and deployment of hierarchical categorial systems. Finally, to make a negative point and to readdress F&L, we know that the vector-processing approach is certainly not committed to concept empiricism, nor to a misfocused and unattainably fine-grained criterion for category-identity across similar but structurally idiosyncratic networks. The vector-processing approach is still a live candidate, and easily the best hope for holism.

(At this point the reader should examine F&L's response: pp. 159–62.)

17

Second Reply to Fodor and Lepore

The following is in response to pp. 159–62.

I'm not getting through to F&L. I take some (small) comfort in the fact that they persevere in construing the connectionist approach to semantics as nothing but Hume's antiquated concept empiricism in modern state-space or vector-algebraic dress. The comfort derives from the fact that, according to the connectionist theory of perceptual recognition and explanatory understanding, when confronted with a novel and puzzling situation, *all* creatures initially activate a vector that is very close to one of its antecedent perceptual or explanatory prototypes. And they may persist in such assimilation for some time, even if this is inadequate to the new situation.

In both of their replies, F&L exemplify this phenomenon. They evidently cannot see that they are now looking at something that does not fit any of their antecedent doctrinal categories. In this reply, I will set my sights on the minimal goal of simply discriminating the new approach from the historical doctrine at issue. Once that is done, the irrelevance of F&L's specific complaints will be evident, and the reader may undertake a properly focused evaluation, at last, of the novel approach proposed.

First and foremost, a trained network's prototype-vector response at the hidden units (a synapse-transformed response to the activation pattern across its input units) is *not* to be seen as just a high-dimensional version of how a voltmeter or a thermometer responds causally to some feature in its environment. The reason is that the trained network's response, unlike the simple measuring instrument's, is always a substantially *ampliative* response. It embodies not just information derived from its current input, but also information that goes well beyond that input, information derived from its many past encounters with other presumptive examples of the category at issue, information now distributed across and embodied within the now "prejudicial" configuration of the synaptic weights that connect the input units to the hidden units at issue. The hidden-unit response is thus always to some degree a speculative and ampliative *hypothesis* about the extra-network environment, rather than a simple information-conservative causal response to some feature in that environment, as in the voltmeter and the thermometer.

That simpler information-conservative causal relation will be familiar to readers of Dretske's (1981) and Fodor's (1987) earlier writings, for it is the basis of their respective accounts of meaning. It will also be familiar as the source of their joint and chronic difficulties in accounting for the possibility of systematic human *mis*conception of the environment, and for the possibility of nontrivial conceptual progress over time. Hume, note well, had a similar problem, since the class of possible human concepts was limited to a base of direct sensory copies plus classical concatenations thereof. Fortunately, the very different ampliative relations displayed in the response characteristics of a well-trained network offer a way to avoid all these problems, Dretske's and F&L's as well as Hume's.

Second, a trained network's hidden-unit representations are *not* primarily sensory, as F&L insist, and they are certainly not tied, node by node, to atomic features of the environment. This last point can be illustrated visually. Thanks to the internal categories it has developed (figure 10.2a), Cottrell's face-recognition network is capable of discriminating male from female faces and of reidentifying, in novel photographs, the faces of the 11 people on which it was originally trained. Subsequent exploration of the coding strategy employed by the mature network revealed that the 80 dimensions of representation severally embodied in the 80 hidden units – as reflected in their so-called "preferred stimuli" at the input layer (i.e., the input pattern that produces the maximum activation at a given hidden unit) – are all highly *diffuse* patterns that encompass the entire visual field. Figure 17.1 shows the preferred stimuli of an arbitrary six of the 80 cells at the hidden layer. Janet Metcalfe, Cottrell's collaborator, coined the term "holons" for these diffuse representational elements.

Clearly, the diffuse and ghost-like coding elements of the face-recognition network are in no familiar sense "sensory simples," nor, demonstrably, are they copies of any input patterns ever presented to the network. (Its past experience is exhausted by the specific faces and nonface objects present in its training set.) Rather, they are dimensions of global input organization, no one of which has ever been explicitly encountered in the network's sensory experience, and many of which are not even remotely face-like (see, for example, the lower left holon). And yet, collectively, these abstract dimensions sustain a coding strategy that allows the network to make real-world facial discriminations at

Figure 17.1 Six of the 80 "holons" that constitute the coding axes of the
hidden-layer activation space of the face-recognition network of figure 10.1

close to 100 percent accuracy. Such diffuse, distributed, and non-
compositional representations are not unique to this case. They are a
standard coding achievement within neural networks generally.

The present network codes any input-layer face image by a pattern of
activations across all 80 cells at the hidden layer, where the activation
level at each such cell represents the degree to which the input face
image overlaps or resembles the idiosyncratic holonic pattern that is the
preferred stimulus of that one hidden-layer cell. Since each cell is unique
in its preferred stimulus, the mature network is performing an
80-dimensional analysis of each input image, according to its
80-dimensional profile of resemblance to each of the 80 holons "embodied" in the 327,680 synaptic weights meeting the hidden units. Those
holons gradually emerged in the course of training, because they
constitute the most efficient coding scheme for collectively representing
the relevant statistical similarities and variances across the large set of
training images – or anyway the most efficient scheme that the network
could find, given its particular training history. And, to repeat, no one of
those hidden-layer cells represents or codes for any "sensory simple"
encountered in its past experience.

Third, the specific representational regime into which the network
settles during training is different every time one performs the experiment; that is, it is different for every network, despite the identity of
their input layers. Depending on the starting configuration of its synaptic
weights, and on the order of presentation of the training photographs,
the naive network will develop a *different* set of holons each time it is
forced anew to develop the discriminative skills described above. That is
to say, the naively reckoned "representational significance" of each of

the 80 dimensions of the hidden-unit activation space will be idiosyncratic for each trained network. No two networks will be exactly the
same in that respect. But at a deeper level, each successful network will
be identical, or closely similar, in having developed an isomorphic
system of hierarchical partitions across its hidden-unit activation space.
(For an analogy, think of a single spatial structure, a left fist for example;
and think of 10 differently rotated 3-D Cartesian coordinate systems,
each one of which can represent perfectly well the family of points that
make up the fist. The *same* objective structure is thus successfully
represented in all ten coordinate systems, but the set of constituting
dimensions is different for each of the 10 cases.) It is these all-important
partitions to which subsequent layers of neurons have become exquisitely and ampliatively sensitive in the course of training. And it is these
shared partitions that sustain almost identical input–output behaviors
across distinct networks.

What is important, evidently, is not the idiosyncratic and backward-
looking causal semantics of any *given* neuronal dimension of this 80-D
space. For any individual network, any neuron, and any training trial,
that could be almost anything. What is important is, first, the global
internal partitions that training has sculpted within that larger space,
whatever the idiosyncratic contents and orientations of its 80 constituting analytical dimensions this time around (see again figure 10.2a).
Second, and equally important, are the ampliative informational/causal
relations that training has established between those internal partitions
of the hidden-layer activation space and the further internal partitions
within the activation spaces of further layers of neurons.

This highlights a fourth divergence from Hume. For what is emerging
here is an internal cognitive economy that ruthlessly and remorselessly
abstracts from the teeming details of its sensory inputs. In principle, the
same internal economy (above the first layer of hidden units) could even
be driven by an entirely *different* set of sensory units, by tactile organs,
for example, rather than by visual ones. That is to say, on the
connectionist model of concepts and concept identity, two creatures
could have essentially the same concepts about external physical objects
– about their shapes, interactions, and law-like behaviors – even though
one creature could only feel them, and the other could only see them.
Once again, the same partitional structures can be successfully represented within distinct coordinate systems, although, in the more radical
case here contemplated, the differences will lie not just in their
rotational orientations but also in the physical sense organs to which
they attach.

For many reasons, then, this is not a Humean concept empiricism.
According to Humean empiricism, we are forever tied to immediately-

given peripheral sensory simples. According to connectionism, by contrast, the whole point of a hierarchy of ampliative coding layers is precisely to transcend the limitations of our peripheral sensory coding. It is to try to "look past" the teeming noise and perspectival idiosyncrasy of one's peripheral sensory input representations to the more stable and more predictive "forms" that lie beyond that mercurial sensory surface, stable forms that are always only partially and imperfectly reflected within that sensory surface, universal forms that might be differently but quite successfully reflected in a variety of alternative sensory manifolds.

If F&L wish to regale me with a deflationary historical analogy, Plato's theory of Forms would be closer to the mark than Hume's. Specifically, I agree with Plato that seeing past the ephemeral is the first goal of learning, and I agree further that it is precisely the "abstract forms" that allow us to make any sense of the relentless flux of the ephemeral. The principal difference between me and Plato concerns the location of those forms (they are inside the head) and their genesis within us: they are gradually sculpted *de novo*, by a deeply *sub*linguistic process, in the course of extended interactions with the environment.

I draw this second and more revealing historical analogy with some hesitation, for I anticipate that F&L will now announce that connectionism is just Platonism served cold the next morning. After all, "Platonism has surely been refuted lo these many centuries; we can, therefore, safely forget about connectionism once more." Evidently, this form of argument would not be genuinely responsive to the challenge currently posed by connectionist models of cognition. But neither was its Humean analog in F&L's initial critique. All of us, F&L included, need to confront connectionist models for what they are: a genuinely novel approach to cognitive phenomena, an approach that must be evaluated on its own merits and not on its superficial (or nonexistent!) similarities with earlier and simpler views.

I close by highlighting a fifth difference between the connectionist approach and Hume's (and any other classical account of meaning for that matter). Classical accounts of meaning have as their target the explication of how content accrues to or is embodied in *linguistic* items (i.e., in sentences and their constituent words), or in the direct mental analogs of linguistic items (i.e., in beliefs and their constituent concepts). Connectionists, however, set their primary explanatory sights on a more general target. The aim of a "connectionist semantics" is to explain how information accrues to or is embodied in brain states generally, as, for example, in lasting configurations of synapses, in lasting partitions across activation spaces, in fleeting activation patterns across neuronal populations, and in unfolding temporal sequences of such patterns.

We are here addressing a form of cognitive economy that has little or nothing linguaformal about it, a form of cognition that is fundamental throughout the animal kingdom, a form of cognition that sustains human linguistic activity as only the latest and perhaps the least of its many cognitive capacities. And yet its manifestly *sub*linguistic elements appear to embody a sophisticated variety of representations whose "semantic" character antedates (and presumably sustains) the idiosyncratic linguistic structures so recently employed by humans. Better, then, that we should focus first on the earlier, more general, and more basic semantic phenomena, and then deal with the semantics of linguistic items as a special, peripheral, and evolutionarily recent case.

One need not agree with the perspective of this research strategy. But neither should one bend one's polemical efforts so as to misrepresent it. In its primary aim, connectionism is not trying to solve F&L's linguistically-focused semantic problem, much less with a disguised version of Hume's concept empiricism. Rather, we are deliberately trying to solve an importantly reconceived set of "semantic" problems, and we are approaching them all with a novel set of analytical resources. Early results are encouraging, as they reveal a tendency for any network to develop a hierarchical system of internal categories, categories that display similarity gradients and other prototype phenomena. So accounting for language does not seem wholly out of reach, especially given the success of Elman's surprisingly simple network, and Christiansen and Chater's, in capturing grammatical competence (see again figure 11.2). Moreover, the emerging semantic and syntactic stories held out by connectionist models are already embedded in an epistemological theory that smoothly embraces concept learning, perceptual recognition, abductive "inference," and even motor control. These elements are either problematic add-ons or glaring absences within Fodor and Lepore's alternative cognitive theory. In all, we are more than comfortable with the contest already under way. Let the respective research programs proceed.

D

Consciousness and Methodology

18
Neuropsychology and Brain Organization: The Damasios

Hanna Damasio and Antonio Damasio have had an enormous influence on how we think about the brain and its organization. They are neurologists, meaning they regularly see human patients; and they are neuropsychologists, meaning their research targets the neural mechanisms for various psychological functions, such as memory, pattern recognition, language, emotion, and reasoning. Human subjects with brain damage (lesion studies) are a unique and highly important source of constraints as we try to figure out how the brain works. Properly studied, they can be the bridge between the behavior of normal subjects on the one hand and networks, neurons, synapses, and neurotransmitters on the other. Depending on methodology, some lesion studies are more significant than others, while some are essentially meaningless. Most importantly, without detailed data on individual brain anatomy derived from techniques such as magnetic resonance imaging (MRI), observations about a patient's behavioral deficits cannot be connected to basic knowledge in the broader domain of neuroscience. And without that, the observations do not take us much beyond the "isn't that amazing" stage. A mainstay of all Damasio lesion research is anatomy, both gross, in terms of locating the lesions in brain areas, and fine-grained, in terms of neuronal pathways, connectivity, and neuronal types. As the neurological case studies accumulate and as the data are interpreted in the light of progress in basic neuroanatomy and neurophysiology, hypotheses about brain specialization and dependencies can be generated.

Many pitfalls beset the lesion approach, and we were initially very attracted to the Damasios' research because of their concern to develop a general methodological design that would avoid these pitfalls and elevate lesion studies to something more than Isolated Tales from the Neurology Ward. For example, for many topics, such as perception and language, it is most useful to restrict studies to patients with single-location brain damage, caused by stroke, surgery for tumor, or focal accidents like sword injuries (uncommon but not unknown). The Damasios' approach is succinctly outlined in the following quotation (1989, 17):

> However, lesions can certainly be used as probes to the operation of hypothetical networks of anatomical regions designed to perform a specified function cooperatively. Given the basic characteristics of the network – in terms of the constitution of its units and their connectional arrangement – lesion probes in different points of the network can help define the cooperative role of the diverse units based on the contrasts of the behavioral performances linked to different sites of damage. The method's power is limited by the lesions' size and by the richness of the "psychological" operations hypothesized for the network the lesion is probing. The smaller the lesion probe capable of creating discriminatory effects (that is, the smaller the lesions capable of causing a functional perturbation that can be related unequivocally to a certain sector of the network), the more the lesion method will have to contribute.

In this context, therefore, the dementias (such as Alzheimer's disease) and closed-head injuries, for example, are less revealing of network function because widespread damage has an impact on many capacities at once. As a probe of network function, therefore, patients with multiple lesions are not as revealing as those with single lesions. For certain other questions, however, the multiple lesions may be a good source of data; for example questions about memory and motor control. Magnetic resonance imaging is a profoundly useful tool for determining lesion site in advance of autopsy; that is in a living human brain. Even tiny lesions can be detected, since the spatial resolution of current technology is in the millimeter range.

Another important anatomical requirement initially demanded by the Damasios and now widely used depends on carefully noting the substantial individual differences in human neuroanatomy. These differences mean that averaging data, for example functional data from positron-emission tomography (PET) scans, across a number of different individuals, has the wholly undesirable effect of downgrading the results. The point is this: if two individuals differ by a centimeter in the location of their respective V1 borders (as in fact they may), then blindly averaging their unseen brain anatomies means that you cannot tell whether any subsequently detected neuronal activity is in V1 or V2, even if you can locate that activity in the PET scans. As the Damasios have pointed out, a given subject's PET scan has to be spatially correlated with his *own* MRI scan if we are to be accurate about precisely what anatomical area is specifically hyperactive in the PET scan. Comparisons between many brains can be extremely useful, but it requires not averaging of brains, as though subjects lined up perfectly, area by area; what is needed before averaging is the matching of areas, subject by subject (Damasio and Frank, 1992).

The Damasios' data adhere additionally to this methodological requirement: the person who does the behavioral testing of the patient should not be the person who locates the lesion on the MRI scan. Keeping the two tasks separate reduces the possibility of finding what you expect and missing what you do not expect. It is a healthy way to maintain the possibility of disconfirmation. Following a patient for many years is another dimension of their methodology that has turned out to pay rich dividends. Often many behavioral tests under many different conditions are necessary in order to limn the subtleties of a range of deficits.

As there are a number of points I wish to illustrate, and because this is best done by reference to a particular case study, let us look briefly at a patient, EVR, who first came to the Damasios' lab more than a decade ago. A brain tumor in the ventromedial region of EVR's frontal lobes (basically directly above the eye sockets) had been surgically removed earlier, with bilateral lesions as a result. Following his surgery, EVR seemed very normal and scored as well on standard IQ tests as he had before the surgery (about 140). He was knowledgeable, answered questions appropriately, and so far as mentation was concerned, seemed unscathed by his loss of brain tissue. EVR himself voiced no complaints. In his day-to-day life, however, a very different picture emerged. Once a steady, resourceful, and efficient accountant, now he made a mess of his tasks, came in late, failed to finish easy jobs, and so forth. Once a reliable and loving family man, his personal life was a shambles. Because he scored well on IQ tests and because he was knowledgeable and bright, EVR's problems seemed to his physician more likely to be psychiatric than neurological. This diagnosis turned out to be entirely wrong.

The case of EVR is by no means unique, and there are a number of patients with similar lesions and comparable behavioral profiles. After studying EVR for some time, and comparing him with other cases of similar damage, the Damasios began to devise new tests to determine what about EVR's emotional responses were not in the normal range. For example, when shown horrifying or disgusting pictures, his galvanic skin response (GSR) was flat. Normal individuals, in contrast, show a huge response while viewing such pictures. On the other hand, he could feel fear or pleasure in uncomplicated, more basic, situations. During the following years, new and more revealing tests were devised to probe more precisely the relation between reasoning logically on the one hand and acting in accordance with reason on the other. There was no doubt that EVR could give the correct answer to questions concerning what would be the best action to take (e.g., defer a small gratification now for a larger reward later), but his own behavior often conflicted with his stated convictions (for example, he would seize the small reward now, missing out on the large reward later). That his "pure reasoning," displayed verbally, and his "practical decision-making," displayed in choice, were so at odds suggested to the Damasios that the real problem lay with EVR's lack of emotional responsivity in situations that involved some understanding of the meaning and implications of the events. That is, EVR would react normally to simple conditions such as a loud noise or a threat of attack, but failed to respond in more complex situations, whose significance might involve more subtle or culturally-mediated features, such as the social consequences of failure to complete jobs or the future consequences of a sudden marriage to a prostitute.

The basic idea in the Damasios' work on consciousness is that representation in changes of body state, comprising visceral feeling as well as somatosensory signals (both external "touch" sensations and sympathetic system changes in skin) and muscle and joint signals, is necessary for self-representation. More correctly, they envisage a complex to-ing and fro-ing of signals between thalamo-cortical states and changes in the body as being the crucial pathways for self-representation. This in turn is necessary for unimpaired consciousness and for sensible decision-making. Body-state representation systematically integrates diverse changes in information originating in the sympathetic system. The cases of EVR and others with similar lesions (ventromedial frontal) were instrumental in the formation of this hypothesis. The point is not that these patients feel nothing at all. Rather, in practical situations requiring of an individual some rather sophisticated cognitive analysis, feelings are not generated in response to his analysis because his analytical processes and his visceral responses (within the heart, gut, skin, and blood chemistry – the "gut feelings") are literally disconnected. Normally, ventromedial frontal cortex would connect to areas containing body-state pathways; in these patients, the pathways are disrupted. It is this set of complex responses, involving future-consequences-recognition, visceral changes, and feelings, that the Damasios see as inclining the person to one decision rather than another. That is, in the context of acquired cognitive-cum-emotional understanding about the world, they bias sensible decisions. When EVR is confronted with a question ("Should I finish this job or watch the football game?"), his brain's body-state representation contains nothing about changes in his viscera, hence he is missing important clues that something is foolish, unwise, or problematic. His frontal lobes have no access to information about the visceral valence of a complex situation or plan or idea. Therefore, some of EVR's behavior turns out to be foolish and unreasonable. (For a much more complete account, see Damasio, 1994; Bechara et al., 1994.) Where does consciousness come in? As they see it, unimpaired consciousness requires a complex interplay of signals between cortical areas and integrated body-state representations, and when there is loss of such interplay, there is selective loss of awareness.

Are there cases where loss of integrated body-state representation results in loss of awareness? Yes, in so-called "anosognosia," or "unawareness of deficit." In these cases, patients typically have right-hemisphere damage (involving damage to somatosensory areas, including somatosensory areas I, II, insula, thalamus, and hypothalamus), seem unaware of events in the left region of space, are unaware of deficits in sensation and movement on the left side, may refuse to acknowledge the left arm or leg as their own, and seem unconcerned when their deficits are explained to them. (See also Bisiach and Berti, 1995.) Because anosognosia rarely results from left-hemisphere lesions, the Damasios hypothesize that standardly it is the right somatosensory areas that are dominant for the integration of body-state representations. This theory thus predicts that sufficiently sensitive tests might reveal, in anosognosic patients, some subtle deficits of body-representation integration in right hemispace.

This research is important for many reasons, but in this context it may be worth emphasizing that it strikes me as a wonderfully rich example of co-evolutionary progress in science. The claim that body-state representation is the underpinning for self-representation is not itself new (see William James, 1890). What is new is the idea that body-state representations interact with the cognitive processes of evaluation and planning, with the result that feelings can be generated by mental events such as imagining the consequences of a socially complex act. Moreover, this is an essential ingredient in what we call rational deliberation. Additionally, the constellation of data – from many levels of organization, macro and micro – make it seem genuinely plausible. And finally, this idea is exciting because it holds out the possibility of generating further and more revealing empirical tests of network hypotheses, using, as probes, studies of human patients with single lesions.

19
Conceptual Analysis and Neuropsychology: John Marshall and Jennifer Gurd

What the Marshall–Gurd duo and the two of us share is a quite deep if rather plain conviction. The facts are the facts; linguistic analysis may tell you what normal speakers believe, but it cannot be a reliable guide to facts about the world, to the real nature of things. Marshall and Gurd make this point very forcefully, and Marshall in particular has been making it in discussion and in print for years. Curiously, even after the passing of ordinary-language philosophy, most Anglo-American philosophers still call themselves analytic philosophers. Even more curiously, many philosophers, including some of those not overtly hostile to empirical data, bemoan our work as "not philosophy," or as undermining the discipline, or as "scientism tainting the autonomy of the humanities." What is going on here?

Probably lots of different things are going on. First, analytic philosophy is an oddly ambiguous enterprise – ambiguous as between analyzing language practice on the one hand and genuinely theorizing on the other. When strictly adhering to the ideas of the later Wittgenstein and his acolytes, the strategy is to analyze concepts such as "voluntary" and "involuntary" as they exist in the vernacular. This is meant to unmask latent confusions, to clarify, and thereby to solve the philosophical part of the problem. Extreme versions of this approach say that there is no problem left once the concept has been analyzed. Extending the use of a concept to include scientifically motivated uses would, in all likelihood, be condemned by strict adherents as a "category error," ostensibly a very bad and foolish thing (see, for example, Hacker, 1987).

Marshall and Gurd are surely right that "conceptual analysis" so construed is a very narrow, if occasionally useful, enterprise. It is a kind of anthropological enterprise, and it should be possible to complete the project in a few years – no more than a decade or so. In fact, however, analytic philosophers rarely limit themselves just to analyzing and clarifying concepts. Typically, they are also engaged in theorizing about what is the case in the world. In other words, they want to know what is true. That of course is altogether laudable, but the trouble arises when such theorizing is carried out under the guise of conceptual analysis, and without significant basis in the relevant empirical science. Quite regularly this detachment from science is explicitly excused on grounds that, after all, the task is conceptual analysis, not empirical discovery. Now, either one can restrict oneself to linguistic analysis, in which case only the linguistic facts are relevant, or one can theorize further about the nature of things, in which case a much wider class of facts is relevant. Pretending to do linguistic analysis while theorizing using "pure reason" is really just armchair scientific speculation. Done in ignorance of the available relevant science, it is unlikely to be very rewarding.

As it happens, too much contemporary philosophy (philosophy of science excepted) consists in looking at neither of these domains of fact, but in chewing on the cud of what does and does not seem conceivable, or likely, or imaginable, or some such. This rigmarole sometimes gets called "transcendental argument," and its results are supposed to be forever beyond the reach of any experimental test. However, because what is or is not conceivable depends on one's idiosyncratic beliefs, these arguments amount to autobiographical statements rather than advances in understanding. I hasten to repeat that clarification and disambiguation are clearly important and highly useful. The be-all and end-all, however, they manifestly are not.

What, then, should philosophers do? It is a huge field and there is lots to do, lots of different things to do. So far as issues about the nature of knowledge and the mind are concerned, clarify by all means; speculate by all means; but don't suppose that philosophy yields a unique, suprascientific avenue to the truth about the world, or that intuition and heartfelt conviction can be anything more than a starting point for pursuing the truth. My own particular philosophical work I see as partly in the theory-building business, as, for example, in the work on the nature of representation and computation with Sejnowski (1992), and the work on the organization of the visual system (with Ramachandran and Sejnowski, 1994). Some of it (e.g., Churchland and Ramachandran, 1993) aims to undo the mischief of other philosophers who pay scant attention to the relevant data but have their own "conceptual" axes to grind. Some of it is synoptic and synthetic, as in my work on reductionism with PMC (1991) and in my work on consciousness (PSC, 1983). Some of the work involves wrestling with problems about which we know so little that we are not sure whether we are even asking the right question, as with the sections on time and the brain in Churchland and

Sejnowski (1992). I have a particular fascination with questions about brain function, and with how the details at the microlevel constrain theorizing at the macro level, but naturally I do not expect all philosophers interested in the nature of the mind/brain to share my passion for the microdetails.

The two places where we find ourselves disagreeing with Marshall and Gurd are (1) reduction as a research strategy, and (2) the significance of basic neuroanatomy and neurophysiology for understanding how the mind/brain works. Some of our answer to the issue of reductionism and multiple realizability is presented in our earlier comments (pp. 219-238). As remarked there, the best that can be said for the notion of "level" is this: At many spatial and temporal scales, evident structure inspires hypotheses to explain what is going on. The three so-called "Marr levels" (computational, algorithmic, and implementational) correspond to three kinds of question that might be asked of *any* organization at *any* spatial/temporal scale: (1) What is this doing? (2) How is it doing it? (3) What are the material bits (at the appropriate spatial scale) it does it with? (See also Churchland and Sejnowski 1992.) Despite his pretensions, Marr's levels do not correspond to any global chunking of human cognition. That was an a priori dream. But to get clear on all of this, more needs to be said on Marshall and Gurd's observation that "functions come first," in the sense that unless one starts with *some* taxonomy of psychological functions, you cannot interpret lesion data at all.

Why bother locating brain lesions? Why bother with autopsies, MRI scans, and so forth? For us, it is as basic as trying to understand what happens when someone loses vision. We could of course give a purely behavioral account, but it is important to understand whether the lesion is retinal or cortical, whether the onset of lesion was abrupt, as with some strokes, or slow, as with tumor, and whether the damage is in a single region or distributed across many areas. As indicated earlier when discussing the Damasio methodology, there are a number of rock-solid reasons for wanting to locate the lesion. These reasons are at the heart of why lesions studies can be scientifically interesting, as opposed to believe-it-or-not tidbits.

The point is this: If lesion studies are to be useful, we want to know what implications they have for how the brain performs that function. We want to know how the many interlocking networks work, and lesion studies can serve as tests for hypotheses about network organization as we compare and contrast focal lesion cases. Demonstrating that a highly specific cognitive deficit, such as global loss of fear, is correlated with a specific brain region (as in the case of patient SM, who has bilateral amygdala destruction) is critical – as is the fact that unless the damage is bilateral the deficit does not occur. These facts put powerful constraints on where and how we then pursue the relevant neuroanatomy and neurophysiology. These facts raise questions that take us back and forth between higher and lower structural levels. Hypothesis space is utterly vast, and artifacts can easily bedevil a purely behavioral approach. It simply makes good, practical research sense to constrain theories about brain function by using neural network models and basic neuroscience along with neuropsychology and experimental psychology.

To best demonstrate this, we shall consider again the cases of EVR and other patients with similar lesions and deficits. Brevity, however, means painting in bold strokes.

With what emotion-sensitive region in limbic structures does the frontal (ventromedial) region damaged in EVR connect? There are large projections from amygdala, hypothalamus, and brain stem structures that carry signals about body state, and in particular about visceral changes (see figure 19.1). Where do neurons from ventromedial regions project to? There are large projections back to amygdala, hypothalamus,

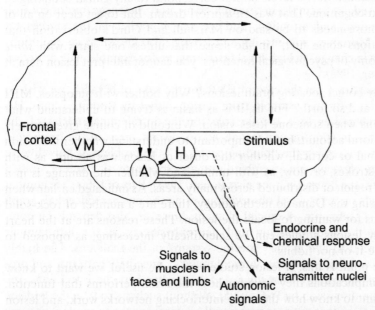

Figure 19.1 Some of the connections mediating emotional responses in humans. Note especially the interaction between the ventromedial (VM) areas of frontal ("practical, social") cortex and the amygdala (A), which interacts with a variety of visceral, muscular, and chemical activities throughout the body.

and somatosensory cortex. What does this imply about the processing of signals from the body "proper" and the feeling of emotions? It implies that the state of the body proper is a critical element in self-representation and in the representation of the emotional significance of outside events (e.g., as threatening, pleasing, embarrassing, etc.)

Is the involvement of ventromedial regions in emotional perception related to the role of serotonergic neurons in frontal cortex and the management of depression and phobias with serotonin enhancers? Probably yes. Ventromedial areas are likely crucial, especially for strong feelings such as those experienced in obsessive-compulsive disorder, where the terror of resisting the impulse is frankly pathological. How does this connect with developmental disorders presenting as reduced affect? Certainly a connection suggests itself. If the serotonergic system is damaged in early development by exposure to substances such as cocaine, then it would be surprising not to see deficits in affect somewhat comparable to that seen in EVR-like patients.

Does neuroscience help us understand neuropsychological data? Surely the answer is yes. To-ing and fro-ing between neuropsychology and basic neuroscience has become the rule, not the exception. It is displayed, for example, in research on memory, language, motor control, perception, and attention, and we saw it earlier in the studies on EVR. Moreover, some to-ing and fro-ing (also known as co-evolution) results in changes in high-level taxonomy, as, for example, with attention (Posner, 1995).

Departing from the case of EVR for the sake of breadth, we wish to consider a further example from recent studies by Rodolfo Llinas. His research points to a unique role for the intralaminar nuclei of the thalamus in coordinating signals across diverse areas of the brain, and thus in addressing the "binding problem," the problem of how diverse sensory elements are assembled into an experience of coherent, unified objects (see figure 19.2; see also Bogen, 1993). Part of Llinas's argument depends on macrolevel observations using the magnetoencephalograph (MEG) technique. A crucial element, however, also depends on comparing the neuroanatomy and neurophysiology in the intralaminar system (ILS) and in the "specific system" of the thalamus. The highly distinctive firing patterns, intracolumnar-connectivity patterns, and projection patterns are what suggested the binding hypothesis to Llinas (see also the discussion by PSC, 1995). Without such microdata, the bedside observation that patients with small bilateral lesions to the ILS become comatose, while unilateral lesions of the ILS produce only neglect of the contralesional side, would seem but a curiosity rather than what it is, a highly significant test for the Llinas network hypothesis.

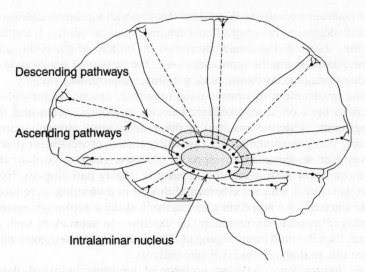

Descending pathways

Ascending pathways

Intralaminar nucleus

Figure 19.2   The ascending and descending connections that unite the
intralaminar system (ILS) with the many different areas of the cerebral cortex.
(After Llinas.)

As to a further possible "fit," notice that, given the Damasio
hypothesis concerning anosognosia and the role of body-state representation, one would predict that, *ceteris paribus*, right ILS lesions will
be more disruptive than left ILS lesions. To my knowledge, data on this
prediction is not yet available.

To conclude, Marshal and Gurd's claim that "function comes first" is
true as far as it goes. But this is rather like saying that "physics starts
with middle-sized objects." What comes first, however, need not be
unrevisable or uncorrectable or inviolable by what comes second, third,
and so on. As neuroscience advances, the possibility emerges that we
shall achieve a deeper understanding of what functional taxonomy is
behaviorally adequate, and what array of functions really are supported
by the nervous system.

None of this gives the least support to a 1990s version of phrenology.
As the Damasios say (1989, 17), "That cortical centers, as traditionally
conceived, could not form the basis for complex psychological functions
in neuropsychology has long been apparent." Areas of specialization are
evidently not discretely localized, and functions are certainly distributed, some perhaps quite widely. As the Damasios emphasize,
localization of damage does not entail localization of function; that is,
localized damage with specific behavioral sequelae ". . . does not mean
that a function disturbed by the lesion was somehow inscribed in the

tissue destroyed by the lesion" (1989, 16–17). Specialization with some distributed aspects, however, there certainly seems to be.

Martha Farah has convincingly shown the failure of the "dedicated module" inference in her powerful paper (1994). Part of her strategy is showing that neural network models, trained to perform a certain task, such as grapheme-to-phoneme transformation, attention shifting, or pattern recognition, can be lesioned by random removal of some of the hidden units, with the result that the performance of the lesioned network looks very similar to the performance of dyslexics, prosopagnosics, or neglect patients respectively. As she correctly cautions, the nets in question do not show what must be the brain's response to a lesion, but they are a demonstration that a neurally-friendly hypothesis can account for the lesion data at least as well as a dedicated module (boxology) hypothesis – better, in fact, because the network hypothesis accords closely with some general features of brain organization: distributed, analog, interactive processing.

More specifically, the Fodorian notion of a module, as encapsulated and unaffected by results of processing elsewhere, cannot be inferred from localized damage, because there is often some residual capacity, and there is often some recovery of function. Quite simply, network hypotheses square far better with such data than do modularity hypotheses. For example: A classic prosopagnosic (cannot recognize individual faces) may well be able to identify a photograph of his mother, even though he cannot recognize his children, his wife, John F. Kennedy, or the Queen of England. A Broca's aphasic may still be able to utter a few words and recognize many typical grammatical failures; a cortically-lesioned subject with loss of sensation in a hand and arm may nevertheless feel something when she rubs her neuropathic hand with her good hand (Weiskrantz and Zhang, 1987). Given evidence elsewhere in neuroscience and psychophysics, it is highly improbable that Fodor-style modules exist anywhere in the nervous system. The machine-shop analogy, in which dedicated instruments perform highly specific and unique tasks, is deeply inappropriate for the brain. How exactly function is specialized while being somewhat distributed is something we shall come to understand in time. To a first approximation, it can already be understood in terms of artificial neural nets.

20
Do We Propose to Eliminate Consciousness?

As a sort of epilogue to the foregoing discussion of the Damasios and Marshall and Gurd concerning neuropsychology, I (PSC) wish to address an issue on which there has been nontrivial confusion. We are probably to blame for much of this, of course, and it is a relief to have again the opportunity to correct misperceptions. Keith Campbell (1986) expressed one attitude towards our view very clearly: "Eliminativism should be stamped out." John Searle (1992) also finds the idea terminally silly. How can we have been as silly as all that? Well, we weren't, not really.

For the record, what eliminativist claims come to is essentially this: As science advances, certain "natural" categories that figured in an earlier theory turn out to have no role and no place in the replacing theory that is taken to provide a correct account of a certain range of phenomena. If those categories are deeply entrenched in common sense, and if they are also routinely used in observation, then the new theory of what is observable will be different from what the ancestor theory assumed to be observable. Now, to put not too fine a point on it, the world is as it is; theories come and go, and the world remains the same. So theory modification does not entail that the nature of the world itself is modified *ipso facto*. It is our understanding of the nature of the world that gets modified. So anyone who thinks that eliminative materialism means that some part of the *dingen an sich* – say, whatever it is that we now think of as "qualia" or "propositional attitude" – is eliminated by mere tinkering with theory is certainly confused. If vital spirit is real, no theorist can make it disappear. The point is, however, that molecular biology can explain biological phenomena perfectly well without appeals to vital spirit. Thus, no serious biologist thinks vital spirit is real. The problem of what distinguishes living from nonliving things was real enough, but its solution is very different from what was assumed in the centuries before modern biology.

Since phenomena are *always* apprehended under an interpretation, theory revision may entail a revision of what phenomena are believed to exist and of what properties they are observed to have. This feature of theory revision often gives people the heebie-jeebies, because they assume they have a theory-neutral access to the world. They are especially wont to suppose they have a theory-neutral access to their own mind-brains. So when one suggests that the category "consciousness" may be fragmenting (PSC, 1983) and that it may be replaced by a set of different categories, people may assume that we are denying there is any phenomenon there to be explained.

This is just a mistake. Of course there exist phenomena to be explained. We are in no doubt that there is a nontrivial difference between being asleep and being awake, between being in a coma and being fully functional, between being aware of a stimulus and not being aware of it. We wonder how to explain, understand, and taxonomize those phenomena, and we suspect science may have some surprises for us. (On the related issue of the usefulness of high-level categories, see earlier, pp. 219–20, 239–40.)

In 1986, I (PSC) agreed with Keith Campbell that some term other than "eliminative materialism" would be preferable. (The expression was originally coined by an avowed opponent of the position, Richard Cornman.) PMC and I stewed quite a lot about this word when he was preparing his book *Matter and Consciousness* (1984) and I was writing *Neurophilosophy* (1986a). We thought that "revisionary materialism" was closer to what we wanted to convey, inasmuch as we take it to be an empirical question how much revision a theory and its concepts will undergo, where outright elimination occupies but one end of a wide spectrum. We experimented with the expression at a few colloquia and conferences, but it did not take very well either. In the end, with mixed feelings, we decided to stick with "eliminative materialism" because it was so indelibly fixed in the literature (see also Bickle, 1992).

With the advantage of hindsight, we feel the expression "eliminative materialism" is in some respects an invitation to misunderstanding. Accordingly, to redress the error, we propose we call the view sketched above and defended in our various writings "good-guy materialism." It has a pleasant ring, it prejudices the reader in its favor, and it leaves open, as it should, *how much* revision our current ideas will undergo as psychology and neuroscience proceed. We have no ideological stake in the revision being massive or minor, though our expectations lean toward the former. Science will proceed as it will, and there is no point getting terribly exercised in predicting just how much revision we can expect. What we do believe is that our current framework is not sacred, that it is neither manifestly nor divinely given, and that "obviousness" is a familiarity phenomenon rather than a measure of metaphysical truth. That said, let us all wait and see what happens.

Marshall and Gurd, reflecting on the implications of a deeper understanding the mind/brain, point to "the danger of pursuing science without regard to moral science..." (p. 182). I recall Bill Lycan urging this very point some 10 years ago in discussion, and it has come to public awareness with the publication of *Descartes' Error*, by Antonio Damasio (1994). Many difficult and highly practical questions must now be addressed by philosophers, especially as cognitive neuroscience reveals more about such matters as rationality and choice.

A detailed explanation of the neurobiological mechanisms subserving choice and decision-making is not likely to be available soon. Nevertheless, impressive developments are clearly evident in this domain (Damasio, 1994). In the foreseeable future, it is probable that a general understanding will emerge, at least of the critical circuitry and neuroactive chemicals, along with the basic principles concerning the role of what we now refer to as reasoning and emotion. Even this much knowledge raises momentous questions concerning social policy (Wright, 1995). The issues are inescapable because socially dangerous choices are an ever present reality of human social life, and because punishment and restraint, as well as moral education, are ethical issues *par excellence*.

As with any scientific and technological advance, there is the danger of social misuse, as well as the possibility for social benefit. This dual-faced potential obtains whether the knowledge involves using fire, making metals, or pursuing the Human Genome Project. The case at hand is importantly different, however, because here the knowledge involves us and our brains – it involves the very thing that makes us what we are. The following is but a small sample of the kinds of question we shall need to confront. What does such understanding portend for our venerable concepts of free will and responsibility? Under what conditions, if any, might it be more humane and fair, as well as more effective, to directly intervene in the nervous system rather than impose long prison sentences or execution? If there is a morally appropriate role for such intervention in rehabilitation or prevention, what are its scope and limits? What are the relevant ethical and moral considerations here? Assuming there is middle ground between the "quick fix," pill-popping approach of the technophiles and the old-ways-are-best intransigence of the traditionalists, how do we begin to characterize that middle ground? These questions, one and all, are singularly troubling to contemplate, and their seriousness and magnitude can seem overwhelming. Yet they will not just go back into the bottle; they are questions already brewing in the minds of general readers of neuroscience as well as of legal practitioners. (For an introduction, see PMC, 1995, chapter 11.)

Like Marshall and Gurd, we expect that new knowledge of the nature of the mind/brain could well usher in distinctly humanizing trends. Already, the "biologizing" of such mental complaints as chronic depression and obsessive compulsive disorder and their treatment with serotonin enhancers like Prozac, for example, have brought enormous relief to many sufferers. For both of these complaints, psychoanalysis was frequently ineffective, expensive, and sometimes harmful. In a more general sense, the developments in cognitive neuroscience may well be positively humanizing rather than dehumanizing, as is sometimes feared (Wilkes, 1984; Campbell, 1986).

It is worth noting that despite the dire forecasts concerning the dehumanizing implications of Darwin's theory, in many respects the replacement of creationist biology with evolutionary biology has been liberating. Women were not created from Adam's rib; original sin and expulsion from paradise is a myth, not fact; women are not responsible for the "fall" of humankind; and, anyhow, there was no "fall," just the tough facts of a biologically competitive world, red in tooth and claw. It allows us to rethink sexuality, as not inherently shameful but as a biological function, well fostered by brain and body mechanisms. Neuroembryology allows us to understand when a fetus has a nervous system sufficiently developed to make it reasonable to consider it a person. Progress in understanding many diseases, to take a very different example, liberates us from the longstanding idea that disease is just punishment or demonic possession. Progress in understanding the absence of any significant biological basis for "race" makes us realize how insignificant a trait is skin color in predicting other biological features (Gould, 1995). Ignorance simply supplies false premises for our moral deliberations, and there is clearly no humanity in that.

E

Moral Psychology and the Rebirth of Moral Theory

21
Flanagan on Moral Knowledge

Flanagan's advocacy of the new approach to moral knowledge is highly welcome, for the proper community to make the wisest use of and generate the maximum theoretical profit from the newly emerging models of cognition is exactly the community of moral philosophers rather than cognitive scientists. The history of moral philosophy already contains several approaches to the subject that anticipate major aspects of the emerging cognitive perspective – Aristotle's construal of moral knowledge as a battery of slowly developing practical skills, Dewey's forthright moral pragmatism, and current explorations in "virtue ethics" are the most striking. Moreover, moral philosophers are uniquely well placed to perceive the explanatory opportunities available and to evaluate the competing accounts responsibly. As in the philosophy of science, the neurocomputational perspective will have a lasting and liberating impact. But in the moral sphere, that impact will fall primarily on metaethics and on moral psychology. Just as substantive science will still have to be done by real scientists, substantive ethics will still have to be done by real moral theorists.

Flanagan and I (PMC) agree that moral knowledge and scientific knowledge are not fundamentally different in kind. They are sustained by the same sorts of cognitive machinery; they develop according to similar principles; and they reflect an equally robust reality. Yet some important differences between scientific and moral knowledge remain, says Flanagan, and he is determined to revisit and re-evaluate them. As he sees it, the first contrast lies in the conflicted nature of the manifold "aims" of moral activity and moral reasoning. Think, for example, of the familiar conflicts between the aims of intrapersonal and interpersonal moral reasonings. And within the latter class, think of one's diverse and often conflicting moral commitments to family, friends, profession, community, country, and the whole of humanity. Does science confront such conflicted aims? Is science the scene of such endless arbitration and accommodation? Presumably not.

Flanagan's second contrast concerns what he calls the local nature of moral knowledge, as opposed to the presumptively universal or nonlocal validity of scientific knowledge. The rationale for this claim lies in Flanagan's useful expression for the proper subject of moral knowledge, "human *ecology*." As with the ecology of a tropical rain forest, or a continental grassland, or an underwater continental shelf, the human ecology is exquisitely complex and can take many different forms, depending on the local economic circumstances, social organizations, technological developments, geographic location, and idiosyncratic history. In the case of a natural ecology, it is obvious that the behavioral "skills" that will make an individual fern a flourishing and well-integrated ecological citizen are utterly dependent on the details of that enveloping natural ecology. In this sense, a fern's "biological virtues" are always "ecosystem relative."

Similarly, a human's moral virtues must always be turned to and measured against the abiding features of the local social economy in which he or she is unavoidably embedded. I am aware that a long tradition in moral theory resists such sensitivity to the existing ecological surround, and not without some reason. But my sympathies on this point lie with Flanagan, for the relativism hereby endorsed does not mean that anything goes, nor is that relativism inconsistent with objective but highly abstract moral principles that assume various closely-related but distinct concrete forms as they are applied to distinct societies at distinct periods of history. Quite the contrary in both cases. The empirical facts of the local social ecology will sharply constrain what reason discovers to be successful modes of behavior; and moral knowledge, like any other form of knowledge, must always seek the maximum level of generality achievable. That said, it remains true that different times and different cultures will often inspire and require – morally require – of their human participants a somewhat different profile of moral virtues. In this sense, if I understand Flanagan correctly, moral knowledge (while still objective) is local in character. And scientific knowledge, on the face of it, is not.

Flanagan has a third criticism to present, but I shall postpone addressing it until the end. I here accept his dual claim that moral knowledge is essentially conflicted and deeply local. What I wish to argue is that, despite casual appearance and official myth, both of Flanagan's claims are true of scientific knowledge as well.

To make this position even remotely plausible, let alone illuminating, I need to back up one giant step and dismantle a related myth. Recall the ancients' distinction between *praxis* and *theoria*, roughly between "practical or behavior-oriented knowledge" and "theoretical or fact-oriented knowledge." Philosophers both past and present have tended to put moral knowledge in the first class and scientific knowledge in the second. And why not? Both present themselves as prototypical instances of the relevant categories.

But this way of carving things up betrays two confusions. The first concerns its wanton misrepresentation of both moral and scientific knowledge, even relative to the revered distinction at issue. And the second concerns the integrity of the distinction itself. Let us take the first point first.

Only a tiny proportion of the general population (or even of academics) ever becomes intimately familiar with the substance of, and smoothly adept in the practice of, any given scientific or engineering discipline. It is robustly prototypical of any field of scientific knowledge that it is *not* a part of the average man's practical life. Such knowledge is prototypically distant, arcane, and practically irrelevant, save only for such impact as it may occasionally have through the ministrations of some equally arcane and impenetrable high-tech industrial plant (producing TVs, pharmaceuticals, or airliners, for example).

For the relatively rare person who does spend her life in the extended deployment of scientific knowledge within research, industry, or both, however, that arcane and practically irrelevant knowledge is the well-oiled vehicle of her daily labors. For her, the properties and entities that are so distantly theoretical for others have become the directly observable features and the readily manipulable tools of her professional workspace. This practical facility, in both perception and manipulation, is an essential feature of becoming a successful scientist or engineer. As Kuhn has emphasized, mastering a scientific theory is a process that barely begins by memorizing a set of discursive laws. The real work is done as one acquires the manifold skills of applying, extending, and and exploiting it, and, in general, of "moving effectively around" the peculiar world to which that theory gives access. Scientific knowledge, accordingly, is an inextricable mixture of fact-oriented, perception-oriented, and behavior-oriented knowledge. It seems otherwise only to people who don't have it or whose encounter with it ended in a handful of two-hour written examinations in the classroom.

Moral knowledge is a similarly inextricable mixture, and here the case is even more easily made. The gradual development of moral character invariably involves the development of a categorial framework with which to classify action types, virtue types, office/role types, character types, and types of crimes and other misbehaviors. Within that framework, general truths, rules, and guidelines are formulated, for use in dealing with social conflicts, discursive reasonings, and moral instruction. Some moral theorists – notably Kantians, contractarians, rule utilitarians, and Christians – portray such discursive rule-systems as the primary embodiment of moral wisdom. That is, they portray moral knowledge as being primarily a *theoretical* achievement! They are wrong, of course (as Aristotle could have told them), but only by exaggeration. Moral knowledge is again a mixture of both *praxis* and *theoria*.

We need a new taxonomy here, one that cross-classifies the ancient dichotomy. Pro tem, I propose the following.

Moral knowledge	**Scientific knowledge**
An inextricable mix of *praxis* and *theoria* focused on the *social* world	An inextricable mix of *praxis* and *theoria* focused on the *natural* world

The significance of this redrawn taxonomy becomes another step clearer when we acknowledge that the original distinction between *praxis* and *theoria* is both superficial and artificial. The brain draws no distinction between them; both kinds of knowledge are embodied in vast configurations of synaptic weights; both display learned categorial structures in neuronal activation space; both serve as filters intervening between sensory input and motor output. If one wants to discriminate moral from scientific knowledge, therefore, one is better advised to look to discriminating subject-matters rather than to discriminating modalities.

From this perspective, the genuinely conflicted situation of the specifically moral agent is mirrored in the genuinely conflicted situation of the practical agent in general. The latter aims to maximize nourishment, bodily health, longevity, protection from the elements, reproduction, recreation, personal safety, the production of tools, the control of resources, and a thousand other nonsocial aims, all of which depend for their conceptualization and successful achievement on the agent's "factual" knowledge, and all of which stand in polydimensional practical *conflict* with each other. Here, as in the social domain, becoming an effective agent is in part a matter of learning to juggle and make coherent a tangle of urgent but conflicted aims. Once again, a superficial contrast disappears upon closer inspection.

If all knowledge is irredeemably practical, at least in prospect, and if we count as scientific knowledge any knowledge that addresses the natural world, as suggested above, then, despite the presumptive dichotomy drawn two paragraphs ago, moral knowledge must be just one *species* of scientific knowledge, since the social world is a subset of the natural world. I embrace this consequence, and it brings me at last to

Flanagan's second claim, the one about the "local" nature of moral knowledge.

The fact is, much prototypically scientific knowledge is local in exactly the same sense. A marine biologist's systematic grasp of the submarine ecosystem lining the west coast of British Columbia and the south coast of Alaska embodies objective knowledge of a highly idiosyncratic reality. A land biologist's grasp of the scorched ecosystem of California's Mojave Desert embodies objective knowledge of quite another. Their respective skills in navigating those very different practical environments are further testament to the local nature of their systematic insight. Similar points can be made about geologists, archaeologists, chemists, and even planetary and stellar astronomers. Granted, the scientist always seeks understandings that will transcend the local and apply, perhaps in modified form, to additional domains. But so also does the student of moral reality, and occasionally he also is successful. What serves in the scout troop may turn out to serve equally well in the boardroom.

I am agreeing with Flanagan's locality thesis here, but I am trying to locate it comfortably within a larger conception of human cognition, a conception that portrays moral knowledge as one of the more dramatically local of a considerable spectrum of cognitive cases, a spectrum that locates "prototypical" examples of science toward the other end of the spectrum, perhaps, but locates them still within a common continuum.

Flanagan's final criticism concerns my allegedly too-casual assumptions concerning the progress of moral knowledge over the centuries. Looking back on human history, Flanagan evidently sees less moral progress than I do, and looking forward, he seems to anticipate less. His alternative vision sees ongoing and occasionally welcome adjustments to changing ecological circumstances, perhaps, but little in the way of progress, such as modern science has apparently achieved.

I am currently ill equipped to take issue with Flanagan on this point, though I confess to a strong impulse to do so. (Look at the distance that separates our social, economic, moral, and political organization from that of the baboons, with whom our ancestors once competed.) Let me concede, for the moment, that he may be right. But if the overall conception of moral cognition that we have here agreed on does not allow me to celebrate much actual moral progress, it does invite celebration of its possibility. For now, I shall make do with that. After all, it is clearly possible to make progress in natural science generally, and social reality is just one aspect of natural reality.

References

Bechara, A., Damasio, A., Damasio, H. and Anderson, S., 1994. "Insensitivity to Future Consequences Following Damage to Human Prefrontal Cortex." *Cognition*, **50**: 7–15.

Bickle, J., 1992. "Revisionary Physicalism." *Biology and Philosophy*, **7**: 411–30.

Bisiach, E. and Berti, A., 1995. "Consciousness in Dyschiria," in *The Cognitive Neurosciences*, M. S. Gazzaniga, ed. Cambridge, MA: MIT Press: 1331–40.

Bogen, J. E., 1993. "Intralaminar Nuclei and the Where of Awareness." *Society for Neuroscience Abstracts*.

Campbell, K., 1986. "Can Intuitive Psychology Survive the Growth of Neuroscience?" *Inquiry*, **29**, 2: 143–52.

Christiansen, M. H. and Chater, N., 1994. "Generalization and Connectionist Language Learning." *Mind and Language*, **9**, 3: 273–87.

Churchland, P. M., 1970. "The Logical Character of Action Explanations." *Philosophical Review*, **79**, 2: 214–36.

Churchland, P. M., 1979. *Scientific Realism and the Plasticity of Mind*. Cambridge: Cambridge University Press.

Churchland, P. M., 1981. "Eliminative Materialism and the Propositional Attitudes." *Journal of Philosophy*, **78**, 2: 67–90.

Churchland, P. M., 1984. *Matter and Consciousness*. Cambridge, MA: MIT Press. (Revised edition, 1988.)

Churchland, P. M., 1988. "Folk Psychology and the Explanation of Human Behavior." *Proceedings of the Aristotelian Society: Supplementary Volume LXII*, D. W. Edgington, ed.

Churchland, P. M., 1989a. *A Neurocomputational Perspective: The Nature of Mind and the Structure of Science*. Cambridge, MA: MIT Press. Chapter 9, "On the Nature of Theories: A Neurocomputational Perspective" and chapter 10, "On the Nature of Explanation: A PDP Approach."

Churchland, P. M., 1989b. "Theory, Taxonomy, and Methodology: A Reply to Haldane's 'Understanding Folk.'" *Proceedings of the Aristotelian Society, Supplementary Volume LIII*, D. W. Edgington, ed.

Churchland, P. M., 1993. "Evaluating Our Self Conception." *Mind and Language*, **8**, 2: 211–22.

Churchland, P. M., 1995. *The Engine of Reason, The Seat of the Soul: A Philosophical Journey into the Brain*. Cambridge, MA: MIT Press.

Churchland, P. M. and Churchland, P. S., 1990. "Intertheoretic Reduction: A Neuroscientist's Field Guide." *Seminars in the Neurosciences*, **2**, 4: 249–56.

Churchland, P. S., 1983. "Consciousness: The Transmutation of a Concept." *Pacific Philosophical Quarterly*, **64**: 80–95.

Churchland, P. S., 1986a. *Neurophilosophy: Toward a Unified Science of the Mind-Brain*. Cambridge, MA: MIT Press.

Churchland, P. S., 1986b. "Replies to Comments on *Neurophilosophy*." *Inquiry*, **29**: 241–72.

Churchland, P. S., 1995. "Can Neurobiology Teach Us Anything About Consciousness?" in *The Mind, the Brain, and Complex Adaptive Systems*.

H. Morowitz and J. Singer, eds. *SFI Studies in the Sciences of Complexity*, Vol. XXII. New York: Addison Wesley: 99–121.

Churchland, P. S. and Ramachandran, V. S., 1993. "Filling in: Why Dennett is Wrong," in *Dennett and His Critics*, B. Dahlbom, ed. Oxford: Blackwell: 28–52.

Churchland, P. S., Ramachandran, V. S. and Sejnowski, T. J., 1994. "A Critique of Pure Vision," in *Large-Scale Neuronal Theories of the Brain*, C. Koch and J. Davis, eds. Cambridge, MA: MIT Press.

Churchland, P. S. and Sejnowski, T. J., 1992. *The Computational Brain*. Cambridge, MA: MIT Press.

Clark, Andy, 1989. *Microcognition*. Cambridge, MA: MIT Press.

Clark, Andy, 1993a. *Associative Engines*. Cambridge, MA: MIT Press.

Clark, Andy, 1993b. "The Varieties of Eliminativism: Sentential, Intentional, and Catastrophic." *Mind and Language*, **8**, 2: 223–33.

Clark, Austen, 1993. *Sensory Qualities*. Oxford: Oxford University Press.

Cottrell, G., 1991. "Extracting Features from Faces Using Compression Networks: Face, Identity, Emotions and Gender Recognition Using Holons," in *Connectionist Models: Proceedings of the 1990 Summer School*, D. Touretzky, J. Elman, T. Sejnowski and G. Hinton, eds. San Mateo, CA.: Morgan Kaufmann.

Crick, F., 1994. *The Astonishing Hypothesis: The Scientific Search for the Soul*. New York: Charles Scribners.

Damasio, A., 1994. *Descartes' Error: Emotion, Reason, and the Human Brain*. New York: G. P. Putnam.

Damasio, H. and Damasio, A., 1989. *Lesion Analysis in Neuropsychology*. Oxford: Oxford University Press.

Damasio, H. and Frank, R., 1992. "Three-dimensional In Vivo Mapping of Brain Lesions in Humans." *Archives of Neurology*, **49**: 137–43.

Dennett, D. C., 1987. *The Intentional Stance*. Cambridge, MA: MIT Press.

Dennett, D. C., 1991. *Consciousness Explained*. Boston: Little, Brown.

Dretske, F., 1981. *Knowledge and the Flow of Information*. Cambridge, MA: MIT Press.

Elman, J. L., 1989. "Representation and Structure in Connectionist Systems," CRL Technical Report. San Diego, CA: Center for Research in Language, UCSD.

Elman, J. L., 1991. "Incremental Learning, or the Importance of Starting Small," CRL Technical Report. San Diego, CA: Center for Research in Language, UCSD.

Elman, J. L., 1992. "Grammatical Structure and Distributed Representations," in *Connectionism: Theory and Practice*, S. Davis, ed. Vol. 3 in the series *Vancouver Studies in Cognitive Science*. Oxford: Oxford University Press.

Farah, M. J., 1994. "Neuropsychological Inference with an Interactive Brain: A Critique of the 'Locality' Assumption." *Behavioral and Brain Sciences*, **17**: 43–104.

Flanagan, O., 1991. *The Varieties of Moral Personality*. Cambridge, MA: Harvard University Press.

Fodor, J. A., 1975. *The Language of Thought*. New York: Crowell.

Fodor, J. A., 1987. *Psychosemantics: The Problem of Meaning in the Philosophy of Mind*. Cambridge, MA: MIT Press.

Fodor, J. A. and Lepore, E., 1992. "Paul Churchland: State Space Semantics," in *Holism: A Shopper's Guide*, Fodor and Lepore, eds. Oxford: Blackwell: chapter 7.

Fodor, J. A. and McLaughlin, B., 1990. "Connectionism and the Problem of Systematicity: Why Smolensky's Solution Doesn't Work." *Cognition*, **35**: 183–204.

Fodor, J. A. and Pylyshyn, Z., 1988. "Connectionism and Cognitive Architecture: A Critical Analysis." *Cognition*, **28**: 3–71.

Giere, R. N., 1994. "The Cognitive Structure of Scientific Theories." *Philosophy of Science*, **61**, 2: 276–96.

Gorman, R. P. and Sejnowski, T. J., 1988. "Analysis of Hidden Units in a Layered Network Trained to Classify Sonar Targets." *Neural Networks*, **1**: 75–89.

Gould, S. J., 1995. "Ghosts of Bell Curves Past." *Natural History*, **104**: 12.

Hacker, P., 1987. "Languages, Minds, and Brains," in *Mindwaves*, C. Blakemore and S. Greenfield, eds. Oxford: Blackwell: 485–505.

Hecht-Nielsen, R., 1990. *Neurocomputing*. Menlo Park, CA: Addison-Wesley: 122.

Hempel, C. G., 1965. *Aspects of Scientific Explanation*. New York: Free Press: chapter 9.

Hinton, G. E. and Shallice, T., 1991. "Lesioning an Attractor Network: investigations of acquired dyslexia." *Psychological Review*, **98**: 74–95.

Hornick, K., Stinchcombe, M. and White, H., 1989. *Neural Networks*, **2**: 359–66.

James, W., 1890. *The Principles of Psychology*, Vols. I and II. New York: Dover.

Kuhn, T. S., 1962. *The Structure of Scientific Revolutions*. Chicago: Chicago University Press.

Lehky, S. and Sejnowski, T. J., 1988. "Network Model of Shape-from-Shading: Neuronal Function Arises from Both Receptive and Projective Fields." *Nature*, **333**: 452–4.

Lehky, S. and Sejnowski, T. J., 1990. "Neural Network Model of Visual Cortex for Determining Surface Curvature from Images of Shaded Surfaces." *Proceedings of the Royal Society of London*, **B240**: 251–78.

Llinas, R. and Ribary, U., 1993. "Coherent 40-Hz Oscillation Characterizes Dream State in Humans." *Proceedings of the National Academy of Sciences*, **90**: 2078–81.

Lockery, S. R., Fang, Y. and Sejnowski, T. J., 1990. "A Dynamical Neural Network Model of Sensorimotor Transformation in the Leech." *Neural Computation*, **2**: 274–82.

Mead, C. and Mahowald, M., 1991. "The Silicon Retina." *Scientific American*, May.

Minsky, M. and Papert, S., 1969. *Perceptrons*. Cambridge, MA: MIT Press.

O'Toole, A. J., Deffenbacher, K. A., Valentin, D. and Abdi, H., 1994.

"Structural Aspects of Face Recognition and the Other Race Effect." *Memory and Cognition*, **22**: 208–24.

Posner, M. A., 1995. "Attention in Cognitive Neuroscience: An Overview," in *The Cognitive Neurosciences*, M. S. Gazzaniga, ed. Camridge, MA: MIT Press: 615–24.

Rock, I., 1983. *The Logic of Perception*. Cambridge, MA: MIT Press.

Rosenberg, C. R. and Sejnowski, T. J., 1987. "Parallel Networks that Learn to Pronounce English Text." *Complex Systems*, **1**: 145–68.

Rumelhart, D. E., Hinton, G. E. and Williams, R. J., 1986. "Learning Internal Representations by Error Propagation," in *Parallel Distributed Processing: Explorations in the Microstructure of Cognition*, D. Rumelhart and J. McClelland, eds. Cambridge, MA: MIT Press: 316–62.

Searle, J., 1992. *The Rediscovery of the Mind*. Cambridge, MA: MIT Press.

Smolensky, P., 1990. "Tensor Product Variable Binding and the Representation of Structure in Connectionist systems." *Artificial Intelligence*, **46**: 159–216.

Weiskrantz, L. and Zhang, D., 1987. "Residual Tactile Sensitivity with Self-directed Stimulation in Hemisanaesthesia." *Journal of Neurology, Neurosurgery, and Psychiatry*, **50**: 632–34.

Wilkes, K., 1984. "Pragmatics in Science and Theory in Common Sense." *Inquiry*, **27**, 4: 339–61.

Wright, R., 1995. "The Biology of Violence," in *The New Yorker*, 13 March: 68–77.

Index

Abrahamsen, Adele 33, 142
Achinstein, Peter 107–8, 117
activation
  of nodes 67
  patterns 104, 111, 130, 225, 227
  of prototypes 23, 99–100,
    110–17, 211–12, 247
  space 23, 71–3, 90, 99, 121,
    232–3, 245, 248, 264, 268, 276
  vector 88, 252, 260, 272, 275
Adams, E. M. 111
alchemy 98
Allfrey, V. 137, 140
amygdala 171, 292–4
analogy 23, 37, 61
analysis, levels of 18–38, 41, 44,
    222, 224–5
analytic/synthetic distinction 146,
    155, 157, 161, 267
Archimedes 269
Aristarchos 222
Aristotle 199, 222–3, 230, 247, 302,
    305
artificial intelligence 226, 241, 259
  see also connectionist AI
astronomy
  Copernican 118
  crystalline spheres 98
attribution theory 33
autism 60–1

Baier, Annette 203
baseball 69

Bates, Elizabeth 240
Bayesianism 59
Bechtel, William 18, 32–4, 121
behaviorism 57
Bennett, Jonathan 60
Bensley, R. R. 139
Berkeley, George 160–2
Berthet, J. 140
Bickle, John 22
biochemistry 128
  see also cell fractionation
biology 53, 137, 177, 230
  molecular 57, 78
bodily humours 22
Bok, Sissela 199
Boltzmann machine 241–3
Boolean functions 158–60, 274–5
boundary conditions 19
Bower, Gordon 41
brain injury 178, 183–5, 188–9, 245,
    285–9, 292–6
  patient EVR 287–9, 293–4
  patient SM 292
Brainvox 163
Brazier, Mary 82
bridge laws see reduction of
    theories
Bromberger, Sylvain 107
Buchner, E. 132, 265
Burton, Robert 38

caloric fluid 22, 26, 29, 230
Campbell, Keith 297–8

Cartesian Theater 169
Cassirer, Ernst 176–9
categorical imperative 193
Causey, Robert 18, 20, 22, 37
cell fractionation 137–41, 267
central nervous system *see* nervous system
cerebellar cortex *see* cortex, cerebellar
cerebellum 66, 188
Chater, N. 237–8, 244, 283
Chomsky, Noam 145, 155, 181, 183
Christensen, Scott M. 33
Christiansen, M. H. 237–8, 244, 283
Clark, Andy 268
Clark, Austen 247
Claude, A. 138–40
Clement, Catherine A. 249
co-evolution 17–18, 23–9, 32, 36, 41–2, 50, 56, 188, 222, 294
co-evolution$_M$ 25–8, 30, 34–7
co-evolution$_P$ 27–8, 32–7, 44
co-evolution$_S$ 26–9, 32–5
explanatory pluralism 27–9, 31–2, 35–6, 41–2, 44
Coffa, J. A. 116–17
cognition 39, 41, 49–52, 55, 72, 81, 86, 118, 125, 130, 177, 185, 187, 189, 196, 205, 225–7, 230, 234–5, 240, 246–7, 251, 260, 266–8, 269–70, 282–3, 288, 292, 302, 306
cognitive science 87–94, 96–7, 101, 145, 153, 242, 302
theory of cognitive dissonance 33
Coleman, L. 200
colliculi 164, 166
color 25, 60, 67, 149–51, 154, 158, 160, 166, 170, 247
color cube 249–50
combustion 33, 44
commensurability 17
continuum model 21–3, 26–30, 34

incommensurability 21, 25, 29, 31–2
common sense psychology *see* folk psychology
computer 185–9, 227
computer model 66, 70, 81, 82
computer science 67, 70
concept 58, 61, 82, 147–8, 151–3, 155–62, 170, 187, 199, 200–1, 268, 279, 281–2, 290–1
concept acquisition 61, 87, 159–60, 199, 268
concept empiricism *see* empiricism, concept
conceptual change 87, 92, 123, 130, 143, 269, 279
connectionism 18, 39, 41, 67, 86–94, 99–100, 109–10, 117, 121–32, 135, 137, 141–3, 153, 158–62, 188, 224–5, 230, 234, 238, 248–51, 265–6, 269–70, 281–3
connectionist AI 87, 109
consciousness 114, 163, 165–6, 168–9, 171, 174, 213, 248, 288–9, 291, 298
content 145–62, 272
calibrational 93–4, 96–7, 99
identity 145, 151–62, 272–7, 281
similarity 145–51, 153
translational 93–4, 96–7
continuum model *see* commensurability
control neurons 97
convergence zones 168, 172
Copernicus 118
Cornman, Richard 298
cortex 180, 288–9
cerebellar 65–6, 188
cerebral 248
early sensory cortices 166–8, 171, 173, 274
frontal 293–4
multiple cortical regions 171
post-rolandic parietal cortices 171
somatosensory 171, 294

cortex *cont'd*
  subcortical nuclei 171–2
  supplementary motor cortex 181
  visual 44, 163–6, 172, 227
Cottrell, G. 228–9, 245, 279
Crick, Francis 66–8, 179, 248
cued recall *see* memory

Dalton, John 230
Damasio, Antonio 80, 292, 295,
  297, 299
Damasio, Hannah 292, 295, 297, 299
Darwin, Charles 21, 180, 300
deductive-nomological model of
  explanation *see* explanation
Dennett, Daniel 33, 60, 90–1, 98,
  173, 240–1, 251, 253–5
Descartes, René 181, 189
Dewey, John 192, 204, 207, 210,
  213, 302
directed attention 65
DNA 140
Down's syndrome 61
Dretske, Fred 279
drive-reduction theory 57
dualism 51, 180, 189
Duve, C. de 140

early sensory cortices *see* cortex,
  early sensory
Eccles, John 181
Einstein, Albert 251
electromagnetic fields 230
elimination of theories 29–34, 53,
  222
eliminativism 145, 158, 224, 254,
  297
  see also materialism, eliminative
Eliot, George 181
Elman, Jeff 235–8, 244–6, 283
emotion 49–52, 55, 64–5, 163, 171,
  178, 255, 285, 287, 294, 299
empiricism
  concept empiricism 274, 277–8,
    281, 283
  logical 18–19, 21–2, 61, 105,
    147–9, 152, 156, 158–62

Enc, Berent 20
epistemology 38, 49, 61, 64, 70, 73,
  78, 123, 158–9, 193–4, 196, 283,
  302
  sentential 104, 109, 113, 254
Eratosthenes 222
Essen, D. Van 96–7
ethics 49, 63, 78, 192–3, 208–10,
  212, 299
  descriptive-genealogical 194–5,
    204–5
  normative 194–5, 205, 211–13
  see also moral philosophy
explanation 19–20, 22, 26–7, 31–2,
  37, 41, 43, 86–94, 97, 101, 105,
  107–18, 123–32, 186, 197, 212,
  250, 252–9
  deductive-nomological (D-N)
    model 19, 21, 112, 116–17,
    123, 125, 257–61, 263–4
  intentional 33–4
  prototype-activation (P-A)
    model 22, 99, 110–15, 197,
    257–60, 263
explanatory pluralism *see* co-
  evolution
explanatory understanding 21–3,
  100, 104–9, 111–18, 121, 123,
  126, 247, 257–61, 263–6, 278

face-recognition experiment 228–
  9, 244–5, 247, 249, 280
Farah, Martha 296
fermentation 128, 132–5, 143, 265
Feyerabend, Paul 20–1
Fish, Stanley 213
Flanagan, Owen 49
Fodor, Jerry 20, 88, 92–3, 226,
  234–5, 240, 259, 296
folk psychology 18, 26, 31–4, 43,
  51–3, 55, 57, 78–9, 86–93,
  98–100, 104, 177, 179, 182,
  224–6, 230, 240, 250–5
foveal vision *see* vision, foveal
Fraassen, Bas C. van 107
free will 17, 63, 299
Frege, Gottlob 58, 157

Freud, Sigmund 70, 78, 82
functionalism 180, 182, 185, 240

Galileo 26, 182, 222, 267
Gazzaniga, Michael 39, 42
genetics 230
  biochemical 36
  gene-control networks 129
  Mendelian 36
  transmission 38
Gentner, Dedre 249
Gestalt psychology 57, 111
Gettier problem 109
Gibbard, Allan 212–13
Giere, Ronald N. 129
Glenberg, A. M. 31
global knowledge detection 87
Goldman, Alvin 49, 61
Goldstein, Kurt 178
Goodman, Nelson 61
grammatically competent
  network 235–8, 244–6, 283
Greenwood, John 33
Gregory, Richard 240
Gurd, Jennifer 297, 299–300

Hacking, Ian 136
Harden, A. 134
Harman, Gilbert 60
Hatfield, Gary 55
Hebb, D. O. 70
Hempel, Carl G. 104–6, 109, 115,
  117, 257, 259
hidden layer 109, 114, 249
hidden units 44, 71, 74–7, 81, 111,
  123, 142, 243, 246, 248–9, 275,
  279, 281
Hinton, G. E. 126, 242–6
hippocampus 43
  lesions of 80
Hirst, William 42
Hoerr, N. 139
Hogeboom, G. H. 138
holon 279–80
homunculi 115, 169–70, 173
Hooke's Law 117
Hooker, Clifford A. 22

Hopfield net 243
Hornick, K. 234
Hubel, D. H. 71, 246
Hume, David 63–4, 158, 161,
  278–82
Humphreys, P. 111
hypothalamus 171, 289, 293–4

identity of meaning see content,
  identity
illusory conjunctions 60
images
  mental 163–5
  role in explanation 22
impetus 26, 29, 31
incommensurability see
  commensurability
inference 23, 60, 111, 127, 131, 145,
  156, 161–2
information processing see
  psychology
insula 171, 289
intensionality 146, 148
intentionality 17, 33, 34, 153, 155,
  251
internalism 27
intertheoretic integration see unity
  of science
intertheoretic relations see
  reduction of theories
intralaminar system (ILS) 294–5
  see also thalamus

Jacoby, L. L. 41
James, William 54–6, 62, 79
Jeffrey, R. C. 111
Johnson, Mark 195

Kahneman, Daniel 59
Kant, Immanuel 60, 81, 176
Kauffman, Stuart A. 129
Kay, P. 200
Kepler, J. 43
Kitcher, Philip 79, 107, 118
knowledge
  account of see epistemology
  moral 192–7, 205–10, 302–6

knowledge *cont'd*
  scientific 193, 195, 205–6, 302–6
Koch, C. 42
Köhlberg, Lawrence 210, 212
Köhler, Wolfgang 70, 78
Kohonen net 243
Kolmogorov, A. N. 234
Kornblith, Hilary 49
Kosslyn, Steven 241
Kuhn, Thomas 20, 60, 124–5, 135, 254, 304

Lamarck, Jean Baptiste Pierre Antoine de Monet 95
Land, Edwin 149, 154
language 147–8, 169, 173, 177, 183, 185, 188, 203, 240, 246, 266, 283–5
  natural 52, 93–6, 100–1, 122, 125–32, 141, 143, 155
  ordinary 51
  philosophy of 176, 180–2, 290
Lashley, Karl S. 70
lateral geniculate nucleus 163–4, 227
Latour, Bruno 136
Laudan, Larry 32
Lavoisier, Antoine-Laurent 44
learning 25, 39, 54, 79–80, 87, 88, 92, 94, 101, 123, 159, 183, 227, 241, 247, 249
  Hebbian 243
  moral 196–212
leech 49, 65, 245
Lehky, S. R. 44, 246
Leslie, Alan 60–1, 63, 80
Lewes, G. H. 181
light *see* color; electromagnetic fields
linguistics 50, 75, 240
  linguistic model of representation *see* representation, linguistic model
Llinas, Rodolfo 65–6, 241–2, 247–8, 294
local coding 71
Locke, John 58

Lockery, Shawn 245
luminiferous ether 22
Lycan, William 299
lying/truth-telling 195, 198–204, 211–12
Lykken, D. T. 38

McCauley, Robert 20, 29–30, 41
McClelland, James L. 126–7, 142
Mahowald, M. 245
Marr, David 186
  Marr levels 292
Marshall, John 297, 299–300
materialism 55
  augmentative 100
  eliminative 26–7, 53, 56, 61, 87, 254–5, 298
Maxwell, James Clerk 230
Mead, C. 245
meaning *see* semantics
mechanics
  Aristotelian 30
  Newtonian 22, 29–31, 44, 181, 223–5, 251
  quantum 22, 31, 44, 251–2
  statistical 19
Medin, Douglas 79
memory 25, 39–43, 128, 167–8, 179, 183, 185, 241, 285
  associative 104
  cued recall 40
  short-term 245
  spacing effect 39–40
  trace 30
  working 37, 166, 173
mentality
  philosophically relevant (PR) 51, 64–77, 80, 246
  see also mental states
mental states 60–1, 80, 89–90, 145, 149, 154, 157
Metcalfe, Janet 279
Milgram experiments 63–4
mind
  mind-body problem 17, 181
  philosophy of 33, 149

mines and rocks 39, 91, 109,
113–14
Minsky, Marvin 243
Mitchell, P. 129
mitochondrion *see* cell
fractionation
Moore, G. E. 176
morality 198, 201–13, 300, 302–6
moral network theory 192–4,
198–201, 204–5, 210–11
moral philosophy 63, 64, 192–5,
302–6
see also ethics
Mother Teresa 208
motor control 72
Mountcastle, Vernon 65–6
mouse eating sesame seeds 89–90,
99
mousetrap 182–3, 185
multiple constraint satisfaction 68,
76
soft constraints 131–2, 135–7,
140–2
multiple instantiation 17, 20, 186
multiple realization/realizability 55,
79, 291

Nagel, Ernest 18, 32, 43
Nash, Ogden 242
naturalism 49, 78–9, 195, 206, 241
natural selection 54, 87, 179
Neisser, Ulric 43
nervous system 43, 54, 64–8, 70–1,
77, 79, 81, 149, 176, 299
NETtalk 18, 39–42, 72–6, 245, 249
Neuberg, C. 133–5
Neumann, John Von 187
architecture 187
neural networks 22, 44, 70, 80, 142,
162, 188, 193, 196, 211, 232, 235,
241, 243, 246, 269, 272, 274–6,
280–1, 296
neurocomputationalism 22, 24, 39,
41, 44, 69
neurophilosophy 48–52, 57, 63–72,
77–9, 176, 239, 248

Newton, Isaac 29, 43, 44, 181,
223–5, 251, 267
Nisbett, Richard 63
node activation 67
Nolfi, S. 94–5, 250

observation vocabulary 145–7, 152
oculomotor system *see* vision
Oppenheim, Paul 20, 104–6, 109,
115, 117, 257, 259
O'Toole, A. J. 244
oxygen 44

Palade, G. E. 138
Papert, S. 243
parallel distributed processing
(PDP) 67–9, 71–6, 81, 187–9,
241–3, 246
parietal
lobe 184
operculum 171
Parisi, D. 94–5, 250
Peirce, Charles Sanders 254
Pellionisz, Andras 65–6, 241–2
perceptual recognition 60, 67, 69,
72, 88, 110–11, 114–15, 118, 123,
166–8, 177, 181, 188, 197,
232–40, 245–7, 260–3, 259, 278,
283, 285
Perner, Joseph 60
phase spaces 104
phlogiston 26, 29, 44
phosphorylation 129, 135
phronesis 199
physicalism 36, 43, 180, 186
Piaget, Jean 210, 212
pineal gland 181
Plato 207, 223, 247, 282
pluralism, explanatory *see* co-
evolution
Popper, Karl 122
positivism 125–8, 131
practical jokes 199, 201
pragmatism 27, 28, 32, 33, 36,
106–8, 112, 118, 208, 250, 254
PR mentality *see* mentality, PR

prototype-activation model of
explanation *see* explanation
prototype vector 22–3, 110, 113,
122, 141, 161, 197, 260, 263,
265–6, 278
psychoanalysis 57
psychology 18, 24–6, 28–9, 33–4,
37–41, 43–4, 50–61, 64, 67–73,
77–80, 82, 182, 224, 226, 239,
244, 250–2, 255
Ptolemy 223
Puckett, Kirby 69
Pylyshyn, Zenon 240
pyruvic acid *see* fermentation

qualia, sensory *see* sensory qualia
qualia inversion 149–51
Quine, Willard Van Orman 61–2,
146, 148, 161–2

radioactive decay 111
Railton, Peter 106, 111
Ramachandran, V. S. 56, 241, 291
rationality 19–20, 60, 63, 122–3,
207
raven paradox 109
Rawls, John 63, 209
reading 183
realism
neurobiological 69
reasoning 88, 132, 137, 141–2, 173,
195, 285, 287, 299
bank-teller study 59
moral 302
see also inference; rationality
reaction of theories 18–38, 41, 43,
50, 53, 55–7, 79, 222, 251
bridge laws 19
microreductionism 19–20, 24–5,
28, 30, 35–8, 42–3
reductionism 30, 31, 55, 78,
180–2, 184–9, 250, 291
see also co-evolution
reflective equilibrium 63
Reid, J. 114, 118, 261
relativity *see* mechanics, quantum
representation 56, 60, 71–3, 76–7,

80, 87–101, 110, 113, 122–32,
142, 145–9, 157, 167, 171–2, 179,
186, 225, 258, 260, 263–4, 283
inner 52, 77, 79, 88
internal 88, 179, 188
linguistic model 87–94, 125, 128
of sensory qualia 25, 241
sentential model 52, 87–94,
97–100, 104, 115, 117, 141
Ribary, U. 247
Richardson, Robert 20, 32, 34, 43,
132, 142
Rorty, Amelie 49
Rosch, Eleanor 58
Rosenberg, Charles 39–42, 72, 75,
81, 245–6
Ross, Lee 63
Rumelhart, David E. 126, 142,
242–3
Ryle, Gilbert 89, 91

St. John, M. F. 127
Salmon, Wesley C. 106–7, 111, 117
Schaffner, Kenneth 35
Schneider, W. C. 138–9
science
history of 21, 28, 31–2, 51, 57,
143
philosophy of 27, 55, 121–2, 125,
128, 131–2, 136, 142, 265,
269–70, 291, 302
sociology of 136
scientific
discovery 36, 38, 100
laws 19
progress 19, 21, 29, 33, 100
revolution 18, 26, 28–9, 34–5,
143
Scriven, Michael 107, 117
Searle, John 297
sea slug 49, 54, 65, 224, 234
Sejnowski, Terrence 20, 31–2,
36–7, 39–41, 44–5, 48, 52, 69–77,
80–2, 86, 88, 242–6, 291–2
selection pressures 23–4, 36
self 168–73, 211
Sellar, Wilfrid 61

semantics   145–9, 151–62, 272–4,
    278–83
  semantic network   244–6
  state space   151–62
sensory qualia   17, 25, 149–51,
    159–60, 177, 247, 274–5, 279,
    282
sentence   90, 99–100, 104–5, 116,
    122–3, 126–31, 145–9, 235–6,
    257, 282
  sentential model of
    representation   see
    representation, sentential
    model
Shallice, T.   244, 246
Sherrington, Charles   64
similarity   61–74, 76, 248
  gradient   109, 283
  judgments   61–2, 73–4, 76
  representation of   61, 73–4
  spaces   61–2, 72–3
simplicity   123, 260
Sintonen, M.   107, 117
Smith, Edward   79
Smolensky, Paul   126, 234, 242
socialization
  moral   201, 204–6
spacing effect   see memory
speech act   107, 199, 203
Spinoza, Benedict de   189
Stahl, Georg Ernst   21, 33
stereoptic vision   see vision,
    stereoptic
Stokes' Law   139
subjectivity   165, 168–74
Sutherland, S.   187
symbol system   88, 92, 101
synapse   282
  synaptic connection   66, 88, 189,
    225, 242, 247, 277
  synaptic value   80
  synaptic weight   104, 109, 117,
    121
  transmission   226

telos   223, 230
temporal lobe   184

tensor-network theory   66–7
Thagard, Paul   21
thalamus   57, 166, 168, 171, 188,
    247, 289, 294
thermodynamics   19, 230
Tootell, Roger   167
transition between theories   see
    scientific revolution
Treisman, Anne   60, 67
Turing machine   71, 127, 234
Turner, Dale R.   33
Tversky, Amos   59, 61–2, 74

unity of science   32–3, 55, 78
  intertheoretic integration   25–7,
    53–7, 78

vector   80
  activation   88
  coding   71–3, 76, 81, 234, 241,
    246–7, 251, 275–6
Vershure, Paul   75–6, 81, 249
vestibular nucleus   81
vestibulo-ocular reflex (VOR)   66
vision   44, 68, 179, 188, 292
  foveal   65
  oculomotor system   65
  stereoptic   241, 245
  visual fixation and tracking   65
  visual recognition   57
  see also visual cortex
Vygotsky, L. S.   143

weight space   80
Wiesel, T. N.   71, 246
Wilkes, Kathleen   254–5
Williams, Ronald J.   242–3
Wimmer, Heinz   60
Wimsatt, William   20, 22, 29, 32, 35,
    42
Wittgenstein, Ludwig   118, 176,
    182, 189, 290

Young, W. J.   134

Zaffron, R.   107
  Zaffron point   107–8, 117–18, 259